REBELLION IN PATAGONIA

REBELLION IN PATAGONIA

Osvaldo Bayer

Translated by
Paul Sharkey and Joshua Neuhouser

Introduced by
Scott Nicholas Nappalos and Joshua Neuhouser

Rebellion in Patagonia

ISBN: 978-1-84935-221-5
E-ISBN: 978-1-84935-222-2
Library of Congress Control Number: 2016930453

Kate Sharpley Library
BM Hurricane
London WC1N 3XX
UK
www.katesharpleylibrary.net

AK Press   AK Press
370 Ryan Ave. #100   PO Box 12766
Chico, CA 95973   Edinburgh EH8 9YE
USA   Scotland
www.akpress.org   www.akuk.com
akpress@akpress.org   ak@akedin.demon.co.uk

The above addresses would be delighted to provide you with the latest AK Press distribution catalog, which features books, pamphlets, zines, and stylish apparel published and/or distributed by AK Press. Alternatively, visit our websites for the complete catalog, latest news, and secure ordering.

Cover design by Josh MacPhee
Indexing by John Barker
Printed in the USA

CONTENTS

INTRODUCTION

By Scott Nicholas Nappalos and Joshua Neuhouser

Rebellion in Patagonia is one of the true classics of Latin American social history, both for the clarity of Osvaldo Bayer's prose as well as for the importance of the events it describes. Here Bayer uncovers the story of the 1920–1922 strike wave by Patagonia's rural peons, led by a Spanish anarchist named Antonio Soto, and its culmination in a massacre dwarfed only by the disappearances that occurred under the 1976–1983 military junta—but ordered by a democratically elected president. He evokes the heyday of the early-twentieth century anarchist movement, which was truly international: exiled Russian revolutionaries and German World War I veterans make their appearances in these pages, as does a deported organizer for the Industrial Workers of the World (IWW), who happened to share an apartment with the future secretary of the Peninsular Committee of the Iberian Anarchist Federation (FAI). There are Tolstoyan pacifists who turn to violence; illiterate Chilean peons who commemorate the execution of Francisco Ferrer, the Catalonian founder of the Modern School movement; and a sex strike by Patagonia's prostitutes.

1

The reader can jump directly in with little knowledge of South American history—Patagonia is only slightly less alien to the Buenos Aires book-buying public than it is to those of us in the English-speaking world, so most of the required background information already comes included—but some may require more context, especially as the history of Argentina before the Perón era is largely unfamiliar to most North Americans.

The Patagonian rebellion was, in many ways, the culmination of a long series of social struggles that date back to the end of the nineteenth century. Prior to this time, Argentina was an isolated agrarian country with land ownership patterns that had remained largely unchanged since the colonial era, but the growth of global capitalism and the demand for the country's agricultural products pulled it into the world system, while the influx of immigrants that began in the 1850s brought the latest European social theories with them—including socialism and anarchism.

The first immigrants were skilled laborers who generally arrived for concrete economic reasons, as Argentine society was defined by a degree of economic mobility up until the 1880s. The arrival of French leftists fleeing from the repression of the Paris Commune brought the first organized socialist effort with the founding of a section of the First International, though it had little impact. Anarchists began organizing around 1879 as part of the Bakuninist section of the First International. Notably, Errico Malatesta came to Argentina and helped found some of the earliest resistance societies, which were the form class struggle took in late-nineteenth century/early-twentieth century Argentina. These resistance societies emerged out of the mutual aid organizations that helped new immigrants navigate a country with no real safety net or infrastructure to receive them. They retained the cooperative mutual aid model but united it with collective actions aimed at improving the conditions of the working class. The first unions were formed in urban areas in 1887 and socialist and anarchist publications rapidly proliferated throughout Argentina in the following decade. Rent strikes began around the same time and workers organized against the social ills rampant in the country's overcrowded and destitute slums, such as addiction, crime, prostitution, and disease.[1]

The anarchist movement fully asserted itself as a unified working class force in the 1890s with a general strike in the city of Rosario in 1895 and a strike wave in support of an eight-hour workday in Buenos Aires in 1899. In 1901, thirty-five delegates representing some seven thousand resistance societies from across the country came together to found the Argentine Workers' Federation (FOA), which was based around the principle of autonomy from all political parties. General strikes, boycotts, sabotage, and rent strikes were endorsed as tactics and the new federation resolved to found free libertarian schools and union hiring halls. The federation's second congress, in 1902, consolidated these anarchist positions, leading the socialists to leave the organization. Out of the federation's 7,620 resistance societies, only 1,230 left, forming the nucleus of the General Union of Workers (UGT).[2] By 1905, the UGT had adopted a form of neutral syndicalism, neither anarchist nor socialist, influenced by France's General Confederation of Labor (CGT), while the FOA—having changed its name to the Argentine Regional Workers' Federation (FORA) to make explicit its internationalist orientation and its rejection of nation-states and borders—voted at its fifth congress to adopt anarcho-communism as the ultimate goal of the organization. The FORA pushed for a strict division between revolution and the day-to-day demands made by unions. Its congresses were also extremely progressive for their time, taking up issues such as gender equality, the rights of prisoners, internationalism, and the social causes of disease in urban areas at a time when such positions were rare, especially in the labor movement.

The growth of the labor movement did not go unnoticed by the ruling class. Military intervention became a commonplace measure to repress strikes, but it was clear that the movement was challenging the ability of the state to control it. The government approved the Residency Law in 1902, which gave the government free license to deport foreign activists. Anarchists—many of whom were immigrants—were explicitly targeted by this law and were rounded up, held incommunicado, and summarily deported. This measure was followed by a 1904 labor code that sought to legalize, regulate, and control unions and strikes, some of the first legislation of its kind in the world. It failed in practice, however, because it was rejected by both capital and labor—capital refused any concessions to labor, while labor refused any attempt to restrict its freedom of activity. Six years later, the Argentine government's repressive powers were further expanded with the Social Defense Law, which provided strict penalties (including prison time) for organizing demonstrations without a permit, publicly using anarchist symbols, coercing others to join a strike or boycott, insulting the Argentine flag, or defending any violation of this law, either verbally or in writing.

The year 1909 proved to be a turning point in the history of Argentina's anarchist movement. The police chief of Buenos Aires, one Colonel Falcón, ordered the military to open fire on a May Day demonstration, killing somewhere between four and ten workers and wounding many more. This tragedy managed to unite Argentina's divided working class. Over sixty thousand union members accompanied the funeral procession of the slain workers, while the FORA and the UGT came together to declare a general strike. After one week, the strike managed to force the release of eight hundred imprisoned workers, though it was unable to secure the resignation of Colonel Falcón, who was later assassinated by a little-known FORA member, a Russian immigrant named Simón Radowitzky who had survived the massacre. The joint general strike encouraged Argentina's unions to move towards unity: in the months following the massacre, the UGT joined together with a group of independent unions to form the Argentine Regional Workers' Confederation (CORA), although the repression that followed the assassination of Colonel Falcón prevented further unity talks with the FORA from taking place.

As an aside, Radowitzky is one of the most interesting figures in the history of Latin American anarchism: he participated in the Russian Revolution of 1905 as a teenager and fled to Argentina after its defeat. Following his assassination of Colonel Falcón, he was sent to the infamous Ushuaia prison in Tierra del Fuego—known as the Argentine Siberia—where he was tortured and raped by the warden throughout his years of imprisonment. The anarchist movement's campaign to secure his release from prison was finally successful in 1930, though a nationalist coup later that year forced him to move to Uruguay, where he resumed his organizing work until he was once again imprisoned. After being freed, he moved to Brazil, where he engaged in anti-fascist organizing before going off to fight in the Spanish Civil War. After Franco's victory in 1939, he fled to France, where he was placed in a concentration camp. He then made his escape, evading the pending Nazi invasion by just under twelve months. That June he settled in Mexico, where he worked in a toy factory until his death in 1956, but he remained active in the anarchist movement and wrote for Mexican anarchist publications.[3]

The centennial of Argentina's independence from Spain, celebrated in 1910, was marked by a perhaps inevitable clash between the year's triumphant nationalism and the restless labor movement. On May 8th—less than a month before the centennial celebrations, scheduled for May 25th—seventy thousand people took to the streets of Buenos Aires to protest the mistreatment of inmates in the National Prison. The CORA and the FORA separately resolved to begin a general strike on May 18th if their demands, including the repeal of the Residency Law, were not met. The government began making arrests on May 13th—in all, over two thousand union members were imprisoned—and a state of emergency was declared the following day. The police organized nationalist gangs to raid union halls, the offices of left-wing newspapers and immigrant-owned businesses. But the strike still went forward. During the centennial celebrations, the trolleys of Buenos Aires could only advance under armed guard and anonymous saboteurs ensured that the electric lights that had been installed to illuminate the city would remain dark.[4] "The government won," FORA organizer and anarchist historian Diego Abad de Santillán would later write. "But history will remember that, to celebrate Argentina's independence, it was necessary to turn Buenos Aires into a military camp, with a state of siege and overflowing prisons."[5]

By 1910—also an election year—it was clear that Argentina's oligarchy could not continue ruling as it had; things would have to change in order for them to stay as they were. The National Autonomist Party had dominated Argentine politics for the previous thirty years, protecting the interests of Argentina's commercial and land-owning oligarchy, ensuring domestic stability and moving the country past the civil wars of the nineteenth century. But it was only able to maintain its grip on power through widespread electoral fraud and disenfranchisement—it's estimated that only 20 percent of the native-born male population voted during the 1910 elections—and by the turn of the century, the party had begun to collapse under the weight of factional infighting.[6] The violence seen during the centennial made it clear that the vaunted stability of the so-called Conservative Republic ushered in by the National Autonomist Party could not last without major changes, and so one of incoming president Roque Sáenz Peña's first actions in office was to pass an electoral reform establishing the secret ballot and compulsory suffrage for all adult male citizens.

Though the intention behind this reform was to provide the ruling oligarchy with democratic legitimacy, the Sáenz Peña Law, as it came to be known, in effect handed the country over to the Radical Civic Union, Argentina's main opposition party. Formed in the 1890s, when an economic crisis divided Argentina's oligarchy into competing factions, the Radical Civic Union staged a series of unsuccessful coups at the turn of the century. After its founder, Leandro Alem, committed suicide in 1896, leadership of the party passed into the hands of his nephew Hipólito Yrigoyen, who worked to expand the party's base beyond the intra-elite struggles of its early years. Following the party's final coup attempt in 1905, Yrigoyen decided to change his strategy from military conspiracy to grassroots organizing, recruiting urban professionals, small business owners and other middle-class elements to join the Radical Civic Union. Yrigoyen's populist attacks on the country's oligarchy appealed to those Argentines who found themselves unable to advance, while local Radical committees organized street corner meetings and free concerts, opened medical clinics, and distributed food to the needy in an attempt to win over the country's working class. By the time Argentina's first elections with universal male suffrage were held in 1916, the Radical Civic Union had positioned itself to easily crush the conservatives. The final results were not even close: Yrigoyen was elected by a thirty-three-point margin.

Once in office, Yrigoyen strove to paternalistically present himself as the "father of the poor" by integrating an immigrant workforce into the framework of Argentine nationalism, providing workers with access to credit and a rising standard of living, and expanding the country's middle class by founding universities and opening up new opportunities in the public sector bureaucracy. His populist reforms sought to shore up support from a battered and militant working class and channel it into institutional change that could cool off an explosive situation, yet without undertaking land reform or altering the basis of Argentina's export-oriented economy. This political strategy is familiar to us now, but the Radical period in Argentine history occurred many years before similar center-left attempts to co-opt working class radicalism, such as the New Deal in the United States or the Popular Fronts in Western Europe.

During these years, Argentina's labor organizations continued to advance towards unification. The first unification congress between the FORA and the CORA—much-delayed by state repression—was finally held in December 1912, although the organizations would not merge until September 1914, when the CORA dissolved itself and joined the FORA. But this unity would not last long. During the ninth congress of the FORA, held in April 1915, a resolution was approved that made the labor federation officially non-ideological, thus rejecting the union's previous anarcho-communist line. "The FORA is an eminently working-class institution, made up of affinity groups organized by trade which nevertheless belong to the most varied ideological and doctrinal tendencies," the resolution stated. "The FORA therefore cannot declare itself to be partisan or to advocate the adoption of a philosophical system or a determined ideology."[7] The adoption of this resolution provoked a split; the anarchists withdrew from the federation in May of that year and formed the FORA V—after the FORA's fifth congress, when the resolution in favor of anarcho-communism was adopted—leaving the syndicalists in control of what came to be known as the FORA IX, after the resolution of the ninth congress.

Another difference between the two FORAs had to do with their composition—the FORA V had a strong base in Argentina's largely immigrant workforce, while members of the FORA IX were overwhelmingly native-born Argentines, with some affiliated unions (such as the Maritime Workers' Federation) even going so far as to ban immigrants from joining.[8] With a reformist orientation and a rank-and-file who were largely eligible voters, building an alliance with the FORA IX became a clear priority for the Radical Civic Union as it sought to win the working-class vote. When Yrigoyen took office in 1916—just one year after the split in the FORA—he adopted a policy of largely giving the FORA IX a free hand while maintaining the fierce repression employed by his predecessors during strikes organized by the FORA V.

The first labor dispute faced by his administration occurred just one month after he took office, when the sailors, stevedores, and boilermen of the Maritime Workers' Federation (FORA IX) went on strike to demand that their wages be adjusted to the rising cost of living. Yrigoyen invited the union's leaders to meet with him at the Casa Rosada and promised to refrain from using the police to protect strikebreakers, thus giving the workers the breathing room needed to settle the dispute with their bosses. The strike ended one month later with a victory for the union.[9] This would generally set the pattern for future strikes under the Yrigoyen administration— at least for those organized by the syndicalists. Things would be very different for socialist and anarchist-led strikes.

In December 1918, the United Metalworkers Resistance Society (FORA V) declared a strike at the Vasena factory, demanding higher wages, an eight-hour workday and the right to overtime pay. The Vasena family proved to be intransigent; they not only hired strikebreakers but used their connections to the Radical party to obtain the weapons permits needed to arm them. But the metalworkers received the solidarity of the city's unions and merchants—railway workers refused to unload raw materials destined for the Vasena works, while local shopkeepers donated food, coal, and other necessities to the strikers—and so the strike dragged on for over a month. By the beginning of 1919, there were nearly daily clashes between strikebreakers and the police on one side and strikers and their neighbors on the other. When the police killed four workers on January 7th, rioting and wildcat strikes across Buenos Aires led the FORA V to declare a general strike (the FORA IX declared its solidarity with the dead but declined to stop work). Barricades rapidly went up across the capital and workers sacked grocery stores and distributed goods to the populace. The Vasena works, trolleys, and police vehicles were torched as a clash broke out between the people in arms on one side and the police and nationalist gangs on the other—though these events are often spoken of for the bloodiness of the repression, they also represented a moment in which the Argentine labor movement attempted to assert itself and directly create an anarchist society through popular revolts. The government required a full military mobilization to regain control of the situation and, as the events described in this book show, the political situation would remain volatile for years to come.

Once the army restored order—at the cost of an estimated seven hundred lives—gangs of rich and middle class Argentines organized a pogrom, taking out their anger at the strikers on the Jewish community of Buenos Aires.[10] This pogrom—the so-called Tragic Week—also marked the rise of Argentina's nationalist movement, a proto-fascist political tendency that sought to expel immigrants, end collective bargaining, and overthrow the democratically elected government. On January 15th, 1919, Rear Admiral Manuel Domecq García—who had armed and organized the "civilian volunteers" responsible for the pogrom—announced the formation of the Argentine Patriotic League, whose goal it would be to repress future outbreaks of working class unrest.[11] Attracting military officers, policemen, large landowners, and right-wing intellectuals to its cause, the Patriotic League quickly became one of the most prominent nationalist organizations in Argentina and worked hand-in-glove with the police to violently break strikes across Argentina, but most infamously in Buenos Aires, La Palma, La Forestal, Villaguay, Gualuaychú, and Patagonia—where anarchists affiliated with the FORA V led a strike that ended in one of the worst massacres in Latin American history.

Though born in the heat of the immediate postwar political struggles, the nationalist movement would outlast its anarchist and Radical opponents to become the single most important tendency in twentieth-century Argentine politics. During the early years of the movement, anti-Semitic, anti-feminist, and anti-democratic ideas surged in popularity, while Mussolini, Hitler, and Charles Maurras became heroes of the Argentine right. "Let my compatriots—be they Radicals, conservatives or progressive liberals—put their hand in the fire if they did not make Mussolini's slogan 'Rome or Moscow' their own in those years," wrote the nationalist intellectual Juan Carulla in 1951.[12] By 1924, Leopoldo Lugones—Argentina's greatest modernist writer and once a man of the left—had embraced the far right, calling on Argentina to follow the example of Italy. In his infamous "Ayacucho Address" (so-called because it was delivered on the centennial of the Battle of Ayacucho, which secured the independence of South America), Lugones lamented the loss of what he considered to be the nobility and heroism of the Wars of Independence and suggested that violence could restore an aristocratic order in Argentina: "Just as the sword has accomplished our only real achievement to date, which is to say, our independence, it will likewise now create the order that we need," he said. "It will implement that indispensable hierarchy that democracy has to this date ruined—which it has in fact fatally derailed, for the natural consequence of democracy is to drift toward demagogy or socialism."[13]

Lugones's proclamation of the "hour of the sword" would have to wait six more years, however, as the prosperity of the mid-1920s and the relative conservatism of the Alvear administration slowed down nationalist organizing. But when Yrigoyen returned to the Casa Rosada in 1928 and the bottom fell out of the world economy the following year, all the conditions were in place for a military coup. On September 6th, 1930, troops led by General José Félix Uriburu—and was accompanied by two nationalist organizations, the Republican League and the League of May—forced Yrigoyen from office and instituted a military dictatorship.[14] Once in power, General Uriburu attempted to create a corporatist state, although political opposition and his own declining health forced him to step down prematurely, deferring this dream until Juan Perón's rise to power a decade and a half later. Incidentally, the FORA IX's successor organization, the Argentine Syndical Union (USA), would participate in the 1945 general strike that secured Perón's release from prison and his ascension to the presidency one year later. The union then dissolved itself and joined the Peronist General Confederation of Labor (CGT), closing out a cycle in which the "pure syndicalist" wing of the labor movement joined the state forces that continued to brutally murder and repress their former comrades.

Following the 1930 coup, many of Argentina's anarchists went into exile in neighboring South American countries, many of which had militant anarchist movements of their own—there would be anarcho-communist revolts in Brazil, Uruguay, Paraguay, and Bolivia up through the 1940s, including the 1931 declaration of a revolutionary commune in the Paraguayan city of Encarnación.[15] With the establishment of the Second Republic in 1931, many FORA members—including Diego Abad de Santillán and Simón Radowitzky, who both make cameo appearances in *Rebellion in Patagonia*—made their way to Spain. Members of the FORA and Uruguay's FORU played an important role in the following years, both in the international debates surrounding the CNT as well as in the civil war itself. And though decimated by repression—Diego Abad de Santillán estimated that, after three decades of FORA activity, over five thousand militants were killed and over 500,000 years in prison sentences were handed out—the union was able to survive under Argentina's succession of military regimes, maintaining a workplace presence until the last military dictatorship in the 1970s.[16]

But by the second half of the twentieth century, when Osvaldo Bayer wrote *Rebellion in Patagonia*, much of this history had been forgotten by the general public and Argentina's once-vital anarchist movement had become a shadow of its former self, having largely been sidelined by Marxism and Peronism. Due to Patagonia's distance from Buenos Aires, the 1920–1922 strike wave and subsequent massacre were particularly shrouded in mystery. Bayer himself heard about the events in Patagonia for the first time from his parents, who lived two blocks from the Río Gallegos jail during the repression that followed the strike. They told him that, late at night, they could hear the screams of the strikers being tortured by the prison guards—"My father was never able to overcome the sadness the deaths of all those people caused him," Bayer would later say.[17] Inspired by his father's stories of the strike, Bayer moved to Patagonia in 1958 and founded *La Chispa*, billed as Patagonia's first independent newspaper. In its pages, he defended the region's workers and indigenous people, but was run out of Patagonia by gendarmes in 1959. In the early 1970s—after abandoning journalism to reinvent himself as an anarchist historian, writing acclaimed books and articles on figures such as Simón Radowitzky and the infamous insurrectionist Severino di Giovanni—Bayer returned to the south to track down the remaining survivors of the massacre. His research would result in his magnum opus, the four-volume *The Avengers of Tragic Patagonia*, later abridged as *Rebellion in Patagonia*. The first volume was a bestseller and film director Héctor Olivera approached Bayer to make a movie based on the books. And that's when the trouble began.

Here it's worth giving some background on the political situation in Argentina at the time. In 1973, Juan Perón returned to Argentina after nearly twenty years in exile and retook the presidency months later. Though many on the left fondly remembered the pro-labor policies of his first two presidential terms (1946–1952 and 1952–1955), Perón merely represented the left wing of the nationalist movement that had massacred Argentina's genuine left in the early twentieth century and his support for unions was merely a means towards his ultimate end of creating a corporatist state modeled on Mussolini's Italy. Any hopes that his return from exile would benefit the left were dashed the day his plane touched down—as Peronists gathered to greet their leader at the Ezeiza International Airport, snipers associated with the right wing of the movement opened fire on the crowd, killing at least thirteen people and wounding some three hundred more. Once in office, Perón fully backed the Peronist right, giving paramilitary organizations a free hand to liquidate Argentina's independent left. When he passed away less than a year later, the presidency passed to his wife Isabel, who only intensified the persecution of the left.

On October 12th, 1974, Isabel Perón censored the film version of *Rebellion in Patagonia*—which had won the Silver Bear at the 24th Berlin International Film Festival just months before—and Osvaldo Bayer's name appeared on the blacklist of the Argentine Anticommunist Alliance (AAA), a Peronist paramilitary organization responsible for the assassinations of over one thousand leftists in the years preceding the military takeover. Bayer fled to West Germany, while Luis Brandoni (who played

Antonio Soto in the film) ended up in Mexico. Héctor Alterio, who played Commander Zavala (the fictionalized version of Commander Varela), was in Spain when he received word of the AAA's threats on his life and he opted not to return to Argentina. Jorge Cepernic, elected governor of Santa Cruz the previous year, was forced from office and imprisoned. According to Bayer, Cepernic asked the prison warden if he deserved to be in prison for having promoted progressive legislation during his aborted term as governor and the warden replied, "No, you aren't a prisoner because of your legislation, you're a prisoner because you allowed *Rebellion in Patagonia* to be filmed."[18] After the military forced Isabel Perón from power, the government continued its persecution of Bayer and his works—in April 1976, Lieutenant Colonel Gorlieri ordered all copies of *Rebellion in Patagonia* to be burned "so that this material cannot keep deceiving our youth as to the true good represented by our national symbols, our family, our Church and, in sum, our most traditional spiritual heritage, as synthesized by the motto 'God, Fatherland, Family.'"[19]

And so history repeated itself. The repression unleashed on Argentina's independent left by a populist president supported by moderate union leaders was echoed by the repression unleashed by Isabel Perón on those who attempted to bring the story to light some fifty years later. "This whole episode meant heartache for me and, with my family, eight years of exile," Bayer wrote in 2004, thirty years after the film was banned. "But, with the passing of time, the truth is ever greener. Whenever I reread the decree of President Lastiri banning *Severino di Giovanni*, or that of Isabel Perón, with *The Anarchist Expropriators*, or the names of those who intervened to hide the massacre in Patagonia from the people, and I see my books in bookstores and the film of *Rebellion in Patagonia* being screened in special showings, I can't help but smile: the truth provides a path through the darkness, it can't be killed forever."[20]

PRELIMINARY NOTE

In *Rebellion in Patagonia*, Osvaldo Bayer has synthesized the material presented in the four-volume *The Avengers of Tragic Patagonia*, whose first three volumes were published in Argentina between 1972 and 1974 and the fourth published in West Germany in 1978. The final volume had to be published abroad as both the author and the editor were forced into exile following the 1976 military coup.

The author has striven to ensure that *Rebellion in Patagonia* contains all the essential information covered in his previous four-volume study. An abridgment was necessary; it will be easier for the Latin American public to learn of the tragic events surrounding the most extensive strike of rural workers in South American history through a more synthesized study. The appearance of a one-volume edition is also more convenient from a publishing standpoint, as it has proven impossible to reprint a work as long as *The Avengers of Tragic Patagonia*.

Rebellion in Patagonia closes a cycle that began with the 1928 publication of José María Borrero's *Tragic Patagonia*, which dealt with the massacre of the indigenous people of southern Argentina and the exploitation of the region's rural workers. Borrero promised a follow-up volume titled *Orgy of Blood* that would deal with the massacre of rural workers during the 1921–1922 strikes. Borrero's second book—for a variety of reasons—was never published and was perhaps never even written. *Rebellion in Patagonia* deals with the same subject that would have been covered by Borrero's book—a subject that, for over fifty years, has remained taboo for researchers into the great deeds of Latin America's nearly unknown social history.

The Exterminating Angel

> "Kurt Wilckens, strong as a diamond,
> noble comrade and brother…"
> Severino Di Giovanni,
> *Los anunciadores de la tempestad*

By 5:30 a.m., it's already clear that January 25th, 1923 is going to be a sweltering day in Buenos Aires. A blond man gets on the trolley at Entre Ríos and Constitución and pays the workers' fare. He is heading towards the Portones de Palermo station, near Plaza Italia. He is holding a package, most likely his lunch or his tools. He seems calm. Shortly after boarding, he begins reading the *Deutsche La Plata Zeitung* that he has been carrying under his arm.

He gets off at Plaza Italia and heads west along Santa Fe, in the direction of the Pacífico station. After passing the station, he arrives at Calle Fitz Roy and stops in front of a pharmacy on the corner.

It's now 7:15 a.m. and the sun is already beating down hard. There's a great deal of foot and automobile traffic. The pharmacy faces the barracks of the 1st and 2nd Infantry. But the blond man doesn't look in that direction: his eyes don't leave the door of the house at Fitz Roy 2461.

Is today going to be the day? The answer seemed to be no. Nobody leaves the house. Minutes go by. Had he already left? Does he have any suspicions?

No, here he comes. A man in a military uniform leaves the house at 7:55. But it's the same as before: he's leading a little girl by the hand. The blond man makes an imperceptible gesture of exasperation. But then the military man stops and talks with the girl. She says that she doesn't feel well. He lifts her up in his arms and carries her back inside.

After a few short seconds the military man leaves the house again, alone this time. He's dressed in standard uniform with a saber at his side. He walks towards Calle Santa Fe on the same side of the street as the blond man. His firm character can be seen in his energetic stride. And now he heads towards his appointment with death on a beautiful, if a bit sweaty, morning.

He is none other than the famous Lieutenant Colonel Varela, better known as Commander Varela. Argentina's workers despise him above all other men. They say he's bloodthirsty, they call him the Butcher of Patagonia, they accuse him of having murdered 1,500 defenseless peons in the south. He forced them to dig their own graves, had them strip naked, and then executed them by firing squad. He gave orders for his subordinates to beat the union leaders with the flats of their swords before killing them, always with four shots each.

Does Commander Varela live up to the legend? He does in the eyes of the blond man waiting for him.

Not that the blond man is a relative of any of the executed workers. He has never even been to Patagonia, but neither has he received so much as five centavos in payment for the assassination. His name is Kurt Gustav Wilckens. A German anarchist of the Tolstoyan persuasion, he is an enemy of violence, but he believes that, in extreme cases, the only response to the violence of the mighty should be more violence. And he will follow through on this belief with an act of vigilante justice.

When he sees Varela coming, Wilckens doesn't hesitate. He moves to intercept him and hides in the doorway of the house located at Fitz Roy 2493. There he waits. Even now he can hear his footfalls. The anarchist leaves the doorway to confront him. But it won't be that easy. In that precise moment, a little girl crosses the street and begins walking in the same direction as Varela, just three steps ahead of him.[1]

Wilckens has run out of time: the little girl's sudden appearance threatens to ruin all his plans. But he makes his decision. He grabs the girl by the arm and pushes her out of the way, shouting, "Run, a car's coming!"

The girl is bewildered, frightened, hesitant. Varela stops to watch this strange scene. Instead of throwing his bomb, Wilckens advances on his prey while turning his back to the girl, as if to protect her with his body, but she is already running away. Facing Varela, Wilckens throws his bomb on the pavement, between him and the officer. There's a powerful explosion. Varela is taken by surprise and the shrapnel tears apart his legs. But Wilckens has also been hit and a sharp pain shoots through his body. He instinctively retreats to the doorway and climbs three or four steps, taking a moment to pull himself together—the enormous explosion has knocked the wind out of him. It takes just three seconds. Wilckens immediately descends the staircase. The anarchist then realizes that all is lost, that he can't flee, that he has a broken leg (his fibula has shattered and the pain in his muscles is agonizing) and that he can't move his other foot because of a piece of shrapnel lodged in the instep.

As he leaves the doorway, he comes across Varela. Though both of his legs are broken, he manages to remain upright by leaning against a tree with his left arm while trying to unsheathe his saber with his right hand. Now the two wounded men are once again face to face. Wilckens approaches, dragging his feet, and pulls out a Colt revolver. Varela roars, but instead of scaring the blue-eyed stranger, it sounds like a death rattle. The officer is collapsing, but he's not the type to surrender or plead for mercy. He keeps tugging at the saber but it refuses to leave the scabbard. There's only twenty centimeters left. Varela is still certain that he'll be able to unsheathe it when the first bullet hits. His strength abandons him and he begins to slowly slip down the tree trunk, but he has enough time left to curse the man who shot him. The second bullet ruptures his jugular. Wilckens empties the chamber. Every bullet is fatal. Varela's body is left wrapped around the tree.

The explosion and the gunshots have caused women to faint, men to flee, and horses to bolt.

Lieutenant Colonel Varela has died. Executed. His attacker is badly wounded. He makes a final effort to reach Calle Santa Fe. People are beginning to show their faces. Fearing the worst, Varela's wife goes down to the street and the poor woman catches sight of her dead husband, his body broken so dramatically.

Several neighbors approach the fallen man, lifting him up to carry him to the pharmacy on the corner. Others follow the strange foreigner who looks like a Scandinavian sailor. They keep their distance because he still carries his gun in his right hand. But two policemen have already come running: Adolfo González Díaz and Nicanor Serrano. They draw their guns when they're just a few steps away from Wilckens but they don't need to act because he offers them the butt of his own revolver. They take it away and hear him say, in broken Spanish, "I have avenged my brothers."[2]

Officer Serrano—"Black Serrano," as he's known at the 31st Precinct—responds by punching him in the mouth and kneeing him in the testicles. His hat—one of those traditional German hats with a wide brim, a cleft crown and a bow on the ribbon— falls off. They take him in with his head uncovered, awkwardly trying to stabilize himself with his wounded legs, like a shorebird with broken feet.

And so begins the cycle of revenge for the bloodiest repression of workers in twentieth century Argentina, save only for the period of the Videla dictatorship. The first chapter was written two years earlier, in the midst of the cold and the relentless gales of Patagonia, far to the south, with the most extensive strike of rural workers in South American history.

CHAPTER ONE

ARGENTINA'S FAR SOUTH

"In general, Argentines have the impression that
Santa Cruz is not part of our fatherland."
Lieutenant Colonel Varela,
Report to the War Ministry on the campaign
against the strikers
February 1922

What had happened in Patagonia? Or, better said, what was Patagonia in 1920?

To simplify things, we can say that it was an Argentine territory that was worked by Chilean peons and exploited by a group of landowners and merchants.[1] In other words, on one side we have those who were born to obey and on the other those who made their fortunes because they were strong by nature. And, down south, "strong" almost always means "unscrupulous." But that's the way things have to be: Patagonia is a land for strong men. At those latitudes, kindness is a sign of weakness. And the weak are devoured by the wind, alcohol, and their fellow men. For all

their faults, those white men who came to conquer Patagonia were
pioneers. It was there that they arrived, made their plans, sought
their fortunes, and harvested their riches, drinking the waters of
abundance. He who stays and carries on and whose feelings do not
waver will get rich. With nobody's help. Have pity on those who
want to take away what's rightfully theirs, what they've won in the
battle against nature, distance, and solitude!

In this battle, they depend on their sheep, horses, and chilotes.[2] The chilotes are a dark, nameless people; wretches born to
huddle in the mud, to never have a peso to their name. They work
to buy alcohol and the occasional gift for their women. Their
aspirations in life end there. They are the opposite of those who
have risked everything to come to Patagonia with the sole goal of
getting rich, "progressing."

This is the difference: some have been drunk on resignation
or indifference since they were children. Others are dominated
by a sole passion, one that is just as natural in those inhospitable
lands: ambition.

Among the ambitious, we can find individuals who have led
truly fantastic lives … and who have made fortunes that are just as
fantastic. It's enough to mention just one—the life and fortune of
Mauricio Braun, for example.

In 1874, a Jewish family disembarked at the port of Punta
Arenas: a man, a woman, and their four children. The father, Elías
Braun; the mother, Sofía Hamburger. They came fleeing Tsarist
Russia, where irrationality was used to maintain privilege and the
people, brutalized by slavery, looked to blame anyone for their
dismal lot except for those who had enslaved them. Hence the
brutal pogroms against the Jewish minority. Encouraged by the
church and the decadent Russian nobles who posed as nationalists,
the mob, morally and physically intoxicated, fell upon that cursed
race, upon the "Christ-killers," and unleashed orgies of blood. Just
as others hunt rats, so the Russians hunted Jews. Armed with little
more than clubs, they would surround a Jewish village or neighborhood and take the lives of others in revenge for all the injustices

they themselves had suffered. Each Jew they beat to death was like an orgasm of pleasure. Their masters exploited them, it's true, but every once in a while he gave them the freedom to kill a Jew. And then he gave them the right to rape the Jew's wife, who needed to surrender her body next to her husband's corpse on those terrible nights if she wanted to save her life and those of her children.

That was the ghastly image imprinted on the hearts of Elías and Sofía Braun when they made landfall in South America. Don Elías was a realist. He knew that there's only one way to overcome prejudice: to have money and power. Only then would he be respected in spite of his race. With the realism and lack of sentimentality he had earned through experience and suffering, Elías Braun got to work. He started with a warehouse in Punta Arenas. But if Elías was a man with a knack for business, his son Mauricio would outdo him in every way. He got his start in business when only a teenager. Everything was looking up. The past was to be forgotten. In this spirit—and despite their origins—the Braun family became Catholic the moment they stepped foot in a Catholic country.

In 1920, on the eve of the labor unrest in Santa Cruz, Elías Braun's son Mauricio Braun owned the Tierra del Fuego Development Corporation in partnership with his sister Sara Braun, controlling a total of 1,376,160 hectares—an astronomical figure that would be difficult to exceed anywhere in the world. This figure comes from an article entitled "Mauricio Braun, Rancher," written by Emilio J. Ferro, president of the Patagonian Federation of Rural Societies. It appeared in an issue of the magazine *Argentina Austral*, which was published by the Braun-Menéndez/Menéndez Behety Group. This particular issue was entirely dedicated to Mauricio Braun. The article also states that the Development Corporation possessed some 1.25 million heads of sheep, producing 5 billion kilos of wool, 700,000 kilos of leather, and 2.5 million kilos of meat.

But let's look at Mauricio Braun's properties in Patagonia, citing as before the laudatory issue of *Argentina Austral*:

He directly controls the 100,000-hectare Coy-Aike ranch, near the Coyle River in Santa Cruz. In Chubut, he founded the 117,500-hectare Quichaura ranch, the 77,000-hectare Pepita ranch, the 57,500-hectare Laurita ranch, and the 10,000-hectare Laura ranch. Together with the Anchorena family, he purchased the 90,000-hectare 8 de Julio ranch. In partnership with Ernesto von Heinz and Rodolfo Stubenrauch, he settled the 50,000-hectare Tapi Aike ranch. In 1916, he purchased 20,000 hectares in southern Santa Cruz from Rufino Martínez, christening the plot San Elías.[3] The Tres Brazos, Cancha Rayada, La Porteña, Montenegro, Gallegos, Chico, and Dinamarquero ranches are his as well. He controls 25 percent of the capital stock in the Laurita, Glencross, and Victorina ranches. He controls 20 percent of the San Julián Sheep Farming Company and 30 percent of the Aysen Development Company. He also controls 30 percent of the Monte León and La Carlota Argentine Ranching Company. Together with Santiago Frank, he settled the La Federica ranch near Lago San Martín. Alongside Segard and Company, he has invested in the Huemules ranch. In partnership with Pablo Lenzner, he settled the El Líbrum ranch between Río Gallegos and Lago Argentino. He settled the Los Machos ranch in San Julián with Juan Scott and the La Vidalita ranch with Erasmo Jones. With Guillermo Bain, he settled the 60,000-hectare La Josefina ranch in Cabo Blanco. With Donato Bain, he settled the 40,000-hectare Colhuel Kaike ranch in Las Heras. Together with Angus Macpherson, he settled the 58,000 hectares near Lago Buenos Aires that make up the San Mauricio ranch, named in his honor. He has invested in Hobbs and Company, which founded the Lago Posados ranch and which had Lucas Bridges at its head. [...] He assisted Hobbs and Company in settling the 90,000-hectare El Ghio ranch. [...] In 1915, he and Rodolfo Suárez, in partnership with Capagli and Company, acquired the 56,250-hectare María Inés ranch, located to the west of Río Gallegos.

But this wasn't the extent of Mauricio Braun's property—he owned much more. By the turn of the century, he had become the owner of the Cutter Cove Mining Company, which dealt in copper, and the Bank of Chile and Argentina, which had its headquarters in Punta Arenas and branch offices in the Santa Cruz port towns of Río Gallegos, Santa Cruz, and San Julián. From there he acquired the South American Export Syndicate Ltd.'s meatpacking plants in Río Seco, Punta Arenas, Puerto Deseado, and Río Grande (Argentina) and Puerto Sara, Puerto Borries and Puerto Natales (Chile). He then founded the La Austral insurance company and invested in the power plant in Puerto Santa Cruz, the electric company in Punta Arenas and the telephone companies in Magallanes and San Julián. He also owned the La Magallanes shoe factory and the Lavaderos de Oro Development Company.

The Brauns weren't the only ones who were all-powerful in southern Chile and Argentina. There were two other characters who had also amassed mountains of gold in just a few short years. One of them, an Asturian named José Menéndez, has been accused of decimating the indigenous habitants of our far south in José María Borrero's book *Tragic Patagonia*. The other, José Nogueira, was Portuguese. These two, Menéndez and Nogueira, transformed themselves from humble shopkeepers to powerful businessmen in a matter of years.

Elías Braun, the Russian Jew who had disembarked at Punta Arenas, was more than just a good businessman. As under monarchies, Braun, Menéndez, and Nogueira pooled their fortunes—not only as partners, but also as families. They had no racial complexes. And so Sara Braun—the eldest daughter of Elías Braun—married the Portuguese immigrant Nogueira, while Mauricio Braun married Josefina Menéndez Behety, the daughter of the Asturian José Menéndez, forming the Braun-Menéndez family. Nogueira died shortly thereafter and Sara Braun inherited a tremendous fortune, which she allowed her brother Mauricio to administer.

Power in Patagonia hinged on the following formula: land plus wool production plus commercialization plus control of transportation. Menéndez, Nogueira, and Braun understood this when they sought to take control of the seaways. How they pulled this off is explained perfectly by Frigate Captain Pedro Florido, the former governor of Tierra del Fuego, in his article "Don Mauricio Braun, Shipping Magnate":

When the young Mauricio Braun first came ashore in Punta Arenas, so began his future career as a shipping magnate, a story that is inseparable from that of progress in Chilean and Argentine Patagonia. Another ship arrived one year later, bringing a young Spaniard and his wife. Like Mauricio, they would forever be part of the history of the region's progress and would even become part of his family, though no one suspected it at the time. This model couple, José Menéndez and María Behety, had decided to come to that distant port town in search of better prospects than those that had been offered them by the thriving city of Buenos Aires. Completing the trinity was a renowned Lusitanian who had been already been working in the region for some years as a shipwright and a guide, as he knew Tierra del Fuego's symphony of inlets, bays, fjords, and channels—off-limits to the novice sailor—like the back of his hand. Here we refer to José Nogueira, the owner and operator of a fleet of 100–400 ton schooners, which he used for fishing, seal hunting, and trading with the region's Indians, not to mention the man who had the privilege of introducing Falkland sheep to Patagonia's ranches. Mauricio Braun started working in Nogueira's offices when he was fifteen and quickly rose through the company thanks to his business skills and his knowledge of many languages, which made him stand out and earned him the respect of his bosses. As the years passed, our young hero took a fancy to Don José's daughter, Josefina Menéndez Behety, and soon married her. As his sister had married Nogueira, he became the son-in-law and brother-in-law of his superiors, who would later become his business partners: first Nogueira and then Don José. Though they became partners in 1908, at first José Menéndez was his rival as Don José had dedicated himself to the maritime sector after his arrival in Punta Arenas. One of his first actions in this line of work had been to purchase a maritime supply business from Captain Luisito Piedrabuena. In this manner, José Menéndez, José Nogueira, and Mauricio Braun, who quickly became a partner in Nogueira's firm, anticipated the theories of the great maritime philosopher Ratzel, who said in 1904, "If you would rule on land, harness the sea."

The firm of Mauricio Braun and Scott was incorporated in 1904, shortly thereafter acquiring the schooner *Ripling Wave*, which they used to bring supplies to the distant ranches of Tierra del Fuego and the Strait of Magellan, returning with bales of wool. But Mauricio Braun didn't stop there. As Punta Arenas was a required stopover between the Atlantic and Pacific Oceans, in those days, maritime activities constituted the town's main source of commercial activity, wealth and progress and the shipping magnate's strong personality and drive consequently won him considerable prestige and influence. The Mauricio Braun & Blanchard Trading and Shipping Company was incorporated in 1892, with Mauricio providing 80 percent of the initial capital stock [...] but the fierce competition between the various shipping firms, especially that owned by his father-in-law José Menéndez, forced him to overhaul the propulsion systems he had been using. [...] Technical requirements and business rivalries took precedence over romanticism [...] as progress and economic logic know nothing of sentimentality. The new company acquired many small passenger and cargo steamboats to serve the coasts of Patagonia and Tierra del Fuego. Punta Arenas, Ushuaia, Río Grande, and other port towns in Santa Cruz were regularly served by the steamboats *Lovart*, *Magallanes*, *Keek-Row*, *Patagonia*, *Porvenir*, *Araucanía*, and *Cordillera*, among others. José Menéndez's acquisition of the 350-ton steamboat *Amadeo* was the warning shot that motivated the firm of Braun & Blanchard to follow in the wake of Mauricio's father-in-law and keep the competition going.

Braun & Blanchard also acted as a shipping agent for British shipping lines, acquiring a fleet of tugboats—*Antonio, Díaz, Laurita, Armando, Carlos,* etc.—along with a shipyard of the dimensions and characteristics needed to provide these boats with the logistical support they required. But the last word had yet to be said. While his father-in-law, a powerful adversary, was increasing the tonnage of his ships and extending his shipping lines beyond Buenos Aires and Valparaíso, Braun founded the Magallanes Whaling Company in 1904. [...] He built the factory and principal whaling station on Deception Island, meeting the demand for blue whales and other, smaller cetaceans with his flagship *Gobernador Borries* and his other whaling vessels, all of them christened with the names of distinguished Chilean admirals: *Montt, Uribe, Valenzuela,* etc.

The rivalry between the shipping companies owned by Braun and José Menéndez was legendary, and it was this competition that created the regular steamboat lines serving Chile and Argentina. [...] Mauricio and his father-in-law didn't mix business with family, and if that sturdy Asturian had an overpowering character, his son-in-law, whom he confronted on the seas, was every bit his equal. By 1907, we can see that Braun & Blanchard were no longer content with only providing services along the coasts of Tierra del Fuego and the most southerly reaches of Chile and Argentina, and so they extended those services right up the Chilean coastline, leasing the Norwegian ships *Alm* and *Westford.* The following year, they bolstered this line with *Chiloé* and *Magallanes,* which had been built in the United Kingdom for carrying cargo and passengers. They acquired other vessels later on, all of them named after provinces of Chile: *Valdivia, Llanquihue, Santiago, Tarapacá,* and *Valparaíso.*

Of course, every maritime industry needs a shipyard to carry out repairs. And so Braun built one in Punta Arenas.

But, at the end of the day, son-in-law and father-in-law were drawn together. The historian Juan Hilarión Lenzi, in another article paying homage to Mauricio Braun, has this to say on the matter:

> The trading and shipping ventures operating under the name of Braun & Blanchard—which served as a holding company—competed with those operated by José Menéndez, both in the region of the Strait of Magellan as well as throughout Patagonia. Father-in-law fought against son-in-law in the world of business. Neither Don José nor Don Mauricio gave any quarter. Their family ties and personal relationships did not interfere with their business plans, but it wasn't logical to insist on conflict when their final objectives were the same. The two tycoons eventually arrived at an arrangement and agreed to form a company that would expand and reinvigorate their field of action. José Menéndez and Mauricio Braun merged their respective companies on June 10th, 1908, forming the Patagonia Import and Export Company. The company's initial stock was 180,000 pounds sterling. The subsidiaries of Braun & Blanchard in Río Gallegos, Santa Cruz, San Julián, Puerto Madryn, Trelew, and Ñorquinco and Menéndez's holdings in Río Gallegos, Santa Cruz, and Comodoro Rivadavia also merged their operations.

Besides the branch offices in these towns, the Patagonia Import and Export Company—popularly known as La Anónima—also incorporated larger ships into its fleet.[4] It acquired the *Asturiano* and the *Argentino* in 1914, with the *Atlántico*, the *Americano*, and the *José Menéndez* coming later.

But the power of Mauricio Braun was barely one-tenth of that exercised by his father-in-law José Menéndez, the tough, ravenous Asturian who served as the true Tsar of Patagonia until his death. A man who has yet to find his true biographer, who will either describe him as egotistical, brutal, and unscrupulous, dominated by an insatiable desire for wealth, or as a leader who fought for progress without caring who was tramped underfoot along the way.

José Menéndez passed away in 1918, leaving a large part of his fortune to King Alfonso XIII of Spain, which provoked the ire of Argentina's socialists and anarchists. Control of La Anónima passed into the hands of Mauricio Braun.

We have consulted the publications of the Menéndez-Behetys and Braun-Menéndezes rather than those of their detractors. Here we're not interested in the origins of their fabulous wealth so much as we are in the political power granted by their economic strength.[5] It's clear that those who had acquired such immense wealth in such a short time would not allow a group of madmen flying the red flag and speaking of concessions to come along and occupy their ranches. Their fellow landowners felt the same.

Through the example of the Braun-Menéndez family, we can understand who controlled the economy in Argentine and Chilean Patagonia, as well as the power that this inevitably represented…in the face of so much wealth, to whose interests were the region's poor civil servants, policemen, judges, governors, etc. going to respond?

Now let's see the hands into which the rest of the territory of Santa Cruz had fallen. The concession of 2,517,274 hectares of formerly state-owned land granted to Adolfo Grünbein (1893) was then divided among the ranchers Halliday, Scott, Rudd, Wood, Waldron, Grienshield, Hamilton, Saunders, Reynard, Jamieson, MacGeorge, MacClain, Felton, Johnson, Woodman, Redman, Smith, Douglas, and Ness from England; Eberhard, Kark, Osenbrüg, Bitsch, Curtze, Wahlen, Wagner, Curt Mayer, and Tweedie from Germany; Bousquet, Guillaume, Sabatier, and Roux from France; Montes, Rivera, Rodolfo Suárez, Fernández, Noya, and Barreiro from Spain; Clark from the United States; Urbina from Chile; and Riquez from Uruguay. In other words, not a single Argentine.

The Grünbein concession took 2,517,274 hectares of land out of the hands of the public trust. Adolfo Grünbein purchased 400 kilometric leagues at the price of 1,000 gold pesos per league. Of these, 125 leagues were turned over to the Bank of Antwerp.

The turn-of-the-century oligarchic government thus condemned Patagonia to be ruled by large landowners and to be and to the medieval system of primitive methods of exploitation. It condemned Patagonia to sheep farming, the most harmful and injurious form of production. But what was established by the oligarchic regime was later embraced, or at least tolerated, by the Radical and Peronist governments, as well as by all of Argentina's military dictatorships. In Patagonia, military governors are honored with monuments, banquets, and tasteless poetry for having promoted a handful of public works while leaving the great landed estates intact—and, in the end, these public works were largely carried out to benefit the landowners. None have thought to promote immigration through the construction of ports, irrigation systems, and factories. And, fundamentally, none have thought to promote agriculture among the region's indigenous inhabitants instead of planning for their total extermination. The only initiatives, rather, have been of a military nature. With warships and barracks, the government attempted to forge a sense of patriotism that can only be felt through shared traditions and a day-to-day commitment to the land. But that would be to speak of wasted opportunities. Reality was and is different.

What invites ridicule is the idea, still being peddled today, that the repression seen during the 1921–1922 strike was carried out in defense of our national heritage and against those who, flying the red flag, wanted to "internationalize" Patagonia. Without any need for a red flag, Patagonia was already internationalized—not just by foreign landowners, but also because all of her raw material wealth was sent overseas.

In other words, the intervention of the Argentine Army did not occur to defend the nation's interests, but to preserve the status and privileges of foreign companies and to protect an unjust feudal regime that still chokes southern Argentina, slowly turning it into a desert.

And it will be in that desolate landscape where the sparks will fly between the two poles of the region's rudimentary social structure: the serfs and the great medieval landowners.

CHAPTER TWO

THE WHITES AND THE REDS

"A handful of ranchers were the masters of
Patagonia, paying in scrip or Chilean currency"
Colonel Pedro Viñas Ibarra, who, as a captain,
commanded one of the columns repressing
the strikes in Patagonia.

The slaughter of Patagonia's workers will occur under the watch of
President Hipólito Yrigoyen, the first president of Argentina elected
by universal, secret, and compulsory voting.[1] The leader of a movement with deep popular roots, a *caudillo* loved by the petite bourgeois
and proletarian masses (with the exception of those class-conscious
workers who identified as anarchists or socialists), Hipólito Yrigoyen
and his Radical Civic Union successfully used constitutional methods to destroy the regime—but not the power—of the landowning
and mercantile oligarchy. Though timid, his reformism successfully managed to democratize Argentina and increase the political
participation of the masses, while he made genuine attempts at a
more independent foreign policy and a fairer redistribution of the

country's wealth. But this same timidity, this propensity for dialogue and compromise, was not enough to overcome the crises faced by his administration. When the industrial workers of Buenos Aires rose up, he allowed the oligarchy to repress them with the army and the armed commandos of the upper crust, resulting in the bloodshed of the Tragic Week of January 1919. And when Patagonia's agricultural workers firmly demanded a series of concessions and the movement threatened to go beyond mere unionism—according to the information available in Buenos Aires—he lets the army defend the feudal order with blood and fire.

Yrigoyen thus became the involuntary executioner of Argentina's social movements. Ironic, but not coincidental. What hadn't occurred under the pre-1916 oligarchic regime—during which repression never reached the level of collective massacre—would transpire under the populist government of Yrigoyen (to reduce repetition).

1920. The distant territory of Patagonia is in crisis. Since the end of the Great War, wool prices have fallen and unrest has increased. The British market is saturated. Two and a half million bundles of wool from Australia and New Zealand that were shipped to London have gone unsold. Patagonian wool hasn't even had that much luck: it hasn't even left the port. The London bureau of the Havas news agency issues a report stating that "significant stocks of low quality South American wool have been offered at low prices to the Central Powers." The good times of the war, when money flowed freely into hands that were already full, have ended in Patagonia. This is the fate of all regions that are condemned to produce a single product: when the price of wool rises, there's prosperity; when it falls, as occurred from 1919 on, there's unemployment, poverty, repression, depressed wages, economic crisis, resignation among small producers and traders, and panic among large landowners. The latter has already asked Yrigoyen for help, though the president proved to be far from sympathetic. The Radical president instead dared, on two consecutive occasions, to move against the sacred interests of the true masters of Patagonia.

He reinstated customs offices in the far south to control imports and exports and then ordered land claims to be reassessed. The latter meant that many ranches were considerably reduced in size, as their owners had taken possession of much more land than they actually owned.

These two measures cut down on a number of rights and prerogatives that had been acquired per se, but also created a defensive atmosphere among large landowners that united them in resistance to anything that smelled of tax collectors and government agents.

It was Dr. Ismael P. Viñas, the new judge in the Patagonian territories of Santa Cruz and Tierra del Fuego—a man with a Radical background and a personal friend of Yrigoyen—who broke with the tradition that all of Patagonia's public servants and judges either answered to ranching interests or were their direct agents. Before the surprised eyes of the representatives of the region's corporations, Viñas initiated legal proceedings for tax evasion against one of the region's largest ranching concerns, The Monte Dinero Sheep Farming Company. The resolute judge also initiated proceedings against The San Julián Sheep Farming Company for their illegal seizure of the property of Donald Munro, who had passed away at the turn of the century and whose fields, as he lacked heirs, should have been turned over to the National Education Council.

This was unthinkable for the large ranching concerns and their agents. It was clear that something had changed in Argentina. The Yrigoyen administration had decided to defend the government's interests against the creeping influence of those who controlled the country's sources of socioeconomic power. But this radicalism showed its limitations at each step. Though he backed Judge Viñas, Yrigoyen also allowed for the inconceivable: the government of Santa Cruz remained in the hands of an ultra-conservative, Edelmiro Correa Falcón, who—though it's hard to believe—simultaneously served as the secretary of the Santa Cruz Rural Society, the landowners' federation. President Yrigoyen could have immediately designated someone else to serve as governor, as Santa Cruz was then a territory and not a province—it was under the direct control of the federal government, in other words, and did not enjoy political autonomy.[2]

As if afraid of rattling the mighty too much, Yrigoyen did not replace Correa Falcón. The ultraconservative continues holding the reins of the territory's government bureaucracy and police apparatus, both of which will be used against the Radical judge.

We shall see how the judge will be supported in this conflict by the sparse middle class of Santa Cruz—small business owners, white collar workers, and artisans—as well as by unionized workers. A crude class alliance in this distant territory will form a sort of anti-oligarchic front aimed at destroying the medieval regime to which they are subjected. When the hour of decision comes, however, this class alliance will break apart and the entire middle class will defect to the side of the landowners, letting the workers alone fall victim to the savage repression.

But first let's study the forces in Buenos Aires that are playing tug-of-war over Argentina's first popularly elected president.

When Patagonia's landowners asked Yrigoyen for support in facing the wool crisis, the president was surrounded by a series of enormous problems. Though he hadn't lost his calm, he was constantly being attacked in both international and domestic politics and on economic, social, and political issues.

Internationally, Yrigoyen had once again fallen out of favor with the Allied nations. Foreign Minister Pueyrredón had left Geneva during the inaugural meeting of the League of Nations after being the sole delegate to vote against the war reparations imposed on defeated Germany. The Argentina of Yrigoyen thus remained true to its policy of neutrality, showing its desire to maintain an independent line, that of a sovereign nation.

And the summer that comes at the end of 1920 will be a hot one in every sense of the word. The peso reaches a record low: 100 dollars buy 298.85 Argentine pesos, scandalizing the haughty columnists at the traditional newspapers, the fearless defenders of the oligarchy's privileges. They blame the populist government. They don't explain that the falling value of the German mark also affects the value of pounds sterling and strengthens the dollar, and that Argentina's economy has become more independent of the British sphere and is slowly beginning to fall under the influence of the true winner of the First World War: the United States.

Domestically, the price of bread has jumped once again, this time to sixty centavos per kilo, which makes these same columnists remember in passing that, before the coming of the populist government, this essential foodstuff cost barely thirty centavos.

Labor conflicts are on the rise. There's a near-general strike among agricultural laborers, primarily in the provinces of Buenos Aires, Santa Fe, Córdoba, Chaco, and Entre Ríos. The ranchers, the small independent farmers, and the large and small property owners don't turn to Yrigoyen for defense. They don't trust him. Neither do Argentina's businessmen nor the representatives of powerful foreign corporations. They know that they have a firm ally, their only friend but a strong one: the Argentine Army. If the army hadn't defeated the workers of the Vasena metal works with fire and blood, who else would have saved the country from the anarchist and Bolshevik hordes in January 1919? Did Yrigoyen even try? Did anyone see any white berets on the streets repressing the rebel workers?[3] All those individuals whose actions stand out in the uncontrolled class struggle of the first three decades of the twentieth century have been graduates of the National Military College. It was Colonel Ramón Falcón who trained the police and worked to break up the major labor organizations until 1909, the year in which he fell victim to the bomb thrown by the anarchist Simón Radowitzky. It was General Dellepiane who became the hero of the Vasena metal works, where proletarian cadavers were piled into wheelbarrows. It is Lieutenant Colonel José Félix Uriburu who will give subversive anarchism the *coup de grace* in 1930, together with men like Colonel Pilotto and Major Rosasco.[4] And later on, it is General Justo who will put an end to the dreams and vagaries of proletarian revolution with severe repression and a continuous state of siege.

But in the wake of the Tragic Week, or Red Week, of January 1919, the upper and upper-middle classes—that is, everyone with something to lose from a workers' uprising—start preparing to defend themselves, even though they know they can count on the army as a strong ally. The genius behind this movement is Dr. Manuel Carlés, the president of the Argentine Patriotic League. A talented organizer, his paramilitary organization spreads across the country, forming a true army of white guards. The organization's brigades are formed by bosses, managers, foremen, police officers, retired military men, and the so-called good workers. Respectable people, in other words. Well-armed, they patrol Argentina's small towns and countryside. If a property owner has a problem with their laborers, the Argentine Patriotic League comes to their aid. They are prepared to do whatever is needed to defend what's theirs. Carlés has also organized women's brigades, led by young Catholic women from good families who recruit their followers from among factory workers and domestic workers.

Manuel Carlés tours the country, sounding the alarm about the threat posed by organized labor and the Yrigoyen administration, despite having been an employee of the federal government not long ago. On December 5th, 1920, Carlés gives the following florid speech:

We are the only country in the world whose authorities, barely concealing their contempt, allow for public sedition against our national identity. Saturated with the insults of sectarianism, the greatest atrocities against the right to work and the moral honor of the fatherland are treated as if they were but the sound of falling rain.

The Patriotic League acts with complete independence: they use the newspapers to issue orders to their members, openly calling on them to take up arms, repress strikes, provide support for besieged capitalists, etc.[5] One example will be enough: this communiqué was issued on December 5th, 1921 by the Patriotic

League brigade in Marcos Juárez, Córdoba in the midst of a peon strike:

> The brigade has mobilized all of its members, who are preparing themselves to defend their collective interests from the anarchist agitators who made their appearance last night and who have since been interfering with the harvest. These outlaws have been threatening the workers and resort to violence at the first sign of resistance; they immediately tried to storm the police station when a group of their agitators was arrested. Such a state of affairs justifies the serious measure of mobilizing the brigade. Divided into defense sectors, we stand ready to repel this aggression. The town's police force is small, but fortunately we form a large and determined group that is willing to guarantee the right to work, even if by force of arms. Today we called upon the ringleader of the subversive movement—a foreigner, naturally—and we have given him a period of two hours to leave the region. If he fails to do so, we will follow the instructions issued by the central committee for these situations. Dr. Carlés has addressed the brigade, endorsing our actions and offering us the tools we need to reach our noble goals.

It's clear that the League has been given a free hand: they run workers out of town, carry firearms, attack unions, break up protests. It's a counter-union, a union of the bosses. The only difference is that the government and the police don't allow the workers to carry firearms.

And quite rightly. Nobody can disagree—at least from the point of view of those who have something to lose—that everyone should defend themselves as best they can. Fear justifies everything. News of the massacres of nobles, capitalists, and landowners by revolutionaries in Russia has kept the lords and masters of Argentina up at night. It's time for neither hesitancy nor the Christian spirit. Each class must defend what's theirs. This true around the world but especially so in Argentina, with the country's strong union movement and anarchism's unshakable hold on broad sectors of its working class. But the government doesn't seem to have taken notice of the muted class warfare that has taken over the streets and countryside. And so Yrigoyen is criticized by the workers for allowing illegal paramilitary organizations to operate with impunity and by the bosses who rebuke his lack of energy in suppressing strikes and acts of terrorism.

Now let's examine the forces that will come into conflict in the distant territory of Santa Cruz. On one side, we have the Río Gallegos Workers' Society (affiliated with the Argentine Regional Workers' Federation, or FORA), which organized stevedores, cooks, waiters, hotel staff, and farmworkers. Their enemies were the city's bosses, organized in the Río Gallegos Commerce and Industry League, the Santa Cruz Rural Society (bringing together all the region's ranchers), and the Argentine Patriotic League, which, as we have said, united property owners, trusted employees, etc. and was a paramilitary organization directed against the proletarian left.

Let's start with the workers. Their central organizations in Buenos Aires were totally divided.

There were two FORAs: the FORA V (orthodox anarchists)[6] and the FORA IX, in which syndicalists, socialists, and the addicts of Russia's Bolshevik revolution prevailed.[7] The latter promoted dialogue with the Radical government—one of its leaders, Maritime Workers' Federation Secretary-General Francisco J. García, had open access to Hipólito Yrigoyen's offices. The anarchists of the FORA V called them chameleons, while the FORA IX, in turn, considered the anarchists to be sectarians.

But the working class wasn't just divided into different organizations, but also different ideologies. Among the socialists, there was the classic division between social democrats and partisans of the dictatorship of the proletariat, as represented by the Socialist Party and the International Socialist Party, which would soon change its name to the Communist Party. The anarchists, in turn, assumed three different positions: the orthodox anarchists were split into a moderate wing (which had a voice in the newspaper *La Protesta*) and a leftist wing (represented by the newspapers *El Libertario*, *La Obra*, and later on *La Antorcha*), while another group of anarchists who sympathized with the Russian Revolution was grouped around the newspaper *Bandera Roja*, and included Julio R. Barcos, García Thomas, etc. These latter were the so-called anarcho-bolsheviks.

None of these divisions that caused such heated polemics in Buenos Aires were visible in the Santa Cruz Workers' Federation, which had its headquarters in Río Gallegos. Its leaders didn't concern themselves with ideological differences and instead focused on standing up to the power of the bosses, the government, and the police. There's no doubt that danger had united them. We can say that, deep down, they all had an anarchist background, though many were still blinded by the triumph of the Russian Revolution.

The Río Gallegos Workers' Federation had a short life. It was founded in 1910 and would end its days among the mass graves of its members in the summer of 1921–1922. The founder of this labor organization was a blacksmith named José Mata, described by the police as a "suspected anarchist militant." He was born in Oviedo, Spain in 1879. He had several children, whose names speak for themselves: Progreso (Progress), Elíseo (Elysium), Alegría (Happiness), Libertario (Libertarian), Bienvenida (Welcome). The first labor dispute in Santa Cruz took place in November 1914 on the Mata Grande ranch, owned by the Englishman Guillermo Patterson. The leaders of this first strike were the Spaniard Fernando Solano Palacios and the Austrian Mateo Giubetich. They demanded that their bosses stop charging migrant farmworkers for their meals and for the combs and shears broken during the shearing, as well as demanding that medical examinations be voluntary, or rather that this expense stop being the responsibility of the workers. They also demanded 85 pesos per month plus food expenses for cart drivers instead of the 90 pesos minus 30 centavos per meal they were currently being paid. The shearers should also have their meals included, they demanded.

The strike then spread to the Los Manantiales and Florida Negra ranches, which were owned by the Englishmen Kemp and Hobbs. The police intervened in defense of the English ranchers and arrested the movement's two leaders. The judge invoked the Social Defense Law, an anti-anarchist measure that sentenced them to prison time and the seizure of 1,000 pesos of their property as reparations for lost profits. But the problems didn't end there, as the strike then spread to all the ranches located near San Julián. The movement's leadership fell to the interim secretary of the San Julián Workers' Society, a forty-eight-year-old Chilean carpenter named Juan de Dios Figueroa. Shearing stopped throughout the region and the bosses responded by bringing in scabs by ship from Buenos Aires. When the scabs disembarked, a battle broke out on the beach. The scabs were backed by the police. This first conflict ended in the total defeat of the strikers and the region's anarchists were hunted down, leading to the arrest of sixty-eight people, an unprecedented number for San Julián. Nearly all of them were foreigners: forty Spaniards, twenty Chileans, one Englishman, one Italian, one Russian, four Argentines, and one Frenchman.

At the beginning of 1915, and as an aftershock of the first strike, the workers of The New Patagonia Meat Preserving and Cold Storage Co. Ltd.—the Swift meatpacking plant of Río Gallegos—stopped work. Once again, police repression helped defeat the movement, and strike leaders Serafín Pita (Uruguayan) and José Mandrioli (Italian) were imprisoned.

The subsequent movements would also be strangled by police repression. But the region's labor organizations, instead of being destroyed, were strengthened by these defeats. It's worth mentioning the strike declared on April 20th, 1917, the first attempted general strike in Río Gallegos. It was organized by the workers to demand an end to the practice of corporal punishment inflicted by foremen on underage farmworkers. It was a strike carried out in solidarity, in other words, which speaks to the altruistic spirit that motivated the proletarians of these distant lands.

In April 1918, a general strike was declared in Puerto Deseado. The demands of the employees of La Anónima (owned by the Braun-Menéndez family) and other companies were supported by the railway workers of the Deseado-Las Heras line, the only rail line in Santa Cruz.

There was always contact and solidarity between the anarchist workers' organizations in Argentine and Chilean Patagonia, solidarity that managed to overcome the enormous distances separating the two countries and the unreliable means of communication connecting them. Collaboration was so close that many union leaders operated in both regions, such as the libertarian Eduardo Puente, who participated in the April 1918 demonstrations in Puerto Deseado and later played a role in the strikes that December in Punta Arenas, the southernmost city in Chile. The Magallanes Workers' Federation (Chile) declared a general strike in protest against "the high cost of living and the economic monopoly of a single family we all depend on"— the Braun-Menéndez family, naturally. Striking workers were attacked by the gendarmerie, leaving many dead or wounded. Soldiers sacked the union's office, destroying their furniture and archives, and arrested the three main strike leaders: Puente, Olea, and Cofre. But the popular outrage was so great that the authorities decided to come to an arrangement with the union. They agreed to all of the strike demands and released Olea and Cofre. Puente, however, was deported. He was sent back to Río Gallegos, where the workers were in a state of great agitation. The Workers' Federation was making the biggest moves it had ever made. And the fight wasn't over higher wages but the freedom of one man: Apolinario Barrera.

This is how it happened: Simón Radowitzky, the young anarchist who had killed Colonel Falcón in 1909 and had been sentenced to life in Tierra del Fuego, the "Argentine Siberia," escaped from his island prison. He had the help of Apolinario Barrera, the manager of the anarchist newspaper *La Protesta*, who had come down from Buenos Aires specifically for this purpose.

After a legendary escape, they were captured in Chile and taken to Punta Arenas on the cruiser *Zenteno*, left shackled to an iron bar on the deck for twelve days. From there, an Argentine Navy transport took them to Río Gallegos, where Aponinario Barrera was turned over to the police and Radowitzky was sent back to the gloomy Ushuaia penitentiary.

Meanwhile, the governor, in turn, ordered that Puente also be arrested and sent to Ushuaia. The Workers' Federation called a general assembly of its members on January 14th, 1919 to decide on whether or not to organize a general strike calling for the release of Apolinario Barrera and Eduardo Puente. But the assembly never got the chance to make its decision, as the police, under the command of Commissioner Ritchie, surrounded the union offices, barged in, and arrested the entire leadership committee (nine Spaniards and one Russian). Another group of workers immediately took over the committee's duties and declared a general strike.

Something unexpected happened on January 17th, something that had never been seen on the streets of Río Gallegos: a demonstration by working-class women. They demanded the immediate release of the men who had been imprisoned because of their union activities. According to the police, the women, who had taken over Calle Zapiola and Calle Independencia, refused orders to disperse. They allegedly hurled abuse at the representatives of law and order, threw stones at Commissioner Alfredo Maffei and attacked Officer Ramón Reyes from behind.

Things only got more serious from there. Sergeant Jesús Sánchez arrested the demonstration's organizer, the Spaniard Pilar Martínez (a thirty-one-year-old widow and a cook by trade). But according to the police report, the woman—a brave Galician flower—gave him "a sharp kick in the testicles, producing a painful contusion rendering him unfit for duty for two days." The police report, signed by Commissioner Ritchie, adds that this crude act committed by a representative of the weaker sex was witnessed by Submissioner Luis Lugones and the civilians Antonio

Adrover, Pedro Rubione, and Augusto Guilard, who immediately offered to testify against the woman.

The medical report, issued by Dr. Ladvocat, shouldn't be missed: "Sergeant Jesús Sánchez complains of a sharp pain in his left testicle that is exacerbated by the slightest pressure. But it will heal without any long-term consequences for the patient." His honor was saved! Heaven forbid that this police officer should lose the virility that he demonstrated so well by beating women.

This affair ended with the formal dissolution of the Workers' Federation and the fleeting triumph of the governor, who just a few days later will have to come to the rescue of Colonel Contreras Sotomayor, the governor of the Chilean province of Magallanes, then facing a strike by the workers at the Borries Meatpacking Plant in Puerto Natales. These workers were supported by the Última Esperanza Farmworkers and Meatpackers Union, led by the anarchists Terán, Espinosa, Saldivia, and Viveros. The workers occupied the city and administered it through workers' councils.

Despite the internal situation in Río Gallegos and the popular rebellion in Punta Arenas that threatened to spill over the border, the governor of Santa Cruz sent all the troops at his disposal to Puerto Natales, where Major Bravo reinstated the Chilean deputy mayor at his post.

And so the first cycle of workers' uprisings in the extreme south of the continent came to an end. The Río Gallegos Workers' Federation also ended the first stage of its existence with the final closure of its offices by Judge Sola and the imprisonment of its leaders, who would be released just five months later. And it is Antonio Soto who will lead the new Río Gallegos Workers' Society in the second stage of its existence, right up to its final defeat at the hands of Lieutenant Colonel Varela.

CHAPTER THREE

DAWN FOR THE WRETCHED

"For his exploiters, the value of a man can't match
that of a mule, a sheep, or a horse."
Manifesto of the Río Gallegos Workers' Society
November 1920

The strikes in Punta Arenas, Puerto Natales, Puerto Deseado, and Río Gallegos were enormously significant for those living in the south. They opened the eyes of the bosses to the possibility of a revolutionary strike that could threaten the private property system at any moment. The days had ended when some people gave the orders and others did nothing but obey. And they realized that, to defend themselves from this danger, they needed unity and, above all, the support of the federal government, which could provide police reinforcements and deploy the armed forces. For the workers, these episodes showed that a movement without organization was condemned to fail. More than anything else, the men of the Río Gallegos Workers' Society criticized themselves for their lack of coordination with their sister organizations in Puerto Natales and Punto Arenas on the Chilean side of the border.

To understand the background to the coming tragedy, we need a clear explanation of the behavior of two men: Judge Viñas and the journalist José María Borrero. The first represents the Radical Party in all its zeal for change and progress; the second, with his charismatic personality, is the spokesman for that stratum of Santa Cruz society caught between the landowners and the workers. A stratum that is almost entirely made up of Spaniards: small landowners, small business owners, tavern keepers, hotel and restaurant owners, white collar workers, independent artisans, etc. This petite bourgeoisie sees their existence threatened by the large consortiums—like the Braun-Menéndez family's La Anónima— true regional monopolies in the sale of such staple products as food, clothing, etc., and possessing the capital and logistical infra- structure needed to destroy any potential competition.

With the meager resources at its disposal, the Patagonian middle class depends on its clientèle, the workers. They even sup- port the labor movement to a certain extent, because higher wages means more purchasing power and therefore higher sales volumes.

This middle social stratum has just one weekly newspaper to speak for it: La Verdad, whose owner and editor is José María Bor- rero. On their side, the landowners have the biweekly La Unión.

Two dissimilar men arrive in Río Gallegos at almost exactly the same time, though by very different routes. The first is the afore- mentioned Judge Ismael Viñas, appointed by President Yrigoyen for a three year term, while the second is the Spaniard Antonio Soto, who ended up in the far south as a stagehand for a travel- ing Spanish operetta company: he set up the scenery, arranged the seating, cleaned up afterwards, and even played the occasional minor role when needed. He decides to stay in Río Gallegos and, within a matter of weeks, becomes the secretary of the Workers' Society, steering it in a frankly revolutionary direction.

The fuse of the coming tragedy will be lit by Judge Viñas through his aforementioned legal proceedings against two English ranching companies: The Monte Dinero Sheep Farming Company and The San Julián Sheep Farming Company.

The acting governor and secretary of the Rural Society, Correa Falcón, uses all the resources at his disposal—the police, the government bureaucracy, and the newspaper *La Unión*—to obstruct the judge. José María Borrero defends the judge's unprecedented stand against the power of the landowners in the pages of *La Verdad*, while two lawyers, Juan Carlos Beherán and Salvador Corminas, provide legal support. This group of men makes contact with the Río Gallegos Workers' Society and holds frequent meetings with Antonio Soto and other union leaders. And so there are working-class manifestos written by Borrero, a lawyer.

A protracted power struggle between the judge and the governor ensues. Viñas accelerates the legal proceedings and orders Monte Dinero's assets to be auctioned off. The governor retaliates by ordering the arrest of the auctioneer and a group of the judge's friends, including José María Borrero, Corminas, and Beherán. When Viñas orders the seizure of the assets of San Julián, the other English ranching company, Governor Correa Falcón once again intervenes with the police to prevent them from being auctioned off.

The president soon learns of the conflict. Even though Judge Viñas is a loyal Radical, the federal government knows that supporting him would bring the country into conflict with English capital at a time when Yrigoyen doesn't want any more problems than he already has; the British legation has been closely following events as they unfold.

Neither has the depression in the wool market been properly dealt with. The time is not right for Yrigoyen to involve himself in land conflicts in Patagonia. For him, that time will never come.

Judge Viñas will be disowned. He will emerge defeated from his attempt to fight British capital. The victor will be Governor Correa Falcón, along with all the interests he represents. But the war is just getting underway and the judge has only lost two battles.

In addition to this internecine strife between the representatives of the executive and legislative powers, which the landowners and merchants of Santa Cruz were following with concern, there was also an atmosphere of latent rebellion among the workers in the region's small towns and rural areas. Worried, Governor Correa Falcón informs the interior minister in April 1920 that "some individuals have arrived from the capital and other parts of the country to spread new ideas, beginning a campaign aiming to subvert the territory's public order." He encloses a copy of an anarchist pamphlet titled *Justicia Social*, which had been widely distributed among the region's farmworkers.

Correa Falcón, who has a nose for labor disturbances, is not overreacting. That June, at the La Oriental ranch near the province of Chubut, an unmistakably subversive strike breaks out. Two Russian anarchists—Anastasio Plichuk and Arsento Casachuk—and one Spaniard—Domingo Barón—stir up the farmworkers and proceed to carry out an occupation of the ranch. But Correa Falcón, with the help of the Chubut police, acts with exemplary speed and vigor. He steps in and breaks the strike. The two Russians and the Spaniard—with the stigma of having violated Article 25 of Public Safety Law 7029—receive a few good blows to their swollen, revolutionary heads and are thrown in the hold of a naval transport on its way to Buenos Aires, where President Yrigoyen will sign their deportation orders under Residence Law 4.144.

Correa Falcón also knows that there is another threat right there in Río Gallegos: Antonio Soto, the new secretary-general of the Workers' Society.

A Spaniard, Antonio Soto was born in the Galician city of El Ferrol on October 11th, 1897, the son of Antonio Soto and Concepción Canalejo. He arrived in Buenos Aires at the age of thirteen. When his father passed away, he and his brother Francisco entered a life of misery and privation not uncommon in Argentina at the time of the centennial. Antonio was rarely able to attend elementary school. Instead, he learned a variety of trades—like many other children in those days—and was educated by poverty, exploitation, and corporal punishment. He was attracted to anarchist and anarcho-syndicalist ideas from a young age. In 1919—when he was twenty-two years old—he joined the Serrano-Mendoza theater company, which toured the ports of Argentine Patagonia and then continued on to Punta Arenas, Puerto Natales, Puerto Montt, etc., bringing the dramatic arts to the south's most isolated southern villages.

A true popular rebellion breaks out in Trelew, Chubut in January 1920. It all started when retail workers go on strike in protest against the governor, the police, and powerful businessmen. Almost the entire population of the city joins the movement. The situation is aggravated by mutual recriminations and, as in every small town, personal issues came to the fore.

In the midst of this conflict, Antonio Soto, the stagehand of the Serrano-Mendoza theater company, makes his appearance by rallying the people behind the striking workers. This earns him his arrest and expulsion from Chubut. It's the first entry on his police record.

He arrives in Río Gallegos soon afterwards. He is attracted to the town's working class atmosphere. Before and after theatrical performances, he goes to the headquarters of the Workers' Society and listens to the speeches of Dr. José María Borrero, who speaks like the gods and always leaves the audience stunned. Borrero encourages Soto to stay in Río Gallegos and join the union; he realizes that Soto is a man of action with the proper ideological background, as well as someone who knows how to express himself in assemblies. And so when the theater leaves town, Soto stays behind.

The future leader of the rural strikes finds work as a stevedore, or as he calls himself, a "beach worker." By Sunday, May 24th, 1920, he has been elected secretary-general of the Río Gallegos Workers' Society.

This is Antonio Soto. According to his police file, he is 1.84 meters tall, has clear blue eyes, dirty blond hair, and a lazy right eye.

He receives his baptism by fire as a union leader that July. Together with unions from elsewhere in Santa Cruz, the Río Gallegos Workers' Society launches strikes in every port and hotel in the territory. They demand higher wages. It isn't easy. Particularly in Río Gallegos. The stevedores lose their strike. The hotel workers' union moves forward, however. The bosses give in, accepting the workers' conditions—with the exceptions of the owners of the Hotel Español and the Grand Hotel, who resort to hiring scabs. So Soto and a compatriot enter one of the hotels and use their fists to try and convince the holdouts to stop work.

When the hotel owner complains to the police, Soto and his colleague are arrested. Representatives of the Workers' Society then approach Judge Viñas, asking him to release the two men. The time has come for the judge to put the governor in check. Viñas orders the two workers to be immediately released, even though the police have already initiated criminal proceedings against them for forcible entry, assault, and property damage. We shall soon see the consequences of this decision.

On August 24th, the police chief, Commissioner Diego Ritchie, informs Governor Correa Falcón that:

> The police have discovered that the local Workers' Federation is working with its counterparts in Buenos Aires, the port cities and Punta Arenas (Chile) to launch a general strike that is to begin next month, a movement that could take on a revolutionary nature ... dynamite is being prepared in one or more of the territory's ports.

Commissioner Ritchie—who insists that the strike will include rural peons—puts in a request for machine guns.

Two weeks later—on September 7th, 1920—the police chief's concerns grow and he sends the governor another report:

> Faced with the threat from the workers and anarchists, I deem the situation in the territory to be quite serious, as there's no doubt

that the general strike being planned will unavoidably become a seditious movement, given the unrest in the workers' camp and the territory's numerous anarchists and repeat offenders, whose ranks are being swelled by the dangerous elements expelled from Punta Arenas in the aftermath of that city's revolutionary strike.

In his urgent request for reinforcements, the police chief provides the following interesting details:

The territory's police force consists of 230 troopers (including the border patrol), who are stationed at 46 precincts, sub-precincts and detachments spread across a 282,000 square kilometer territory that is home to some very important ranches and four large meat-packing plants—*the Swift plant in Río Gallegos, the Swift plant in San Julián, the Armour plant in Puerto Santa Cruz and the Puerto Deseado Meatpacking Plant, owned by a local ranching company.* Río Gallegos alone has a population of around 4,000 residents, with more in important towns like Puerto Santa Cruz, San Julián, Puerto Deseado, and Las Heras. It's easy to see how difficult or even impossible it would be to defeat a movement such as the one being prepared with our badly paid and understaffed police force.

He then requests infantry troops from Buenos Aires or a war-ship carrying an expeditionary force, adding that the police under his command are keeping a close watch on the movement's ringleaders.

On December 15th, 1920, Governor Correa Falcón complains to the interior minister that Judge Viñas "favors the workers" and has been a party to "extortion" against the business community of Río Gallegos. This is what happened: after the July hotel workers' strike had been lifted, the Río Gallegos Workers' Society declared a boycott of the hotels that had refused the union's demands. The boycott was well organized: taxi drivers refused to take passengers to those hotels, union members talked to hotel staff and encouraged them to stop working—or, rather, pressured them to stop work—and hotel guests were stopped in the street and had the conflict politely explained to them. And the streets of that small city were inundated with flyers in those days.

As we have said, these two hotels were the Grand Hotel and the Hotel Español. The owner of the latter, Serafín Zapico, seeing that he would either have to give in or be forced to close the hotel, asked Judge Viñas for advice. Viñas agreed to straighten things out for him, telling him the next day to go to the headquarters of the Workers' Society, as Soto and other union members had agreed to meet with him. The distressed businessman did as he was told and Soto informed him that the only way to resolve the matter would be to rehire the four hotel workers who had been fired during the strike, paying their lost wages, and accepting the conditions demanded by the union. Zapico consulted with Viñas, who also told him that this was the only way to end the conflict. And so Zapico bowed his head and paid up.

Things wouldn't be so easy for Manuel Albarellos, the owner of the Grand Hotel. Despairing of the "blockade" imposed by the Workers' Society, he also turned to Judge Viñas, who gave him the same advice he had given Zapico. According to Albarellos's subsequent statement to the police, when he entered the building he was surrounded by union members who insulted him and threatened him, saying that they could only reach an arrangement if he paid a 3,700-peso fine.

The desperate hotel owner—3,700 pesos was a substantial sum in those days—went back to Judge Viñas, who told him not to give up and promised to settle the matter. Viñas—after meeting with the labor leaders—told the hotel owner that he was able to get him a "discount" and that he would only have to come up with 2,500 pesos. To complete his cavalry, the reluctant hotel owner, accustomed to treating his workers like slaves, had to swallow his pride and make the payment in person at the union headquarters. The hotel owner, specialized in attending to the needs of the well-to-do, had to hand the money over to Soto, who made a show of counting it out before an assembly of jubilant workers. Soto told him that he could go, that the "blockade" would be lifted.

There's no doubt that for these proletarians, accustomed to the lean side of life, these triumphs must have felt glorious.

Governor Correa Falcón makes all this known to the federal government, sending a detailed report to Interior Minister Ramón Gómez, popularly known as Tuerto Gómez. The minister's reaction is typical of the Radical administration: he orders it to be filed away. For him, the best way to solve a problem is to leave it unsolved. And this would also allow the judge, a loyal party member, to remain in good standing. The government already took the side of the governor in the case of the English ranches. And so now it's time to take the judge's side, even if only by omission. Besides, it's a policy of the Radical administration to give the unions a free hand as long as they don't go too far.

Under the leadership of Antonio Soto, the Río Gallegos Workers' Society receives a great impetus. It acquires a printing press, begins to publish the newspaper *1° de Mayo* and sends delegates to the ranches of the interior to explain the basics of organizing and fighting for concessions. These delegates bring up names like Proudhon, Bakunin, Kropotkin, Malatesta. They all have an anarchist background and constantly bring up the example of the October Revolution in Russia.

It's genuinely strange—and why not exciting?—to find the red flag flying over the headquarters of a small union that nevertheless embodied the hopes of the dispossessed in distant Río Gallegos, a town of barely four thousand inhabitants, far removed from all major cities and thousands of kilometers from the cauldron of rebellion that Europe became in the 1920s. It's incredible how these men, who not only lacked proven leaders but also had a complete lack of organizational experience, nevertheless put their best foot forward in order to not lose the hurried pace that the Russian Revolution had imposed on the proletariat.

And just as strange is another incident that will directly lead to many of the events that followed. In September 1920, the Río

Gallegos Workers' Society asks the police for permission to hold a memorial for the Catalan pedagogue Francisco Ferrer, the father of rationalist education who was executed eleven years beforehand at the Montjuich Castle. In an act that brought shame upon the human race, the most conservative faction of the Catholic Church had influenced Alfonso XIII to do away with a teacher who used reason to destroy myths and who opposed religious obscurantism and militaristic irrationality above all else.

The memorial is scheduled for October 1st. In the days leading up to the event, the Workers' Society distributes flyers throughout the city and surrounding ranches. The text of these flyers says more than any later interpretation of these events:

THE RÍO GALLEGOS WORKERS' SOCIETY
1909—OCTOBER 13—1920
TO THE PEOPLE

It has been eleven years since this day moved the entire world.
It has been eleven years since the lowest and most cowardly attack on Free Thought was carried out in the thousand-times-accursed Montjuich Castle (Barcelona).
Francisco Ferrer, the founder of the Modern School, who taught children the path of light, was cravenly executed by those Tartuffes who commit all class of infamies in the name of Christ.
But Francisco Ferrer will live forever in our hearts and we shall always be ready to spit this crime in the face of its perpetrators.
Glory to the martyrs of Human Liberty!
Glory to Francisco Ferrer!
Farmworkers: You have the duty to come to town on October 1st and pay homage to the Martyr of Freedom.

FRANCISCO FERRER
Cravenly executed on October 13th, 1909

On September 28th, Diego Ritchie refuses to issue a permit for the event. The workers aren't intimidated and, without stopping to blink, declare a forty-eight-hour general strike.[1] And this isn't a bluff. Here's what Amador V. González has to say about the strike:

September 30th dawned to a city in a state of siege. Though there was no reason to adopt such measures and martial law had not been declared, pedestrians were banned from gathering on the streets or in doorways, the armed forces poured out of the barracks to show off their Mausers and prison guards patrolled the city by automobile, frightening residents from north to south, as if the city was a warzone. On the 1st, armed men surrounded the offices of the Workers' Society and passersby were stopped and sent in another direction. The offices of the Workers' Society were closed down and the homes of its secretary and treasurer ransacked, but under what law? As a preliminary measure, the Workers' Society ordered the suspension of all previously scheduled demonstrations and declared the general strike to be indefinite until the authorities recognized their error in allowing the police chief to use such extreme measures against a peaceful and orderly commemoration.[2]

The confrontation is ruthless. The government and police use force and the workers use the strike, that powerful measure of civil disobedience.

Faced with Correa Falcón's offensive, the workers turn to their friends Borrero and Viñas. They gather in the offices that the lawyer shares with Dr. Juan Carlos Beherán and prepare to appeal Commissioner Ritchie's decision.

In their statement to the judge, they make use of an impressively original argument. They write:

We protest against the prohibition of a demonstration scheduled for today—*October 1, 1920*—to commemorate the anniversary of the execution of Francisco Ferrer, whom the believers in the religion of labor hold as a martyr of freedom and a symbol of their ideas, just as believers in the Catholic religion pay homage to St. Francis of Assisi or the Maid of Orleans, recently beatified as St. Joan of Arc, or as believers in the Mohammedan religion pay homage to Mohammed, or as believers in the religion of patriotism pay tribute to the heroes of the Reconquista, the War of Independence, or the Emancipation.

Judge Viñas receives the appeal at three in the afternoon and immediately orders Commissioner Ritchie to explain his motives. And he also informs him that the court will remain open past its normal hours as a way of letting him know that his response must be immediate.

The barracks arguments used by Commissioner Ritchie show a devastating inconsistency:

By banning the meeting to be held today, the police department has understood that it was to commemorate the memory of a person held to be a martyr for his anarchist ideas, as Francisco Ferrer is universally considered to be a fanatic of that cause which is currently threatening to dissolve our contemporary social order. This gives the planned homage the hallmarks of inviability inherent in that class of protests that have been prohibited to protect the social order. Moreover, Your Honor, this is fundamentally a protest against an execution carried out by a foreign nation. Whether legal or illegal is not for us to judge for reasons of international courtesy; a judgement cannot be made by our constituted authorities, cannot take part, not even to grant a permit for protests against the decisions made by the Spanish court system, as it is not subject to our appeals. Nor was this event organized with a respectable aim, such as that of the improvement of living conditions for the working class. The character of the demonstration is purely political and falls outside our remit.

Viñas doesn't waver. Not only does he reverse the commissioner's decision, he also criticizes his ideas, demonstrating a
rational spirit and a respect for the ideas of others:

The Public Safety Law has long been the subject of judicial decisions and has just as long been the cause of errors, with a lack
of knowledge of our social history leading to many blatantly
unfounded assertions. The flyer distributed by the workers only
states that the event will commemorate the execution of the
person mentioned, describing him solely as the founder of the
Modern School, nothing more. There is no mention of any political tendency on the flyer that could be considered anarchist or
libertarian, which are admittedly new developments in the history
of ideas and whose consequences in the history of events are even
more recent. The scientific conception of anarchism, its theories
and the nature of its attacks are not only extremely vague and
confusing to the masses, but also to sociologists and law profes-
sors. When these fundamental doubts present themselves before
the court, the duty of the law must be to prevent any restriction of
the freedom of assembly guaranteed in the Constitution.

Reading this decision, we have to give Viñas his due. It's clear
that he had a special sensibility. It was truly exceptional and daring
to sign the defense of a labor demonstration in this way, and even
more exceptional still for a homage to Ferrer in regions where the
government was controlled by the mighty—and just one year after
the Tragic Week, when it was the duty of all well-born Argentines
to hunt down revolutionary workers.

He orders the ban to be lifted and for the governor to be
informed of his decision.

The governor is notified on October 2nd. Correa Falcón,
neither stupid nor lazy, drafts his own resolution: "Acknowledge
receipt of the judicial decision and, as the date on which the permit
for a demonstration had been requested has since passed, place the
permit on file."

Even though the opportunity to pay homage to Ferrer has passed, the workers cannot contain their enthusiasm for the judge's decision. They feel defended; their ideas have triumphed over the government officials whom they accuse of being mere lackeys of commercial and landowning interests. The Workers' Society lifts the strike. Now the offensive will be taken by the merchants and the property owners of the Commerce and Industry League. They find a leader in Ibón Noya, a rancher and the owner of the Buick Garage, an auto parts store. And their counteroffensive will also begin with boycotts. The first thing they do is organize an advertisers' boycott of a newspaper called *La Gaceta del Sur*, which published an article praising the strike.

The Workers' Society responds to this blow with an even heavier one: a boycott of three local businesses. They distribute flyers among the population encouraging them not to purchase from three local grocery stores. With this measure, they aim to divide the alliance of the bosses, since other grocers will double their earnings as long as nobody patronizes the three boycotted businesses.

Correa Falcón summons Soto to the police station to end the conflict with the Commerce and Industry League. But the anarchist tells Commissioner Ritchie that a police station is hardly an ideal location to resolve labor issues.

Correa Falcón realizes that words are of no more use and goes all in. On the night of October 19th, the Workers' Society holds an assembly. So he acts. First measure: agents are stationed outside the doors of the union headquarters so nobody can leave. Second measure: the police chief himself directs the raid, which will be carried out by prison guards. The workers are forced against the wall with their hands up and—once they have been patted down for weapons—they are thrown out of the union offices and lined up in full view of their neighbors. Then, escorted by bayonets, they are marched in single file to the nearest jail and locked up with the common criminals to soften them up.

In the meantime, Correa Falcón covers his back, wiring the following message to the interior minister:

A group of labor agitators held a meeting without the permit required under existing regulations. The group, which for some time has been characterized by their extortionate tactics and the aggressive nature of their propaganda, disobeyed police orders to disperse. The police arrested ten individuals on violations of the public safety and social defense laws, as red flags and banners were confiscated, as were a large number of flyers calling for consumers to boycott local businesses. The municipal government and the Commerce and Industry League passed measures in support of the police action and have ensured that the populace will not suffer from shortages in the event of a strike. These measures have been welcomed by public opinion. Preliminary depositions have demonstrated the guilt of those arrested. I hope that you will inform me if they should be turned over to the federal government, given that they are foreigners to a man.

The governor's plan was perfect. Only the immigrants were processed and he took advantage of the government's confusion by offering the interior minister a way out: put them aboard a battleship, send them all to Buenos Aires and apply Law 4.144, expelling them from the country. Dead, the dog is cured of rabies. Great problems require great solutions.

This plan would have been very easy to carry out under a conservative government. But now Hipólito Yrigoyen was in power and such cavalier treatment of the lives of others, even if they were nothing more than poor immigrants, was being slightly curtailed.

There was one big fish among those arrested at the union offices: Dr. José María Borrero. According to Correa Falcón, there were three men responsible for everything that had been happening in that sleepy Patagonian town: Judge Viñas, the fiery Borrero, and the Spaniard, Soto.

Those arrested were all Spaniards, which Borrero and his friends skillfully frame as an attack on the Spanish community. They complain to the Spanish consul and the federal government.

With its offices closed and the majority of its leaders jailed, the Workers' Society immediately launches a general strike. Judge Viñas orders Correa Falcón to immediately free the arrestees, but he refuses to carry out the judge's orders.

With battleships available to take the arrestees away, the governor impatiently awaits the response of the interior minister. But the response of the federal government is truly disappointing for Correa Falcón: "If the preliminary depositions aren't strong enough to begin legal proceedings against the arrestees locally, they should be released, keeping them under discreet surveillance in order to avoid civil disturbances." This means that Correa Falcón must either turn the prisoners over to his enemy Viñas or grant them conditional freedom. He chooses to take a different path. He still has plenty of room to maneuver and sees no reason to admit defeat, though he only has a few weeks left in office—his replacement, Captain Ángel Yza, has already been named. He finds his inspiration in the interior minister's telegram, which states, "If the preliminary depositions aren't strong enough…" This suggests that he still has an opportunity to build his case, which can take several days. And Santa Cruz is very far away from the capital—between telegram and telegram, the prisoners could spend a great deal of time in the shadows.

But the situation deteriorates. The strike spreads like an oil spill throughout the countryside. The Workers' Society distributes the following manifesto to nearby ranches:

> Greetings, comrades. The police have arrested a group of workers and refused to release them, even when so ordered by the judge. Such an abuse of authority has forced us to call a general strike, and so we urge you to stop work and come to the capital as an act of solidarity until our comrades walk free.
>
> Regards, The Strike Committee.

The strike upsets the government of Santa Cruz. The police are on the move. Groups of workers are broken up, even when doing nothing more than walking down the street, with the nightstick encouraging the reluctant. All suspicious-looking Chileans are run out of town. Upon receiving news of a group of Chileans gathered at the Hotel Castilla,[3] they carry out a raid, pulling no punches, and identify all those present. Taverns are raided if they offer haven to Chileans coming in from the countryside or allow them to hold meetings. Their owners are often subpoenaed or "delayed" at the police station. This produces solidarity between workers and small business owners, uniting them in open conflict with large companies such as La Anónima.

Correa Falcón has arrested twenty-seven people. But he knows that he can't get greedy and so he tactically decides to set some of them free—but holds on to those whom Viñas ordered him to release.

This is celebrated by the Workers' Society as a partial triumph. They issue a manifesto that, despite the best efforts of the police, is passed from hand to hand among the peons and the poor:

To the workers

Comrades: We are approaching victory with giant steps. Fifteen of our imprisoned comrades have already been set free. There are still twelve left in jail. Our interim governor, the secretary of the Rural Society, has rebelled against the law and refused to obey the binding orders of the federal government to release eight of them. But his time will come and justice will triumph over caprice. The strike continues, as does the boycott, and neither will be lifted until all of our comrades are free. They are trying to turn our righteous stand into a question of nationality. Reject this nonsense, comrades—workers don't see an enemy in a man who doesn't share his nationality, but instead a fellow victim of capital, which corrupts and dominates everything. Men are all equals, no matter where they were born, and we therefore cannot let differences of nationality come between us. Forward, then, until we achieve our hard-won victory. If we remain united, we will defeat all the difficulties created by our enemies.

—The Strike Committee

But Correa Falcón continues with his tactical blows. The next will target the El Antártico printing press, where the workers print their flyers. The police will claim that they were provoked—that they were fired upon from the direction of the printing press—and then they will break into the shop, arrest those present, and destroy all the propaganda they find.

A group of Spanish nationals send a complaint to the Interior Ministry stating that "the police are beating people in the street." This claim is backed by the Puerto Deseado newspaper *El Orden*, which reports that "the police commit outrages and abuses against the workers, provoking unrest in the population at large."

After a great deal of back and forth, the federal government sides with Judge Viñas and orders Correa Falcón to release all the detained union members. They all go free on October 29th—except for two.

The Workers' Society celebrates this development but orders the general strike to continue:

> Our comrades Muñoz and Traba remain imprisoned. Both of them have been beaten and deliberately wounded by the police. Their tormentors have kept them locked up in foul dungeons to hide this brutal and unspeakable abuse. Well then—as long as these comrades remain imprisoned, the strike will continue and we will not lose heart. Comrades, we therefore beg you to help us bring work to a standstill by circulating these resolutions on the ranches. Victory will be ours because we have reason on our side: a force that triumphs over all obstacles. Our enemies will fall from the weight of their own crimes, just as rotten fruit falls from the tree that nurtured it.

The campaign is a complete success: all of the detainees are released by November 1st.

The finale of this turbulent prelude to the Spartakiad launched by the Workers' Society is an attempt on the life of the organization's secretary-general, Antonio Soto. It occurs on November 3rd,

1920. Soto is walking in the direction of Antwerp House to speak with a workers' delegate when a suspicious figure lunges from a doorway and rapidly stabs him in the chest. The knife pierces his clothing but strikes the pocket watch that Soto carries in his left coat pocket. Soto collapses from the blow and pretends to reach for a gun. His attacker flees at full speed. Soto has received some cuts to the chest, but he is alive.

Those who sent the assassin thought well. By eliminating Soto, they would have decapitated the Santa Cruz labor movement.

The Workers' Society has won a battle by securing the release of its prisoners, but now it's time to make demands. Its workers have shown discipline, a spirit of sacrifice and clear class consciousness. This can be taken advantage of, as could the fact that many farmworkers came into town during the strike.

The labor organization prepares two campaigns: better pay for retail workers and a full list of demands for farmworkers. Here Antonio Soto proves himself to be a very gifted organizer. He sends emissaries to the countryside, holds meetings around the clock, rallies the new recruits, and instructs activists on the ABCs of unionism. When their demands are rejected, a strike breaks out across the territory.

In November 1920, Governor Correa Falcón sees control slip from his fingers. The rural strike extends across Santa Cruz. Work has completely stopped in Río Gallegos and the ports are paralyzed. There's a growing sense of unease among the landowners. The work stoppage threatens the sheep breeding season, but a solution remains elusive. The tougher Correa Falcón gets, the more rebellious the workers become. *La Unión* reports that, "In the early days of the strike, there were over two hundred strange men wandering the streets confusedly, staring at people without understanding what was going on." These men are none other than the farmworkers who have answered the call of the Workers' Society.

The bosses, their children, and high-ranking employees decide to form a volunteer militia whose first action is to offer their services to the local jail "for the sake of order and as a guardian of morality," as the aforementioned newspaper will put it.

But neither the Patriotic League nor the Rural Society nor the Commerce and Industry League nor the volunteer militia will be able to bring the strike to an end. They find themselves forced to seek out the union leaders and open negotiations.

On November 6th, three leading ranchers—Ibón Noya, Miguel Grigera, and Rodolgo Suárez—announce that they have been unable to reach an agreement with the strike committee. They then issue the following manifesto:

> To the people of Río Gallegos and the farmworkers:
>
> We the undersigned, owners of haciendas to the south of the Río Santa Cruz, have resolved, in spite of the difficult times we are experiencing as a result of the crisis in the international beef and wool markets, to:
> 1. Negotiate directly with our workers on our own ranches.
> 2. Pay our workers a minimum salary of 100 pesos per month, to be paid in Argentine currency, plus meals.
> 3. Negotiate salaries in excess of this amount with individual workers in accordance with their duties.
> 4. Work to gradually improve the food and hygienic conditions in the workers' quarters.

The first point is entirely out of question for the workers. The bosses have decided not to recognize their labor organizations. The situation becomes tenser still. Soto is unfamiliar with the countryside and so he puts his trust in questionable individuals with unquestionable energy. During this first strike, the two *de facto* leaders of the rural movement had little union experience. The first, El 68, is a former inmate at Ushuaia, where 68 was his inmate number. It became his nickname after his release. The other, El Toscano, is an irrepressible daredevil who has also had his share of run-ins with the law. They are both Italians. El 68, whose real name is José Aicardi, is an accomplished rider, as is El Toscano, the alias of Alfredo Fonte, a thirty-three-year-old cart driver who came to Argentina when he was only three. They both come across more as genuine *gauchos* than as Italian immigrants.

They are aided by two Argentines: Bartolo Díaz (known as El Paisano Díaz) and Florentino Cuello (nicknamed Gaucho Cuello). They're both brawlers, always on hand when there are blows to be delivered. But they're also the ones who recruit the most chilotes to the union, charging them 12 pesos in yearly dues and handing out union cards. Both men are extremely popular on the ranches and know the countryside like the backs of their hands.

Gaucho Cuello is from Diamante, Entre Ríos, where he was born in 1884. In 1912, he stabbed someone back home—it seems their wounds were quite serious—earning him five years in the Río Gallegos prison. He stayed in town after his release in 1917 and was working on the Tapi-Aike ranch when the strike broke out.

These four men are largely responsible for the complete work stoppage on the ranches of southern Santa Cruz. The ringleader is undoubtedly the mysterious El 68. They are also joined by a Chilean named Lorenzo Cárdenas: a brave, determined, cold-blooded man. This group of organizers is rounded out with the German anarchist Franz Lorenz; the Paraguayan Francisco Aguilera; Federico Villard Peyré, a French anarchist and the delegate representing the Menéndez Behety's La Anita ranch; the Americans Carlos Hantke (who also goes by the name of Charles Manning), Charles Middleton (easily identified by his gold teeth) and Frank Cross; the Scots Alex McLeod and Jack Gunn; an Afro-Portuguese by the name of Cantrill; a handsome Uruguayan cart driver nicknamed Palomilla; John Johnston, another American; a Spaniard named José Graña, etc.

They make up the active minority that goes from ranch to ranch to organize occupations. They take the landowners, administrators, and foremen hostage and swell their ranks with the peons.

All of the ranches south of the Río Santa Cruz are paralyzed. On November 18th, *La Unión* runs an article that captures the tense atmosphere:

> With work stoppages on every ranch and the intransigence of the landowners, a new, more fundamental problem arises. The economic interests of the territory and its population depend on a rapid solution. What will become of Río Gallegos if the meat-packing plants don't reopen? What will ranches do with almost half a million heads of unsellable livestock? And Puerto Natales, in Chile, will also be unable to dispose of its livestock. Ranchers have already suffered heavy losses from the strike launched by their peons during the breeding season.

It is the ranchers who will take the first step towards reaching an agreement. They make a new offer to the workers on November 17th. This time, they include the following clause:

> The Río Gallegos Workers' Society will be acknowledged as the sole representative of the workers and its delegates will be authorized to visit our ranches once per month. At this time, they will be permitted to discuss any grievances with the ranch owner or foreman as well as to meet with union members.

The following day, expectations run high in Río Gallegos. There isn't enough space in the Workers' Society headquarters for everyone. The offer is gone over point by point, only to be rejected. The agreement must be clear, its clauses must leave no room for doubt and points that contain little more than generalities cannot be endorsed. The workers draft a counter-offer, signed by Antonio Soto:

CAPITAL-LABOR AGREEMENT

For the purposes of mutual assistance and sustenance, as well as for the dignity of all, the ranchers south of the Río Santa Cruz and the farmworkers represented by the Río Gallegos Workers' Society agree to the following clauses and conditions:

FIRST: At the earliest possible opportunity and within the limits imposed by specific local and regional conditions, the ranchers must implement the following reasonable improvements to the living conditions of their workers:

a) No more than three men will be required to share any given four square meter room. Bunks are to be prohibited and they must be given cots or beds, complete with mattresses. Rooms must be properly ventilated and will be disinfected on a weekly basis. Each bedroom must be equipped with a bathroom and enough water for the workers to wash themselves after work;

b) Lighting costs will be borne by the employer, who will be required to issue each worker with a monthly supply of candles. Each common area will be supplied with a stove, lamp, and benches, to be paid for by the employer;

c) Saturday afternoons will be set aside to allow the peons to wash their clothes. If this is unfeasible, another day can be substituted;

d) Meals will consist of three courses, including soup, dessert and coffee, tea, or mate;

e) Beds and mattresses will be supplied by the employer, and workers will be responsible for purchasing their own clothing;

f) In the event of strong wind or rain, work will stop until the weather improves, unless there is an emergency recognized by both parties;

g) Each ranch must be equipped with a first aid kit with instructions in Spanish;

h) If a worker is fired or is otherwise no longer needed, their employer will be required to return them to the location at which they were hired.

SECOND: The ranchers commit to pay their workers a minimum salary of 100 pesos, to be paid in Argentine currency, plus food expenses. They must also commit to not reduce any salaries that currently exceed this amount. Any raises made will be at the discretion of the rancher, provided that they are in accordance with the abilities and merits of the worker. They must also hire one assistant cook if they employ between ten and twenty workers, two assistant cooks for ranches with between twenty and forty workers and a baker if the number of workers exceeds forty. Drovers hired on a month-to-month basis will be paid an additional 12 pesos per day if they make use of the ranch's horses and an additional 20 pesos per day if their provide their own horses. Shepherds hired on a month-to-month basis will receive 20 pesos for every foal they deliver, while shepherds hired on a daily basis will receive 30 pesos.

THIRD: The ranchers will hire at least one drover per ranch, depending on its size. Bimonthly inspections will be carried out to look after the needs of the drover(s), with preference given to family men in proportion to their number of children, which will encourage population growth and the country's development.

FOURTH: The ranchers recognize the Río Gallegos Workers' Society as the representative of the workers and agree to allow a delegate to be appointed on each ranch to act as an intermediary between the employers and the Workers' Society. This delegate will have the power to arrange temporary settlements for pressing issues that affect the rights and responsibilities of both the workers and their employers.

FIFTH: The ranchers will do everything in their power to ensure that all of their workers are unionized, but they will not force them to join a union nor are they required to refuse the labor of nonunion workers.

SIXTH: The Workers' Society commits to lift the present farmworkers' strike and will order its members to return to work once this agreement has been signed.

SEVENTH: The Workers' Society commits to immediately endorse regulations and instructions for its members that are designed to bring about greater harmony between capital and labor, which together form the foundation of existing society. It will use flyers, conferences, and conversations to encourage the

values of order, hard work, and mutual respect among its members—values that should not be forgotten.

EIGHTH: This agreement will come into effect on November 1st and the strike will end with all workers receiving payment
for the days missed, with no reprisals on either side.

Faced with this response from the workers, the ranchers reply
that, "Having exhausted our options and being unable to overcome our disagreements, we regard our mission to be over."

Negotiations break down. If we analyze the workers' offer,
we can reach a number of conclusions about the true situation of
Patagonian farmworkers.

The system of bunks[4] was not just used in Patagonia, but in
many parts of the country. It was the "custom" in rural areas. The
living quarters for peons—especially on smaller ranches—were also
used to store obsolete gear or farm machinery. The menu consisting
solely of capon—along with the health problems that accompany
it—remains in place to this day on virtually every ranch in Patagonia. In many cases, the living quarters remain exactly the same as
they did half a century ago. But the greatest impediment to progress
in Patagonia—and this cannot be refuted—is the inhumane treatment of workers and the lack of thoughtfulness towards the land's
primary source of wealth: human beings. Just as it was fifty years
ago, only single men are hired as shepherds or peons. Ranch owners
want no families—unless that means a "household," as they call it,
where the woman handles domestic chores for the landowner and
her husband is a cook. But broadly speaking, the entire workforce
is made up of single men who live at the ranch from Monday to
Saturday and then head into town on Sunday to spend all their
earnings on getting drunk in bars or brothels. The economics of this
system are poorly understood by the ranchers. Farmworkers become
itinerant; there's nothing to tie them down and they go wherever
they receive higher pay or wherever life is better.

This is why the third clause of the workers' offer showed great
wisdom in asking for drovers to be selected from among family

men, "with preference given to family men in proportion to their number of children, which will encourage population growth and the country's development." What a shame that none of this was ever implemented and was instead drowned in blood and crushed by the logic of lead and steel.

All in all, there was nothing outrageous about the workers' demands, and later on we shall see that the ranchers largely recognized this. Their reformist motives could be seen in the seventh clause, in which the Workers' Society "commits to immediately endorse regulations and instructions for its members that are designed to bring about greater harmony between capital and labor…"

Here we can detect the hand of Borrero at work, and perhaps that of Viñas. We say this because Borrero was always eager to show that the Workers' Society was not an extremist organization. As for Viñas, the phrase "harmony between capital and labor" hints at the Yrigoyenist mindset that Perón would later inherit. Of course, this harmony would be torn apart by gunfire and end up crucified on the posts of Patagonia's endless barbed wire fences.

The Workers' Society accompanied their list of demands with a manifesto titled *To the Civilized World*, again showing that they only sought to win a series of concessions and had no revolutionary aims:

To the civilized world:

A general strike has been declared in the countryside. It will be total and absolute: no work will be done, not even the transportation of livestock, which is the region's sole resource.

We cannot yet tell what the consequences of this strike will be nor the dimensions it may assume, especially as urban workers are standing firm in their support for their rural comrades, showing solidarity with their just and legitimate aspirations.

And so the Río Gallegos Workers' Society wishes to absolve its membership of all responsibility for any later developments, placing this responsibility into the hands of the ranchers south of the Río Santa Cruz. With the honorable exceptions of the Clark brothers and Benjamín Gómez, they have displayed what is either the crassest ignorance or the most refined malice, accompanied by an utter lack of humanitarianism, altruism, fair-mindedness, and equity. They propose to carry on treating their workers with the same brutality they have shown up until today, confusing them with serfs or slaves and treating them as just another vulgar product on the market, like mules, sheep, or horses. At the present time, ranchers feel that one man can always be replaced by another, at no cost to themselves, while the replacement of an animal constitutes a financial setback and pains them more than the loss of a fellow man or the needs of a family in distress.

It is shameful to have to say such things in the twentieth century, but since these are the conditions that can be observed by anyone visiting the region's ranches, even the ones closest to Río Gallegos, we must expose this situation to everyone who considers themselves to be civilized and let opprobrium and shame fall on the heads of those responsible.

And, lest it be argued that our claims are exaggerated, allow us to recount what has happened so far.

As part of the labor negotiations occurring in the territory, the workers put forward a list of demands on November 1st, and it took the ranchers a full sixteen days to respond, and only then after a great deal of maneuvering.

Consistent with their desire to harmonize the interests of the parties involved, the workers put their own demands on hold and studied the ranchers' offer. They then decided to draw up their own capital-labor agreement, which is transcribed below.

This was then followed by the list of demands signed by Antonio Soto. The manifesto concluded by stating that the eighth clause was "imbued with humanitarian sentiments, sacred and sublime. By requiring both parties to refrain from reprisals, it puts into practice the greatest of precepts: love one another, forget your resentments, discard your hatreds, and set aside your ill will." And then it made an appeal:

WORKERS:

Now, more than ever, we must display our unyielding will to assert our dignity and be regarded by society as the most efficient champions of progress and civilization. We must marshal our forces, move forward and staunchly defend our vulnerable and unrecognized rights. Whenever we see a comrade who is fearful or hesitant, let us not burden him with reproaches or threats, but instead strive to strengthen his resolve, lift up his spirit, and offer him the fraternal and loving embrace of his fellow unfortunates.

Now, more than ever, we must display our cultivation and education, of which so few proofs have been offered, by setting aside violence and coercion and neither using nor abusing the use of force. Let the latter become the final symptom of the lack of conscience on the part of the bosses, as it is widely known that whenever they are presented with the just demands of the workers, they see a terrifying specter and immediately turn to bayonets, rifles, and men in uniform. They cannot be too certain of the justice of their cause when they resort to such measures.

Let us counter the strength of arms with the strength of our arguments, the righteousness of our conduct, and the integrity of our actions, and victory shall be ours. —The strike committee.

The manifesto speaks for itself. It tells workers to "love one another," and leaves the use of force, of "bayonets, rifles, and men in uniform" to the bosses, who of course will use them, surpassing all expectations. Such as when Commissioner Micheri bends his saber out of shape by beating chilotes who speak of nothing but love for their fellow man. And when Varela orders his men to open fire on this shapeless mass of wretches, let us then remember the phrase about countering "the strength of arms with the strength of our arguments."

As the days slip by, the atmosphere south of the Río Santa Cruz becomes increasingly tense. The strike shows no sign of lifting and the landowners continue to worry. On November 24th, the latter head down to the port to receive two "wealthy landowners and influential businessmen," as *La Unión* refers to them. They are none other than Mauricio Braun and Alejandro Menéndez Behety, stopping by on the steamship *Argentino* on their way to Punta Arenas for the unveiling of a monument to Magellan donated by Don José Menéndez.

They come bringing good news: workers recruited in Buenos Aires are on their way to replace their disobedient counterparts.

La Unión pompously announces the establishment of the Free Labor Association, a sort of union of right-thinking, deferential workers:

> A large number of workers from throughout the region have taken the initiative to found a Free Labor Association, allowing the working man, currently tyrannized by the absurd sectarianism of malicious, belligerent gangs, to exercise his freedom to adjust his conduct to his circumstances and interests.

Antonio Soto is unsettled by this offensive, but he has someone to cover his back: that mysterious individual known as El 68, who fluently speaks the language of gunfire.

So when the first "free" workers arrive from Buenos Aires and head towards the Douglas ranch to replace the strikers—traveling under police escort—they are met by armed horsemen at a place along the road to Punta Arenas known as Bajada de Clark. The horsemen fire into the air, disappearing and reappearing like guerrillas. The scare is so great that the tractors carrying the strikebreakers and their police escorts immediately turn around and head back towards Río Gallegos. Correa Falcón immediately orders Commissioner Ritchie to patrol the area with four cars and fifteen policemen. But they simply waste gasoline—there's no trace left of the rebel gauchos.

Soto is amused, but deep down he knows that to some extent he has sold his soul to the devil: having friends like El 68 or El Toscano is neither very wise nor very anarchist. These two men have done a little of everything and can't be accused of being naïve. They know that the only gospel they can bring to the police and the powerful is violence; they laugh at those poetic souls who believe in the "sovereign will of assemblies" and respect the opinions of others. They monopolize decision making and impose their preferred methods, even into the second strike: They rally the peons, organize them into armed gangs, and attack the ranches, holding their owners, administrators, and sympathizers hostage, all the while confusing the police by traveling far and wide.

The Bajada de Clark incident has a demoralizing effect on the ranchers. On December 2nd, they come back to the workers with a counteroffer: they accept the union's second list of demands, with the sole exception of the part about delegates being assigned to each ranch. The bosses offer their own version of the clause:

> The ranchers recognize the Río Gallegos Workers' Society as the sole representative of the workers and agree to allow a delegate to be appointed on each ranch to act as an intermediary between the employers and the Workers' Society. This delegate will have the power to arrange temporary settlements for pressing issues that affect the rights and responsibilities of both the workers and their employers. On each ranch, these delegates will be appointed by the workers with the approval of the employers, taking seniority and behavior into account. The employers reserve the right to veto the delegate of the Workers' Society and the workers recognize that holding the position of delegate is not a guarantee of job stability.

This counteroffer is accepted in principle by the rural delegates in a referendum organized by the strike committee, but it's here that the workers become divided. Antonio Soto and the strike committee reject the counteroffer.

Amador González, a worker at the *Gaceta del Sur* newspaper who had thrown his weight behind Antonio Soto and the Workers' Society, comes out in favor of lifting the strike. He is seconded by Ildefonso Martínez and Bernabé Ruiz, who, as representatives of the FORA IX, one of the two labor organizations in Buenos Aires, are very important men for the Patagonian labor movement. The two delegates, Martínez and Ruiz, also maintain contact with the Maritime Workers' Federation, which owes its importance to its presence in every port along the coast of Patagonia. Both men launch a furious campaign against Soto for opposing the agreement.

In the meantime, an important change is about to occur in the world of politics. Captain Yza—the new governor of Santa Cruz, appointed by Yrigoyen and ratified by Congress—has announced in Buenos Aires that all of the government functionaries who served under Correa Falcón will be replaced, including Commissioner Ritchie, who will be replaced by Oscar Schweitzer.

This news is greeted as a victory by Borrero and Judge Viñas, as it represents the total defeat of Correa Falcón. And it actively encourages the continuation of the strike.

Antonio Soto goes for broke and gathers all the workers together. The conflict between the two tendencies in the union—syndicalist and anarchist—comes to a head in that December 4th assembly. The majority backs Soto's decision to continue the strike. But Soto is well aware that he can only pull this off if the union's entire leadership supports the strike. So the union also elects new leaders, almost all of them Spaniards holding libertarian ideas. Soto is re-elected as secretary-general.

From this moment on, the workers will have new enemies in the syndicalists and the *Gaceta del Sur* newspaper, which, as we have said, came out in favor of accepting the ranchers' offer.

The newspaper is unsparing in its attacks on Soto. For example, the article "Unionism? Anti-Unionism!" reads as follows:

The workers of Río Gallegos, who have the idiosyncrasy of paying homage to the absurd, have set an awful, terrible precedent. Led by their personal feelings, the workers have let themselves be steered towards disorganization and a grotesque authoritarianism imposed by an inept union leadership. Although the reverence shown to shameless demagogues has always been the greatest threat to the Workers' Society, Antonio Soto stands out for his mental obtuseness and his practical ignorance of unionism even among those who make up the union's unreasonable and idiotic leadership, claiming that their shrewdness elevates them above neophyte workers. More than anyone else, he bears the responsibility for the union's unraveling. His disciples have embarrassingly hoisted him up on a pedestal and worship him as if they have seen the Messiah.

Further along, they criticize the "illogical frequency of the union's strikes and its absurd boycotts." It's important to note that the "syndicalists" aren't just attacking Soto but also the strikes and boycotts organized by the Workers' Society—and that they are doing so in the middle of a general strike, a life or death struggle for the union's future.

When this issue of *Gaceta del Sur* appears on the newsstands, Correa Falcón wastes no time in sending a copy to the interior minister. He also takes the opportunity to attack Judge Viñas for good measure, arguing that his defense of Soto and the labor organization was responsible for everything that followed.

But the strike keeps going despite all these setbacks, and with ever greater intensity. El 68 and El Toscano continue stirring up the peons and cutting fences. The ranchers are afraid and begin preparing their exodus to Río Gallegos.

What position should they take? They are at a loss. At first, they had no interest in reaching a settlement because the wool market was in crisis and so the strike represented an opportunity for them not to pay their workers. But now the very existence of their ranches is at stake, as is the private property system as a whole. The days slip by and the strikers remain unstoppable. Correa Falcón is seemingly impotent, with too few police at his disposal to teach the subversives a proper lesson. There has to be another way: putting pressure on the government, for example.

The ranchers—led by Alejandro Menéndez Behety—send desperate messages to Yrigoyen. The press in Buenos Aires speaks of predations and has begun using the word "bandits" to refer to striking peons. But the strike advances. First it spreads to Puerto Santa Cruz, then San Julián, where something happens without precedent in those latitudes: somebody bombs the home of the "prominent citizen" Juan J. Albornoz, local president of the Argentine Patriotic League. But it's in Puerto Deseado where the truly unexpected will occur, with blood spilled and gunshots exchanged.

CHAPTER FOUR

HAPPY ENDING:
A GOOD PRELUDE TO DEATH

"He who is not for the fatherland is an
enemy of the fatherland."
Río Gallegos Rural Society,
May 27th, 1921

"Workers of the world, unite!
In one solid block, in the close embrace of our
exploited brethren, we shall march down the path that
leads to the emancipation of the slaves of capital."
Río Gallegos Workers' Society
May 18th, 1921

The movement in Puerto Deseado was unique. Far from being a simple confrontation between workers and their bosses, the conflict pitted the majority of the town's population against the "Argentine Circle," an organization of far-right notables that had the full support of the police and treated the town's politicians like their playthings. And it's striking that here is where the battle between the left and the right was at its purest. The left was made up of small shopkeepers, immigrant artisans, and the entirety of the working class—including the unionized workers of the Puerto Deseado-Pico Truncado railway line—while the right consisted of professionals, ranchers, and high-ranking employees of the Braun-Menéndez and Argensud companies. It all started when the immigrants asked the interior minister to officially recognize Puerto Deseado as a municipality. This would not only give immigrants the right to vote but also control of the local government, as they were the majority of the town's population. And so power would slip from the hands of the Argentine Circle's highly exclusive membership. As the latter were neither stupid nor lazy, they were well aware that they were about to lose their truly oligarchic power through a simple legal maneuver. So they sent Yrigoyen an unusual telegram: "The Argentine Circle of Puerto Deseado is against giving the town municipal status, as it would put the local government into the hands of the immigrant majority. No country in the world would allow its political process to be controlled by foreigners."

The animosity between the two groups increases; there's open hatred for the police and the powerful. On December 2nd, the workers at La Anónima go on strike, as do the railway workers. The police respond by locking up the secretary-general of the Workers' Society. One week later, the strike has not only held up but even managed to spread. Despite the communication difficulties involved, local union leaders are in close contact with Antonio Soto in Río Gallegos. Hotel, bar, and café employees have all gone on strike by December 9th. Businesses that hire scabs are boycotted. There are violent incidents across town: blows are exchanged at the Spanish Society—which serves as the headquarters for the strike committee and the pro-municipality activists—and the Colón Bar. Nothing moves. The police patrol the streets in twos, while hotel owners personally serve their guests. Puerto Deseado seems to be on the verge of a civil war. An arbitration committee made up of doctors and bank managers fails in its attempts to reach an agreement with the strikers. From Río Gallegos, Correa Falcón calls for an end to insubordination. The police don't take their time. They lock up the organizers San Emeterio and Christiansen. But the workers stand firm: they call for a general strike, beginning on December 10th at 8 a.m. They don't have access to a printing press to make their flyers and so they write them by hand on Canson paper. It pays off. The streets are empty.

The patriots of the Argentine Circle realize that their days are numbered. The numbers don't lie: Puerto Deseado has a population of 1,570 and only 80 are adult Argentines.

The explosion comes on December 17th. The unions and the pro-municipality committee are scheduled to meet at the offices of the Spanish Society, but the police turn everyone away. Word spreads that the meeting will take place in the graveyard. They are honor-bound to gather at 5:30 p.m. More than three hundred men begin marching towards downtown.

News of the approaching strikers terrifies the members of the Argentine Circle, who take refuge at the police station, bringing their weapons with them. The police chief asks the Coast Guard for reinforcements.

There are contradictory accounts about what happens next. The strikers will later say that their procession was perfectly calm, while the police will claim that they "hurled abuse at shopkeepers, businessmen and members of the White Guard and broke the windows of the offices of the Argentina del Sur Company." And the police will childishly add that two of the protesters shouted, "Death to the Argentines, lovers of order! Down with the Argentine Circle!"

The procession continues forward and the two or three soldiers trailing behind do not dare to stop it. Soon everyone gathers in front of the police station. Inside, the cream of the Argentine Circle take up their positions next to the police and the Coast Guard, refusing to be intimidated by loudmouthed immigrants and anarchists. They open fire the moment the crowd gets within range. This is evidently the language they speak. No one is left on the street, save the corpse of a twenty-one-year-old railway worker named Domingo Faustino Olmedo. A bullet has struck him in the heart. The men of the Argentine Circle aimed well. Excellent marksmanship. A few others have been wounded. Commissioner Alberto Martín will later report that all of the wounds that day were inflicted by Winchester rifles wielded by "citizens who cooperated with the police."

It's time to finish off the strikers before they can regroup. A wide net is cast and the agitators are brought in, one by one.

The police refuse to give up young Olmedo's body, holding it at the station overnight. Only later do they release the body to his mother.

Governor Correa Falcón is pleased. The strikers have been taught a lesson.

All thirty of those arrested are packed into the same cell. None of them are treated like little girls.

But in spite of the police dragnet and the lesson taught with gunpowder, the strike holds. And posters continue to appear, written in pencil or red ink on Canson paper for lack of a printer;

Departmental Workers' Federation—Puerto Deseado

TO WORKING PEOPLE! COMRADES!
Thirty of us have been jailed by the capitalist tyrants. But there are still enough of us left to sustain and rejuvenate the struggle against this increasing tyranny.
LONG LIVE THE STRIKE!
—The Strike Committee

Governor Correa Falcón sends the Interior Ministry a telegram explaining "the truth" behind the events in Puerto Deseado:

On Friday the 17th at 6 o'clock, a group of 250 individuals attacked the Puerto Deseado police station with the intention of freeing two people who had been arrested as threats to public safety. The police, with the help of the Argentine Circle, managed to repel the attack, killing one of the attackers and wounding three others. Luckily, there were no losses sustained by the champions of order. The police conducted themselves impeccably.

This is the approach Correa Falcón will use during his final days in office, an approach that will lead directly to the bloody skirmish at El Cerrito. He knows that El 68 and El Toscano are operating near Lago Argentino. He sends out Commissioner Pedro Micheri, an unscrupulous man, the very prototype of the rogue cop. Micheri receives orders to crush the rural uprising with a heavy hand. This plan is accompanied by insistent calls for military intervention from ranchers and their representatives in Buenos Aires. In Río Gallegos, plans are being made for the creation of a Free Labor Association that will bring in workers from Buenos Aires.

This is the situation at the beginning of 1921, the most tragic year in the history of Patagonia. There's a total work stoppage in Río Gallegos and Puerto Deseado. The few shops that manage to stay open are directly staffed by their owners and supervisors. The Workers' Society has also declared a boycott against three shops in Río Gallegos. And this doesn't just mean that no one shops there but that no one is allowed to engage in any sort of commerce with them—not even butchers, barbers, or milkmen.

There is a violent atmosphere in San Julián and Puerto Santa Cruz, with partial strikes erupting on a day-to-day basis. In Puerto Deseado, a general strike manages to survive the repression. On December 30th, the first of Yrigoyen's troops arrive; sixty soldiers under the command of Frigate Lieutenant Jorge Godoy disembark from the *Ona* in Puerto Deseado.

South of the Río Santa Cruz, the rural strike is all-encompassing. El 68, El Toscano, and their men camp out near Lago Argentino—close to José Pantín's hotels in Río Mitre and

Calafate, which are little more than taverns, and Clark and Tey-seyre's El Cerrito hotel, which is a little bigger. From there they organize raiding parties to attack ranches, carrying off horses, cutting barbed wire fences, and stirring up the peons.

In the meantime, Captain Yza—appointed governor of Santa Cruz several months back—remains in Buenos Aires, where he orders that Correa Falcón's entire staff be replaced by loyal Radicals.

On December 27th, *La Prensa* runs an editorial rightly stating, "Despite the current lack of leadership and the seriousness of the situation, we can still find governors strolling around the Plaza de Mayo."

The one man who will take advantage of Yza's strolls will be Edelmiro Correa Falcón.

Commissioner Micheri sets off for Lago Argentino. Correa Falcón has given him orders to revoke the permits for the "hotels and drinking establishments" owned by the Spaniard José Pantín, who sympathizes with the strikers and allows them to buy all sorts of goods on credit. You have to start here: take away the chilotes' source of sustenance, and complement by the judicious use of the saber and the riding crop, and the problem will go away. Micheri is accompanied by two young men from Buenos Aires—both fervent nationalists—who can't wait to confront the chilotes and show them what Argentines are made of. Their names are Ernesto Bozzano and Jorge Pérez Millán Temperley. The latter is something of a fanatic, a scion of high society who will later become one of the key players in these bloody events.

Commissioner Pedro José Micheri—a thirty-four-year-old from Corrientes—has been given a free hand to carry out his mission however he sees fit. Arriving at Lago Argentino on December 24th, he discovers that Christmas will be celebrated with horse races and card games at a place called Charles Fuhr. He immediately heads out to stop the games from taking place, but when he arrives, after a few shouts and a search for weapons, he gets to talking. At an inquiry conducted four months later, the police officer Martín Gray, who accompanied Commissioner Micheri, will confess that Micheri placed bets on the horses and "played cards all day on the 25th while police officers kept an eye on the games, accompanied by two bribe-takers assigned by Micheri." Micheri also sends Officer Balbarrey a message explaining that any permits requested for horse races at Charles Fuhr should be granted, as long as the kickback doesn't drop below 1,000 pesos.

From there, Micheri goes off to visit the rancher Gerónimo Stipicich, assuring him that he's come to protect his ranch from being attacked by strikers. In return for this protection, Micheri is given sixteen red fox pelts. A good tip.

Sergeant Sosa informs Micheri that sixteen armed strikers have been seen at Pantín's hotel in Calafate. Micheri heads over with his men. He confronts the strikers and brusquely tells them, "You have twenty-four hours to get back to work or leave Lago Argentino or I'll beat you black and blue, bathe you in your own blood, and then force you over the Cordillera."[1] The strikers quietly hear him out and then ask for an extension of four days, as they have a delegate in Río Gallegos who they say will negotiate an end to the strike. Micheri agrees, provided they don't butcher any livestock taken from the ranches.

He nevertheless arrests the manager of the Pantín hotel, who offered the strikers goods on credit, and revokes his business license. He intends to close all of the businesses extending credit to the strikers. He then does the same to the stores owned by Severino Camporro—a Galician anarchist who not only offered them credit, but also urged them to carry on the strike to the last man—and the Spaniard Sixto González, whom he arrests as an "instigator and propagandist." Officer Alberto Baldi will later testify that Micheri personally beat González on the head with his riding crop.

He is brave, this Micheri. With ten officers like him, you could break any strike. He continues his campaign against the business owners who support the strike with all the toughness he's shown until now. He sends an agent to the Río Mitre Hotel along with a warning to its manager—the Yugoslav Nicolás Batistich—to immediately clear everyone out of the establishment for "having harbored strikers." Batistich has a compatriot named Doza deliver a letter to Micheri. When Doza arrives, Sergeant Sosa warns Micheri that the messenger is a spy for the strikers. Micheri strikes Doza on the back with the flat of his saber, arrests him, and marches him out in front of the police station, hoping that the strikers will kill him themselves.

Accompanied by fifteen policemen armed with Mausers, commissioner Micheri rides off to defend the Menéndez-Behety's La Anita ranch. Upon arriving at Cerro Comisión, he approaches a store owned by the Spaniard García Braña, who sells food and drink to the peons. Micheri shouts for Braña to come out. He's one of those shopkeepers who likes to talk things over and explain his point of view, defending himself with words. But Micheri cuts him off, saying, "I already know you're a professor, say everything you need to say." And without hesitating, he firmly beats the Spaniard on the back with his saber. While this is happening, Officer Nova takes two bottles of whiskey from the store for his men.[2]

One less supporter of the strike.

From there, Micheri rides off to visit his friend Gerónimo Stipicich, who asks him to evict the five Chilean cart-drivers who have been occupying and collecting firewood at the Cerro Buenos Aires ranch for the last couple days. Micheri doesn't need to be asked twice.

He and his men approach the peaceable cart-drivers and beat them with the flats of their sabers, forcing them to take their carts to the police station, where they are made to unload all their firewood (it will come in handy during the winter). He also charges them a fine for "grazing rights." Then he tells them to get out.

The Chileans leave with their pockets and carts empty, their backs warmed by the beating. It's hard to imagine that they'll ever return.

Commissioner Micheri presses on with his epic tour around Lago Argentino. He has taken a dislike to Batistich, the manager of the Río Mitre Hotel. He wants to inspect the premises to see if Batistich has carried out the order to evict his guests. When they're within sight of the hotel, they notice that there's a group of people out front who rapidly go inside and lock the doors. Accompanied by Officer Garay, Sergeant Sosa, and the gendarmes Bozzano, Gardozo and Pérez Millán, Micheri approaches and demands that they open the doors. But the men inside aren't easily intimidated. They don't open up. Micheri repeats the order. He's livid. But the only response from inside is a gunshot fired from the window. There's a great deal of confusion. The police, led by Micheri, only stop running when they're five blocks away. The hotel's occupants take advantage of their momentary victory to flee to the hills. At the inquiry held months later, Micheri will declare that once the gunfire ceased, "the gang fled."

From there, Micheri heads straight to La Anita. He arrests a number of people along the way. Micheri's methods for getting people to confess are not very refined. He primarily makes use of his saber, holding it with both hands so as to better caress the flesh with the flat of his blade. He beats one of the suspects with such enthusiasm that it actually bends the blade. But he doesn't get upset: he asks one of the gendarmes to straighten it out and then gets back to business. To make things better, one of the suspects, a Spaniard named Pablo Baquero, was among those who had barricade themselves inside the Río Mitre Hotel and then fled to the hills. Micheri likes to do things personally and gives Baquero special treatment. "You Spanish son of a bitch!" he shouts. "Was something grabbing you by the ass that kept you from coming out like I told you?" And then he gives him a thorough beating.

As all those arrested were farmworkers on Stipicich's ranch, the commissioner—whose arms have already gotten sore—gathers them together and tells them, "I'm going to release you, but if Mr. Stipicich sends for you, you must do whatever he says and work for nothing."

Micheri arrives at La Anita, where he oversees the shearing and leaves a well-armed guard at the request of the administrator, Mr. Shaw. Just as he's getting ready to leave—on January 2nd—word arrives that El 68 and El Toscano have attacked the El Campamento ranch, another Menéndez property. According to the police report, the strikers—led by "a Piedmontese Italian" (El 68)—made off with 3,000 pesos in merchandise, weapons and cash. They destroyed the ranch's automobile before they left with the peons and horses, taking the ranch administrator along as a hostage.

Commissioner Micheri knows that the strikers are on the prowl near El Cerrito. He gets two automobiles ready. He will ride in the first, driven by José Alonso, as will Officer Balbarrey and Corporal Montaña. The second—a vehicle borrowed from Stipicich and driven by his chauffeur, Rodolfo Senecovich—will carry Sergeant Sosa, Corporal Bozzano, and Pérez Millán Temperley. They leave at eight in the morning, well-armed with Mausers.

As they approach El Cerrito, they spot a number of men looking for cover. Micheri smiles and orders Alonso to keep driving. He trusts in his saber and his bullets. But he has miscalculated. El 68 and El Toscano are waiting at El Cerrito, and uniforms don't scare them. The two Italians give the order to stop the automobiles.

Accounts of the bloody events that follow will vary greatly. According to Balbarrey and Montaña—as well as Officer Martín Garay, who is not present but will collect evidence later on—when Commissioner Micheri sees that he's being expected, he speeds down the road towards Río Gallegos, signaling for the other automobile to follow.

They hear the order to stop when they're within two hundred meters of the hotel. Micheri, brave as always, stands up in the automobile and starts shooting left and right. But El 68's men don't flinch; they answer with a hail of gunfire. Bullets fly all around the commissioner and his companions, but they manage to make it through. But then a well-aimed Winchester shot takes out a rear tire. Micheri thinks that he's reached his end and orders

Alonso to keep driving. The vehicle laboriously zig-zags forward. Four strikers get into an automobile and follow Micheri. But while these farm boys may be excellent riders, they're lost behind the wheel. They take off with such force that the car rolls over. Though shaken, they remain undaunted. They run over to Valentín Teyseyre's automobile and resume the chase. Some kilometers away, the back wheel falls off Micheri's car and everyone gets out and runs. Micheri is badly wounded; he has one bullet lodged in his shoulder and another in his chest.

The other car had been following just two hundred meters behind Micheri. They stop, turn around and are about to drive off in the other direction when they receive a hail of gunfire. El 68 gives the order to shoot them all, without mercy. The chauffeur, Senecovich, panics and tries to move forward through the bullets.

The car lurches forward until, directionless, it turns towards the hotel and crashes into a post. Pérez Millán Temperley, despite his leg wounds, is the only passenger who manages to free himself from the wreck. Senecovich tries and fails to stand up: he has been shot in the hip. In the front seat, next to the chauffeur, Sergeant Sosa lies dead. In the back, Corporal Bozzano clings to life for a few minutes more. Two dead, and Senecovich gravely wounded. The strikers take him inside the hotel and lay him down on a cot, next to Pérez Millán.

Back at the first car, the other four policeman have been caught by their pursuers. Micheri and his men surrender. They are taken prisoner and turned over to El 68. When they get back to the hotel, Micheri is surrounded by strikers shouting, "And now? What'll we do with him? He's not so brave now, is he? Where's the tough guy now?"

The Chilean Lorenzo Cárdenas wants to immediately shoot the prisoners. He says that there needs to be a purge if the strike is to succeed. But opinion is split. El Gaucho Cuello, who commands the group of Argentines, doesn't want trouble. He asks El 68 not to kill the policemen: he argues that they should be taken hostage and their fate decided later.

El 68 isn't in a position to argue with Florentino Cuello, nor with the other Argentine strike leader, El Paisano Bartolo Díaz. He gives in.

And then the hotel restaurant empties out, leaving only El 68. Two ranchers—a German named Helmich and the Comte de Liniers—are brought before him. They were both taken hostage after coming to the hotel to do some shopping. After witnessing the shootout, they believe that they're in their final hour and they ask to meet with the strike leader. Both Liniers and Helmich tell the former prisoner of Ushuaia that they're willing to sign the new labor agreement and that they will concede to all of their demands. El 68 doesn't accept their offer. He replies that if they sign while being held hostage, the authorities in Río Gallegos will claim that they were coerced into doing so.

The other Argentine strike leader, El Paisano Bartolo Díaz—a wily gaucho who's always watching his back—asks El 68 to release the two ranchers. He agrees, on the condition that they write a letter to the Río Gallegos Workers' Federation stating that they voluntarily accept the new labor agreement.

The time has now come to move on. El 68 and El Toscano give the order to pack up. As they're getting ready to go, they hear the sound of a motor. It's Commissioner Ritchie, Correa Falcón's acting police chief. He's arrived from Río Gallegos to provide back up for Micheri.

Two cars pull up. Commissioner Ritchie, Sergeant Peralta and Agent Campos ride in the first, on loan from La Anónima and driven by a chauffeur named Caldelas. The second gets a flat just a few kilometers from El Cerrito. But Ritchie's car also comes to a halt, just four hundred meters short of the hotel, when they run out of gasoline. Ritchie orders Campos to retrieve a gasoline can and refill the tank.

El 68's men, having watched the policemen climb out of the car, charge forward on horseback to stop them. When Ritchie sees the cavalry coming, he orders his men to take cover behind some nearby rocks. When they ask him to surrender, Ritchie responds by opening fire. He's a fine shot, a cool-headed man who knows that these Chileans are worth nothing. But the peons dismount, take positions behind the rocks and return fire. Ritchie realizes that they'll soon be surrounded and orders Campos to keep filling the tank while the others cover him. And then a barefaced Galician worker named Zacarías Gracián approaches to hunt for policemen. Ritchie greets him with a bullet to the face. Gracián falls, and Ritchie and his men take advantage of the confusion to get into their car. But the peons and their Winchesters bathe them in bullets. Ritchie is shot in his right hand and Sergeant Pereya's arm dances from a bullet in the wrist. The commissioner realizes that it's now a matter of life or death and starts the car, pulls a U-turn and drives off, leaving Campos standing there with the gasoline can in his hand.[3] He's promptly cut down by El 68's men.

When Ritchie passes by the second car, he tells its occupants to follow him. They take refuge at Pablo Lenzer's ranch and wait there for reinforcements.

The strikers at El Cerrito hastily finish their preparations for departure. They know that the weight of the entire Río Gallegos police force will soon fall on them.

Arguments can be heard in the midst of their preparations. Pérez Millán says that he won't be able to ride with his injuries. And the chauffeur, Senecovich, loudly demands care. Lorenzo Cárdenas wants to finish both of them off himself. Pérez Millán is saved by Armando Camporro, a striker who takes him by the arm and helps him into the saddle.[4] But Senecovich remains on his cot, accused by Cárdenas of being a police agent who reported on the strikers at Stipicich's ranch to Micheri.[5] And what should be done with this man who not only can't ride, but can't even stand up? Lorenzo Cárdenas quickly solves the problem: he shoots him, avenging the death of his friend Zacarías Gracián.

This enrages many of the farmworkers. They reproach Cárdenas for his decision. But Cárdenas is a man of action and he pays their threats no heed. He's one of those who feel that the movement is no place for introspection. Subsequent developments may prove him right. Those on the other side, those defending order and private property, will act just like the murderer Lorenzo Cárdenas.

The strikers depart, all two hundred of them. They ride off and set up camp in a canyon nine leagues away. There they sleep under the stars, covering themselves with *quillangos*.[6] They are accompanied by their two wounded hostages: Commissioner Micheri, with his two bullet wounds, and Pérez Millán Temperley.

When news of the El Cerrito incident reaches Río Gallegos, it's truly explosive. Especially after the arrival of Commissioner Ritchie, with his wounded hand, Sergeant Peralta—whose right arm will have to be amputated—and the chauffeur, Caldelas, whose face is badly scarred by the glass from the shattered windshield. People are terrified. Ritchie, a strong man who is accustomed to treating the poor like sheep, returns wounded and defeated, his men routed, bearing the news that Micheri has been taken prisoner. These mounted anarchists have even dared to attack Micheri![7]

This news confirms the sense of unease in Río Gallegos, which had already witnessed a Danteesque spectacle on Monday, January 3rd. The town's residents were awoken by gunfire at one in the morning. The shots were fired to draw people's attention to a fire. The La Amberense warehouse, owned by a Belgian named Kreglinger, was burning down. And it was filled with gasoline and oil tanks. The strikers had chosen well. There would be explosions all throughout the night. Those who believed in private property were chilled to the bone. But for the poor, this crackle of fireworks provided splendid entertainment. More than a few think that the time has come to pack up and leave, that Santa Cruz has come to resemble the Russia of 1917.

There is a strong backlash in Río Gallegos. "Unity in the face of danger," exhorts the conservative newspaper. And at the Social Club, a group of Argentines resolve to throw their weight behind Correa Falcón and his defense plans. This meeting brings together thirty-seven citizens, all of them ready to defend Argentina and, in passing, their property. But the Argentines aren't the only ones making preparations. The British community holds their own meeting, also offering their services to the governor.

The situation is chaotic. Steamships no longer arrive. It's announced that once the *Asturiano* unmoors, Santa Cruz will be cut off from the outside world. Not that it matters much: everyone's getting ready to defend what's theirs.

Though he only has a few days left in office, Correa Falcón prepares to defeat the strikers once and for all. He issues a manifesto to the "citizens," posting it on every street corner in Río Gallegos:

> The situation created by the outrageous acts of subversive groups makes it necessary for those men who respect the law and the liberties granted by the Constitution to band together. This isn't a labor dispute, but instead something much more serious: the subversion of law and order, along with all the principles of equality and justice.

He calls on the "honest citizens" to organize themselves, as "the honor, life and property of the populace cannot be left to the mercy of heartless fools." He concludes by stating, "Let us ensure respect for our Constitution and our laws, and let us keep the flag of our fatherland flying high."

He sends a telegram to the interior minister informing him that "those supporting law and order in Río Gallegos have immediately responded, unconditionally putting themselves at the disposal of the government. The majority of these people are Argentine and British."

The British community in Patagonia isn't alone. The British embassy in Buenos Aires has also reacted. Its representative, Ronald Macleay, tells the Argentine government of his concerns regarding the plight of British nationals in rather uncompromising terms:

Things have gotten to such a critical state that British nationals, both in town and in the countryside, require urgent protection. It would be dangerous in the extreme to delay any further in providing this protection. I therefore beseech Your Excellency to treat this matter with the utmost seriousness and to authorize me to telegraph the British consul in Río Gallegos, allowing him to reassure his countrymen that the Argentine government will adopt immediate and appropriate measure to protect their lives and property.

Things are beginning to take a more serious turn. Yrigoyen knows that British interests have immense influence in Argentina and that they won't be shy in defending themselves. The Falkland Islands lie just off the coast and British warships are always on standby.

On January 8th, the War Ministry reports that the Navy is dispatching fifty sailors to Río Gallegos and that "the ministry has a squadron standing by to intervene, should further events make such a measure necessary."

When things are at their most fraught, the *Aristobulo del Valle* arrives in Río Gallegos with twenty-five sailors under the command of Ensign Alfredo Malerba. They are only a handful of men, but Malerba is worth one hundred sailors. He meets with Correa Falcón the moment he comes ashore and resolves to pacify the town with an iron hand.

The following day, Captain Narciso Laprida disembarks from the *Querandi*, bringing fifty soldiers from the 10th Cavalry Regiment with him.

The newspaper *La Unión*, speaking for the region's ranchers, merchants, and government officials, enthusiastically welcomes the military:

Though they are few in number, we have every confidence in their effectiveness because they represent the nation's armed forces. Rebelling against them is to rebel against the fatherland they represent, and those who do so risk being considered enemies of the nation and treated with all the severity of martial law. And so those who respect order, both Argentine and immigrant, could not contain their applause when these bearers of the glad tidings of peace and security marched through our streets.

When Correa Falcón realizes that Malerba is an advocate of order at all costs, he puts him in command of the city's prisons and police force.

He doesn't need to be asked twice. On Sunday, January 16th, he mobilizes his sailors and the entire police force to seal off the town, which, in a matter of hours, is cleansed of anything that smells of strikers. He has no qualms about locking up the leaders along with the small fry. And so the first to fall is José María Borrero, the advisor to the Workers' Society and the managing editor of *La Verdad*. He's soon followed by all of the friends of Antonio Soto, though the man himself could not be located.[8]

Two hours after Borrero was arrested, something disgraceful occurs. Accompanied by their men, Malerba and Ritchie set off for *La Verdad*'s printing press. But the doors are locked. Ritchie approaches the house of a type-setter—which faces the press—to ask for the keys. He's whipped when he refuses and Ritchie orders the doors to be forced open. The next day, Ensign Malerba visits the jail. When he passes in front of Borrero, he tells him that his printing press has been destroyed by persons unknown.

This procedure is not very democratic, but it is incredibly effective. When Borrero is released from jail, he finds his printing press destroyed, his plates smashed, and thirty-six boxes of type ruined. In the subsequent court case, Malerba will state that he had been acting on orders from the Naval Ministry.

This is how Correa Falcón and Malerba manage to leave the movement leaderless in Río Gallegos. Save for Antonio Soto, all of the leaders are behind bars. And Antonio Soto is cut off from his followers. Before, messengers from the countryside were able to slip past the police checkpoints by taking a detour along the banks of the river. But now Malerba has sealed off that route as well.

Furthermore, a curfew has also been decreed:

Public gatherings are prohibited. The population is asked to refrain from bearing arms or using the streets after 9 p.m., as well as to immediately comply with any orders they may receive from sentries or police officers.

Yrigoyen and Minister Gómez are in over their heads with this problem of the rural strike. The British embassy complains once again. Macleay informs Argentina's Foreign Affairs Ministry that a ranch owned by a British national named Juan Cormack was attacked by "armed and mounted strikers, who destroyed shearing equipment and requisitioned horses and supplies." And then he insists that the Argentine government take protective measures.

Chile, too, is worried about the rural strike on the other side of the border. The following document is an undeniable rebuttal of the theory that the strike in Patagonia was fomented by the Chilean armed forces. In a note addressed to the Foreign Affairs Ministry in Buenos Aires and dated January 12th, Noel, the Argentine ambassador in Buenos Aires, writes:

Confidential and Restricted

To the Foreign Affairs Ministry, Buenos Aires:
Chile's foreign affairs minister tells me that he has received some very alarming reports about disturbances in the far south, where bandits have overrun the ranches along the border between Chile and Argentina, 250 kilometers away from Punta Arenas, whose residents are asking for protection. The Chilean government requests that Your Excellency forward any relevant news to the embassy, as well as to inquire if the Argentine government has sufficient forces at its disposal in said region and if it would be willing to order its police forces to work in coordination with

the Chilean police to defeat these bandits. The Chilean government requests an urgent response.

Noel, Argentine Ambassador.

There will be note after note along these lines, showing the
Chilean government's fear that the conflict would spread into
Chilean Patagonia and the Aysén region, a fear stoked in the halls
of power by large landowners with the same names as those on the
Argentine side of the border.

Under the command of Captain Laprida, the 10th Cavalry
Squadron sets out from Río Gallegos on January 2nd, accompanied by Commissioner Ritchie and around twenty policemen.
They go by truck to Robert MacDonald's La Vanguardia ranch
and wait there for their horses.

Laprida remains at La Vanguardia, unwilling to venture
beyond this stronghold. He knows that El 68 and El Toscano,
both of them quite close, are not afraid of a shootout.

Laprida, Malerba, and Correa Falcón telegraph Buenos Aires,
reporting that they do not have enough men at their disposal.

But in the meantime, what are the town's strikers up to? In Río
Gallegos, the strike has become unsustainable. Repression, imprisonment, a ban on meetings, and the loss of Borrero's newspaper
(which often ran union communiqués) would, little by little, lead to
the bosses' victory and a return to work. Antonio Soto understands
that nothing more can be done in the city and, as the syndicalist FORA doesn't respond to his desperate appeals, he calls for the
strike to be lifted in order to save the Workers' Society. He drafts a
long communiqué analyzing the movement and explaining why the
urban workers were defeated. This communiqué closes by stating:

> Men of conscience will eventually judge us and the authorities
> will do us justice because truth and justice will come to light and
> triumph. If we are silenced, other voices will be raised because
> there is no strength that can destroy the union of the workers,
> because it is a beautiful and righteous cause.

There's no alternative: in Buenos Aires, the Maritime Workers' Federation has already come to a separate arrangement. Ships begin to arrive in Río Gallegos once more. The first to arrive is the *Presidente Mitre*, carrying 326 third class passengers. *La Unión*, the mouthpiece of the ranchers, triumphantly reports that the ship has brought in "a full staff for the meatpacking plants." The arrival of the *Mitre* ends a period of seventy days' rest at the ports of Santa Cruz, which the newspaper notes is "equivalent to the time that Columbus took to discover America four centuries ago."

The ship's arrival in Río Gallegos has a tremendous psychological impact on the town's residents, especially its merchants and landowners. Two delegates from the syndicalist FORA also arrive from Buenos Aires on the *Presidente Mitre*: Santiago Lázaro and Francisco Somoza, who will wage a war to the death against Antonio Soto and the Río Gallegos Workers' Society.

Besides the *Mitre*, the *Presidente Quintana*, and the *Asturiano* are also on their way to the coasts of Patagonia.

Antonio Soto decides to travel to Buenos Aires and clarify the situation to the syndicalists. He emerges from hiding and is smuggled aboard the steamship *Asturiano* by the ship's mechanics. During a stopover at Puerto Deseado, the town's sub-prefect learns of Soto's presence aboard the ship and orders the maritime police to bring him ashore. But the ship's entire crew goes on strike and the police, outdone, are forced to retreat. Upon docking in Buenos Aires, the police try to search the ship, but a group of three hundred stevedores get in the way.[9] *La Organización Obrera*, the mouthpiece of the syndicalist FORA, reports Soto's arrival on January 29th. Soto will participate in the union's national congress as the delegate of the Río Gallegos Workers' Society. But Soto has also come to encourage the unionized workers of Buenos Aires to help their fellows in the countryside, then facing the toughest moments of the strike. The labor congress, bringing together delegates from every corner of the country, is held from January 29th to February 5th, 1921. There, Soto will insult the national union leadership. He will criticize the decision of the Maritime

Workers' Federation to allow ships filled with strikebreakers to disembark and sail to Río Gallegos. The entire congress will listen with astonishment to the Patagonian delegate's scathing criticism of the national leadership's lack of solidarity and their abandonment of the labor movement in the south during so difficult a year for the workers as 1920.

Soto will never be forgiven for this speech. Criticizing the bureaucracy of the country's most powerful labor federation is a capital sin. And the bureaucracy immediately hits back. The union's national newspaper, *La Organización Obrera*, publishes the following report on the labor congress on February 12th:

> The delegate from Santa Cruz used the labor disputes on the southern coast as an opportunity to bring up matters that took two hours to address. He made unjustified criticisms of the Maritime Workers' Federation and the national leadership, which drew a vehement response from Alegría, Cisneros, and others, as well as from the national leadership council. In the end, the decisions of the national leadership were endorsed by a vote of 99 to 3, and it was agreed by a vote of 111 delegates that all matters not scheduled on the agenda should be addressed in committee.

As we can see, the Chamber of Deputies isn't alone in referring sensitive matters to committee—unions can do it as well.

But the rural strike will last until the bitter end. El 68 and El Toscano move shrewdly. They're constantly shifting camp and don't seek out confrontation, but when they need to fight, they fight. And they will prove this in their tragicomic clash with Commissioner Francisco Nicolía Jameson and the officers under his command.[10]

As we have seen, the strikers have been camping out in a canyon nine leagues away from El Cerrito. From there, they set out for Juan Clark's El Tero ranch. Their ranks have been swollen by around 450 peons. Keeping with their tactic of staying on the move and disorienting the police, they push forward and set up camp in a quarry, which will later be known as Cañadón de los Huelguistas (Strikers' Canyon). There they remain for several days while El 68 heads to Río Gallegos to meet with Soto. The former prisoner of Ushuaia manages to slip past the police checkpoints and then leaves the capital accompanied by thirty men, a truly daring feat. They attack the ranches they come across on their way back to camp, taking hostages, capturing gendarmes, and requisitioning weapons and horses. Their ranks swell by 150 men, making a total of six hundred strikers in the canyon. They immediately break camp and march towards Lago Argentino, where they carry out an occupation of La Anita ranch. There they capture four gendarmes and thirty shearers.

Unaware of these developments, Commissioner Nicolía Jameson has received orders from Correa Falcón to reinforce the guard at La Anita. Assisted by Officer Novas, he gathers together fifteen well-armed men and they drive off in a car and a truck. They feel safe because they know that Laprida is stationed at La Vanguardia with fifty soldiers, and they're confident they won't see a trace of El 68's men. Upon reaching Calafate, the commissioner lets his men stop at Echeverría's tavern and generously buys them a few rounds. They're a bit tipsy when they resume their journey to La Anita. But when they reach the Río Centinela, they see three cars approach. Sixty riders emerge from the side of the road. Commissioner Jameson orders his men to halt and take up positions.

As the cars approach, a gendarme named Artaza, drunk and unsteady on his feet, begins firing left and right. Facing such a welcome, the strikers stop and fire on the police. Commissioner Nicolía Jameson and his men flee as best they can, piling into their vehicles, turning around and taking off at top speed, leaving behind Artaza, who is too drunk to run, and another two gendarmes named Giménez and Páez. Realizing that they have been left to the mercy of the strikers, Giménez and Páez scream for their lives. Officer Nova, riding in the truck, draws his revolver and forces the driver to stop and pick them up.

Artaza is left on his own and keeps firing until he is cut down by El 68's men.

Officer Nova will later tell his superiors that Nicolía Jameson beat a hasty retreat; that when he saw the strikers, he shouted, "Everybody aboard, let's go!"; that Artaza had left the police station drunk, "having consumed a large amount of alcohol, purchased from La Anónima by Commissioner Jameson."

The car leaves the truck far behind. When Nova finally reaches Echeverría's tavern, he finds "Commissioner Jameson and Officer Garay totally intoxicated, embracing each other and saying farewell." Jameson had bought three bottles and got drunk, as had most of his men, strengthening their spirits while they waited for the strikers. But the latter had given up the chase, as the area was under surveillance by Captain Laprida and his cavalry troops. The police officer's testimony will state that, as he left the tavern, Jameson shouted, "Long live the fatherland! Down with the red flag and long live the flag of Argentina!" He then ordered those present to give a cheer for each officer who had fought that day.

When they arrive at the police station, they find Subcommissioner Douglas ordering Jameson to give a cheer for him and his men. He then orders Nova to fetch three bottles of whiskey from Dickie's ranch "to share among the men who conducted themselves so bravely at the Río Centinela." And then something occurs that clearly shows these men's brutality and total lack of respect for humanity. Two riders were being held at the station on suspicion of being strikers. Jameson has them taken from their cells, orders his men to strip them naked and beats them with the flat of his saber in front of the troops. He then orders them to be left naked all night, though this order is later overridden by Captain Laprida, who arrives half an hour later. But Nicolía Jameson hasn't finished with the day's great deeds. Nobody at the police station feels safe. They all fear an attack by El 68 and El Toscano. And so they decide to head to Lenzner's ranch, where most of the cavalry troops are stationed. There, Captain Laprida turns a German striker over to the police. Nicolía Jameson immediately orders the

German to be taken out back. He handcuffs the prisoner, lowers him halfway into a well and then uses Officer Nova's handcuffs to shackle him to a nearby fence. A true Chinese torture: spending the Patagonian night out in the open, with one's feet in the water. (An investigation will conclude with Jameson's dismissal on March 23rd, 1921 for "misconduct and moral weakness.")

But the "Battle" of the Río Centinela will naturally be seized upon by the press as yet another opportunity for outrage at the savagery of the strikers. Río Gallegos' *La Unión* will refer to the death of Artaza as an "unprecedented and premeditated murder" and a "repulsive crime."

But Correa Falcón has only a few days left in power. After six months of indecision, Governor Yza is finally leaving for Río Gallegos. The ranchers prepare to give him a warm welcome. They distrust him as a Radical, but trust him as a military officer. One editorial in *La Unión* proclaims:

> It takes the authority of a disciplined spirit—such as the we see in Captain Yza, forged in the purest patriotic traditions and strengthened by military life in the bosom of these legendary institutions and by daily contact with the symbols of our nation, which inspire the most fervent and austere feelings of appreciation for the values they represent—to take on the task at hand, which demands not only governmental expertise and the application of time-honored measures, but also the virtue of a civic conscience and the serene, magnanimous understanding of lofty souls.

The news that the new governor is on his way arrives even as Correa Falcón and Malerba carry on with the repression. In Río Gallegos, every democratic right has been revoked. Meanwhile, the Rural Society is extremely active in preparing its defenses. Its members resolve to unite with similar organizations in San Julián and Puerto Santa Cruz. The unification committee is made up of sixteen members (eight from Río Gallegos, four from Puerto Santa Cruz and four from San Julián) and chaired by Ibón Noya.

Governor Correa Falcón is ratified as its managing secretary. But the most important decision the committee takes is to collect 100,000 pesos for expenses and for "the campaign to uphold law and order." These funds are raised by requiring each landowner to pay the Rural Society two centavos per head of livestock. One document that clearly shows the connivance between the police, the army, and the White Guard—the self-defense organization of the ranchers—is the report addressed to the interior minister by Engineer Cobos, sent to Buenos Aires as a delegate of the Santa Cruz Rural Society:

> The White Guard has taken responsibility for supplying meat, automobiles, and gasoline to the local police station and has agreed to pay for repairs. And let me also mention that, for some time, each of the town's five primary retail outlets has been providing them with goods equivalent to 50 pesos per month, free of charge. This arrangement has been in place for years. The White Guard has covered the expenses of a car trip taken by four officers stationed at Tamel Aike who were needed as reinforcements at the police station in San Julián. During the strike, when it was decided to send eleven soldiers to San Julián, their journey was underwritten by merchants and landowners, as was their return trip to Río Gallegos. And, during their mission, they had to be provided with lodging and saddles, along with other supplies and living expenses. We merchants and landowners have paid a total of 8,615 pesos on maintaining and transporting these troops, which does not include the 4,000 pesos provided by the White Guard.

There is little hope left for the workers. Who are the police and army going to defend if they depended on the landowners for food and transportation?

Yrigoyen is slow but neither deaf nor blind. The federal government mobilizes the 10th Cavalry Regiment with orders to pacify the south. The regiment is under the command of Lieutenant Colonel Héctor Benigno Varela.

Varela visits the Casa Rosada to meet with the president and clarify the details of his mission. On a torrid January day, Varela and his young assistant, First Lieutenant Anaya, both of them in dress uniform, enter the cool shade of the president's office. Before them stands an enormous man, twice their own height, who barely seems to be moving. He speaks slowly, taking his time. Anaya is awestruck. Varela listens with a religious silence. The president talks in generalities and the officer listens with growing interest, anticipating the moment in which his commander-in-chief will issue the "secret instructions," the precise orders that must never be repeated outside that mysterious office. But the president takes his time. He speaks of party politics, the struggles of years past, and the republic in general.

Suddenly, the audience is over. The president rises to his feet. Taken aback, Varela ventures one polite and deferential query: "Mr. President, I should like to know what I am to do in Santa Cruz."

Hipólito Yrigoyen, his warm voice inflected with trust and intimacy—as if he were addressing a brother or a son—tells him, "Go, Lieutenant Colonel. Go and study what is happening and do your duty."

And that is it. Varela is at a loss. But the giant offers him his hand. There's no more to say.

"Stop by Dr. Gómez's office and he will give you your instructions."

But Anaya will later state, "Dr. Gómez was waiting for us in his office but didn't add a single word. He merely passed on some telegrams he had received and wished us a safe journey."[11]

Varela is not the type of man who spends his time worrying about if he's being set up. His thoughts are on his soldiers, his plans, his preparations and logistics. Having been ordered, he will act. The 10th Cavalry Regiment shakes to life. Varela has a military soul. He loves action, discipline, duty, and the manliness of command. He is a great admirer of German military discipline and has been diligently studying the German language for years.

The 10th Cavalry Regiment did not exist when it was ordered to move south. The 1889 class had graduated in December and the new class was still being recruited. The soldiers would need to be tracked down. One by one, the former conscripts are taken from their homes and sent to the barracks. We can only imagine the "delight" felt by these young men, their military service completed, who are now ordered back to active duty to crush a strike in Patagonia. Anaya describes this forced recruitment as "a difficult task." He only manages to muster up 150 men and will have to reinforce the regiment with another twenty additional soldiers from the 2nd Cavalry Regiment.

They embark on the *Guardia Nacional* on the night of January 28th, 1921.

The strikers continue their occupation of La Anita. A car passes by, carrying the ranchers Gerónimo and José Stipicich, along with their brother-in-law Duimo Martinovich and Gerónimo's son, only twelve years old. The strikers take them prisoner. El 68 suggests that Stipicich go to Río Gallegos and encourage the other ranchers to sign the labor agreement. His brother and son will be held at the ranch until he returns.

Trembling, Stipicich drives towards Río Gallegos, accompanied by Guillermo Payne, another rancher who was being held hostage. In the meantime, El Toscano heads to the Río Coyle to stir up the workers and bring back food and weapons.

The first thing Stipicich does upon reaching Río Gallegos is send a telegram to the representative of La Anónima in Puerto Santa Cruz. We have reproduced it below as it describes the situation well:

> Mr. Menotti Bianchi: I have just arrived from Lago Argentino. I had set out on the 21st, along with my brother, my son, and several other people. When we arrived at La Anita, we were

greeted by the over five hundred strikers who were occupying the ranch. They held me for six hours, and my brother and son remain in their power. I received permission to leave and seek out some sort of settlement. You can understand my plight. I would recommend settling because the situation is dire—they didn't kill me only because they didn't want to, they told me that I arrived at just the right time, as they were about to burn down La Anita, as well as all of my ranches. They agreed to grant me four days' reprieve. The authorities are powerless. Over fifteen police officers have also been taken prisoner, including Commissioner Micheri, who has been wounded. Many of the strikers are blameless. We must do whatever is in our power to avoid confrontations. As I am in danger, I beg you to inform me of your decision at once, as I must leave tomorrow. Speaking for myself, I am in favor of settling. —Gerónimo Stipicich.

In Río Gallegos, Stipicich will meet with Mauricio Braun, Alejandro Menéndez Behety, José Montes, Ibón Noya, Ernesto von Heinz, and other landowners. The ranchers propose that the workers elect a negotiating committee and that, if no agreement can be reached, a neutral arbitrator be designated. Stipicich returns to La Anita on January 26th.

The strikers agree, appointing a delegate to meet with the ranchers in Río Gallegos.

On Saturday, January 29th, 1921—months after being appointed—the new governor of Santa Cruz finally arrived in Río Gallegos. Yza's first actions disappoint the hardliners. He dismisses Correa Falcón's friends, retaining only those with no reputation for brutality. The curfew is the next to go.

That same day, he meets with the members of the Rural Society to look for a solution to the rural conflict. Stipicich returns, accompanied by the workers' delegate. On Sunday, the ranchers hold a meeting in the presence of the governor. They approve a new list of conditions and unanimously elect Governor Yza as their arbitrator.

In their new offer, the ranchers accept nearly all of the workers' demands. The article on the ranch delegates is worded as follows:

> The employers agree to recognize labor associations as lawful organizations on the condition that they have been granted legal status. Workers are free to join said associations at their own discretion, as only the good conduct and competence of each individual will be taken into account by employers.

This offer was signed by all of the powerful landowners of Santa Cruz, including Mauricio Braun and Alejandro Menéndez Behety. A close reading of the ranchers' offer shows the extent of the strike's success—this agreement was without precedent in Argentina as a whole.

The governor immediately speaks with the workers' delegate and proposes that he travel alongside two government representatives who will have the power to open formal negotiations with the strikers.

In the meantime, Varela receives orders for his troops to disembark from the *Guardia Nacional* in Puerto Santa Cruz rather than Río Gallegos. Yza continues to make decisions that don't favor the landowners: he releases all of the workers who been arrested during the strike, including the controversial José María Borrero, who—despite the destruction of his printing press—immediately resumes his offensive against Correa Falcón and the men of the Rural Society.

The government commission that has gone to Lago Argentino in search of the strikers, and give them word of the ranchers' offer fails to find them. This gives Varela the opportunity to propose his own solution, one that will later prove to be extremely controversial. The strikers have also drafted a new offer to bring to the discussion table:

> Full recognition of the demands presented by the workers.

The workers will not be held responsible, either morally or materially, for any of the events that occurred during the strike.

The label of "bandits" that has been given to the workers must be formally retracted.

Any and all authorities who unjustly targeted workers must be dismissed.

The governor must guarantee that no reprisals of any kind will be taken against those workers who participated in the strike or no agreement will be possible.

But the absence of contact makes direct negotiations impossible. Varela and his troops reach Puerto Santa Cruz on February 2nd, 1921. Years later, Anaya will write about this moment:

The decision to disembark there was dictated by the possibility of the insurrection spreading north, as was expected, thus putting us in position to intercept them. Once the troops had been welcomed by the local authorities, the regiment's commander easily gauged popular expectations, as well as the prevailing disorder and the lack of coordination between local authorities. These observations prompted him to press on towards Río Gallegos, accompanied by his aide-de-camp and one police officer.

Anaya has also told us that, during his trip to Río Gallegos, Varela does not meet with Yza but instead with Correa Falcón, who apparently painted an exaggerated portrait of the crimes of the strikers and the destruction caused by the conflict. Anaya adds that Varela, wishing to corroborate these claims, embarks on "a personal reconnaissance of the nearby ranches that were said to be looted and destroyed (but) those who abandoned their land were the first to provide information contradicting the official reports."

Anaya's writings are very important and must be remembered, as he will later contradict himself when justifying the executions to come. But if exaggerations were made regarding the behavior of the strikers during the first strike, who's to say that the same thing won't happen during the second strike as well?

It is only then that Varela meets with Yza, who has received "instructions from the federal government." Anaya describes them as follows:

> The instructions received by Governor Yza added little or nothing to what we already knew. But they did include a desire to avoid bloodshed at any cost and to peacefully resolve the conflict that was so damaging to the territory's economy. It was a matter of some urgency for the business community in general and the governor in particular to ensure that the shearing go smoothly and for the governor to show himself to be a faithful servant of the president, whose pro-labor policies were well known.

The ranchers, who had been dreaming of a military solution that would solve the problem with saber blows, now realize that they had fallen into the Radical trap. On February 10th, they react with a furious telegram to the interior minister:

> In the wake of the vandalism committed by the rebels, the territory's residents feel obligated to remind Your Excellency of the rights guaranteed by the Constitution. The ranchers have authorized the Rural Society's president to appoint Governor Yza as arbitrator on the understanding that he would reach a satisfactory arrangement with the good elements among the workers. Given the failure of his efforts and the continuing criminal attacks, we have called off our overtures to the strikers and have instead requested that Governor Yza strictly enforce the nation's laws. We have been greatly dissatisfied with his decision to free the instigators and intellectual authors of this conflict, as it is public knowledge that the leaders of the revolt in the countryside are based in the capital. —Ibón Noya.

The ranchers have realized that Yza, as a good Radical, will give more weight to the opinions of his fellow party members. They are correct; Yza will principally listen to Judge Viñas. Besides, the governor—who wants to end the strike at all costs—has realized that the judge is the only one who the workers will obey. Yza will use the judge to contact two of the strike leaders—both friends of Viñas—who will be the ones to finally accept a settlement. They are also two of the only Argentines among the peons: Gaucho Cuello and El Paisano Bartolo Díaz.

They reach a temporary arrangement. No one will be taken prisoner and each worker will be given a safe conduct pass allowing them to return to work. Yza will be the arbitrator and will agree in principle to the workers' offer. In exchange, to prevent the army and the governor from losing face, the workers will appear to unconditionally surrender their hostages, weapons, and horses to Varela.

Gaucho Cuello and El Paisano Díaz take this offer to El 68 and El Toscano, who angrily reject it, declaring that they will never surrender their weapons. So the decision goes to the assembly. El 68 and the Spaniard Graña speak against the offer. Cuello, Bartolo Díaz, the Paraguayan Jara and another Argentine by the name of Lara speak in favor. The chilotes vote to end the strike: there are 427 votes in favor of returning to work against 200 votes in favor of continuing the resistance. When Florentino Cuello and Bartolo Díaz hand over their wounded hostages (Commissioner Micheri and Pérez Millán), El 68 and El Toscano, along with two hundred of their followers, make off with most of the weapons. Later on, Florentino Cuello gives himself up to Governor Yza at the El Tero ranch, along with the remaining weapons—which are very few—and 1,913 horses. There, the police confirm the identity of the strikers who have turned themselves in and issue them safe conduct passes. Florentino Cuello receives Pass No. 1 and is allowed to leave, followed by El Paisano Díaz and the other ranch delegates. To keep up appearances, Yza sends a telegraph to the interior minister stating that "the ringleaders have been arrested and, after being disarmed, have been released by the police, as ordered." But he was merely honoring his word to release all those who turned themselves in.

Everything has ended well: the strikers remain free and Yza will come down on the side of the workers. But nobody suspects that this happy ending is only a prelude to death.

CHAPTER FIVE

THE LONG MARCH TOWARDS DEATH

"The same was done to the Indians in that bloodbath
they call the Conquest of the Desert."
"The Massacre in Santa Cruz,"
La Protesta, January 6th, 1922

"Like the Indian before him, the pariah—without
family, home, religion or fatherland—becomes a
murderer and a vandal, burning crops and
attacking ranches…"
El Soldato Argentino,[1] Vol. II No. 13
January 2nd, 1922

The first strike was nothing more than an overture to the massacre that would follow. It was a rosy chapter in the history of Patagonia when compared to the horror that events will acquire nine months later. Let's see how General Anaya, who participated in the repression of the second strike as a captain, describes the difference:

We have just heard the most objective account possible of the events that shook the far south in 1921. To differentiate it from the events that followed, allow us to refer to it as the "peaceful military campaign," in contrast to what I shall call the "bloody military campaign."[2]

Work resumes and the much-delayed shearing is rushed to completion. But this gives a false impression of what's really going on: the workers have triumphed, plain and simple. This is how the Workers' Society sees it, how the Rural Society sees it, and how the Commerce and Industry League sees it.

Two police officers have been murdered. Landowners, gendarmes and ranch administrators have been taken hostage. Fences have been cut, animals have been slaughtered, buildings have been destroyed.

But that didn't stop Captain Yza and Commander Varela from coming to Patagonia and settling with the strikers, giving them safe conduct passes that allowed them to freely move around the region and work wherever they pleased. And don't forget that they didn't hand over their weapons, as most of them remain in the possession of El 68, El Toscano, and the group that followed them. Aside from a few old rifles and rusty revolvers, Varela turned up nothing. Such is the panorama seen by the landowners and despondent merchants of Santa Cruz.

When Varela returns to Río Gallegos, they even say so to his face. Edelmiro Correa Falcón recounts the story in his pamphlet *The Events in Santa Cruz, 1919–1921*:

Once the 10th Cavalry Regiment's peacemaking mission had concluded, a few individuals happened to encounter Lieutenant Colonel Varela in Río Gallegos. While they drank their tea, one of those present said that it set a dangerous precedent to allow so many weapons to remain in the hands of the rebels, who had nevertheless been issued with a sort of act of indemnity. The lieutenant colonel rejected this view of the situation, adding that his mission had been satisfactorily completed in accordance with the personal instructions of the president—a claim that was later borne out by those who heard these instructions issued. During this same conversation, another one of those present said that the news arriving from the countryside left him convinced that there would soon be a general uprising throughout the territory. The lieutenant colonel ignored this prediction, repeating that he believed his pacification efforts to have been definitive.

But the mighty aren't Varela's only critics. The commander's pacifist stance is even being openly censured within his own regiment. Captain Anaya enumerates these criticisms:

The regiment, which had remained in the barracks in Santa Cruz, was utterly oblivious to what was going on and felt unsatisfied with the peaceful outcome. These feelings were encouraged by the landowners who had abandoned their ranches and wanted to see brutal, indiscriminate repression. The coastal business interests also disapproved of the solution, wishing that the strike had instead been drowned in blood. They mounted a campaign of defamation against the military officer and the governor, whom they claimed had blindly made a pact with insurgents out of ignorance and short-term political gain. Some officers were not unsympathetic to these criticisms, feeling that a humanitarian rather than military solution to the conflict had robbed them of their laurels.

Even before he leaves for Buenos Aires, Varela hesitates. He seems to be under a lot of pressure. Enrique Noya—brother of Rural Society President Ibón Noya—will tell us the following:

When the first strike ended, my brother Ibón told Varela, "When you leave, it will all start again." Varela replied, "If it starts up again, I'll come back and shoot the lot."

In Río Gallegos, *La Unión* mercilessly attacks the settlement reached by Varela and Governor Yza:

> The settlement deals exclusively with the economic aspects of the conflict, constituting a resounding victory for the impositions of the workers that has been facilitated by the authorities themselves. Lacking understanding, and with a total absence of impartiality, they have delivered a Solomonic judgment and indirectly forced capital to accept it.[3] Nothing has been done to address the crimes, thefts, arsons, etc. that were committed during the strike—the perpetrators and their accomplices have not been taken in, not even for questioning.

The bosses had insisted on a hard line, glorifying Correa Falcón and brutish police officers like Ritchie and Nicolía Jameson. They had seen violence as the only possible solution. They could not understand the accommodating policies of the Radical president, as implemented by Governor Yza and Lieutenant Colonel Varela.

So, as we can see, nothing has been settled. There are still three antagonistic forces in a sparsely populated region. There are the bosses, with Correa Falcón as their most visible figure, along with the administrators of British-owned ranches and, perhaps most importantly, Mauricio Braun and Alejandro Menéndez Behety, who are the most intelligent of the lot, the ones with the most influence in Buenos Aires and the ones who have slowly begun to arrange a definitive settlement of the crisis. The second faction revolves around Borrero and Judge Viñas and includes all the members of the Radical Civic Union. It is this group whose support Governor Yza will seek. The third conflicting force is, of course, the labor movement, strengthened by its recent success.

In his role as the mediator between the bosses and the workers, Yza asks the Workers' Society to lift its boycott of certain stores. But Antonio Soto refuses to simply do whatever the governor tells him to do. Yes, the boycotts will be lifted, but only when three conditions are met:

- All of the strikers who have been fired will be rehired and given back pay for all workdays lost to the strike.
- All non-unionized workers will be dismissed.
- The bosses will reimburse the Workers' Society for all costs incurred in printing their manifestos.

In short, Soto demands unconditional surrender. When the bosses learn of his demands, they are truly outraged. *La Unión*, scandalized, can't help but attack the governor once more:

The government's passivity in the face of such extortion essentially authorizes the subversion of law and order and the abdication of authority to the labor associations, which now represent a new power running parallel to the constitutional authorities. Outside agitators, the aftertaste of unrestricted immigration, profess doctrines in which those who were once slaves will take the place of their oppressors. An undisciplined horde, incapable of the honest struggle to earn a living, offers us the sad spectacle of tyranny lurking behind the veneer of economic concessions and forces us to confront the problem of nationality by slandering native-born citizens and supplanting the principles of the law with the imperative of their bastard aspirations. Foreigners, who have formed trade unions for no other purpose than the subversion of order and rebellion against the law and who have found easy living in revolt and social imbalance, proclaim destructive theories in the form of supposed concessions. They must therefore destroy any trace of the national spirit that could oppose their aims. War has been declared against the country's sons, against the *criollos* who have more right than anyone to live in our society, as it is their home, on the simple ground that they rightly rebel against the imposition of these utopias.

This patriotic nonsense is but a sample of the arguments that were rehashed day after day, in every corner of the country, by the Argentine Patriotic League. According to them, Argentine workers weren't the victims of capitalists or landowners, be they foreign or domestic, but instead of immigrant workers who "brought with them ideas that are incompatible with national sentiments."

Syndicalism, liberty, equality, socialism, and universality were all foreign notions. The authentic Argentine, by contrast, was that worker who refused to succumb to this siren song, who was satisfied with his lot and was always respectful to his betters. He had a deep-seated love for his fatherland, always wearing his best on Independence Day, always flying the blue and white high, and always opposing those Spaniards and Italians who wished to swap the nation's symbols for the "red rag."

This argument about "foreign ideas," used to combat socialist and libertarian ideas, was an undeniable success. It has taken root in the Argentine working class. It hasn't just been repeated by every government from 1930 onwards, without exception—no matter if they derived their legitimacy from military coups or from elections—but also within the General Confederation of Labor (CGT) itself, from the mouths of Peronist labor leaders such as José Espejo, Augusto Vandor, José Alonso, José Rucci, Lorenzo Miguel, etc.

All of the philosophical, social, and political ideas that belong to no country in particular, but are instead the heritage of the entire human race, could be silenced with a single word: Argentina!

This argument would nevertheless cast its spell over the entire country and has continued to prove lucrative for the Argentine bourgeoisie up to the present day.

But what's even odder is that, in the Río Gallegos of 1921, every single member of the Argentine Patriotic League—without exception—was a foreigner. The nonsense printed above was written by Rodríguez Algarra, the editor of *La Unión*, a purebred Spaniard with close ties to the Braun and Menéndez Behety interests.

But the secretary of the Workers' Society cared little for these patriotic arguments. Instead, he was preparing a new blow against the frightened supporters of capitalism: a strike at the Swift meat-packing plant in Río Gallegos.

If there was one place in Patagonia that deserved a strike, this was it. Perhaps not because of its wages or working conditions—which were comparable to the rest of the country—but because of the medievalism of its employment contracts. We have in our hands an example of one of these contracts.[4] It speaks for itself. This contract, which workers were required to sign before shipping out from Buenos Aires to Río Gallegos, is pompously titled *Service Leasing Contract* and reads as follows:

Swift & Company of La Plata, Río Gallegos, and San Julián (hereinafter referred to as "The Company"), through its agent in this city, Swift & Company of La Plata, Ltd, with its address at Calle 25 de Mayo 195, and Manuel Pérez (hereinafter referred to as "The Contractor"), have agreed to the following:

The Contractor will provide his services as a manual laborer for the aforementioned Company at its plants in either Río Gallegos or San Julián, for which he will receive an hourly wage of 0.65 pesos, plus an extra 50 pesos per month for room and board. The Contractor commits to do all work required of him.

The Company will advance the Contractor the price of a third-class ticket from Buenos Aires to either Río Gallegos or San Julián, which will be deducted from his first month's wages. The Company commits to pay the Contractor the equivalent of the wages for four hours of work for each day during the period between his departure from Buenos Aires until the first day of the slaughter, as well as during the period from the last day of the slaughter until his arrival in Buenos Aires in his return trip, with the exception of Sundays, holidays, and delays beyond the control of the Company.

Should the Contractor remain employed until the end of the season's labors, or so long as the Company requires their services in any capacity, he will be reimbursed for his travel expenses between Buenos Aires and either Río Gallegos or San Julián. If the Contractor resigns or is dismissed prior to the end of the season for poor performance or incompetence, at the discretion of the Company's administrators in Río Gallegos and San Julián, he will not be reimbursed for his travel expenses, neither from Buenos Aires to either Río Gallegos or San Julián nor in his return trip. To guarantee compliance with this contract, the Company will withhold 30 pesos per month from the Contractor's wages, which will be returned to him upon completion of his contractual obligations. If the Contractor does not strictly fulfill his contractual obligations, or if he directly or indirectly contributes to labor disturbances or otherwise interferes with the Company's business interests, he will forfeit his right to the amount withheld. The Contractor commits to work for the wage established above for the amount of hours required by the Company. If required to work a half day on Sundays, he will do so. The Company commits to provide the Contractor with a minimum of eight hours of work each day for the duration of the slaughter. If the steamship bringing workers from Buenos Aires to either Río Gallegos or San Julián is delayed or unable to depart for reasons beyond the control of the Company, such as strikes, fires, or cases of *force majeure*, this contract may be suspended or canceled at the Company's discretion.

Any claims made against the Company prior to the Contractor's return to Buenos Aires must be presented to the Company's superintendent in Río Gallegos or they will be considered as null and void.

In accordance with the above, the parties have duly signed this contract in Buenos Aires on January 9th, 1921 on the understanding that, in the event of any disagreements between the parties regarding the above clauses, the Contractor agrees to accept the jurisdiction of the competent authorities in Buenos Aires and commits to accept their resolutions.

This, then, was the "contract." If we analyze this condemnation to slavery on the part of a North American company, we can see that a worker who behaved himself—according to the company's criteria—could earn a few pesos—very few, to be sure—while in the process destroying his health in the hellish meatpacking plants of those days. But the worker who protested or "directly or indirectly contribute(d) to labor disturbances or otherwise interfere(d) with the Company's business" would forfeit everything he had earned.

Borrero was not exaggerating when he wrote in *Tragic Patagonia* that a Swift meatpacker, working shifts of up to fifteen and a half hours (in the most unhygienic conditions imaginable, of course), would receive only 28.50 pesos for an entire month of work—332 hours. And that is to say nothing of the worker who dared to speak up: he would be fired and abandoned there in Río Gallegos or San Julián, with no grounds for complaint. He had signed the contract.

But there was one person in Río Gallegos who was not afraid of Swift: Antonio Soto, secretary general of the Workers' Society.

After two or three workers at the plant get the nerve to meet with him and explain their situation, Soto gets things moving. Something happens on March 25th, 1921 that takes the directors of the powerful North American company by surprise: a strike at their meatpacking plant in Río Gallegos.

It's the only thing that was missing: the Swift strike comes hot on the heels of the rural strike and right at the height of the slaughter.

But the men of the Rural Society and Swift & Company aren't going to take it lying down. They call for a hardline approach in the pages of *La Unión*, blaming Soto and the men of the Workers' Society instead of the plant's wretched working conditions. According to *La Unión*, the workers, "by presenting a list of demands contrary to the spirit of the contract, and by refusing to load ships and undertaking other actions that amount to preemptive retaliations, such as demanding to be paid for days squandered in working out a settlement, have shown that outside agitators have intervened in this dispute, distorting the intentions of the true workers."

This time, the employers have the upper hand. The Workers' Society will be defeated. After a week, the meatpackers will meekly return to work. This time, Governor Yza allows the police chief, Captain Schweizer, to settle the conflict however he sees fit. Led by Ibón Noya, the Rural Society meets with Schweizer and tells him that the problem will be easy to resolve if only Soto and company are removed from the picture. The captain gathers the strikers together and tells them that everything can be straightened out if only they distance themselves from the Workers' Society and elect their own strike committee. He also offers to have the Rural Society intervene on their behalf.

The workers, brought in from Buenos Aires, are easily tamed. Penniless and homeless—despite Soto's best efforts—they know they can find no other jobs in town, nor can they return to Buenos Aires. They accept, almost without a second thought. And so a solution is found. *La Unión* is euphoric: "The workers have decided to return to work on the same terms as when they left, with no modifications to their employment contracts one way or another... Those who prepared the demands driving the strike have failed."

Rural Society president Ibón Noya publicly congratulates the police chief, the first step towards reconciling the bosses with Yza's Radical government.

During the strike, Soto had been unable to give his full attention to the meatpackers' struggle because he was facing one of the most dangerous offensives against the labor organization: internal division. Between the victorious conclusion of the first strike and the coming tragedy, Soto must wage a relentless struggle against the union leaders sent from Buenos Aires by the syndicalist FORA and against a faction of workers that have broken away from the Workers' Society to organize non-aligned unions.

The mighty are delighted by this split in the Río Gallegos labor movement and they encourage this sectarianism as best they can. At the beginning of April 1921, *La Unión* prints an exultant article titled nothing less than "Signs of Backlash":

Some unionized workers in Río Gallegos have decided to form an independent organization, allowing them to more spontaneously make decisions that serve their own interests in the trade union struggles in which they are engaged.

The first group to leave the Workers' Society is the printers' union, led by Amador González, whose disagreements with Soto we have already seen. To raise funds for their union they organize a festival, which is promoted in the conservative newspaper. This same newspaper will later run a story on the event, describing it as:

An enjoyable party that has proven to be a great success, judging by attendance, and whose eminently humanitarian purpose is a faithful reflection of the societal ideal that this union is pursuing through its honorable independence from the systematized tyranny currently observed in many other unions. This attitude can be seen in their statement of principles, which speaks with measured eloquence on the standards that must be met by the new organization, which has already won some concessions and which subscribes to the principle of harmony and concord between workers and bosses.

The good workers, in other words. The launch of a "free" trade union triggered the first split from the anarchists of the Workers' Society. The bosses have high hopes: they see the free trade unions as a way to put the rebels in check. As *La Unión* writes, "the attitude of the printers will soon spread to many other unions once we can objectively appreciate the results of their efforts."

The rich don't waste their time. With an admirable persistence, the press hammers away daily at Governor Yza and President Yrigoyen. On the other side of the trenches, Soto is increasingly isolated. He is surrounded by a group of Spaniards who talk much but accomplish little, by strange foreigners with revolutionary nicknames and by silent, smiling chilotes, who could be blown away by a strong wind. In the wake of the first strike, the labor front has split into three factions: the "free workers," who are actually quite scarce, made up of a few shop girls and the habitual, vulgar confidants of management; the emissaries of the syndicalist FORA, sympathetic to the Yrigoyen administration and close friends with Captain Yza; and the proletariat proper, unionized but lacking union experience, led by ideologically confused men who can barely read or write but who are nevertheless driven by a *sui generis* anarchism, close to that of Bakunin and Proudhon and impelled by an undeniable dose of individual rebelliousness, a cry of protest against abuse, and a thirst for trouble, as only surfaces in certain historical circumstances. But in the Patagonia of 1921 it will become an irresistible force—so irresistible that Hipólito Yrigoyen himself will have to once more send in the army.

And so Antonio Soto begins to make his moves. This time he doesn't stay in Río Gallegos. He sets off for Santa Cruz, San Julián, Puerto Deseado, and Lago Argentino. He occasionally travels in a car on loan from the Workers' Society, but also manages to find his calling as a horseman. He organizes every ranch he visits, appointing delegates and launching a campaign to unionize all the peons. In Puerto Santa Cruz, the workers elect a Spanish hotel employee named Ramón Outerelo as their delegate. In San Julián they elect Albino Argüelles, an Argentine belonging to the Socialist Party. But things are more difficult in Puerto Deseado: there the railway workers, led by Portales, are affiliated with the syndicalist FORA.

But while Soto is busy organizing, the Rural Society has the irreplaceable Edelmiro A. Correa Falcón on their side. He is also on the move, setting up affiliates in every town along the coast. He asks only one thing: refuse to comply with the agreement. Reject the power of the union, once and for all. He tells the bosses to prepare for a fight in September. Soto also mentions this same month; continue to struggle, and if the bosses don't comply, paralyze the entire territory when the shearing season begins in September.

Correa Falcón recommends taking up arms, joining the Patriotic League and promoting the Free Labor Association in order to draw in the "good workers." Soto, for his part, recommends discussing political and labor issues in the assemblies in order to create class consciousness. But his rationalism gets in the way: he always says that the violence and brutality of the bosses should be opposed by reason and logic. This is his only failing, as will be proven when the Mausers begin to spit fire and the lungs of the workers are torn apart by lead.

Soto suffers another setback in May 1921. The telegraph workers go on strike in Río Gallegos. Soto immediately offers them the support of the Workers' Society, but the strike has uneven support among the workers. Though there are sixteen strikers who hold out for several days, they are outvoted in assembly and the strike committee is replaced by another that breaks with the Río Gallegos Workers' Society. This defeat—writes *La Unión*—"will force the Postal Federation to reflect on the negative consequences of their relationship with the Workers' Federation." Soto and his men will have a lot of difficult, thorny work ahead of them.

General C. J. Martínez also arrives in Río Gallegos at this time. He has been sent by the Army to scout out locations for a new barracks. During his travels across Santa Cruz, the general is accompanied by none other than Correa Falcón. They are treated like princes on every ranch they visit. His subsequent report will have an enormous influence on the army's actions that summer.

In the meantime, Judge Viñas has decided to spend some time in Buenos Aires. The workers lose a valuable ally. The only friend they have left is José María Borrero, who continues to support them by campaigning against the landowners in the pages of *La Verdad*.

When winter paralyzes the movement, Antonio Soto works on perfecting the boycott system. As we have seen, Yza has failed in his attempts to have him lift the boycott against the businesses owned by Varela and Fernández, Elbourne and Slater, and Ibón Noya. It continues to be strictly enforced. None of the workers purchase anything from them. Nobody supplies them with merchandise, no stevedores unload their cargo. And if the bosses want a settlement, they need to make the first move—they must go to the union offices themselves and fly the white flag.

The boycott is an effective tool because it reveals the contradictions within the business sector. It doesn't favor the workers so much as it does the other, non-boycotted businesses. Soto knows this. The Commerce and Industry League splits between those suffering from the boycott and those benefiting from it. Arguments follow and each merchant tries to resolve things on their own. The first to undertake their "walk to Canossa" are Elbourne and Slater, representatives of British landowners and importers of a wide range of goods. They ask to speak with Soto and agree to rehire the strikers, repaying them their lost wages down to the last centavo. They also agree to fire all scab workers and open negotiations on the last point, which would require them to reimburse the union for all expenses incurred in printing pro-boycott propaganda. The bosses regard this last point as even more degrading than unconditional surrender. They finally work out a solution: Soto suggests that Elbourne and Slater donate an amount equivalent to the union's printing costs to an impoverished family in Río Gallegos. The British merchants, red in the face, comply.

When Soto announces the agreement in an assembly, the Spaniards are euphoric and the chilotes shriek with delight.

But the agreement provokes boundless rage among the men of the Rural Society. Their unofficial mouthpiece, *La Unión*, writes with ill-disguised resentment that the Commerce and Industry League is "a parasitic organization." The article has a tone of desperation, which is a testimony to Antonio Soto's influence:

> There's evidently little spirit of cooperation in our business sector. The solidarity explicitly mentioned in the League's charter is nonexistent, as is its stated intention of joint efforts promoting the common interest. The prevailing view is that individuals should look after their interests as best they can. In the meantime, more ground is ceded to the union each day. The most far-fetched demands are accepted without much resistance

because this has been found to be the easiest and perhaps most profitable way of avoiding even greater losses—after all, prices can always be increased.

The boycott seems to have been very effective against Varela and Fernández, because they publicly agree to the same conditions as Elbourne and Slater—that is, all of the conditions demanded of them except for the last. They also suggest giving 300 pesos to a needy family instead of reimbursing the Workers' Society.

But at an assembly chaired by Soto, the workers say no, absolutely not. While it may have represented a way out for Elbourne and Slater, it won't be so for Varela and Fernández. The fight continues to the death.

"What's happening in the south?" asks *La Prensa* of Buenos Aires in a contemporary editorial. They paint an apocalyptic picture:

Information provided by the government would have us believe that the crimes committed in the south are nothing more than common, trivial offenses with no greater meaning. They attribute reports of assault, murder, theft, and arson to alarmism. But the statements made by both locals and travelers to the region back up these reports of organized banditry and even suggest that the news we have received in Buenos Aires fails to reflect the situation in all its severity.

But all this will be refuted by the statements made by Lieutenant Colonel Varela upon his return to Buenos Aires, which will be published in the very same *La Prensa*:

Lieutenant Colonel Varela, who returned from Río Gallegos yesterday, says that his troops have completed their mission and will soon return home. We spoke with Varela upon his arrival and he told us that the attacks on ranches and commercial establishments, along with all other disorders, ceased just days after his troops disembarked in Santa Cruz and advanced towards the

Cordillera. He added that four hundred strikers gave themselves up around seventy leagues from the coast and that they offered no resistance, even though many of them were armed. Lieutenant Colonel Varela denies that these people were insurgents, arguing that they were simply striking workers who had not committed the outrages of which they have been accused. He said that while they did requisition supplies, they also issued vouchers to the victims of these thefts so that they could be reimbursed by the Resistance Society to which the strikers belong. (…) To the extent that they were armed, their arsenal was quite minimal. There were about one hundred men armed with shotguns and Winchester rifles, all of which were turned over to the soldiers. After considering all aspects of the situation, these individuals were released.

These statements are essential in interpreting these events. Later, with the massacre underway, Varela will make very different statements regarding a similar situation.

Lieutenant Colonel Varela's claims provoke a backlash from the entrepreneurs and landowners of Santa Cruz. *La Unión* writes:

We are astounded by the news we received by telegraph regarding Lieutenant Colonel Varela's statements on the events that have been occurring in our territory. It is possible that, out of goodwill, he believes the declarations made by the armed strikers. But what Varela cannot deny, as this is an irrefutable fact, is that we have seen countless assaults, all manner of thievery and the most repugnant murders. We cannot understand how a military man, whose high rank should place him above all suspicion, can make such enormous mistakes when the most glaring proof of what had occurred could be seen throughout the territory he patrolled.

At the end of April, El Toscano's group (El 68 and his men had crossed the border into Chile and nothing more was ever heard of them) attacks Carlos Henstock's ranch at Paso del Medio and then Luciano Carreras's Las Horquestas ranch. The ranchers are outraged. They feel these attacks are a logical consequence of the indulgence displayed by Lieutenant Colonel Varela and Governor Yza. But they also outrage the Workers' Society, which distances itself from El Toscano and declares that it has nothing to do with El Toscano's depredations. Soto will have to act with an iron hand if he doesn't want to be imprisoned.

As the winter of 1921 sets in, the Río Gallegos Workers' Federation—comprised of sailors and stevedores, cooks, retail workers, agricultural workers, and various other trades—becomes a territorial federation, thanks to Soto's trips to the interior. He also invites Chile's Magallanes Workers' Federation, which is based in Puerto Natales and Punta Arenas, to a Patagonian labor congress. For Soto, a fanatical internationalist, there are neither borders nor flags nor countries nor nationalities, only regions.

For Somoza and Lázaro, the two envoys of the syndicalist FORA, Soto's initiatives conflict with the interests of the union bureaucracy in Buenos Aires, then planning to absorb the anarchist FORA. Besides, the powerful syndicalist FORA had established productive dialogue with Yrigoyen through Francisco Javier García of the Maritime Workers' Federation.

Ever since their arrival in Río Gallegos, Somoza and Lázaro have been hoping that Soto would slip. They're unable to see eye-to-eye. Soto insists on total war against the bosses. The Buenos Aires group advocates moderation at any price. They have too much at stake to get bogged down in such a distant and dangerous movement as the one in Patagonia.

Besides backing the printers who broke away from the Río Gallegos Workers' Federation, the delegates of the syndicalist FORA also encourage the creation of the Drivers and Mechanics Union, which entails another division in the Workers' Federation.

The dismemberment of the labor federation is welcomed by the conservative press. *La Unión*, satisfied that Soto has suffered another setback, writes:

The Drivers and Mechanics Union, a recently organized independent union, has issued a press release explaining their reasons for separating themselves from the Workers' Federation, accompanied by a statement of principles. Their reasoning needs no commentary, as should be obvious to the public. Their press release analyzes, with a certain elevation, the rational methods that should be used by the workers. While explaining the reasons behind their attitude, they moderately present the facts without stooping to sectarian insults, instead correctly emphasizing what is clear to us all—that workers are the victims of those who, despite not being workers themselves, nevertheless rise through the ranks of the union and exploit them in the most malicious and shameless fashion conceivable. This brutality and exploitation is worse than in the days of legalized slavery, but fortunately it seems that experience has taught the working man to defend himself.

By simply reading this editorial, we can draw our own conclusions as to the identity of the union's leaders. We can also conclude that, rightly or wrongly, Antonio Soto was carrying out a relentless struggle against the mighty, who have turned to their most dangerous weapon: sectarianism. Labor activists in Buenos Aires were quite familiar with this problem. The statement made by the national leaders of the anarchist FORA regarding the creation of the new union is transcribed below:

In Río Gallegos, the Drivers and Mechanics Union was founded in the winter of 1921. It is composed of nine individuals: Rogelio El Tuerto Lorenzo, owner of the La Chocolatería brothel; José Moreno, owner of the brothel bearing his name; Roberto del Pozo, who is guilty of embezzling money from the Natales Workers' Federation in Chile; Ildefonso Martínez, Bernabé Ruiz, and Antonio Freyres, three well-known pimps and eternal vagabonds; and Leopoldo Tronsch, an agent of none other than Ibón Noya, president of the Patriotic League. And this group of rogues is completed by the habitual strikebreaker José Veloso. From the moment this shameful group was formed, they have been insistently making insidious attacks on the local Federation, spreading the vilest rumors about the authentic proletarian organization.

Antonio Soto rode out every storm, but now he's on his own. Judge Viñas has gone, Borrero now sides with the Radicals—although he does still come to the defense of the Workers' Federation from time to time—and Governor Yza, not wanting any more trouble, has come to an understanding with the syndicalist FORA. And that's to say nothing of the merchants and landowners: for them, Soto is the source of all evil.

On April 18th, 1921, Soto calls an assembly and puts everything on the line. He publicly offers to resign.

The assembly has a number of issues to address. It opens with the reading of a letter from the Puerto Deseado Workers' Federation, which states that, "Despite the best efforts of Governor Yza to find a solution to the labor conflict, the intransigence of the bosses has made a settlement impossible." In this same letter, the union leaders in Puerto Deseado ask their counterparts in Río Gallegos to send bread, meat, and other basic necessities, which they say the town's workers cannot currently purchase due to high prices.

Despite the poverty of nearly all those present—a remarkable three hundred of them, according to police reports—they pass the hat amongst themselves and vote to allow their leaders to use union funds for the same purpose.

Next up is the matter of the boycott against Varela and Fernández. They vote to "strengthen the boycott until they accept the Federation's conditions." Lastly, the assembly addresses Antonio Soto's resignation as secretary general. According to Aguilar, a police officer sent from Buenos Aires to play the sad role of infiltrator, Soto's resignation is unanimously rejected. Soto's triumph is absolute: not a single vote is cast against him.

In this warlike atmosphere, another important assembly is held at Río Gallegos's Select Cinema on May 10th. It's interesting to examine the details of this meeting because they faithfully reflect how these inexperienced labor leaders resolve their problems in such a thoroughly hostile environment. The first item of business is the request of former prison guard Tomás Villalustre to join the union. His application is rejected by majority vote and the union resolves "to remind Elbourne and Slater of the conditions for lifting the boycott, as they have employed Villalustre as an assistant bookkeeper."

The second issue under debate is the request for assistance made by the striking workers at the Buenos Aires fruit market. The workers unanimously vote to provide them with 100 pesos. They are always generous with their fellow workers. But when it's their turn to suffer persecution, their comrades in Buenos Aires will take their time in returning the favor.

As for the boycott of Varela and Fernández's business, the workers vote to "keep the boycott in place until they completely surrender." There will be no transactions with them at all. Ibón Noya, however, is given a glimmer of hope. They resolve to "keep the boycott in place until Mr. Noya personally approaches the Workers' Society and a settlement is reached."

The assembly is still underway when Antonio Soto is advised that the supporters of the syndicalist FORA, Rogelio Lorenzo and the Drivers and Mechanics Union, have occupied the headquarters of the Workers' Society. Furious, Soto leaves the Select Cinema, still full of workers, and heads back to the union headquarters by himself. He throws the nine squatters out onto the street with his bare hands and then locks the door behind him. This incident is the talk of the town for weeks, adding to Soto's reputation among the workers of Río Gallegos. But Rogelio Lorenzo and his followers won't forget the blows they received.

Once formed, the Drivers and Mechanics Union embarks on a campaign of daily written attacks against the Workers' Society and, in particular, Antonio Soto.

But Soto takes the bull by the horns and invites all of the town's drivers and mechanics to an assembly, asking them to pick sides. The assembly, held on May 18th, is another triumph for the

Río Gallegos Workers' Society. It turns out that the other union has a membership of only nine.

One fact is enough to show the increasingly unbridgeable gulf between the workers and their bosses: the disinterment of the bodies of the police officers who died at El Cerrito.

Three cars and a truck head to the hotel in mid-June. The bodies are dug up and sent to Río Gallegos. A candlelight wake is held in the main parlor of the governor's mansion. A crucifix dominates the scene.

The Rural Society wants the ceremony to be a display of the region's grief. Government officials, merchants, industrialists, landowners, and high-ranking employees all turn out to pay their respects.

The church lends its weight to the silent spectacle and the parish priest presides over the ceremony. *La Unión* describes the candlelight funeral procession:

> The four coffins were carried by hand. The police marching band added a somber accent to the march, which was led by Police Chief Schweizer, the commissioner, and representatives of high society. A considerable number of automobiles brought up the rear. Downtown businesses closed their doors as a sign of mourning as the procession passed and many passers-by stopped to watch, while the melancholy tolling of the church bells interrupted the solemnity of the march. Shops in all the towns along the coast closed their doors at the same time.

Governor Yza isn't present because he has already left for Buenos Aires, where he's scheduled to arrive on June 21st. He is replaced during his absence by Major Cefaly Pandolfi, who will be in charge during the time leading up to the second strike and the repression that follows. Yza will take months to return. His absence can be interpreted in a number of ways.

The Workers' Society didn't sit idly by during the propaganda onslaught unleashed during the reburial of the police officers. At

Soto's suggestion, they voted to exhume the remains of their comrade Zacarías Gracián, who also died at El Cerrito, and bring his body back to Río Gallegos.

Hermógenes Pisabarro was put in charge of making a coffin for Gracián, and Constantino García's carting company handled the transportation, free of charge. The funeral procession through the streets of Río Gallegos was an extraordinary event. It lacked the automobiles that were present during the funeral of the police officers, but instead the people showed up. No church bells tolled, but there were voices singing the anarchist anthem "Hijos del Pueblo." No priests or government officials, but the entire leadership of the Workers' Society was present, led by the young Antonio Soto.

The funeral procession saw the workers close ranks behind the Workers' Society. It was a lesson for the government and the bosses, and even the Radicals understood that, unless something unexpected happens, the workers will do away with everything in September, the fateful month that everyone is anxiously anticipating.

There's also a new newspaper in Río Gallegos: *El Nacional*, run by Arturo Brisighelli, a former employee of the police department and a fervent supporter of the Radical governor. His newspaper directly responds to the increasingly open criticisms of *La Unión*, which will soon be directly edited by Correa Falcón himself. For his part, José María Borrero stops publishing *La Verdad*, which he had used to firmly support the workers. He replaces it with *El Español*, a newspaper focusing on the Spanish community in Patagonia.

The final break between the bosses and the workers occurs in July 1921. Despite temperatures of 21 degrees below zero, the situation has become increasingly heated. The bosses have refused to implement the conditions they had accepted in January. The Workers' Society has openly accused Correa Falcón, the secretary general of the Rural Society, of advising landowners to refuse to implement the Yza settlement during his recent tour through the territory. Complaints by ranch delegates have piled up at the headquarters of the Workers' Society, which finds itself powerless in the face of this offensive. The only thing it can do is to wait for the shearing season to arrive. Besides, protests to the state government have no effect: Major Cefaly Pandolfi simply responds that it would be best to wait for the governor to return.

This tension boils to the surface in a series of four incidents. Someone fires ten shots through the windows of the Puerto Deseado home of Eloy del Val, an accountant for the Patagonia Trading Company. The motive: he has fired several workers. Although nobody is injured, it will cause a big stir and the protests will even reach Buenos Aires, where the bosses asked for more protection. Dr. Alejandro Sicardi, president of the Santa Cruz Patriotic League, is disarmed in the middle of the street by members of the Workers' Society, an incident we will discuss in greater detail later. Seven ranches are attacked by gangs of workers, stealing horses as if they're preparing for another strike. The fourth incident, which succeeds in finally enraging the populace, comes on the night of July 9th—Independence Day.

Río Gallegos bleeds nationalism that day. There's one ceremony after another, all day long. At 1:30 p.m., there's a parade that leaves from the governor's mansion and passes by the church on Calle Roca before heading towards Maipú. All of the important government officials are there, as are the judges and the police. There's a detachment of prison guards and a brass band in the plaza. The church is full of the city's most prominent families, members of the Spanish Society and the Cosmopolitan Society and there are people from the Mary Help of Christians Catholic School and the public schools. Father Crema says mass. Following the pious ceremony, everyone heads towards the statue of General San Martín and, after singing the national anthem, they listen to the inevitably patriotic speech delivered by the young Radical lawyer Bartolomé Pérez. And here it can be noted that the Radicals have gone over to the sunny side of the street. Pérez indirectly distances the government from the workers:

Gentlemen, on days such as today, every Argentine should breathe the spirit of patriotism, contemplate the purity of our past and fix their eyes on the future, lifting their gaze from the earth to the sky where our flag proudly waves, as if knowing that it will forever be distinct from those wretched banners born in the heat of utopian ideals, which will be unable to supplant it so long as there is a single Argentine left alive, or even an echo of the spirit of our nationality and race.

After they finish bathing in the Jordan of outspoken patriotism, these respectable people attend a reception at the Social Club, where they sit through another patriotic diatribe from the mouth of Prefect Milcíades Virasoro Gaun before enjoying what the reporter from *La Unión* describes as "an exquisite sangria." Meanwhile, the poor and the wretched enjoy the gaucho sport of *carreras de sortija* on Calle Zapiola, in front of the plaza.

But that exquisite sangria must have gone down wrong. The highlight of the day's festivities is a grand banquet at the Hotel Español, attended by "one hundred luminaries of high society, including the naval officers whose vessels were in port, a lively gathering at what promised to be a friendly feast," as *La Unión* will later report.

But this ceremony—where high-ranking officials rub elbows with businessmen, ranchers, lawyers, naval officers, and policemen—will be a failure because of just one Spaniard.

Just when the hors d'oeuvres are about to be served, as the guests are unfolding their napkins, one of the waiters tells the cook, Antonio Paris, that one of the diners is none other than Manuel Fernández of Varela & Fernández, boycotted by the Workers' Society. And so Antonio Paris, as stubborn a Spaniard as they come, calls all the waiters together and forbids them from serving the table—adorned with little Argentine flags—at which the cream of Río Gallegos society sits. The desperate pleas of the hotel owner are met with the most absolute intransigence. When Paris says no, it means no, definitively: either Fernández goes, or the entire banquet is off.

There's a great deal of back and forth but the answer is always no. And so the terrified hotel owner must inform his crestfallen guests.

It's an outrage, a real outrage. Everyone, unanimously, takes it as an affront to the fatherland. As an offense to the country's most sacred symbols, committed by a filthy Spaniard. This is evidently anti-Argentine behavior because the nation's colors are right there on the table, naval officers are there in dress uniform, and the whole point of the banquet is to celebrate Argentina.

But it only takes a few words from Nava, the director of the Public Assistance Agency, to defuse the tension. He is so witty and he takes everything so lightly that the guests erupt into nervous laughter and—note the unanimity here—go to the kitchen to serve themselves, under the hostile gaze of the waiters, who had been having the time of their lives.

The guests, very pleased with themselves, behave like gentlemen and serve each other. These great men treat each other chivalrously, as if to show those wretched anarchists that there's something more important than convenience: the fatherland. And the fatherland unites the mighty more than ever that day.

But things won't end there. The offense is too great. Above all, it is an affront to Argentina; the guests make it a point of honor. And it is on that day when the idea emerges to eradicate the cancer that has been eating away at Santa Cruz.

"Face to Face" is the title of the editorial in *La Unión* addressing the incident:

On Saturday evening, something occurred that was nothing more than yet another in a long series of similar incidents that have plagued our city. The employees at a local hotel refused to serve at a banquet on the pretext that they were boycotting one of the guests. It should have been enough for them to see that this was a patriotic gathering, attended by the authorities, for them to refrain from using their petty but annoying tool of proletarian resistance. Refrain they did not, and the slogans of the Workers' Federation—which workers will deny if asked to confess by the authorities, as has occurred on other occasions—outweighed the cordial and refined nature of the gathering. In this way, the workers are setting themselves up as a power in opposition to the established order, showing no reverence for the nation's symbols. It is nevertheless thanks to these symbols and the generous freedoms they represent that organized labor has been allowed such a wide field of action. But it was a mistake to offend patriotic sentiments. This has reminded us that whoever is not a friend of the fatherland is its enemy, and that it would be a prudent measure to pluck out the worm and cauterize the wound in order to prevent wholesale infection. Self-defense is a just response to aggression, and self-defense has no limits when it repels an unjust aggression.

The affair doesn't end in indignation. The Argentine Patriotic League, which had unsuccessfully tried to gain a foothold during the first strike, establishes itself in Río Gallegos once and for all. While reporting on this development, *La Unión* reminds its readers of the behavior of Antonio Paris and the waiters at the Hotel Español, describing their attitude as that of "the clear, disrespectful arbitrariness of the local Workers' Society."

Then, with arguments that no patriot could reject, *La Unión* argues in indignant but clear and energetic language that:

Plain and simple, this incident represents the most serious challenge we have yet seen to law and order, as well as the most blatant disrespect for the fatherland and its institutions, whose freedoms have been unspeakably abused by the more or less authentic labor organizations that have given free rein to all of their class hatred and resentment. The need to contain such intolerance has given rise to the organization of a self-defense force, and Saturday's incident was necessary to effectively end the indifference to these serious questions of social order.

On Sunday afternoon, *La Unión* reports that:

[Following] a brief exchange of ideas, and as the consummation of a common desire, forces aligned to constitute the local brigade of the Argentine Patriotic League, a distinguished organization that responds to a pressing need that affects every corner of our country. The same problems we face are those that have unsettled the League's untiring president, Dr. Manuel Carlés, a healthy example of selfless, noble dedication.

And the mouthpiece of the landowners concludes:

The local brigade of the Patriotic League will receive the spontaneous support of all Argentines and foreigners who wish to cooperate with the organization's patriotic, civilizing work.

Paris and his fellow Spaniards had done well! Now they have to put up with this alliance of the mighty, which will soon be dealing out beatings in the name of patriotism and the fatherland. The Río Gallegos Patriotic League even includes Radicals on its steering committee. Need has brought them together. Ibón Noya presides over this alliance, with the great brute Diego Ritchie at his right hand. Arturo Brisighelli, a man with close connections to the governor and the Radical Civic Union, is elected as the organization's secretary. Santiago Stoppani (the prison's warden), Max Loewenthal, Manuel Fernández (under boycott), Dr. Bartolomé Pérez (Yrigoyen's first supporter in Santa Cruz), Edelmiro Correa Falcón, Nicolás Feller, and Luis Klappenbach are all members as well.

These are people who are ready for anything. The Patriotic League has shown that they are a force to be reckoned with. The bosses grow closer together as they await September. Soto, in turn, decides to purge the labor organization of all the sectarians backed by the syndicalist FORA. To clarify things once and for all, he calls for an assembly to be held at the Select Cinema on

July 19th. According to the police infiltrator, over 230 workers attend. Soto takes the floor to personally demand the expulsion of Rogelio Lorenzo for being "undeserving of membership in the Federation." There's an uproar and the vast majority vote to expel Lorenzo, physically ejecting him from the premises. From this moment on, Rogelio Lorenzo and his followers will be granted complete impunity by the police and will receive support from the Radical Civic Union, even being treated with indulgence by Braun, Menéndez Behety, and the Rural Society.

And while all this is occurring, acting governor Cefaly Pandolfi has yet to make a decision. He closely follows Yza's instructions: negotiate and negotiate some more, deciding on nothing that could exacerbate the situation, and do everything possible to avoid a new strike. He talks at length with Soto in an attempt to convince him to lift the boycott, but to no avail. The situation deteriorates. Even the barbers refuse to serve Manuel Fernández—a fierce, energetic Spaniard with a reputation for eating workers alive—who now must ask his employees to cut his hair.

That July, Puerto Santa Cruz is on fire. The situation is worse than in Río Gallegos. The leader of the local labor movement is Manuel Outerelo—all that need be said is that he's a Spanish anarchist. The orders of the Workers' Federation are strictly enforced.

But Outerelo and the unionized workers have to face none other than Dr. Miguel Sicardi, an unmarried, forty-year-old lawyer who serves as the president of the Fatherland Defense Association and who is the most conspicuous representative of Puerto Santa Cruz's landowners and big businessmen. Sicardi is not a man who shirks his responsibilities. There's nothing more important to him than to tear the labor movement out by its roots.

On June 12th, 1921, the hostility between Dr. Sicardi and the Workers' Society leads to a serious confrontation. The workers hold a protest that day at 2 p.m. A column advances down the street to cries of "Death to the Patriotic League!" As they pass the Hotel Londres, Dr. Sicadri himself shows up, scattering the crowd with gunshots. But a Russian meatpacker named Miguel

Gesenko tackles him, twisting his arm and forcing him to drop his gun. Sicardi then complains to the police that the workers had been shouting "Death to the Argentines!" and so he stepped in to defend the nation's honor with a cry of "Long live the fatherland!" The Puerto Santa Cruz Workers' Federation responds to Sicardi's acrimony with a boycott, "with all of the workers at all of the town's businesses refusing to sell him goods or make deliveries to his house," as *La Unión* indignantly reports, adding heroically that "the local representative of La Anónima, Carlos Borgiali, has committed to personally deliver food to Dr. Sicardi and his family." But the workers solemnly dismiss Borgiali as an intermediary. His truck is met with a picket line of stevedores, construction workers, and Chileans who prevent him from unloading.

"A tougher line will have to be taken," argues an editorial in *La Unión*. And so it goes. Now all of the workers will have to find another shoulder to cry on: they've all been fired. All of the clerks and deliverymen who refused to sell provisions to the family of Dr. Sicardi have been dismissed from the Patagonia Import and Export Company, the Trading Company Limited, and the Southern Argentina Company, as well as from the firms of Sapunar & Co., Jordán Domic and Watson, Godomiz & Co. etc.

We shall now see how the workers will feed their families—in the middle of the Patagonian winter—when the end of the month comes.

The situation is critical. Outerelo travels to Río Gallegos to ask Antonio Soto for advice. Soto's hand remains steady: he orders every union in Santa Cruz to go on strike. "We may die of hunger," he says, "but so will they."[5] And the interim governor responds by continuing to wait nervously. He orders the police not to act, but to wait and wait. This is Yrigoyen's theory of politics: most problems resolve themselves on their own and the rest are never resolved by anyone. Great tragedies can occur in the meantime, of course; his administration has already been stained by the Tragic Week and the massacre of the woodcutters in La Forestal.

The bosses cope as best they can. They open their shops in the morning, serving their customers themselves, and then head to the docks in the afternoon to personally unload the ships. They wait for Joaquín de Anchorena and Manuel Carlés to send "free workers" from Buenos Aires. And the first strikebreakers are on their way aboard the steamship *Camarones*.

Towards the end of July, Correa Falcón will travel to Buenos Aires on a mission from the Santa Cruz Rural Society. He will meet with the landowners living in the capital, bringing them around to the views of Menéndez Behety, Braun, and their colleagues. They agree to support General Martínez and openly criticize Lieutenant Colonel Varela.

As we have already seen, Correa Falcón took General Martínez around Santa Cruz to look for a location for a new barracks. Upon his return to Buenos Aires, Martínez speaks of the sacrifices made by the landowners, denounces the subversive attitude of the working class, and calls attention to the large number of Chileans living in the region.

Preparations are underway for September. Large corporations and business associations bombard the government with demands for troops. Deputy Albarracín proposes that three cavalry regiments be permanently deployed to Patagonia. He requests 1.2 million pesos to recruit one thousand volunteers and another million to build movable barracks. The president of the San Julián Rural Society, Engineer Cobos, presents the interior minister with a memorandum on July 18th; this same memorandum also manages to be surprisingly well distributed among the general population. It calls for the urgent and permanent deployment of infantry troops to all of the region's ports and the larger towns in the interior to "guarantee" the life, interests, and freedom to work of Patagonia's residents, which it argues are seriously threatened by labor disputes of an anarchist nature. At this same time, Correa Falcón meets directly with the federal government and it becomes clear that the balance is tipping in favor of the landowners. The interior minister himself, Dr. Isidro Ruiz Moreno, suddenly responds to Cobos's request for troops by saying that it might be better to "send one regiment" until Congress has the opportunity to vote on the president's proposal (made on January 16th) to create a regional gendarmerie.

The fate of Santa Cruz will be decided in Buenos Aires that August. The mighty have been busy and have acted wisely. They have made use of every tool at their disposal: the government, the army, the Argentine Rural Society, the Patriotic League, the Free Labor Association. They make coordinated moves on three fronts. Alejandro Menéndez Behety and Mauricio Braun take care of the capital; Edelmiro Correa Falcón represents the ranchers, the Patriotic League, and the Río Gallegos Free Labor Association; Cobos works with another group of landowners through the Fatherland Defense Association and the Rural Society in San Julián and Puerto Santa Cruz.

Meanwhile, *La Nación* and *La Razón* report that the situation in Santa Cruz is already catastrophic. Telegrams and memoranda flood the Casa Rosada, the Interior Ministry, and the Chamber of Deputies.

But the bite of poverty is already being felt in the south. There's no work to do, and many peons are let go. Only where the peons have ranch delegates representing them can the bosses be slowed down a little. The stablehands go on strike at La Anita, demanding that the settlement be respected. *La Unión* sounds the alarm, reporting that "anarchy reigns among the workers, who freely commit all types of reprehensible actions." Ibón Noya addresses the Chamber of Deputies, asking for an urgent military intervention. He says that things have gotten to the point that, "if the support of the authorities arrives after September, it may well be too late to avoid a repetition of the unfortunate events seen last year." And he doesn't miss the chance to mention that "what occurred here and what may well occur again is the result of the social decomposition caused by the agitation of undesirable immigrants." (Ibón Noya is a Spaniard and his wife is Chilean.)

They think of nothing but repression. Their only hope is that the army will come and put everything back in place. In the meantime, the price of a kilo of flour has gone up by 1.20 pesos and wholesalers have either stopped supplying essential goods altogether, or only do so at exorbitant prices. It seems as if everything has been disrupted and that someone is moving behind the scenes, setting a trap for the workers, who will walk into it with their eyes closed. But what other options do they have?

A report in *La Nación* by someone identified only as "a resident of Santa Cruz"—but who is none other than Correa Falcón, then in Buenos Aires—foresees dark days ahead for Patagonia. If the military doesn't intervene, "there will be nothing but ruins and desolation."

In Puerto Santa Cruz, a strike has been dragging on for weeks. The workers have nothing left, but their families are receiving aid from the Río Gallegos Workers' Society. The Commerce and Industry League tries to register "free workers" but then complains when nobody signs up. They blame the police—particularly Commissioner Baylon—for not taking action against the strikers. The Río Gallegos Workers' Society opens their own hiring hall and their counterparts in San Julián soon follow suit. The Río Gallegos Patriotic League runs the following advertisement in *La Unión*:

FREE LABOR: Those workers who wish to join the free labor program can register on workdays from 11:30 a.m. to 1:30 p.m. at the offices of the Patriotic League.

In San Julián, the Patriotic League holds a meeting. There's excitement in the air. Its members resolve to "support the maintenance of law and order, no matter the cost." *La Razón* insists that the Radical government has completely abandoned Patagonia to labor subversion. *La Prensa* speaks of "vandalism in the south," giving the impression that looting and murder are everyday occurrences.

In reality, it's what's happening in Buenos Aires that matters. Forty southern landowners make their rounds in the capital, knocking on doors and visiting newspapers. They hold a meeting on August 16th, electing Mauricio Braun, Carlos Menéndez Behety, Piedra Buena, Volkhauser, Pedemonte, and D'Hunval to represent them in a meeting with Yrigoyen. This time around, the individual landowners who live and suffer in Santa Cruz, and who have no agents to speak for them, are content. This time around, Mauricio Braun and Menéndez Behety will show their faces instead of acting through their representatives.

Two days later, a meeting held at the commodity exchange lays the groundwork for the unification of Patagonia's business community. Mauricio Braun, Alejandro Menéndez Behety, Cobos, Watson, Piedra Buena, Berrando, López, and Amaya are appointed to draft the new organization's charter. This new employers' association will have enormous importance, because there will be an "all for one, one for all" in Tierra del Fuego, Santa Cruz, and Chubut. There will be unity in the face of danger. This time, they won't be caught divided and alone. The blow will be well aimed and final. The only solution is a purge that will clean up the region for the next fifty years, at least.

And an editorial in *La Nación* identifies a new type of striker, "the wicked striker"—which is the exact title of the editorial, in fact. And the wicked striker is none other than the working man who goes on strike in Santa Cruz. The learned columnist studies this type from a sociological perspective in what is evidently a groundbreaking study.

The columnist takes the reader on a journey through history, from the Indian raids of the previous century through the epoch of banditry and gaucho rebellions to this new, unexpected villain that has appeared in the south, waving the red flag: the wicked striker. And this is how they describe him:

The telegrams we receive from Santa Cruz—which are more unsettling than those from analogous situations, such as in

Misiones—seems to indicate the arrival of a new danger: the wicked striker. Will he replace the bandit? The news tells of looting carried out by peons who have had enough of their labors, of groups of individuals who show up at ranches and demand room and board throughout the winter while offering nothing in exchange, of other gangs that attack the ranches, destroying their fences and committing serious crimes. And men sharing a criminal background, all of them well armed, are coming together to spread banditry throughout the territory.

Here we have the reappearance of banditry, which was nearly extinct, in a new form: the wicked striker.

There's finally some good news on August 27th. Correa Falcón meets with Manuel Carlés and Don Joaquín de Anchorena. They discuss sending "free workers" to Santa Cruz, which will "provide this territory with labor and allow us to expel untrustworthy elements, stopping the advance of socially destructive theories," as *La Nación* will put it the following day. Carlés and Anchorena guarantee Correa Falcón that both the Rural Society and the Patriotic League have the resources to meet the region's needs.

That same day, the nationalist Anchorena finds the time to write a furious condemnation of a bill drafted by Deputy Guido, a Radical, that would establish a moratorium on the debts owed by small farmers.

On August, 29th, "free labor" scores its first victory in Patagonia. In Puerto Santa Cruz, twenty workers disembark from the steamship *Asturiano*. They will try to get the paralyzed town running again. All hope rides on the Free Labor Association— that is, on the opposition to anything that smells like a union. Argentina's capitalist and landowning class have such faith that they pompously announce the formation of a committee to erect a monument to free labor in the port of Buenos Aires, "a monument that will enshrine the place of free labor in Argentine culture and commemorate its first martyr, the worker José Elías." (According to the FORA, Elías—killed in a shootout at the port—was the bodyguard of Joaquín de Anchorena, who had attacked the strike committee.)

Here is where Argentina's upper class made its mistake: they didn't have the right methods to win over the working class. It would have been much easier to win over a faction within the labor movement: the "good" union leaders. Yrigoyen outflanked them by favoring those union leaders who were able to keep the labor movement within certain bounds and who refused to introduce any demands beyond wages and working conditions. This was a very practical method, one that will be imitated by every government following the 1943 revolution, leading to the disappearance of the classical unionism, combative and aggressive, of the anarchist FORA.

These were tough times and each class took up arms in self-defense. And Yrigoyen was caught in the middle, trying to smooth things over and ride out the storm that had been unleashed on the world with the triumph of the October Revolution in Russia.

And Argentina's courts were full of conservative judges who strictly enforced repressive laws—laws that Yrigoyen hadn't dared to repeal—as a way of crushing the labor movement. The champions of free labor praised, for example, a September 21st decision by Judge Ramos Mejía to apply the Social Defense Law against two Spanish workers who insulted two strikebreakers by calling them sheep and bleating at them. The judge sentenced them to two years in prison because, even though the incident didn't go beyond insult and ridicule, it was nevertheless "an attempt to obstruct the freedom to work."

The situation in Río Gallegos is complicated by something that has nothing to do with local tensions. The U.S. steamship *Beacon Grange*, on its way to supply the Swift meatpacking plant, runs aground at Punta Loyola on September 6th. The ship is a total loss. The Mauricio Braun-Blanchard company, based in Punta Arenas, is contracted to salvage its cargo. But as the Magallanes Workers' Federation had declared a strike in that Chilean city,

Mauricio Braun is forced to recruit workers from small coastal towns with no union presence. So the Chilean union asks the workers of Río Gallegos for support. And so Antonio Soto boycotts the salvage operation. Mauricio Braun puts his workers aboard the steamship *Lovart* and brings them to Río Gallegos. The men of the Workers' Society are waiting for them. At this first encounter, they are very persuasive. They explain that no work should be done because Mauricio Braun needs to come to an understanding with the Magallanes Workers' Federation first.

The Workers' Society distributes flyers in every port in Santa Cruz. This is the first joint action between the labor organizations in Punta Arenas and Río Gallegos, the first and last act of unity between the workers of both countries. The flyers are distributed on September 20th. At 8 p.m. that day, the police escort Braun's workers back to the *Lovart*. They board at 9 p.m. but are told that, due to a technical problem, the ship will be unable to sail until the next morning. The "free workers" head back to town along Calle Buenos Aires. They don't get very far. Close to fifteen union members surround them, firing into the air. The victims run to whatever shelter they can find. And then something unexpected occurs. The police intervene with their usual vigor, as they did in the times of Correa Falcón and Ritchie. The headquarters of the Workers' Federation is ransacked and all those inside are arrested. Interim governor Cefaly Pandolfi wires Yza, who remains in Buenos Aires: "Unionized workers have fired upon free workers. The police have taken several prisoners, among them two Russians."

In those days, naturally, the word "Russian" made this incident doubly threatening.

This isn't the only telegram Yza receives from the frightened Cefaly Pandolfi. In one cable, he reports that a "free worker" in Puerto Santa Cruz, who had recently arrived from Buenos Aires, was shot twice and remained in critical condition. And another reports that "many people are gathered at Lago Argentino. This is symptomatic because there is no apparent reason for the gathering."

Yza himself sends a message to the interior minister on September 26th, asking him to "immediately send the battleship *Almirante Brown* to Santa Cruz; the urgent need for troops can be seen in the telegrams sent from Río Gallegos." Of these telegrams, the most important was the last, the one reporting "the presence of persons unknown at Lago Argentino." And that gathering was attended by none other than Antonio Soto, on horseback.

There had been important developments in the Río Gallegos labor movement.

Soto had come to understand that all of the attacks were directed at him, and that it wasn't just the ranchers, merchants, police, and government officials who pinned everything on him and who argued that his elimination would end the conflict, but that the delegates of the syndicalist FORA had joined in as well. And so he steps down as secretary general and proposes that he be replaced with a man whose brave actions had won him fame among the workers of Río Gallegos: Antonio Paris, the cook from the Hotel Español who sabotaged the official Independence Day banquet.

Soto knows that the fight that summer will be a tough one and that careful preparations will have to be made to ensure that the strike ends in a definitive victory and an agreement that would be respected and enforced. He knows that the struggle will play out in the countryside because there would be no freedom of action in the city. So he decides to travel across the vast expanses of Patagonia, ranch by ranch, and personally explain the situation to the peons. And he's even more sure of his decision after the syndicalist FORA, led by Rogelio Lorenzo and José Veloso, floods the territory's ports and ranches with flyers inviting the peons in the Lago Argentino region—where Menéndez Behety's most important possessions are located—to leave the Workers' Federation and create their own union.

But the Río Gallegos Workers' Society responds directly and straightforwardly on September 16th by issuing its *Manifesto No. 1*, signed by Antonio B. Paris:

TO ALL OF THE URBAN AND RURAL WORKERS

We have a manifesto in our hands, purportedly issued by the Lago Argentino Workers' Committee, calling for an assembly to be held near Puerto Irma on October 2nd with the goal of establishing a Lago Argentino Regional Workers' Federation.

If we were unaware that our enemies have been trying to incite discontent within our ranks, we might naively believe that this manifesto was drafted by the workers, but we have already learned to unmask our enemies. All of the urban workers and many of the rural workers already know who they really are: hustlers, gamblers, office seekers, and phony trade unionists on the payroll of the enemies of proletarian emancipation.

Comrades, can you not see how the capitalist bourgeoisie, in the guise of their charitable societies, rural societies, landowners' associations, trusts, patriotic leagues, and employers' associations, always use every tool at their disposal to enslave the workers? And that we the workers will fight amongst ourselves over questions of form, of amalgamated trade unions versus local federations, and that we will lose the bonds of solidarity that we are morally and materially obliged to uphold? No, comrades: emphatically reject the intervention of this gang of idle ruffians who would offer you rules that they have never followed themselves. Let us continue to fight as we have until now, in an open and determined struggle until victory, like our brave comrades on the other side of the world who knew how to overcome the villainy of Tsarism.

LONG LIVE THE WORKERS' FEDERATION!!!

Antonio Soto understood that victory would not be won by flyers alone. In addition to preparing for the rural strike, it would also be necessary to defeat the sectarians in assembly after assembly. The movement would have to simultaneously reach every corner of the territory and that would be complicated. There were few organizers and communication would be difficult. The mighty had all the resources: the telegraph lines, the police, automobiles, and every newspaper along the coast. It wasn't like the previous year, when the workers could count on the friendship of Judge Viñas, José María Borrero (along with his newspaper, *La Verdad*), and three or four lawyers.

Now there's nobody. Even Borrero—the true driving force behind the first strike but who was now leaning towards the Radicals—had begun to call for calm. The workers had sacrificed a great deal to purchase a printing press and several boxes of type to launch Patagonia's first labor newspaper, *1° de Mayo*, which they would use to communicate with the most isolated regions of the territory.

There's no time to lose; action alone can bring victory. Spring has begun and people need to get ready.

On September 15th, Antonio Soto and his companions are issued with the following credentials:

> The Rural Committee is hereby composed of Antonio Soto as secretary, José Grana as treasurer, Domingo Oyola as scribe and Efraín Fuentes as spokesman. They have been granted broad powers by the union leadership, whose signatures are affixed below.

They set out that same day, heading on an endless tour of the ranches of the cordillera, traveling by automobile and on horseback.[6] It is the last time Soto will see Río Gallegos for a decade.

There is a firsthand account of this tour in the travel diary of Domingo Oyola, a former telegraph operator who was fired during the failed strike at the beginning of the year. He travels in the same car as Soto.

Through this diary, we can glimpse the naivety and idealism of these men who, without knowing it, are starting down the path toward their ultimate defeat:

> 12:30 a.m.: Everything is ready for departure. The cars are filled with gasoline, suitcases with newspapers and flyers. Someone

approaches us and tells us that the police are combing the area and might prevent us from leaving. After handshakes of thanks, we say goodbye. Our comrades in the other car, who were waiting silently for their driver, beg him to get underway. We leave in two cars and speed off into the countryside, in the direction of Güer Ayke. I can see that my comrades are finally at ease. One of them says, "Now we are free. Let them follow us if they want…"

There's such strength in these fighting men! When push comes to shove, they all work together with an iron will, brushing aside the details to focus on the task at hand as if they were one man. There's three of them. We pass through Güer Ayke without being spotted by the police. We stop our Ford to wait for our other four companions, who were no longer visible, and they signal at us with their headlights. They've gotten stuck in a stream. "We're stuck," they say. "The engine cut out and it won't restart." We have to free the wheels from the mud and then push hard. We're three leagues from Güer Ayke, so we can take our time. Two comrades grab shovels and get to work. Others look for pieces of wood to use as levers. The moon has already begun to hide itself behind the mountains. The cold makes the work tougher; the water at the edge of the stream is frozen. Our comrades work feverishly to free the car, ignoring the temperature. They're up to their knees in water and it's hard for them to move. But while performing this task (unpleasant to be sure), our comrades smile at the thought of freeing the car from the stream. Even sacrifice can be satisfying when you act on your convictions.

This is all we have left of the diary of a Patagonian striker. This was the outbound journey; the return trip will be quite bitter.

We have the itinerary of the two automobiles, taken from Antonio Soto's notes, and through them we can imagine those two tiny Fords traveling through the desert, carrying eight madmen drunk on the ideas of social justice and human redemption. What possessed three Spaniards, one Pole, one Argentine, and three Chileans to set off through this wasteland to bring the gospel of Bakunin to those illiterate, God-forsaken peons? They were crazier than any characters dreamed of by Roberto Arlt, beyond the imagination of even Maxim Gorky. A former stage-hand, a stevedore, a mechanic, a former telegraph operator, three shepherds, a former electrician, and a hotel valet go off to fight for social justice and human redemption in the depopulated expanses of Patagonia. A shame that the conversations between these eight messengers of dynamite and fury weren't recorded. If Jesus had happened upon them in the desert, he would have shook his head sadly and told them, "Brothers, you are exaggerating the teachings of the Gospel."

This is their itinerary until October 5th: Barranca Blanca, El Tero, Mac Cormack, Tapi Ayke, Fuentes del Coyle, Cancha Carrera, Primavera, San José, Laurita, Rospentek, Punta Alta, Glenncross, Rincón de los Morros, Douglas, Bella Vista, Buitreras, Paso del Medio, Clark, and two other locations whose names have been erased from the page with the passage of time. But Soto also finds the time to visit Rancho Farías, near Puerto Irene, to preside over an assembly on September 25th. Between 120 and 130 workers attend. The assembly addresses the need for unity and lays plans to prevent the formation of the Lago Argentino Regional Workers' Federation, as desired by the sectarians. It's an unmitigated triumph for Antonio Soto.

Despite their massive propaganda offensive, nobody shows up to the assembly organized by the sectarians on October 2nd. But their failure only makes them more determined. The syndicalist FORA begins to shamelessly collaborate with the police, acting as the pawns of the Radical government in Río Gallegos. And we will see later on how the national leadership in Buenos Aires will wash their hands of the Workers' Federation and abandon its members to their fate when they declare a general strike and are then massacred by the army.

After having triumphed over the syndicalist FORA, Antonio Soto will face another problem: El Toscano has reappeared in the cordillera. After refusing to surrender to Varela at El Tero, this novelesque character had been living on abandoned farms and survived by hunting *guanacos*. He then went to Calafate to recruit followers, selecting five men, each more outlandish than the last. True bandits. There's Ernesto Francisco Martín Reith, a tall, twenty-six-year-old German with long blond hair and a cherubic face. No one knows how he got so far south. He is always accompanied by his comrade Federico Heerssen Dietrich, another twenty-six-year-old German with shaggy red hair and the eyes of a lynx. Frank Cross, twenty-seven-years old, is a former boxer from the United States who came to Argentina four years earlier. He is always armed with three revolvers and a cartridge belt, wears short boots, and drags his heels like a cowboy. The thirty-two-year-old Argentine Zacarías Caro is a scoundrel with a special nose for the police who spent seven and a half years in Ushuaia. The final member of the gang is the Chilean Santiago Días, twenty-two years old, who knows the cordillera well and can vanish as quickly as a rabbit.

El Toscano calls his gang The Red Council (with himself as its self-appointed chairman). All six men wear a red armband "as a symbol of socialism." When spring comes, El Toscano unilaterally declares the long-awaited strike and begins a series of "actions."

At the beginning of October, El Toscano meets with Soto. His plan is to launch an immediate revolt on the ranches and attack all of the police officers stationed in the cordillera. This would create the conditions needed for the victory of the strikers. Immediate action should be taken; the peons would carry out a surprise occupation of the ranches and take the landowners and administrators hostage. Soto disagrees. He says that work should only stop on those ranches whose owners and administrators haven't respected the conditions accepted at the end of the first strike. That they should wait for the ranchers to make the first move and then decide on an appropriate response. That declaring a general strike would play into the hands of the Rural Society. He strongly disapproves of El Toscano's raids, arguing that each action must be approved in assemblies and that everyone involved in the movement should abide by the resolutions of the Río Gallegos Workers' Society instead of going out on their own.

The break with El Toscano is final. From this moment on, Soto will spread the word from ranch to ranch that El Toscano and the sectarians are equally dangerous and that everyone should respect the resolutions of the Federation.

In the early hours of October 1st, there's a feeling of satisfaction in the halls of congress. The federal deputies of the Radical Civic Union have just abolished the death penalty. No one in Argentina will ever be executed again. There's only one man who could have pushed through such an important measure: President Yrigoyen. Men should be punished for their crimes, it's true, but nobody has the right to take the life of another. Only God.

(A twist of fate: five weeks later in Santa Cruz, more workers will be executed than under any conservative government.)

In the meantime, the situation in Río Gallegos continued to deteriorate. For once, the police moved quickly. They seemed to have abandoned their policy of neutrality. They sacked the Federation's headquarters in the wake of the *Beacon Grange* incident and fifteen people were arrested. The Federation wants to seek a writ of habeas corpus but is unable to find a lawyer to represent them. This is how the Federation's newspaper describes the incident:

> On September 20th, the police broke into the union head-quarters without warning and without a warrant, only a "Stop!" and a "Hands Up!" followed by pistol-whippings. They arrested everyone present and then searched their homes using the same methods. Hours and days have passed and the reasons for the police operation and arrests remain official secrets that must be kept from the ignorant public (without the guidance of lawyers or judges, anyways). What are the courts doing? Not even the letter of the law provides support for their actions. Correction is per-mitted but here they punish; a shootout is heard on the beach and they sack the union headquarters, which isn't even nearby. (…) At

least fifteen comrades have spent two days waiting to be booked, others three or four. Habeas corpus may as well be the name of an antediluvian animal because the penal code is unclear on the subject. The lawyers and judges of Río Gallegos don't recognize it. Five comrades remain in jail: Fernado Ulacia, Manuel Rivas, Jacobo Droisef, Nicofor Borinck, and Francisco Saules! How cold-blooded we must be if we continue to tolerate this tyranny!

But the police won't stop there; they're ready to arrest anyone who opposes the arrival of "free workers" in the ports of Santa Cruz. For every Chilean, Spaniard, or Pole who stops work, the Patriotic League will send an Argentine from Corrientes, Catamarca, or Santiago del Estero.

Another shadowy event occurs on October 8th: El Toscano and his men are apprehended by the police near Lago Argentino. Or so the official story goes; the truth is somewhat different. It's a group of unionized workers who spot El Toscano in Río Rico, near the Chilean border. They inform Commissioner Vera, and a group of policemen and peons capture him while he's eating *carne asada*. The participation of union members in his arrest is criticized by the Río Gallegos Workers' Federation and by anarchists in Buenos Aires, who issue a pamphlet titled "Santa Cruz" arguing that they "cannot support" workers who offer assistance to the police.

This incident shows the lack of class consciousness among many of the peons. They had heard Soto tell them that nobody should follow El Toscano because his raids and predations played into the hands of the bosses, harming the labor movement. And so when he's within range, they turn him over to the police.

The reality was that, although El Toscano's actions made the bosses look like the victims, they were content to see the famous bandit behind bars. They had known him by one alias but many names: Alfredo Willrey, Godofredo Fontes, José Villar, Max Miligan, Juan Trini, Hilario Rolis, José Ventura, Antonio Mora, José Rosendo (his real name was Alfredo Fonte). And that was the end of Patagonia's unique Red Council.

The law comes down hard. The police have evidently received orders to act energetically against the workers. Soto continues the hard work of organizing informative assemblies on each ranch and unionizing the peons. He meets with Ramón Outerelo, who tells him that the workers in Puerto Santa Cruz have taken the decision to draft a new list of demands modifying the Yza settlement. Among other demands, they are organizing for the elimination of shearing subcontractors, who provided their own workers and lowered the price of labor. They have presented their demands to the Puerto Santa Cruz Rural Society, which has until October 30th to accept. This puts Soto in an uncomfortable position and he insists that the movement focus on demanding the implementation of the Yza settlement because he predicts that the bosses will reject any new demands, forcing the workers to lose face or declare a general strike, the success of which he cannot guarantee. Outerelo tells him that it's too late to hold another assembly. He tries to win Soto over by telling him of his travels through the countryside, which have convinced him that the workers will unconditionally support a strike. Time is of the essence and the two leaders reach a compromise: the Río Gallegos Workers' Society will fight for the implementation of the Yza settlement through strikes on those ranches that have refused to comply while following events in Puerto Santa Cruz and offering solidarity if needed. If a general strike breaks out, Outerelo will assume responsibility for coordinating actions between different regions of the state. Soto tells The Colonel—his nickname for Outerelo—that he would have to take over the leadership of any strike encompassing the entire territory, as his geographical position makes him a logical go-between with Albino Argüelles—the union leader in San Julián—and a newcomer from Puerto Deseado: José Font, better known as Facón Grande (Big Knife), a reliable but reserved gaucho from Entre Ríos and a cart driver by trade, one of those men who can make eight Percheron horses obey with nothing more than a whistle.

If a general strike is declared throughout the territory, Soto foresees that problems will arise in Puerto Santa Cruz, San Julián, and Puerto Deseado. These three ports are under the influence of the syndicalist FORA. In Puerto Deseado, the railway workers' union, which boasts the most experienced men, answers to Portales; in San Julián and Puerto Santa Cruz, the stevedores side with the Maritime Workers' Federation, which doesn't want any trouble: they have a good rapport with Yrigoyen. There's no room for error. The only ones to mobilize in Puerto Santa Cruz will be a handful of anarchists. Argüelles in San Julián is a socialist, and the socialists want debate, not struggle. And Puerto Deseado, still licking its wounds from the previous year, has remained fairly calm. And so, aside from Río Gallegos, which is fully under the influence of the Workers' Federation, only the workers in the countryside can be counted on. It will be a strike of peons, cut off from the coast, cut off from any communication with Buenos Aires.

At the beginning of October, a number of ranches have begun to comply with the settlement. Wherever this doesn't occur, the workers go on strike. The Fatherland Defense Association of Puerto Santa Cruz addresses the president once more. They point out that the strike will interfere with the shearing and with all the businesses that rely on the wool industry.

But it's no longer necessary for them to protest. The police launch coordinated operations in Puerto Deseado, Puerto San Julián, Puerto Santa Cruz, and Río Gallegos. Anyone with union connections is imprisoned. In Río Gallegos, the headquarters of the Workers' Federation is ransacked and closed down. There the police make their biggest catch: Antonio Paris, the organization's secretary general, the man most hated by the Patriotic League, the one who had the pleasure of not serving the Independence Day banquet. They take him away in handcuffs, badly beaten. All of the Argentines at the police station take pleasure in his arrival. That night, the Patriotic League and the Progress Club are full of amused talk of the Spaniard's arrest, the clubs that were broken against his head, and the special treatment he received at the station, where Sergeant Echazú had some good ideas about how to teach the anarchist to act properly in this country. After the laughter dies down, they congratulate the police on their response to this emergency with a sober gesture of thanks. And *La Unión* will praise the police force for "having conducted a partial purge of the unwelcome elements that, until now, acted with impunity under the cover of apparent legality."

The police dragnets in Puerto Santa Cruz, San Julián, and Puerto Deseado are quite successful as well. It can be argued that every influential union leader has been captured. Soto hears the news while visiting the Bella Vista ranch. They tell him that Paris and his companions were put aboard a Navy transport vessel and that no one knows where they have been taken. They also show him the call for a general strike that was drafted by the few comrades who have remained at large. Soto drafts two communiqués on the spot. The first repeats the call for a general strike:

> Comrades! Stop work until the deportees have been returned to us and until everyone who has been jailed has been released. Let no one accuse us of cowardice! Comrades: Stop work today at 2 p.m., if you have not already done so, and show your solidarity by joining our ranks. With this you will be doing your duty as class-conscious workers.

The second declares:

> To the people of Río Gallegos and workers across the country, greetings! Just when we felt at peace, secure in our work after the tragic events of the recent strike, we see the return of the barbarous reaction characteristic of that den of degenerate pimps and opportunists known as the Patriotic League, with their banner of Free Labor. (…) Rural workers! Let us take up this dignified, manly struggle and refuse to produce anything for these patriotic parasites. The arbitrary deportation of our comrades demands that we bring out the best within us and make sacrifices. A general strike has been declared and its reach must be absolute, both in the countryside and in town. Workers, be aware!

News of the strike spreads like a chain reaction. It is Antonio Soto who gives the order to stop work, rise up, and take over the ranches. He can be found—as we have mentioned—on the Bella Vista ranch, owned by Sara Braun and administered by Mauricio Braun. It's symbolic that this is where the great strike begins. There they unfurl the red and black flag. And there they begin the long march towards death. On horseback.

In the meantime, things have been falling into place in Buenos Aires. The pressure exerted on the government by the Rural Society, the ranchers, the British ambassador, and General Martínez's public statements about the need to finish off the Patagonian labor movement have begun to bear fruit. Yrigoyen gradually begins the bureaucratic process of mobilizing the forces needed to repress the strike.

But Yrigoyen doesn't cave to the ranchers on everything: he insists on sending the much-criticized Lieutenant Colonel Varela. The very man who appeased the workers the first time around. What is Yrigoyen thinking? Why does he send a Radical officer to carry out such an unpleasant task? Even the orders are unpleasant. And here we reach the crux of the matter. These orders are disputed and will continue to be disputed. When he arrives in Santa Cruz, Lieutenant Colonel Varela will tell his men to organize firing squads. He will announce this publicly, just weeks after Congress eliminated the death penalty. On whose authority does he act? Does Yrigoyen approve? How is it that, under a democratic government that has not declared itself at war with enemies foreign or domestic and whose Congress is meeting (albeit in extraordinary sessions), a lieutenant colonel could introduce martial law? Varela was a serious officer, not a madman, and he always did his duty. We have difficulty believing that he would act alone without the president's support. Perhaps the only thing that can be said in Yrigoyen's favor is that, under pressure from the powerful interests involved, Varela may have lost control, exceeded his authority or acted in the moment. Besides, the navy officers received the same instructions as

Varela—act on a war footing—but they don't act with the same ruthlessness.

In the lengthy report that Varela will give his superiors, there is only one brief reference to his orders. Word for word, it says, "In accordance with the verbal instructions I received from the war minister, which were further elaborated upon by the interior minister, the regiment under my command embarked...etc."

So the orders were issued through political channels: the war minister is Julio Moreno, and the interior minister is El Tuerto Gómez.

For his part, General Anaya—then a captain—has this to say on the matter:

In late October, the commander of the 10th Cavalry Regiment—Lieutenant Colonel Varela, the same as during the previous campaign—was summoned to the minister's offices to be informed that his regiment might be redeployed to restore order in Patagonia, the order that had been so controversial during his previous intervention. This mission was confirmed some days later with the same ambiguity as before, only now the orders came from the interior minister: "Go and see what's going on and do your duty." The regiment set sail on November 4th...

Before leaving, Varela seeks an audience with President Yrigoyen, but the commander-in-chief is a very busy man and the regiment's departure cannot be postponed. It seems that Varela has already received his orders but wants the president to confirm them because his mission is of the utmost importance. But, suggestively, the doors of the president's office remain closed to the lieutenant colonel.

The Radical senator Bartolomé Pérez has suggested that the orders to impose martial law and act with the utmost severity came from the president by means of the war minister: "One way or another, the situation must be resolved." We need to understand the difficult situation being faced by the Radical administration:

the party was divided and elections were approaching in Buenos Aires province, where the conservatives had already declared victory, as well as in Córdoba, Tucumán, and Mendóza. And these would be followed by a presidential election and the inevitable internal struggles it would bring. There was also subversive activity in Salta and San Juan, etc.

So Yrigoyen couldn't allow for prolonged strikes or subversion in Patagonia. There was no other solution than to act—or refrain from acting—as he had during the Tragic Week. It was the hour—"unfortunately"—for the guns to speak. The time had come for the government of the middle class to define itself. And so it defined itself in opposition to the workers.

Other Radical leaders have stated, on the contrary, that Varela acted on the direct orders of the army. Or, more specifically, on the orders of the commander of the 2nd Division, General Dellepiane, the man who had personally drowned the Vasena strike in fire and blood.

We will return to the matter of responsibility later on. We will see how everyone will try to throw each other to the wolves and how, over time, Commander Varela will go down in history as the only one responsible for the massacre.

Now for operational matters. The troops are being mobilized. The mighty of Patagonia have gotten their way. They have maneuvered so skillfully that every eye in Argentina is fixed on the south.

It's impressive how quickly and masterfully they were able to shape the image of the Workers' Society (bandits, outlaws, and murderers were the kindest words used). But even more impressive is how the very architects of the repression that followed (Varela, Anaya, and Viñas Ibarra) recognized that this image was false, that their tales of the workers' crimes were nothing but a lie. Let us hear what Anaya has to say in the aforementioned conference at the Military Circle:

Alarm spread through the population and fear exceeded the bounds of reason. Calls for federal intervention got louder. The press in Buenos Aires, whether serious or partisan, added their voices, though their interventions were motivated not so much by patriotism as from the economic interests of their patrons. The correspondents they sent south for this purpose did their job well. For proof of this, you only need to reread the newspaper headlines from those days. They began spreading rumors of rape and looting and other premeditated crimes, all of them supported by the testimony of influential figures with connections to the stock exchange and the government.

This is the perspective of General Anaya, labeled "The Jackal" in the labor press for his role in the repression. Varela's report is more contradictory. During the first strike they were workers fighting for their rights who didn't engage in looting and only requisitioned supplies in exchange for signed receipts. The second time around, they were bloodthirsty foreign agents who wanted to take over Argentina and substitute the red flag for the blue and white. As for Viñas Ibarra, he will affirm that the workers were exploited by their bosses and will justify their demands, but he nevertheless participates in the repression and defends his actions.

As Varela gets his men ready to embark on the *Almirante Brown*, Soto and his men gain some time.

By October 31st, Soto alone has managed to launch revolts on the Buiteras, Alquinta, Rincón de los Morros, and Glencross ranches, in addition to the La Esperanza and Bella Vista ranches.

The movement spreads like an oil slick, and a column of three hundred agricultural workers approaches Turbio and Punta Alta. The Workers' Society's other delegates have stirred up the peons on every ranch from Lago Argentino to Punta Alta.

In short, these men have mobilized every corner of the vast southeastern region of Santa Cruz in just seven days. At first, the movement is entirely without incident. The delegates approach a ranch, speak with the peons, commandeer weapons, and take food as needed in exchange for vouchers signed by Soto. If the owners or administrators are present, they are taken hostage. They also try to take all of the ranch's horses with them, if possible, to avoid being hunted down. But no police detachments are attacked. In Turbio, the workers set up camp just a few meters from a police detachment and pass the night peacefully. Soto wants to prove that he's leading a strike, not an uprising. He knows that conflicts with the police will provoke an outcry and that there will be accusations of treason. Even the Rural Society's newspaper reports, in a tone that will drastically change later, "They plan to march to Río Gallegos. Their only demand is for their prisoners to be released. Reports indicate that the strikers have no destructive intentions." Which is true. The movement only seeks the release of the prisoners. The peons haven't risen up because of demagogic promises but out of solidarity. And this is something we cannot overlook. There can be no talk of demagogy or accusations that the labor leaders were demagogues for having declared a strike. Argentina has never witnessed such a massive sympathy strike before or since. Aside from the Puerto Santa Cruz Workers' Society, which tacked on a series of concessions, the strikers' only demand was the release of the prisoners.

The first hard news of the strike comes from Punta Arenas, where the employees and administrators of the British-owned ranches seek refuge. Chile immediately mobilizes the Magallanes Batallion and closes its border with Argentina. A company under the command of Lieutenant Villablanca and a machine gun detail are posted at Puerto Natales. The carabinieri are also mobilized. One squadron marches to the border and an infantry company watches Tierra del Fuego, as the strike is also being observed on Menéndez Behety's properties in Río Grande.

Chile has a conservative government and the Brauns, Menéndezes, and Montes receive an immediate response to their demands for protection—much quicker than the response they've received from the Yrigoyen administration. But Argentine troops are finally on their way and they will erase every trace of the labor uprising from Patagonian soil.

By November 5th, all of southern Santa Cruz is paralyzed. There's not a single ranch left where people are still working. The workers dominate the roads. They march in columns of sixty, one hundred, two hundred men, carrying the red flag across the desolate land of Santa Cruz. Soto is in Punta Alta with Graña, Sambucetti, and Mongilnitzky, the men who had left Río Gallegos with him. They decide that, while Soto continues leading the rural strike, the three of them should try to enter Río Gallegos to replace the imprisoned leaders and establish a foothold in town. Soto argues that the strike will be lost if it remains isolated from the coast. And so they drive off on the difficult mission of entering the capital. Sambucetti will take over as the organization's secretary general. He will try to meet with the interim governor and ask him to release the prisoners in exchange for ending the rural strike.

These men will divide into two groups but neither will reach their destination.

When Sambucetti, Fernández, and Mongilnitzky try to drive across the Buitreras bridge on November 1st, the police block their path. They appear on all sides, heavily armed. Sambucetti explains that they're on their way to meet with the governor, but the police are short on formalities. They hogtie their prisoners and toss them in the back of their truck like sacks of potatoes. They're beaten all the way back to town. Now they'll be ready to meet with the governor! By the time they reach Río Gallegos, of course, they aren't exactly very presentable, so instead of being taken to the governor's mansion they're thrown in jail. The police enter their cells one by one, enjoying themselves. They only have one question: Where is Antonio Soto?

The police are lucky: in addition to three strike leaders, they've also brought in two Winchesters, a large stack of propaganda, and a great deal of correspondence relating to the strike. But the biggest prize is a red identity card with Cyrillic text that Mongilnitzky had been carrying with him. It's passed from hand to hand. The most influential citizens in Río Gallegos come to look at it with horror and delight: there's finally proof. The great conspiracy. Nobody understands a word, but it's written in Russian: it can evidently only speak of revolution, death, bloodshed, anarchism, maximalism, and, in the end, anti-Argentinism. This identity card is enough to prove, no more and no less, that the Patagonian strike has been inspired by Moscow. It's proof enough for Argentina's newspapers and military officers to speak of a vast foreign conspiracy aimed at destroying the nation's sovereignty. Besides the identity card, they also find some extremely suspicious letters, all of them written in Russian. Though no one bothers to translate them, they evidently constitute proof of a conspiracy. A translation might have proven to be a great disappointment: the identity card was issued by the Leo Tolstoy Library, which allowed its members to read the works of freethinkers, rationalists, and libertarians—Bakunin, Kropotkin, Proudhon—as well as Marx and Engels and literary figures like Maxim Gorky, Panait Istrati, etc. The letters were from his family, although they did include some news of what was happening in Puerto Santa Cruz.

The Río Gallegos police do not feel comfortable with such prisoners. Their admittedly unscientific attempts to soften them up have been unsuccessful. The police are also afraid of the reaction of the workers. So they transfer their prisoners to the *Vicente Fidel López*, a naval transport currently in port. This ends up saving their lives. The lieutenant colonel will arrive a few days later and he will have no tolerance for mysteries—much less identity cards written in Russian.

The other group of union leaders decides to take a detour to the Las Horquestas ranch on their way to Río Gallegos and there they spend the night. Someone tells Commissioner Douglas of the arrival of Graña, Oyola, and Álvarez. The commissioner and his men surround the small property and force everyone to come out with their hands up. It's a good catch: Oyola and Graña are perhaps Soto's two most valuable men. With their capture, Antonio Soto has been left on his own. He will be accompanied by dedicated supporters, but nobody with organizing experience.

The strike continues to spread. Ramón Outerelo has managed to escape Puerto Santa Cruz, reaching Paso Ibáñez. He survives by the skin of his teeth. The entire union leadership has been rounded up in the purge organized by the police and the Patriotic League.

In Puerto Santa Cruz, the union receives a "visit" and all of its assets are destroyed with rifle butts. The library, containing the works of Ghiraldo and all the usual suspects from Russia, is literally shat upon. The typewriter, purchased with the contributions of the day laborers of Puerto Santa Cruz, is taken to the police station, where it will be used to prepare reports on the subversive activities of these foreign anarchists. Years later, the police will proudly explain to visitors that the typewriter had belonged to the "bandits of 1921."

Instead of following Soto's lead and staying away from the ports, Outerelo's men make for the coast. They visit ranches in groups of ten or fifteen men, stirring up the peons, requisitioning supplies and weapons, and organizing columns that converge on Puerto Santa Cruz.

The ranchers flee with their families. The countryside is completely abandoned. Only one family stays to defend themselves: the Schroeders, Germans who own the Bremen and El Cifre ranches. Law-abiding people. They have turned their ranch into a veritable garden. When they hear that the workers have rebelled and are taking landowners hostage, they refuse to abandon their property. The entire family stands their ground, even the women and children. They keep watch day and night. The strikers are nearby. Their oldest son has only recently come back from Germany, where he had volunteered to fight in the Great War. He spent four years in the trenches. A man whose hands don't shake, he knows to aim for the head.

On the morning of November 5th, the alarm sounds. They're coming. A group of ten men following the red flag. They drive a herd of horses before them, as if to shield themselves from attack. There are eight chilotes and one Argentine under the command of a Spaniard named Martínez, a simple, hard-working man who always speaks up in assemblies, criticizing priests and the state in a barely perceptible voice.

The chilotes advance, shouting "Long live the Strike!" and whooping like Indians, perhaps to give themselves courage. They're actually somewhat afraid of these bosses. They pay well and on time, but they're men of few words and hardly any of their workers trust them. They're constantly practicing their aim and they care for their weapons with the same affection that another would pet a beloved dog.

While Frau Schroeder and the children withdraw to the most protected room in the house, the men take strategic positions. The oldest son climbs to the top of the windmill. He has a clear view of the road. He also predicts that the chilotes would only be armed with short range weapons, while he has a shiny new Mauser.

The strikers approach as if there was no danger. The Schroeders let them. They fire a broadside once the intruders are within range. There's not a word of warning. Martínez is shot in the head. So is the Argentine behind him. Good marksmanship. They tumble off their horses and lie in the dirt, as if crucified.

The others beat a retreat. It's time for all that target practice to pay off. Several others are wounded and two horses are killed.

The chilotes fall back five hundred meters from the house, taking cover behind some rocks. They return fire with their revolvers but all of their bullets fall short. The Europeans take their time. Between shots, they carefully wipe down the barrels of their guns so that they don't overheat. Then they take aim, and when they see a dark-skinned face appear from behind a rock, they pull the trigger. The chilotes can't even move their heads. It's more like hunting than combat. Besides, these Germans are well prepared. They know that the chilotes can wait them out for days, hoping the Schroeders will run out of bullets. But there's nothing to worry about. They have several cases of ammunition. And they don't waste a single shot. In the end, the chilotes flee in a rather undignified fashion, dragging away their wounded.

The Schroeders realize that this is their only opportunity. The entire family piles into their automobile and they drive to Puerto Coyle. From there, they send a telegraph to the police stating that they've killed two strikers and wounded "several others." They ask for help in returning to their ranch and continuing the fight, anticipating that the strikers will return. Commissioner Wells, Officer Guadarrama, Sergeant Echazú, and several gendarmes immediately set out from Río Gallegos. The police contingent joins up with the men of the Schroeder family in Puerto Coyle.

When the strikers learn that Martínez and Caranta have been killed on the Bremen ranch, they assign a group of ten peons to take it over. They arrive at five in the morning and capture the gendarme standing guard, but the rest of the police, waiting in the houses, have been warned. There's an intense shootout. The strikers, unable to advance, begin to run out of bullets. The Chilean Roberto Triviño Cárcamo takes the initiative and advances towards the road on horseback, his remaining comrades trailing clumsily behind. But Don Enrique Schroeder shoots his horse out from under him with only one bullet. Triviño falls. The others, thinking he's dead, flee as fast as their horses can carry them. Triviño gets up and starts running. The police find him several kilometers away, hidden in the bushes, and whip him all the way back to the ranch. There they tie him to the windmill, where he will remain until Lieutenant Colonel Varela arrives.

While the cruiser *Almirante Brown* sails towards Puerto Santa Cruz to protect the town's Armour meatpacking plant, Varela heads straight for Río Gallegos. He had set sail from Buenos Aires with the 10th Cavalry Regiment on November 4th and arrived in Punta Loyola—twelve kilometers from Río Gallegos—on the 9th.

Varela's first impressions can be seen in his dispatches:

Work was at a complete standstill. The landowners, administrators, supervisors, and foremen were all being held captive, aside from a few who had managed to escape, leaving their property in the hands of the rebels. It had been this way for quite some time and nothing was known of their fate. It was even claimed that many of them had been murdered, their ranches looted and then burned to the ground. In general, it can be said that the local population was in such a state of nervous excitement that it bordered on desperation. The authorities had done nothing and the police limited themselves to reporting on events as they occurred. With communications severed, the only reliable news was that some police officers had fled, leaving behind their weapons and ammunition, which were then seized by the rebels. This could be confirmed by their later attacks. Some police officers also let themselves be taken prisoner without putting up the least resistance.

Anaya is more categorical:

Nothing had been heard of the police detachments scattered throughout the interior and the government assumed that they had all met the same fate. None of the messengers who had been sent out had returned and it was suspected that they had been captured or, at best, were hiding out until they could slip through the blockade. All of the landowners, either fearing reprisals or out of their own self-interest, had stopped work on their ranches. The administrators and foremen who had not been captured fled to the coast, where their reports have helped fuel the panic. Others, the most frightened (of which there were more than a few), took any chance that came their way to flee farther north. The police in the coastal towns, sharing these fears, only undertook to protect themselves. They were convinced that they were dealing with an insurrectionary movement of such proportions that it would overthrow the legitimate authorities in Santa Cruz and immediately impose a social-anarchist regime, transplanted from other latitudes. These fears were stoked by those who claimed that the strike was part of a foreign plot. The suspicion was that Santa Cruz had been divided up amongst different groups or cells, which seemed confirmed by the simultaneous actions throughout the territory, especially in distant regions that were home to important ranches and where the actions undertaken were perfectly suited to the population's logistical needs. The reports issued by the naval authorities added little or nothing to this picture. In the absence of specific orders, the navy limited itself to monitoring shipping traffic and port activity, which of course had been brought to a halt. Only occasionally could news from Punta Arenas be heard over the wireless, and far from easing tensions, this only managed to increase the alarm. The presence of the *Almirante Brown* was due to the possible destruction of the Armour meatpacking plant, left inactive as a consequence of the prevailing fears, a decision that did little to alleviate the desperation felt throughout the territory.

With respect to Varela's statements, there's no question that work was at a complete standstill. From the outskirts of Río Gallegos to the cordillera, from the 52nd parallel (the southern border with Chile) to the Río Santa Cruz, the movement continued to spread. By then it had reached San Julián and was beginning to show signs of life in Bahía Laura and Puerto Deseado, where Facón Grande was beginning to make his move. It's also true that communications had been severed and almost all of the landowners and administrators encountered by the strikers were taken hostage, but they enjoyed a certain freedom in camp and were even allowed to write to their relatives. What's absolutely false is the assertion that those landowners, administrators, and workers who refused to go along with the strike were killed. There is no evidence—in police reports, death certificates, or internal government reports—that provides support for this rumor. Neither the Rural Society nor *La Unión* could provide the name of a single individual who was killed by the strikers. The case of a rancher named Flekker seems to have been the work of the police. Whether or not rapes were committed is much harder to clarify. Prior to the arrival of the armed forces, not a single report of a rape was filed. Of course, it could be argued that the victims were afraid to speak out. But there was also an absence of third party witnesses. Later—at the end of the strike—there will be a case where the victim won't come forward but there will be witnesses and the two culprits will be shot. In none of the formal protests filed by the British, American, Belgian, Spanish, and German ambassadors is there any mention of rape. As for looting, it undeniably occurred, but to a much lesser degree than during the first strike, when El Toscano and El 68 had been the movement's leaders.

Of course, all these complaints were made by the police and the landowners. The strikers, isolated from the cities, lost their written means of communication and could not defend themselves from the accusations of their enemies. But the press in the coastal towns could print anything that would help them frame the strikers as bandits, murderers, and thieves. Even *La Unión* would later have to make a series of shameful retractions.

But let's return to Varela as he disembarks in Río Gallegos:

> Considering that law and order have been subverted; that the rights to life, property, and personal safety as guaranteed by our Constitution have ceased to exist; and that armed men have openly risen up against the fatherland and against the federal government, threatening the established authorities, sowing destruction, committing arson, and requisitioning horses, supplies, and private property of all kinds, I interpret the situation as being extremely serious.

What happened to Varela? Why is the second strike a subversive uprising "against the fatherland" and "against the federal government" when the first was, in Varela's own words, a labor movement seeking concessions? Especially when you consider that the first strike began with the deaths of five policemen and the second strike, up to this point, has been free of bloodshed? After all, the only deaths were those of the two workers killed by the Schroeders.

Why has Varela changed his mind? Or was it Yrigoyen's orders that have changed?

This is what will confuse the strikers, who are certain that the army will act exactly as it did the first time around—as a peaceful arbitrator. This belief will be Varela's trump card. Surprise them, catch them unawares. Overwhelm them from the start, grab them by the scruff of the neck and make them kiss the dirt.

From the outset, Varela interpreted his mission as one of war. He had to win, vanquishing and annihilating the enemy. But how could he destroy a force that outnumbered his own by ten to one? And how could he do it with two hundred inexperienced soldiers who didn't know the lay of the land and weren't used to the cold winds of Patagonia? There was one key to victory. If Varela planned to triumph over forces ten times more numerous than his own, it was because he knew that the enemy lacked both military organization and a sufficient number of weapons and that, above all, it didn't want war. We defend this hypothesis in the face of the claims made by Varela and Anaya that the strikers were "militarized forces, perfectly armed and supplied with ammunition." This is completely and absolutely false. We can see this in each of Varela's dispatches, which indicate the number of prisoners and weapons captured when the strikers surrender *en masse*. There, beyond all speculation, we should be able to find the truth. The numbers are clear: there's almost always two or three times as many prisoners as weapons, which are almost always very poor— old Winchesters and a very small number of Savages. Even when new, these weapons couldn't match the range of the firearms used by the 10th Cavalry. In recent years, historians have attempted to prove that the Patagonian strikers were armed and organized by the Chilean government, but Varela didn't come across any weapons that would have been issued by the carabinieri or the Chilean Army. There are a few exceptions, however—we've been able to confirm two weapons that seem to have belonged to the Chilean carabinieri. But many things can be found in such a multitudinous movement, such as three Chilean deserters who had abandoned their posts years beforehand, finding work on Argentine ranches and later joining the strike. It also wouldn't be the first time that carabinieri stationed along the border sold their weapons in Argentina in exchange for a few bottles of good Paraguayan aguardiente or Dutch gin. At the time, it was common for policemen to sell their guns, and not just in Chile but also in our country as well. The records are full of these cases, which always occur in isolation.

Varela knows who he is going to fight. He's known them since the first strike. They're chilotes, accompanied by the occasional Spaniard, Russian, or German. People who are out of touch with reality, believing in humanity and getting lost in their analyses of Tolstoy and Bakunin. And they always remain individuals, with no knowledge of weapon use, troop movements, and the fundamentals of combat: manipulating the masses, giving orders and ensuring that they are obeyed, making each soldier into an automaton who would even shoot his own father if so ordered. No, for this you need military men.

If Varela arrived with so few men that they might be best described as reconnaissance units, it's because he knew that the strikers weren't prepared for a fight. It was more of a punitive operation than actual warfare because there wouldn't be any battles aside from the isolated episode of Facón Grande, which can also be disputed. Had Varela sent a handful of soldiers into this region and actually believed that there would be combat against two thousand men who were "perfectly armed and supplied with ammunition"—or, as some modern writers argue, "perfectly trained and commanded by officers of the Chilean Army"[7]—then Varela was either irresponsible or suicidal. He was neither; he knew who he would face, which is why he divided his forces. And the truth is that it was no more dangerous than a stroll through the countryside. Or rather, a safari.

We will now follow Varela's troops until they encounter the strikers. In his dispatches, the officer writes:

> I have decided to act with the utmost speed, organizing three detachments:
>
> Twelve soldiers under Lieutenant Colonel Varela and First Lieutenant Schweizer, heading in the direction: El Cifre—Paso Ibáñez—Santa Cruz.

Fifty soldiers and one nurse under Captain Viñas Ibarra and Sub-lieutenant Frugoni, heading in the direction: Tapi Aike—Fuentes de Couyle—Primavera—Cancha Carrera—Cordillera de los Baguales.

Thirty soldiers and one nurse under Captain Campos, heading in the direction: El Cifre—Laguna Benito—south bank of the Río Santa Cruz.

The first column got underway on November 11th at 6 a.m., the other two on November 12th at 7 a.m.

Daily war report: Lieutenant Colonel Varela—First Lieutenant Schweizer. Having reached El Cifre and confirmed the reports of the events that occurred there, including the attacks on the ranch and the shootout between the rebels and the police, and in light of the news I received on the scene (that Captain Viñas Ibarra had come across groups willing to resist the army in the zone under his command), I resolved to return to Río Gallegos and head south towards Punta Alta, passing through the ranches that, according to the news, would have been attacked.

But Varela remains silent on one very important fact: the campaign's first extrajudicial execution occurs at El Cifre. The victim is the Chilean Luis Triviño Cárcamo, who had been taken prisoner and left chained to the ranch's windmill. Commissioner Isidro Guadarrama has personally told us that when Varela arrived at the Schroeder ranch, he was informed that Triviño had participated in the attack and was an incorrigible striker. That a group of strikers approached the ranch every night in an attempt to rescue their comrade, but were always repelled by the police stationed in the barns. That the strikers then decided to open fire on the barns. That, whenever he heard gunshots, Triviño Cárcamo—still chained to the windmill—laughed at the police, shouting "Long live the Strike!" After hearing all this, Varela said calmly, "That one has had his last laugh, shoot him at once." He then gave Sergeant Echazú the order. Echazú and the police officers fired from close range and the chilote died with his expression somewhere between serenity and surprise. They buried him the following day alongside his comrades Martínez and Caranta, 150 meters from the house. All of this was witnessed by the Schroeder family, who continue living and working on these same ranches fifty years later. This was the first execution of the campaign.

From the Schroeder ranch, Varela returns to Río Gallegos, where he dispatches a column of thirty-one men under the command of First Lieutenant Anello to the Bella Vista and Esperanza Douglas ranches. The column leaves before daybreak on November 14th. Varela remains in Río Gallegos on the 15th and, accompanied by thirteen men, finally leaves at five in the morning on the 16th, heading in the following direction:[8]

> Río Gallegos, Bella Vista, Esperanza Douglas, Punta Alta, Rospensteek, crossing the border at this point and then re-entering Argentina at Cancha Carrera to arrive at Fuentes de Coyle and make contact with Captain Viñas Ibarra's squadron, which should be nearby.

This means that Varela and his troops enter Chilean territory at one point and then leave at another, for which they need the permission of the Chilean authorities. This will be criticized and ridiculed by the newspapers of Punta Arenas, which run articles arguing that Argentina's armed forces should put their own house in order before they come to pacify Chile. *La Unión* of Río Gallegos will then respond angrily that Varela crossed over into Chile for no reason other than that of saving time. Let's continue with Varela:

> Upon arriving in Punta Alta at 9 p.m. on November 16th, I received vague reports that Captain Viñas Ibarra's squadron had encountered the rebels, but no details as to the exact location of the encounter or its outcome.

In other words, the first "battle" had occurred between the Argentine Army and the strikers. In this "battle," as in every other incident in the campaign (save for the events at Tehuelches), the only fatalities were workers. The two versions of the encounter that emerge are completely contradictory. First we will examine Captain Viñas Ibarra's official report on his actions prior to the "Battle" of Punta Alta. He states that at 3 a.m. on November 14th, his troops were being transported by truck to the Fuentes del Coyle ranch,

> where Commissioner Douglas and the region's police officers are gathered. Having heard my orders and placing himself at my disposal, Douglas informs me that he has received news that a group of rebels are looting the Laguna Salada ranch, owned by the Tierra del Fuego Development Corporation and located seven leagues away, near the border with Chile. We venture into the cordillera, a rocky region heavily covered with forests and filled with ravines, which would have made it wonderfully suited to ambushes if the enemy knew how to make use of the lay of the land.

These last few words prove one thing: that if the strikers had wanted to confront the army, they would have had every advantage, but at no time did this idea ever occur to them. Captain Viñas Ibarra continues:

> Two kilometers away from Laguna Salada, I ordered my men to halt and divided them into two groups. One group of six soldiers, under the command of Sub-lieutenant Frugoni Miranda, were to make themselves known to the enemy and draw their attention with sporadic gunfire. This would allow the rest of the troops (the remaining nine soldiers under my direct command) to take possession of the high ground overlooking the ranch from the rear so that none of the rebels could escape. None of the eighty rebels, whose horses were saddled up, saw us take the hill behind the ranch. When we interrupted their looting, they tried to resist the order to surrender.

As we can see, there's a great disparity in numbers. There are eighty strikers confronting fifteen soldiers. And they're only facing six soldiers out front. Eighty of the so-called rebels see a party of just six men approaching. The strikers had also neglected to position sentries, a sign that they weren't looking for a fight and weren't expecting attacks from "the enemy." Viñas Ibarra tells us, however, that:

A few tried to ride off but, finding themselves encircled by sharpshooters, they turned back after ineffectually firing off a few rounds. I ordered them to line up but they regrouped and tried once again to escape, so I ordered my troops to fire into the air to intimidate them. This did the trick and they all unconditionally surrendered.

These "bandits," who were "perfectly armed and supplied with ammunition" and commanded by "Chilean officers"—as they will later be described by partisan historians—evidently had no stomach for a fight. What's certain is that they thought the Argentine Army would solve all of their problems, but they will be sorely disappointed. Let's continue with Viñas Ibarra's report, paying close attention to the "armament" captured:

Outcome: Eighty prisoners, all of them Chileans with no criminal record in Argentina, most of them drawn from the nitrate mines of the north. Some Winchesters, several revolvers, many long knives, and 350 stolen horses (not counting their own mounts).

Observe: in his official report to the War Ministry, Viñas Ibarra says "some Winchesters" (how many—one, five, ten?), "several revolvers" (how many—and are these the weapons to use when taking on an army?), "many long knives" (a weapon clearly ill-suited for the fierce "battles" that the army will wage against the "Chilean bandits").

And so we have the battle of Laguna Salada, a Braun ranch. The next will be the Battle of Punta Alta, where the massacre begins.

Captain Viñas Ibarra's report is difficult to believe, but it will be typical of all of his dispatches throughout the campaign, which always try to prove that Patagonia was facing a Chilean invasion instead of a strike. After capturing another fifty prisoners, "all Chileans," and two hundred horses (he doesn't mention having seized any weapons) along the Chilean border on November 15th, he reports that:

> Towards midnight I received news from a resident of Chile who sought us out after hearing about our activities and our guarantees. He reported that in the south of the territory, near the Cordillera Chica, a group of rebels and their hostages had set up camp.

Viñas Ibarra then explains the operation, for which he had fifty soldiers. The cavalry regiment departs at 4:30 a.m. on the 16th. It is preceded by a scouting party made up of a non-commissioned officer and four soldiers. He writes:

> At 18:30, I heard shooting from the direction of the scouting party's location. I ordered my squadron to halt while I advanced. There was a lagoon in front of a hill, forming a natural barrier, and a line of sharpshooters could be seen. As the gunfire was escalating and two of their horses were wounded, I ordered the scouting party to retreat, take cover behind a nearby hill, and return fire. Returning to my squadron, I ordered Sergeant Agüero to reinforce the scouting party with four men. These eight men were to spread out and draw the attention of the rebels, keeping them stationary and giving me a free hand. Sub-lieutenant Frugoni Miranda, Sergeant Sánchez, and fifteen soldiers would try to take the right slope of the hill and return any fire they receive from the enemy, forcing them to leave the high ground and head towards the pampa to their right. With the rest of the troops,

I took cover in a wooded hollow and observed the attack. A well-entrenched line of no less than one hundred rebels redoubled their fire against our front and flank. The enemy aimed well but, thanks to our good use of the terrain, their fire had no effect. The sub-lieutenant's troops began to fire and the fighting spread. Another two horses were hit by stray bullets. As night was falling and we needed to finish the battle, I attacked with the remaining troops on the enemy's right flank, trying to surround them.

The next passage is worth studying closely:

It was in these circumstances, with night already falling, that the enemy (only one hundred meters away) realized they were about to be surrounded and began shouting "Down with Argentina!" and "Long live Chile!" Love for the fatherland suddenly filled the hearts of our soldiers, who, far from home, were outraged by this insult to the nation. They respond, as if ordered, with a cry of "Long live the Fatherland!" that resounded in all their hearts as if it were an omen of victory. I ordered them to fire and advance. When we were within meters of the enemy, getting ready to use our bayonets, Lieutenant Frugoni arrived with the rearguard. The rebels see their defeat and surrendered.

Outcome: Five dead and four wounded on the side of the rebels, seventy-five prisoners taken, twenty-four hostages (landowners, administrators, and foremen) rescued and 250 horses seized, along with many Winchesters, revolvers, and shotguns, ammunition, and all sorts of supplies. Some fifty well-armed men were able to escape on horseback under the cover of darkness and we were unable to find them as the fugitives knew the lay of the land. Many of the wounded must have been among the fugitives. For our part, only four of our horses were wounded. We stayed at the rebel camp that night and captured another fifteen prisoners, some of whom we came across in the mountains while others were detected when they began treacherously shooting at us from their hiding places. We kept watch and took additional prisoners throughout the night. Nothing weighed on the spirit of the troops. After such constant fatigue, they handled a night in that dangerous camp with composure. The government, the Argentine people, and above all the army owe them their eternal gratitude. I must stress that among our prisoners there was only one Argentine and that he was a recidivist from Ushuaia. All the rest were Chileans, including many carabinieri who claimed to be deserters, but I was later able to prove that this claim was false.

Analyzing Captain Viñas Ibarra's report, we can see much that remains unclear and much that contradicts court documents that he will sign at a later date.

According to Viñas Ibarra's calculations, there were 134 strikers (five dead, four wounded, fifty fugitives, and seventy-five who were taken prisoner) confronting forty soldiers. The strikers, organized into infantry lines, took the soldiers by surprise. They were crack sharpshooters and made use of the natural cover provided by the lagoon, a natural obstacle that the soldiers could not cross. Furthermore, the line of infantry was of "no less than one hundred" men who were well-entrenched in strategic positions. Their shooting was excellent. In spite of all this—according to Viñas Ibarra—only two horses were wounded at the beginning of the battle and another two were lost to "stray bullets"—that is, we don't even know if they were killed by the strikers or by friendly fire. Yet the army surrounds the one hundred sharpshooters belching fire, and fighting erupts after the cries of "Down with Argentina!" and "Long live Chile!" We know the outcome. The soldiers emerged without a single scratch, not even in the hand-to-hand combat against these country folk, who are so good at handling knives. And, furthermore, many of the prisoners were Chilean carabinieri. This claim—if it were true, it would have been serious enough to trigger a protest by the Argentine government—is never mentioned again in Viñas

Ibarra's subsequent dispatches, nor in Varela's report to the War Ministry. The same thing occurs with the cheers in favor of Chile and against Argentina. This was evidently a flourish added by Captain Viñas Ibarra. The Workers' Society never had a single good word to say about Chile—to the contrary, their newspaper ridiculed those who believed in the Chilean flag just as much as those who believed in the flag of Argentina.

But the biggest flaw in Viñas Ibarra's report is the section on the weapons seized. He says that at least one hundred sharpshooters attacked his soldiers, but then says that he seized "many Winchesters, revolvers, and shotguns" without ever mentioning a specific number. Now we'll hear from the other side. We have the account of a Chilean farmworker who survived the events at Punta Alta, originally published in *El Trabajo*, the newspaper of the Magallanes Workers' Federation in Punta Arenas, and later reprinted by labor publications in Buenos Aires.

It was November 11th or 12th. In the solitude of Patagonia, you can never be sure what day it is. Some comrades found me working my land (four square leagues) early that morning. They told me about the call for a general strike and asked me to stop work. As I have a heart and I am a man of courage, they didn't have to ask twice. By nightfall we had joined a group of seventy comrades camped out in the foothills, by the banks of a small stream. We were all outraged by the unjust imprisonments and resolved not to go back to work until the prisoners were freed. Over the next few days, we split up into delegations that went from ranch to ranch to invite the few people who were still at work (mostly out of ignorance of what was going on) to join the strike and to round up all the horses we could find. By the fourth day, no one was still working. While waiting for a delegation that was late in returning, we were surprised by a force from the 10th Cavalry composed of thirty conscripts under the command of the hyena Captain Viñas Ibarra and several police officers. Almost all of us were on foot, far from our horses. One of our comrades fired a shot into the air, which was our agreed signal to verify if a group approaching the camp was one of our own. This was enough to claim that we were bandits, justifying all the murders that were committed in the days that followed. The troops hurried their approach and fired on us without saying a word. I don't know how many fell in those moments of terrible confusion. Even though there were more of us and we could have defended ourselves with our revolvers and *boleadoras* (we only had three Winchesters), and we could have resisted in a way that would have justified the barbaric attitude of the troops, we didn't fight because that was never our intention. We had resolved to avoid any confrontations with the army, and to avoid bloodshed because our quarrel wasn't with the soldiers. We wanted to carry out simple actions that would prevent the ranchers from finishing the season's tasks (shearing and branding) so that the scale of their losses would frighten them and we would be able to secure the release of our imprisoned comrades. But we were very mistaken: the ranchers had decreed our total extermination and these orders had to be carried out no matter what. The orders were irreversible and had to be followed, right or wrong. Small wonder, then, that the officers and even their troops, conscripts—workers and the sons of workers!—lost all sense of humanity and were merciless with their fellow man, executing men who surrendered without putting up the least resistance. When they felt that enough of us had fallen, and were convinced that they were safe from all harm, they charged at us with their sabers drawn. I'm incapable of painting a picture of that horrible scene. You would have to use the most macabre hues, but even that would pale in comparison. I can assure you that the troops felt very satisfied with this prologue to their brave work, which was in no way inferior to what would follow. The plan to drown the rebellion and the rights of the workers in blood came straight from Buenos Aires and was paid for by Menéndez Behety, Braun, Montes, and all the other Patagonian landowners with many thousands of pounds sterling, so the governor and

Colonel Varela performed wonderfully. Those who paid for the massacre can't complain.

Those left standing were taken prisoner. The wounded were given the *coup de grace* with either bullets or sabers, depending on the whims of their executioners. I myself had been shot in the right elbow and in the chest. Upon seeing those maddened hyenas at work, I got the happy idea of playing dead, as those panthers in the shape of men were so ferocious that neither clamors nor pleas would move them. I spent the rest of the day in a heap of corpses. When night fell and the camp went quiet, I was able to silently drag myself over to the bushes. There I rested a little and gave some respite to my painful wounds, which had been aggravated by my difficult journey. Finding strength in weakness but seemingly suffering even more, even regretting that I hadn't let them finish me off, I continued dragging myself until I reached lower ground, where I curled up to rest in a little hollow. I don't know if it was from fever or fear, but I was sure that I was being watched on all sides. Terrified, weakened, and nearly lifeless, I continued fleeing to nowhere in particular, seeking the darkest and most isolated resting places. When the light of the new day began to pierce the darkness, the need to find a good hiding place passed through my absent mind. Luckily I found myself at the foot of a stony hill. Eighty meters up, I came across some caves that must have once been, or perhaps still were, mountain lion dens. I settled into one of them and used pieces of my shirt to bandage my broken and enormously swollen elbow as best I could. I used my undershirt, sweater, and vest to bandage the wounds in my chest, where were not as painful. (The man who is looking after me, a charitable comrade who understands these things, fears that my arm may never be the same again. My chest wounds have already healed. We're like dogs that can heal themselves by doing no more than lick their wounds!)

Having taken care of my wounds, I tried to sleep. No luck! For the first time in my life, I regretted having been born in Argentina! The pain from my wounds, the thirst that was devouring me and the vision of the horrible carnage I had witnessed and suffered ensured that my attempts to sleep were in vain. My head was a Dantesque scene, haunted by a thousand dreadful ghosts. And there I lay until the sound of a gunshot woke me from my trance. More and more gunshots followed. I didn't know the reason for the shooting until days later, when I came across two companions in misfortune. They told me of what I had not been able to witness myself on the day of the attack and in the days that followed. I have heard their stories and those of other wretches like us who also managed to save themselves from the massacre elsewhere. Genuine stories, whose truth has even been sworn to under oath as more than a few have been reluctant to believe them, but not I.

Let me pause for a moment to allow a comrade, who had been shot in the leg, to speak. He says that after the strikers were defeated, those few left among the living were lined up and interrogated by Viñas Ibarra, who asked them for the name of their leader. But in reality, they were not actually a regiment of men with a commander, however, but a group of comrades who had gathered in the forest to take shelter from the wind and the cold. As no one answered, Commissioner Douglas stepped forward. Douglas is a celebrated and criminal individual who took part in many massacres of workers, as well as that crime that occurred at the Education Council in Buenos Aires. He accused Pintos of being the ringleader, as the comrade's constant sermons had always interfered with the plans of Douglas, who, like all police, is always on the take. Douglas took advantage of this opportunity.

One insinuation is enough for Viñas Ibarra to say, "Two steps forward...aim...fire..."

Comrade Pintos fell to his knees but didn't die, so Douglas drew his pistol and gave him what they call the coup de grace. Walking a few steps down the line of prisoners, Douglas recognized someone else. This time it was Comrade Lagos. Taken out of the line two steps, Douglas fired two shots, one in the side and the other head on. Our comrade fell, and as his wounds weren't fatal, when he regained consciousness he noticed that the troops had backed away a few meters. The group of conscripts that was closest to him was busy gathering firewood. Understanding that they were planning to burn the corpses, Comrade Lagos waited until they had gone off in search of more firewood and then dragged himself out from among the dead and was able to make it to the forest. Thanks to his quick thinking, he is happily among us once again, although his condition remains quite serious. Other comrades who also hid in the forest told me that, a moment later, a truck arrived carrying picks and shovels. The few comrades who were left, those who weren't killed but were instead only tortured, were forced to dig a mass grave for the thirty-six victims. As night was already falling, the truck returned to Río Gallegos to take our comrades to prison, leaving forty conscripts at the site to finish the task.

Here ends the account of the peon whose name has been omitted to keep him from being identified by the police on either side of the cordillera. It's clear that these two accounts cannot be reconciled, although the peon's version includes the names of two victims whom we have been able to confirm. It's also true that the strikers shot into the air to identify themselves when approaching the camp. It's possible that these shots were the ones heard by Viñas Ibarra before he began his indiscriminate attack. The lack of victims among the soldiers, although they were fewer in number and could have been easily surrounded by a force three times larger, makes the peon's account more believable. The same thing can be said about Viñas Ibarra's failure to cite the number of weapons seized by the army, while the peon mentions an exact number: three Winchesters.

But let's continue hearing the evidence. Captain Viñas Ibarra's reports to the War Ministry will be blatantly contradicted by his later statements before the court in Río Gallegos.

All of the dispatches written by Varela and his officers are characterized by their ambiguity: the number of enemy "combatants" never coincides with the sum of the prisoners and the dead.

Remember that Viñas Ibarra says that he was attacked by one hundred sharpshooters, that he took seventy-five prisoners, that another fifty escaped, and that there were five dead and four wounded, which makes a total of 134 men. He will turn over only thirty-five prisoners to the authorities in Río Gallegos, although he says that some of them were released after agreeing to return to work. But according to a message sent by Varela to interim governor Céfaly Pandolfi, these thirty-five men also included prisoners taken at Laguna Salada, where Viñas Ibarra began his operations. And with these disparities in the numbers, we can't be sure what happened to many of the prisoners. As we have seen, Viñas Ibarra's report to the War Ministry states that "among our prisoners there was only one Argentine and that he was a recidivist from Ushuaia. All the rest were Chileans, including many carabinieri who claimed to be deserters, but I was later able to prove that this claim was false." This flagrantly contradicts the list of prisoners sent to Río Gallegos, which states that, of the total thirty-five, two were Argentines, twenty-seven Chileans, one was French, there was one Uruguayan, one Russian, one Austrian, two Spaniards, and one Italian. The list also includes the ranches on which they worked as peons, or lists them as "itinerant" if they were shearers. In this list of prisoners taken at Punta Alta and Laguna Salada, there are no "carabinieri" or "deserted carabinieri." (What this list also makes clear is that thirty-three of the thirty-five prisoners were single and only two were married, a result of the ranchers' demand that peons be unmarried and childless, which undoubtedly contributed to the depopulation of Argentine Patagonia.)

Let's hear some other accounts of the "Battle" of Punta Alta before moving on. Sub-lieutenant Jonas writes in his memoirs that thirty strikers were shot, their wrists bound with wire beforehand.

In Puerto Natales, we had the opportunity to speak with Virginio González, a seventy-two-year-old shearer who told us that he was at Punta Alta in November 1921. His name even appears on the list of prisoners signed by Lieutenant Colonel Varela: "Virginio González, Chilean, twenty-two-years-old, single, itinerant."

The elderly Virginio González told us that he belonged to the group nominally led by the Argentine Pinto, but whose true driving force was a German named Otto who could barely speak Spanish. He had fought in the First World War and had been in Argentina for just one year. Otto, two or three Spaniards, and one Russian were the only ones who were familiar with social issues and could explain anarchism to the Chileans. Virginio González told us that they knew the troops were on their way because two comrades had come to warn them; that Pintos was the only leader at the camp because Otto and the others had gone off to organize other ranches; that Pintos told everyone to stay calm because it was the army that was approaching and not the police. Many sat down and others left camp to receive the troops. One of them fired a shot into the air as a greeting, as was customary in Patagonia in those days. The troops immediately scattered and opened fire on the welcoming party, as well as anything else that moved.

They started shooting like lunatics. We realized that they were scared and that they weren't going to stop until they had wasted all their bullets or until they realized that we were defenseless; the few Winchesters we had were in the hands of the delegation we had sent out to organize the nearby ranches. The only one who had a Mauser was the German, Otto, who had been given it because he had served in the war. The army's attack claimed many victims. We lay on the ground until the sergeants and Captain Viñas shouted at us to surrender with our hands up. Then they took us to a corral. When we got up, we saw many of our comrades lying on the ground, probably dead or wounded. They grabbed us one by one, beating us with the flats of their sabers as they herded us into the corral on horseback, as if we were livestock. Then they made us line up and shout out our name and nationality. All of us Chileans were taken aside. When they got to Pinto, Commissioner Douglas shouted, "This one's the ringleader, my captain!" They took him away. We had no idea what happened to him. Later, in jail, I heard that Commissioner Douglas had him shot. They took us all to the Fuentes de Coyle ranch and held us in another corral. One by one they put us in the livestock crush, which was surrounded by soldiers and policemen who beat us with the flats of their sabers. But one Russian worker by the name of Simón[9] suffered a fate even worse than that of the Chileans. *He was forced into the livestock crush three or four times and the last time he had to crawl on all fours. He was beaten terribly, which made the soldiers shriek with delight.*

Virginio González's account coincides on almost all points with what we heard from Commissioner Isidro Guadarrama, whose testimony we consider to be quite valuable for its dependable information. Though he's a man who defends and completely justifies the army's intervention, he nevertheless bears witness to every detail of the campaign. He says that the survivors of the events at Punta Alta were given an exemplary lesson. He describes the use of the livestock crush, with the soldiers climbing up the bars of the machine to enthusiastically beat the chilotes. "More than one chilote lost an ear," he says. "You should have seen how meek they got after a good thrashing."

Commissioner Guadarrama's account also coincides with that of the shearer Virginio González in terms of how the prisoners were treated in the Río Gallegos jail. When they arrived, the chilotes were beaten every night, without exception, by the peerless prison guards of Río Gallegos. González says that they were beaten with lead-filled nightsticks—that is, the same ones then being used by the prison guards in Ushuaia.

On November 19th, 1921, *La Unión* of Río Gallego runs a story by their correspondent in Punta Arenas stating that one hundred strikers were killed at Punta Alta, a number that they will later reduce to ten. *La Unión* of Punta Arenas, also under the influence of the Menéndez interests, reports that "five strikers were killed, two were wounded and 140 were wounded following the clash at Punta Alta."

As to the identification of the bodies, Commissioner Samuel Douglas Price (who has been accused of the murder of Pintos) states in his report that it was impossible to identify them because the troops feared another attack from the strikers. According to this report, the incident occurred at a place known as Corrales Viejos de Punta Alta. Douglas mentions five dead, ten wounded and thirty-eight prisoners, contradicting the reports made by Viñas Ibarra and Varela, which mention thirty-five prisoners. Douglas says that thirty of them were Chileans, while the list of prisoners drafted by the officers mentions twenty-seven. Which means that we have three missing Chileans. But as will be very clear before this all comes to an end, three chilotes here or there don't really matter. Besides, Viñas Ibarra's report is also untrustworthy: it mentions forty-five prisoners captured at Punta Alta, while only thirty-five make it to Río Gallegos. In his report to the War Ministry, he says, word for word, "Day 20: forty-five prisoners captured following the battle at Punta Alta are taken to Río Gallegos." So Viñas Ibarra must have lost ten Chileans along the way.

La Unión of Punta Alta reports that, among the dead at Punta Alta:

> The body of Juan Nasif has been duly identified and brought to Río Gallegos, but it has not been possible to identify the four remaining bodies as the authorities responsible for this task noted the presence of isolated groups of strikers nearby and had to stop work out of fear of being captured.[10]

But the piece of evidence that will perhaps shed the most light on the events at Punta Alta—as its details coincide with those given in previous accounts—is a letter published in *El Trabajo* of Punta Arenas on December 20th, 1921, when the massacre at the La Anita ranch had already occurred. Thanks to this letter, we have been able to learn the names of some of the other workers killed by Viñas Ibarra's troops:

The army caught us by surprise at 5 p.m. on the 14th and we kept silent because we figured that we would be questioned but we were shot at instead, which caused panic in our ranks. Seeing ourselves being attacked so savagely, Comrade Saldivia waved a flag to signal that we weren't trying to resist and to see if we could get them to stop shooting so there wouldn't be so many victims. But it was all in vain because the "brave soldiers" aimed the barrels of their guns at Comrade Saldivia who then fell lifeless to the ground. When those brave men saw that the workers continued their primitive attitude of patiently waiting for death with their arms crossed, they approached, made us kneel in the muddy ground, and then searched us and took everything we had, threatening to shoot anyone who protested on the spot.

After taking all of our money and valuables, they made us burn all our papers, even our military service cards. We had no choice if we wanted to live. Once they finished robbing us, not even leaving us our handkerchiefs, they began interrogating us while shouting that we were murderers, along with any other insult that came to their minds, asking us for the name of the criminal mastermind of the movement, when in reality the only criminal masterminds were the soldiers who were murdering peaceful and innocent workers. Then they took some of us aside to answer their questions, like that comrade who said that he didn't know anything because he had only been there one day and that was enough for the bloodthirsty Douglas to put a bullet in his head, killing him instantly. After this crime, he kept demanding that we tell him if Pinto was present and since nobody answered he approached us and recognized Pinto, who had the same luck as the other comrade, with the difference that, after killing him, Douglas ranted at us, as if possessed, "This was the ringleader who incited you to do these things!" Then he made Comrade Benjamín Borquez step forward in front of all seventy of us who had been detained there and forced him at gunpoint to burn everything he was carrying except for a check, which the commissioner took. In all, the comrades murdered at Punta Alta were Félix E. Pinto, Juan Álvarez, Oscar Mancilla, Miguel Saldivia, and several others that I don't remember because there were thirty of us who went missing.

The allegation that soldiers stole the peons' belongings will be repeated throughout all regions of the territory where executions occurred and will be corroborated by the public statements of Sub-lieutenant Jonas. The most highly prized items were the quillangos that the peons used to cover themselves when sleeping out in the open. A very poor enemy, a miserable little war.

In the end, how many people died at Punta Alta? Were there thirty-seven casualties, as the FORA's publications say? Five, as Viñas Ibarra says? Thirty, as stated by Sub-lieutenant Jonas? Thirty, as reported by *El Trabajo* of Punta Arenas? Five at Punta Alta and ten at Fuentes de Coyle, as reported by the Chilean government? Our investigation has only been able to uncover the names of six dead workers: Félix E. Pinto, Juan Álvarez, Oscar Manuel Mancilla, Miguel Saldivia, Juan Nasif, and Julio Nicasio Freyer (this last name was provided by *La Unión* of Punta Arenas, which reported that he was one of those wounded at Punta Alta and that he managed to cross the border before dying of his wounds in Punta Arenas).

Six names, not many and far too few for such an anonymous mass. In the executions to come we will have even less luck.

But we still have yet to hear the most pathetic account of the events at Laguna Salada and Punta Alta. It was written by one of Varela's soldiers. This account is something of a synthesis of the two perspectives: it contains the official story that the workers shot first, but then goes on to mention facts ignored in Varela's official report. It's a naïve account, lacking in rhetorical flourishes, but it exposes the army's cruelty and moral vacuum.

We owe this valuable testimony to the tireless efforts of the Permanent History Center in the town of Adolfo González Chávez. For now, we have reproduced the section of the text that covers the Laguna Salada and Punta Alta incidents and we will return to it later as we follow events in chronological order:

Don Ramón Octavio Vallejos, born in the city of Necochea on November 2nd, 1900, is a long time resident of Adolfo González Chávez, having arrived there with his father in 1909. He warmly shook our hands; his own are the calloused hands of a man used to working the land. He has dark skin and his black hair is covered by a broad-brimmed brown hat. He has an aquiline nose and thin lips. He stares at us with his penetrating eyes but barely participates in the conversation. But his expression is frank and he enjoys the chat. A spry, elderly *criollo*, he wears a brown jacket, gray trousers, an olive green shirt and a black bow tie. Asked about his part in the events that came to be known as the Patagonia Tragedy, he tells us:

"I did my military service in the 10th Cavalry Regiment, 3rd Squadron and was stationed at Campo de Mayo in 1921.[11] I remember the socio-political climate that year, when the country was rattled by strikes and there wasn't a day that passed without talk of a mobilization. Most of us had already been discharged when November came. Already back in civilian clothes and celebrating the end of our military service, an order was suddenly issued for us to once again take up arms. There was a lot of discontent, but we hid it from our superiors. The 3rd and 1st Squadrons embarked from Buenos Aires on November 2nd, which was even worse because it was my birthday. We took all of our equipment, weapons, and tools with us on the Guardia Nacional, everything except our horses, which were given to us by rich ranchers in Río Gallegos. Our superior officers were Héctor Benigno Varela; Captains Campos, Barras, and Viñas; and Sub-lieutenant Frugoni Miranda. The non-commissioned officers who directly commanded my squadron were Corporals Sosa and Esperín (sic).[12] Our voyage lasted seven days and we arrived in Río Gallegos late at night on November 9th. They gave us leave on the second night and almost all of us went to a brothel, where we got into a huge fight with the police, but since it was dishonorable for soldiers to be put under arrest, we agreed to go to the peons' quarters that we were using for a barracks, report ourselves to the sergeant, and turn over our insignia.

The brothel's girls, who were on good terms with the strikers, filled us in on the situation, as our superiors had told us little or nothing about why we had been deployed there. We also learned from them that almost all of the ranches belonged to English companies and that it was these landowners who had asked the troops to come, as they were opposed to the settlement negotiated by our superior officer, Héctor Benigno Varela, on an earlier expedition.

A few days later they took us to a ranch, whose name I don't remember, to supply us with horses. There our superior officers gave us a speech, hammering the idea into us that the striking workers were bandits who had been looting ranches and that we must treat them like common criminals, giving them no quarter. We had our first skirmish by the roadside as we were climbing a low hill. The workers took us by surprise, firing at us with short-range weapons from the high ground. We immediately returned fire, but as we were at the foot of a rocky slope, it was difficult for us to aim properly. They promptly surrendered, so the engagement only lasted a few minutes. We took them to a ranch with their hands up. The landowner gave our commanding officer a list of workers suspected of being strike leaders; I know that there were executions that night because we heard many gunshots, but none of us had any part in it. It's possible that it was our officers who carried out the executions. I also don't know the names of the executed workers.

We left the ranch the following day. I think it was still November, it's hard to remember the exact date after so much time. After riding for several leagues, we came across a wooden corral that was being occupied by the workers, who welcomed us with a hail of bullets. Aware of the limited range of the weapons used by the strikers, our superiors ordered us to retreat a few meters before returning fire. They immediately began to feel the effects of the higher quality and longer range of our weapons and a white flag appeared in the corral. We took them all prisoners, some two hundred workers in all. The order was to shoot anyone who moved.

We took them to a ranch owned by an Englishman. It felt more like a cattle drive. They moaned in unison from our beatings and whippings. The riding crops we used had three metal rings. At the ranch, the Englishman gave our superiors a list of the most dangerous strikers and they were taken aside. We put them in the stocks, which I believe were already at the ranch because we didn't bring them with us or make them ourselves. I can't say for certain what happened to those unhappy men, but I'm sure that many were executed on the spot. I don't recall them being tried before being shot, because the executions generally occurred immediately after the strikers were taken prisoner.

In the course of my research, I visited the Punta Alta ranch in December 1972. The ranch's director, Ernesto van Peborg, told me himself that he had read my previous publications on these events and was interested to know that his very ranch was where the first "battle" had taken place between the strikers and the soldiers commanded by Captain Viñas Ibarra. As the latter's dispatches are very detailed, we were able to locate the exact spot of the mass grave with the help of the ranch administrator, Man, aerial mapping, and the contemporary documents we had brought with us. The remains of Pintos and his comrades were found buried near Punta del Monte, a location where there used to be a wooden corral and exactly where Commissioner Guadarrama, director of the province's land registry had indicated on a hand-drawn map. This location, on the road to Turbio, was difficult to access and required the use of an all-terrain vehicle.

We also spoke with three valuable witnesses to the executions at Punta Alta and the events involving the strike column led by Pintos.

The first was Ángel Vargas (Chilean, born in Valparaíso in 1905, currently working as a truck driver in Río Gallegos). He was present during the "Battle" of Punta Alta and appears on the list signed by H.B. Varela of the strikers handed over to the authorities in Río Gallegos on November 21st, 1921, where he is listed as Prisoner #15: "Ángel Vargas, Chilean, sixteen years old, single, itinerant."

We met with Vargas in December 1972 in his home on Calle Santiago del Estero in Río Gallegos. He welcomed us in but warns us that, despite the passing years, he still doesn't want to discuss some of the things he had witnessed because he's Chilean and because there were still many people alive who were implicated in what he called "the tremendous crime that was the repression of the second rural strike." He only wanted to talk about his personal experiences and stick to the facts, without commentary.

Ángel Vargas arrived at the Esperanza Douglas ranch (now named Sofia) in November 1921, accompanied by an eighteen-year-old Yugoslav named Antonio Peric Zlatar. The next morning, Antonio Soto and a group of strikers came to the ranch and called all of the peons to the canteen. Nearly sixty men from the ranch and surrounding areas showed up. Then Soto spoke, informing them that many of their leaders had been taken prisoner: Sambucetti, Mongilnitzky, and Severino Fernández had been captured at the Buitreras bridge and Graña, Oyola, and Restituto Álvarez at Las Horquetas. Soto added that El Toscano, Ulacia, and a few others were imprisoned in Río Gallegos and that a general strike had been called to secure their release. The slogan was "Freedom or Strike." He then gave organizing instructions, "form groups, gather together everyone from the ranches, and take the horses with you." Vargas continued:

> I remember one thing that Soto said, and which I still don't agree with today. He said that we should go on strike voluntarily, but that if we didn't, the ranch delegates would force us to comply. He also said that if we needed food or clothing during the strike,

we could appropriate them from the ranch storehouses and the Workers' Society would back us.

Vargas paused for a moment and then explained:

In my eyes, it was wrong to take things that weren't ours. Soto—who was a tall young man who spoke well—also told us to take hostages from among the administrators, foremen, accountants, and landowners we came across. If there were any women, we had to leave one or two peons behind to chop firewood for them and ensure they had meat. Comrade Pintos led our column. He assigned teams to tour the ranches and stir up the people. As I had just recently arrived from Chile, I didn't understand anything that had to do with the strike but I joined the column because I had no other option. I later regretted having not slipped away. Pintos headed off towards Punta Alta, near what is now Río Turbio. Along the way, we came across some Turks in the pampas who were selling things from out of their carts. There were two of them; one was named Emilio Amado. They both had beards. Our delegate, Ramón Lagos, forced them to unhitch their horses and follow us. One of them was later killed by the army. And so we reached Punta Alta, setting up camp at the place known as Corrales Viejos. This was the base of operations for the commissions that went out to organize the nearby ranches. We were cooking over the campfire one morning when we heard the alarm: "The carabinieri are coming!" This was confusing, because it was actually the Argentine Army. The soldiers approached on foot over open ground, about thirty or forty meters apart. They began shooting at us and we only had four Winchesters to defend ourselves. I remember running towards the woods and seeing tree branches being torn apart by their bullets. I saved myself by making terrific leaps. One bullet grazed my boots, leaving a mark on my foot. We surrendered with our hands up and they took us to the corral. Then they brought in the others. I saw Commissioner Douglas, who had a revolver and a sword. The two Turks were hiding in the woods and it was Douglas who found them, shouting, "Sons of bandits!" He killed one of them on the spot.[13] The other Turk screamed and started pleading for his life. Douglas shot him and broke his clavicle, but as he wouldn't stop begging to be spared, the officer recognized him as a Turkish merchant from Río Gallegos and asked him, "What are you doing here? Who brought you?"

The Turk pointed straight at Lagos.

Commissioner Douglas then shot Lagos without blinking. Lagos fell to the ground, shouting, "Oh, my mother!" He lay there motionless. But the bullet had only grazed his thick skull.

In the meantime, one of the officers ordered his men to gather firewood to burn the corpses. As Lagos was beginning to stir, Commissioner Douglas shot him again but again failed to injure him. (From what Lagos later told me, the bullet was stopped by the silk handkerchief he wore around his neck and didn't even reach his shirt.) Douglas made him stand up and told him, "I'll take care of you in a minute." But he didn't fire any more shots.

They took away all of our documents and burned them and cut off our hair. We had to remain on our feet, without moving. We were being watched; if we moved, we would be shot by the sentinels. We stayed that way all night. We remained terrified until they brought us to Fuentes de Coyle.

They lined us up outside the shearing shed. This is when the dance began. We had to tell our name, nationality, and the ranch we worked on to a scribe they had brought with them, a civilian. When we finished, the civilian told us to step inside. There were two rows of soldiers, White Guards and police officers, armed with sabers, whips, and riding crops. We had to walk between them and enter the livestock crush. I watched how they beat the man in front of me, an elderly man who collapsed from the beating, which only encouraged them to redouble their efforts. I tried to get in front of the old man, but a soldier drew his saber and slashed at my face. I'll never forget it. I was able to block the blow with my forearm because I was carrying my bindle over my shoulder, but I couldn't stop another soldier from hitting my face hard with the flat of his saber. The blow was so hard that my skin peeled off three days later. I came away half blind from pain and rage. Then they kept us lined up for fifty hours without eating or drinking. This was when they began to take certain people aside and some very strange things happened that I don't want to talk about so I won't compromise myself.

We asked him what happened to Pintos. He told us:

They shot him in the corral in Punta Alta. First they questioned a Chilean named Oscar Mansilla, who acted properly and said that he didn't know him. Then they shot him in the back. They let him suffer until Mansilla himself asked to be put out of his misery. Commissioner Douglas recognized Pintos and then he was shot. He managed to say, "I am Ar..." From the little I knew of him, he seemed to be a good man. Of the approximately one hundred men who were at Punta Alta, about thirty of us were taken back to Río Gallegos.

(Varela's list of the prisoners taken at Punta Alta lists thirty-five names.)

Before finishing, he told us of Julio Freyer, who was wounded at Punta Alta and managed to escape to Puerto Natales and then to Punta Arenas, where he died from the gangrene that had infected his wounds. He said that Freyer was a very cheerful person and that at Punta Alta he worked as a valet to the deputy administrator of the Esperanza Douglas ranch, an Englishman. When the army attacked, Freyer was shaving and the Englishman was holding the mirror and towel for him.

The second witness to the Punta Alta incident we interviewed was Antonio Peric Zlatar, a Yugoslav born in 1903 who now lives in Puerto Santa Cruz, where he works as a shearing contractor. We met with him on the Carmen ranch. When Soto arrived, Peric was eighteen years old and working on the Esperanza Douglas ranch with Ángel Vargas. He repeated Soto's instructions, which we have already transcribed above, stressing the part about how "the strikers could take things from the ranch storehouses as long as they really needed them." But he said that Pintos opposed the requisition of goods from the ranches, that he was an honest man. He drew us a map of Punta Alta: an elevated wooden corral for branding livestock with a stand of oaks off to one side and a large meadow in front. He said that they didn't have any long-range weapons, that there were only four Winchesters in the entire camp. He said that when the soldiers advanced, it was a young boy named Vargas, only sixteen years old, who shot into the air to sound the alarm, that at first the soldiers were flying a white flag but then they started shooting. Peric managed to hide among the oaks when he heard the shooting start and there he stayed until the soldiers marched off with their prisoners. There he came across Freyer, who had a wounded leg. He helped him across the border at Morro Chico at two in the morning because the carabinieri were on alert and were handing over fugitives to the army. The wound on Freyer's right knee was quite serious. Peric left him in Puerto Natales before continuing on to Punta Arenas, where he remained in hiding for some time.

He told us that he later had the chance to speak with Ravena, an elderly, one-eyed man who had been with them at Punta Alta. Ravena told him that nine bodies were dumped into the well and that he was forced to cover them with branches. Of the dead, Peric knew a Chilean shepherd from the Marckach Aike ranch, a Russian who was completely innocent, a peon from the La Uruguaya ranch, Pintos and the Turk Nasif, whom Douglas killed after finding him in a rotting tree trunk. Lagos was shot twice but didn't die, though he was left with a scar across his scalp.

The third witness we interviewed from Pintos's column was a Spaniard named Eulogio Alonso, now seventy-five years old and the current owner of the Alonso and Covadonga hotels in Río Gallegos. Mr. Alonso told us:

I joined Félix Pintos's column because that was what the Workers' Federation told me to do when the conflict started. At the time, I was working on Ibón Noya's Paso del Medio ranch at the time. We left Río Gallegos, spreading word of the strike ranch by ranch. There were no attacks on people or property, that I can assure you. Whenever we took something from the ranch storehouses, we always left behind a signed receipt. We set up camp at Punta Alta, a place where there was a wooden corral for branding, very close to the Punta del Monte ranch. There was also a sort of little ranch near the corral. There were two Turks in our group: Nasif, from Río Gallegos, and Amado, from Lago Argentino. The former was later murdered by the soldiers. Our column was heading to the La Anita ranch, where we were going to join up with the other groups organized by Antonio Soto.

I was miraculously able to save my life, purely by luck. That day, I had gone to search the Punta del Monte ranch for supplies with the German, Otto, and a few other people. We arrived at the ranch close to nightfall and were about to head back when we saw a peon who had been at the camp. His first name was Bautista and, if I remember correctly, his last name was García. He was on the run and told us that the camp had been attacked by either the police or the army and that several people had been killed. They had approached from the direction of Fuentes del Coyle and encircled the striking peons. A few saved themselves by fleeing towards Chile. So we decided to split up. I thought the most intelligent thing to do was to head towards Río Gallegos to find out what was really going on. I set off on horseback and managed to enter the city, hiding at the house of a friend of mine named Valeriano Fernández. I knew they were looking for me because I was part of the delegations that had gone out to spread word of the strike. But the persecution diminished as time went by, especially after the defeat of the strike. Thanks to the intervention of the hotel owner Genaro Lafuente and the shearing contractor Nicolich, I was able to get my hands on a safe conduct pass and start working again.

Of the original group at the Punta Alta camp, five people died in the shootout and I think they executed between sixteen and eighteen.

Varela didn't fail to properly choose his methods to strangle the strike as quickly as possible: the bullet, the whip, the saber, the stocks. And he cleaned up Patagonia once and for all.

Patagonia's peons will be the ones to pay the price for everything: the crisis, Yrigoyen's internal difficulties in Buenos Aires, the slump in the wool market, and Correa Falcón's conflict with Judge Viñas and José María Borrero in Río Gallegos. Neither Viñas nor Borrero show their faces in the moment of danger. The former will be conversing with his colleagues in Buenos Aires, while the latter, having given up publishing, will be preparing to buy a ranch near Puerto Deseado. Correa Falcón, meanwhile, will become the architect of victory, working behind the scenes to manipulate the spectacle that will be seen from Buenos Aires: arsons, rapes, thefts, foreign anarchists spreading devastation throughout Patagonia. The Argentine Army, meanwhile, advances under the command of Commander Varela, mounted criollos riding criollo horses and searching for the foreign usurper, the red, the vermin who wants to turn our sacred fatherland into an "immense wasteland" (as Manuel Carlés says, and as General Anaya will repeat years later).

Varela, meanwhile, decides to head back to Río Gallegos instead of making contact with Viñas Ibarra at Fuentes de Coyle:

Day 18—Río Gallegos. Given the current situation and the news that the subversive movement was spreading north, I decided to issue the following proclamation, which was distributed throughout the territory:

PROCLAMATION: ARGENTINE REPUBLIC—
GOVERNMENT OF SANTA CRUZ

To the landowners and ranch administrators: In order to foster a return to calm in the countryside and to make it possible for work to resume on the ranches, the undersigned believes that it is his duty to indicate that it would be best for everyone to return to their post and try to resume work with whatever resources they currently have available. Everyone must do their part to defend their interests, whether by repelling any attacks directed against them or by using whatever resources they have at their disposal to normalize a return to work. Everyone must henceforth make it clear to their workers that any individual who takes part in a subversive movement, whether as an instigator or as a supporter, as well as any individual who is currently armed or who has used their weapons against their fellows, will be punished to the fullest extent of the law.

Ranches will be protected by federal forces and any attacks on them will be considered an attack on the federal government. It is particularly recommended to discover the political affiliations of any persons traveling near one's ranch and to verify the reasons for their journey, examining the personal effects they are carrying with them. Landowners and ranch administrators can efficiently contribute to eliminating vagrancy by strictly forbidding so-called migrants from staying on their property for longer than twenty-four hours, except under special circumstances such as illness or any other situation that would logically imply a longer stay. Once this period has expired, the migrants can be required to help out with work on the ranch.

Ranchers must submit a list of their employees by December 15th, as well as on the first of every month following that date, indicating any changes and detailing their wages and the benefits they have been granted.

It is strictly prohibited to come to an understanding with labor organizations, which are from here on out officially banned. Their representatives and members must not be allowed to visit ranches or any of their dependencies, nor will they be allowed to issue manifestos, communiqués or any other sort of propaganda.

All workers on each ranch must be registered with the police and carry a safe conduct pass indicating their background and political affiliations. These safe conduct passes will be an indispensable requirement for being hired and without them they must be turned away from each ranch. When presented with these documents, landowners and ranch administrators must use them to note the date on which the worker in question is hired, as well as his wages. They must also note the date on which the worker in question leaves the ranch, the duration of his employment, the form in which he was paid and his reason for leaving.

Aside from the present provisions, all of the territory's ranchers are morally obligated to provide the police with any relevant information, which is both in their interests as well as those of society as a whole, as well as being a sincerely patriotic act and a gesture in support of public order, respect for national sovereignty, and the country's general progress.

Río Gallegos, November 22, 1921. Héctor B. Varela, Lieutenant Colonel, Commander of the 10th Cavalry Regiment.

This proclamation clearly shows that the Argentine Army took the side of the ranchers and declared the workers to be their enemies: in plain terms, it decrees the dissolution of Patagonia's unions. The army hasn't come to pacify but to destroy the strikers, outlawing labor organizations but not the Rural Society. Varela shows no interest in who is right or why a strike has broken out, he doesn't ask if the bosses implemented the terms of the agreement that he himself had negotiated during his first expedition. He gives unlimited power to the bosses, granting them the right to run migrant workers off their land after twenty-four hours.

There's no question that this proclamation erases all the rights won by the workers over years of struggle, leaving them at the mercy of their bosses and the police, even requiring them to register themselves. Varela couldn't have been unaware—he himself has said as much in writing—that the police were immoral, that they lived from bribes and that, of course, they were the uniformed agents of the region's landowners.

What right does Varela have to impose laws? Who gives him the power to make this proclamation, if neither Congress nor the president has declared a state of emergency in Santa Cruz?

We do not believe that Varela would take these measures on his own; he has evidently received instructions to such effect. At no time does Yrigoyen dispute these measures, much less the extrajudicial executions to come.

In the meantime, Outerelo and his men have begun a major operation: the occupation of Paso Ibáñez—now known as Comandante Piedra Buena—a town near Puerto Santa Cruz inhabited by only eight hundred people.

On November 16th, around four hundred strikers ride into Paso Ibáñez.

They bring their hostages with them—ranchers, administrators, and even the director of the Armour meatpacking plant—and hold them in the town's movie theater.

This terrifies nearby Puerto Santa Cruz, where the cruiser *Almirante Brown* watches over the aforementioned meatpacking plant. The men of the White Guard—under the command of a lawyer and notary named Sicardi, a police commissioner named Sotuyo, and the navy men—immediately prepare for action. They advance on Paso Ibáñez along the south bank of the Río Santa Cruz, observing the strikers' movements by telescope. Outerelo decides to resist. He places bales of wool at the entrance to the town and all along the main street and the riverbank. As the sailors open fire, Outerelo orders the captured policemen and the most exploitative ranchers to be lined up in front of the bales.

This stops the attack. Outerelo seizes the opportunity to send a delegation of workers, along with two hostages, to negotiate a satisfactory settlement in Puerto Santa Cruz.

They raise the white flag. They only ask for the prisoners to be released, for the deportees to be returned, for the "free laborers" to be sent back to Buenos Aires, and for their demands to be recognized. But the commanding officer of the *Almirante Brown* washes his hands of the matter and says that he doesn't have the power to negotiate. He suggests that the strikers cross the river and surrender, but Outerelo doesn't want to give himself up so easily, although he lacks the weapons and ammunition that would be required to resist an armed attack. Even *La Unión* is optimistic, stating that the strikers have no weapons.

The navy resumes fire on the strikers at Paso Ibáñez. One hostage is killed. His death is attributed to Outerelo's men, of course, but a wrongful death suit will later be filed against the Navy by the wife of the deceased—a ranch administrator—and the truth will come out. In Claim No. 429, submitted to the Interior Ministry on January 10th, 1922, Angelina Crocce de Molina demands compensation for the death of her husband Pablo Molina, "killed by sailors from the *Almirante Brown* during the skirmish at Paso Ibáñez on November 21st, 1921." Statements made by the landowners held hostage prove that Molina died from "wounds caused by Mauser bullets fired by the naval troops." This testimony is interesting: among other things, the landowners say that the wounded man received immediate medical care from Outerelo's right-hand man, the Chilean José Escoubiéres. And that, throughout the occupation of Paso Ibáñez, the strikers "were not drunk but sober."

From Río Gallegos, Varela exchanges messages with the commander of the *Almirante Brown*, who asks him to travel to Puerto Santa Cruz and direct the operations himself. Varela will arrive on November 23rd. In the meantime, Commissioner Sotuyo hunts down everyone in Puerto Santa Cruz who is not a sworn partisan of the bosses. He claims to have uncovered a conspiracy, thereby giving him the right to imprison, bribe, and murder with impunity. *La Unión* describes this conspiracy in chilling detail:

> A Russian secret society with anarchist leanings has been uncovered in our town. The police have seized a copy of their statutes, along with a large quantity of revolutionary manifestos and gunpowder, sulfur, and other items. Their manifestos are incitations to violence and destruction. This group arrived last year at the

time of the last strike, attracted by the Armour meatpacking plant. As of today, the Puerto Santa Cruz Patriotic League has been officially constituted,[14] filling the town with enthusiasm. Business leaders, their employees, and all of the town's healthy elements stand ready to help the police and organize themselves to defend the town from any possible bandit attack, as well as to handle the transportation of the troops and other urgently needed services. Subcommissioner Sotuyo will work energetically to ensure peace and order.

Had Outerelo used those three days to occupy Puerto Santa Cruz, he would have had no difficulty in doing so given the numbers at his command. But he had neither firearms nor ammunition, only some low caliber revolvers and a few Winchesters.

When Varela arrives at Paso Ibáñez, a delegation of strikers and hostages ask to meet with him and negotiate a settlement.

And Varela, as brave as always, agrees. Colonel Schweizer, then a Lieutenant First Class and Varela's adjutant, has given us an account of this episode. When Varela learns of the peons' desire to negotiate, he heads out to Paso Ibáñez himself, accompanied only by Lieutenant Schweizer and Mr. Hirsch, the managing inspector of La Anónima, there to represent commercial and ranching interests. They are welcomed by Outerelo, Avendaño, García, and a fourth man known only as the North American. Varela rides into the lion's den; as he passes through, the rebel peons stare at him, enraged. They show off their weapons (knives stuck in their belts, the odd rifle) and line up their hostages—all of them men—in front of the bales of wool to show the officer what he would be risking if shots are fired. The workers take Varela and his two companions to a corrugated metal shed. This is the moment of truth for Varela. One of the union leaders—Avendaño—is wearing a hat. Varela tells him curtly, "Don't you know that one does not address an officer with one's hat on?" It produces the desired effect. Avendaño mumbles an apology and removes his hat. This is enough for Varela to see that these men don't want war but are instead desperate for a settlement. They begin to talk: the workers offer to end the strike and release their hostages if the following conditions are met:

- The return of all those deported and freedom for all those imprisoned in connection with the social conflicts along the Patagonian coast since October 25th.
- The departure of the so-called free laborers from the Patagonian coast, along with any other strikebreakers, who are to be returned to their point of origin.
- The acknowledgment, without discussion, of the note addressed to the business community by the Puerto Santa Cruz Workers' Federation in July.
- The acceptance by the landowners of the list of demands that has already been presented to them.
- An agreement not to engage in reprisals against the workers who have participated in the current strike.

Five points to discuss. Outerelo knows that, in negotiations, you have to make five demands to obtain half as many concessions.

Varela's only response is unconditional surrender. He's only a few meters away from half a thousand rebels, yet Varela, with an expression that exaggerates his contempt for these indecisive leaders, repeats his demand: unconditional surrender. And then he shows them a proclamation of death: execution by firing squad.

Outerelo, Avendaño, García, and the North American withdraw, with the proclamation of death in hand, to talk with their people. Then Varela suggests to Schweizer and Hirsch that they launch a surprise attack on the spot. He is carrying a hidden revolver and could eliminate the leaders once they reappear. With the ringleaders gone, the chilotes would immediately surrender and the hostages could be rescued, avoiding any possible casualties among the troops, as well as the destruction of the town. He has balls, that Varela.

The young Lieutenant Schweizer replies that if so ordered, he will obey. But Hirsch begs Varela to reconsider, telling him that he has a family waiting for him in Puerto Santa Cruz and that the chilotes would tear them to pieces. Afraid, he begs Varela again and again not to do it. Varela turns to Schweizer and says, with total contempt, "See, First Lieutenant, you can't do these things with civilians present."

For his part, Avendaño wants a settlement, no matter the price. Outerelo thinks of his comrades elsewhere who are also on strike and insists on pushing forward, without being frightened by the proclamation. The leaders reach an agreement: they will hold an assembly that night and accept the will of the majority. They immediately release the hostages to placate Varela.

Varela stands firm and tells them, "If you don't unconditionally surrender, my hand won't shake." And he walks off with his back straight, as if trying to make up for his short stature. With that, Varela has won his war.

The proclamation that Varela showed the strikers at Paso Ibáñez, and which would shape the Argentine Army's conduct in Patagonia, read as follows:

> Having closely scrutinized the settlement that you have proposed, it is my duty to inform you that I cannot accept your terms as they stand, as their illegal nature places them outside my jurisdiction.
>
> If you agree to immediately and unconditionally surrender and turn over all of the hostages, horses, and weapons in your possession, then I can guarantee your safety and that of your family and will commit to plead your case before the authorities and campaign on behalf of the workers in general.
>
> If I have not received the unconditional surrender of all of the armed strikers in the territory of Santa Cruz within twenty-four hours of your receipt of this proclamation, then I will proceed to:

1. Compel you to submit through the use of force. The officers under my command will be ordered to treat all armed strikers as enemies of the country in which they reside.
2. Hold you personally responsible for the lives of each and every one of the prisoners you are currently holding against their will, as well as for any incidents that may affect the civilian population of the territories you occupy or may come to occupy.
3. Punish, with the utmost severity, anyone found bearing arms without the written permission of the author of this proclamation.
4. Execute, without trial, anyone who fires on the army.

If it proves necessary for the army to resort to the use of force against the strikers, be warned that there will be neither negotiations nor suspensions of hostilities.
Signed: Varela, Lieutenant Colonel, Commander of the 10th Cavalry Regiment

Such was the proclamation issued by the Argentine Army to repress a strike during the administration of Hipólito Yrigoyen. The fourth point allows for the execution of prisoners—a violation of federal law and the Constitution, which Yrigoyen was otherwise so careful to respect. But clearly the law and the Constitution can be thrown out the window when the heat is on.

The strikers, almost all of them unarmed, release their hostages to Varela, who is waiting on the other side of the river. It's meant as a conciliatory gesture, but Varela doesn't seek pacification but total submission. He has realized that his enemy doesn't want a fight. Hundreds of peons flee by truck, by car, and by horse, leaving nearly all of the goods they had seized from the ranches at Paso Ibáñez. Avendaño heads towards Río Chico with the rest of the group, who intend to turn themselves over to the army at a more favorable opportunity. Outerelo, still determined to win, goes off to look for the groups of strikers camped out near San Julián, focusing on the area near the Bella Vista ranch in Cañadón León (now known as Gobernador Gregores), where he hopes to meet up with Albino Argüelles' men. Varelas states in his report:

> This orderly retreat, which ignored my proclamation and the offers made within, in itself constitutes an acceptance of combat and a challenge to the army's troops in the field.

He regards them, in other words, as enemy combatants. And, as he stated in the proclamation, the army would neither negotiate with nor accept the surrender of combatants. Anyone who could not escape would face the death penalty, plain and simple. Carte blanche for the army.

Varela crosses the river and occupies Paso Ibáñez.

Meanwhile, Captain Anaya disembarks in San Julián with fresh troops from Buenos Aires. He is accompanied by four other officers, eighteen non-commissioned officers, and forty-five soldiers, who constitute the 4th Squadron of the 10th Cavalry Regiment and who include a machine gun detail (note the high number of non-commissioned officers compared to the number of soldiers).

While still at sea, on board the *Guardia Nacional*, Anaya receives the following message, which is key in understanding the instructions that Varela gives his officials:

> Captain Anaya: You are to march along the left bank of the Río Chico and Río Chalia in the direction of Lago Viedma. The rebels have retreated from Paso Ibáñez and are heading west—try to head them off. It's best to give no quarter to the ringleaders. They have many horses.
>
> Signed: Varela

"Give no quarter to the ringleaders." These are Varela's orders to Anaya. And in the coming "battles," the soldiers will seemingly shoot smart bullets because all of the ringleaders appear to die. Anaya will be ruthless in carrying out the instructions of his beloved commander.

Varela and his men march towards Corpen. Avendaño's group, instead of fleeing due north, follow a strange route: they go first to Paso Río Chico (they are the ones who occupy La Anónima) and then follow the banks of the river to Corpen. And, eight leagues from Paso Río Chico, Varela and the strikers make contact. And, once again, there are varying accounts of what happens. Varela's report states:

> The chase continued that morning under my supervision. We set out for Río Chico by way of Corpen. As we approached, I sent an automobile towards Paso Río Chico to make contact with Captain Anaya's squadron, which, according to the orders I had given, should have been approaching from that direction. The automobile returned shortly thereafter to inform me that a group of rebels was advancing on Corpen; there were more or less one hundred individuals on horseback accompanied by several trucks carrying their supplies. I immediately headed out to intercept and subdue them, which I managed to accomplish some eight leagues west of Paso Río Chico. After they catch sight of our trucks, the rebels got into firing position. I ordered my troops forward and, after a brief shootout, they surrendered at 1400 hours and I took sixty-five of them prisoner. Six men died during the skirmish, including their leader, Avendaño. We also seized two trucks filled with goods that had been taken from people's houses in Paso Ibáñez.

As we can see, Varela does not explain the "shootout." A man who is normally so careful about recording details has nothing to say about how the skirmish begins. The army is traveling by car and truck. So are the strikers. How do they run into each other? He doesn't say. As we shall see, the truth is quite different.

In reality, Avendaño and the motley assortment of somber men who accompanied him had lost even their will to flee. Avendaño was an Argentine and was one of those who had worked hardest to reach a settlement with the ranchers. In the assembly at Paso Ibáñez, he was the one who suggested releasing the hostages in order to placate Varela. And so they were released.

We don't know how many were shot at Río Chico and Paso Ibáñez. What we do know is that Avendaño was not killed at Río Chico, but was instead taken to Paso Ibáñez. There he was imprisoned. The last person to see him alive—Juvenal Christensen, who later became the general manager of the Armour meatpacking plant in Puerto Santa Cruz—has told us that Avendaño had lost all hope, begging everyone who talked with him to intervene and save his life. But he was taken from his cell the next day and nothing more was ever heard of him.

The FORA report on the incident states that Avendaño was tied to a barbed wire fence and then shot in the head.

Another two leaders were shot at Paso Ibáñez: Antonio Alonso and Manuel Sánchez. According to the Maritime Workers' Federation's report, Alonso was stripped naked, tied to a post, and then repeatedly caned to get him to talk. Then they had him dig his own grave and shot him. As for Manuel Sánchez, five hundred residents of Puerto Santa Cruz, Paso Ibáñez, and Río Chico pleaded for his life to be spared, but Captain Campos said that he could only exchange his life for that of another. In the end, five non-commissioned officers took him away by car, destination unknown.

But of all these executions, perhaps the most unjust was that of the Spanish fisherman José Rogelio Ramírez, a father of five. Though he participated in the strike, he did no more than drive Outerelo and Descoubiére around in an automobile they had commandeered.

The English rancher Guillermo Lewis (owner of the Cañadón Toro ranch, fifty-two years old and a resident of Argentina for the previous twenty-four) has provided some revealing testimony (File V, No. 113, Page 1,679, 1922). He states that he was taken to Paso Ibáñez on November 16th,

1921 by eight strikers led by Descoubiére. But then he states that he was allowed to visit his family on the Semino ranch. It was José Rogelio Ramírez who drove him to the ranch. When the strikers decided to hand their hostages over to Varela, José Rogelio Ramírez went to the Semino ranch to look for Lewis's family, arriving in time to reunite them aboard the cutter *Alfa*, which was headed to Puerto Santa Cruz. Lewis adds that, during the occupation of Paso Ibáñez, the Chilean leader Descoubiére "took special pains to avoid damage to local residences, strictly prohibiting alcohol and punishing any excesses."

But let's return to José Rogelio Ramírez. He and Avendaño are captured by Varela at Corpen. From there they are taken to Paso Ibáñez, where the dance begins. José Rogelio Ramírez is savagely beaten each night and told to confess the crimes of his fellow strikers. But the soldiers soon get tired, as the Spaniard proves too tough to turn informer. They choose the usual procedure. They take him for a drive and there's one problem less by the time dinner's ready.

Ramírez's widow—a Spaniard named Pura Fernández, the mother of five young children—is not the sort of woman to hold her tongue. She does everything she can to recover her husband's body, but to no avail. Deeply hurt, she decides to return to Spain.

In September 1922, the official newspaper of the Maritime Workers' Federation publishes a photograph of Pura Fernández accompanied by an article openly accusing Lieutenant Colonel Varela and the Argentine Army of executing her husband.

With Avendaño's group disbanded and its leader killed, Varela prepares to relentlessly hunt down and exterminate Outerelo's group. Outerelo flees towards Cañadón León (Gobernador Gregores) along the right bank of the Río Chico. Varela's men follow:

December 1. Having crossed the river and established from their tracks that the main group was continuing towards Bella Vista, I press on and continue the chase in that direction. Following a brief shootout, I subdue the most important group of rebels near the ranch at 1500 hours. This was the group that held the town of Paso Ibáñez for eleven days. We seize 430 prisoners, four thousand horses, around two hundred long-range weapons, thirty revolvers, a large quantity of ammunition, and 50,000 pesos worth of stolen merchandise. Eleven individuals were killed in the skirmish, including the ringleader Outerelo, one of the most dangerous agitators in the seditious movement.

This is the full extent of Varela's curt report, which nevertheless contains two interesting details: though typewritten, it contains two handwritten corrections made by the officer himself. The number of prisoners has been hastily modified to 430 and the number of horses to four thousand. The original numbers are illegible.

Analyzing this report, we can see that, in contrast to his other dispatches, Varela doesn't even bother to say that the workers shot first. He simply mentions a "brief shootout" and twelve dead strikers. But it turns out that—according to Varela himself—there were 430 strikers, while the military forces were made up of Varela, Sub-lieutenant Rafael A. Loza, and only thirty-one soldiers, a ratio of thirteen to one. There are nevertheless twelve casualties among the strikers—and Loza will later admit that there may have been another two—and none among the troops.

Let's look at the entry in Sub-lieutenant Loza's campaign diary for December 1st, the day on which the strike leaders in central Santa Cruz were killed:

The chase continued until 1500 hours, when an automobile was sighted on the pampas. Its passengers tried to drive off when they noticed our presence, but we caught up with them. The automobile was transporting the group's spies. We took them prisoner and forced them to lead us to their camp. After twenty minutes' march, we spotted their camp, which was located one hundred meters from Cañadón de los Leones. Measures were taken to prepare for any possible resistance. Rebel fire from the nearest hill was answered by Corporal Díaz's subdivision. The shootout lasted five minutes at the most, leaving twelve dead on the ground,[15] including the group's main leader, Ramón Outerelo. Based on information we received later, two of the wounded who had hidden themselves in the brush must have died some time afterwards. After the strikers surrendered, we proceeded to free the ranchers captured by the ringleaders and assign responsibilities, separating the dangerous prisoners from the rest. The first group included those individuals who had formed part of the ranch delegations and taken part in the attacks on houses and commercial establishments, while the second group contained those individuals who had allowed themselves to be swept along by the first.

We then confiscated their weapons, munitions, supplies, and stolen goods. Sentries were assigned to watch over the prisoners and grooms to care for the stolen horses, which amounted to more or less four thousand animals. There were around 430 prisoners.

This action determined the success of Varela's campaign. With the total defeat of Outerelo, the "coordinator" of the strike movement, the workers of Santa Cruz were left in disarray. The only leaders left were Soto in the south, with his back to the cordillera, and José Font—Facón Grande—in the north. The courageous Varela will hunt them as if they were butterflies, but instead of simply collecting them he will trample them underfoot as if they were poisonous spiders.

Varela's triumph at Bella Vista was easy. Too easy for us to believe his curt report or Sub-lieutenant Loza's longer but equally implausible report.

Let's look at some other accounts of the dismal events at the Bella Vista ranch in Cañadón León (Gobernador Gregores).

We have, for example, the account of General Anaya—the officer who sent Sub-lieutenant Loza towards Cañadón León—whose report contradicts Varela's, especially regarding the number of dead:

Crossing the river, Varela presses on towards Bella Vista. His determination to overtake the column of strikers pays off and, after a couple hours, he surprises their rearguard and sows confusion in their ranks. This confusion becomes disastrous for the strikers as they realize that other troops are approaching their right flank. Attracted by the sound of gunfire, Anaya's squadron arrives in time to assist in accepting the strikers' surrender and assigning responsibilities. The spoils of this skirmish include 480 prisoners, four thousand horses, 296 rifles of various calibers, abundant ammunition, forty-nine revolvers, and a splendid haul of clothing, food, drink, and anything else they were able to carry away from the ranches they looted, even musical instruments. Fifteen or twenty of the strikers paid with their lives, among them a certain Outerelo, the infamous agitator who led the group. The task of assigning responsibilities after their unconditional surrender was long and difficult. Although the prisoners accused each another of their crimes, and despite doubts about releasing the guilty, eighty-seven strikers were turned over to the territory's judicial authorities, after which they confessed and were sentenced.

As we can see, the number of dead isn't even consistent between the military reports. But it's even worse than that. We have already seen Varela's official report. That report was written in February 1922. But in the campaign diary that Varela sends the War Ministry, he states that there were only eight people killed in the skirmish:

Supported by one official, thirty soldiers, and ten civilians (among them chauffeurs and guides), I pursued the rebels across the countryside, ambushing and subduing 420 of them fifty leagues outside of Puerto Santa Cruz. The army seized three thousand horses, 260 rifles, thirty revolvers, and 50,000 pesos worth of merchandise, most of it stolen from La Anónima. (…) Eight rebels were killed, including Outerelo, the ringleader.

Here is the key to understanding the "battle." The correspondent from *La Nación* will report that there was only one shot fired and five hundred men were taken prisoner during the action at Cañadón León, which occurred at Tomás Hospitaleche's Bella Vista ranch on December 1st, 1921. And the newspaper's correspondent seems to be correct. There was neither a battle nor a skirmish, as Varela would have us believe.

Colonel Schweizer—Varela's adjutant on this campaign—has told me how Outerelo died. As the column of strikers approached the Bella Vista ranch, one of the trucks they were using to carry ammunition and a large supply of victuals ran out of gasoline or had some other sort of problem. After arriving at the ranch, Outerelo and three of his men return with either gasoline or tools. But Varela's advance party had already reached the vehicle and was preparing their ambush. The strikers, led by Outerelo, get out of their car and approach the truck. It was then that they were ordered to halt. As Outerelo and his men tried to return to their car and flee, they were shot by Varela's soldiers. (Another account states that they were never ordered to halt, but were simply shot as they approached the truck.) The troops then marched towards Bella Vista under the cover of a white flag and frightened the strikers into surrendering. Leaderless and completely disoriented, they agreed. Varela immediately seized their weapons and took aside the eight primary culprits (these are the ones that Varela will list as having been killed in the "skirmish," a figure he will later round up to twelve; the other four—Outerelo included—were those killed in the ambush). Then things get messy. The party had ended for the strikers. What Captain Anaya refers to as "assigning responsibilities" will begin. But we will deal with this later when we analyze the number of executions at Bella Vista, perhaps the place—aside from La Anita—where the executions were most thorough.

The anarchists will interpret the events at Bella Vista differently; the report published in *La Antorcha* reads as follows:

En route to the interior, the strikers set up camp on rather uneven ground. They see several cars approach, one of them flying a white flag. Comrade Outerelo, a soldier, and a civilian get out of one of the cars. Outerelo tells the workers that everything has been arranged and that there's no reason to resist, as the freed hostages managed to get the police to agree to their demands. But they had either treacherously deceived him or threatened him with execution. There were some comrades, but only a few, who didn't believe his story and left camp, destination unknown. And so began two hundred murders and more than one martyrdom. On the strength of the assurances given by Outerelo, who had stayed behind to negotiate, knowing that Varela would arrive soon, the strikers handed over their weapons and their nearly five thousand horses.

So according to the anarchists, Outerelo had gone to negotiate with the troops and then returned with surrender conditions, accompanied by a military emissary and a civilian. And that once the workers surrendered, he was shot by Varela himself.

In any case, if we compare this account with the military dispatches, it's possible that the "four spies" in the automobile captured by Sub-lieutenant Loza were given white flags and told to convince the other workers to surrender. Or maybe it wasn't Outerelo who was shot when the truck was ambushed, but some other labor leader. And so the only question is if Outerelo was killed in the ambush or if he was executed later on, after having arranged the conditions for surrender.

But what can be seen at Bella Vista is that the workers had not launched a revolutionary strike, nor had they considered confronting the army. They instead expected Varela to arrange a settlement, just as he did the first time around.

Now let's see what happened when responsibilities were assigned, as Captain Anaya put it. We'll examine the anarchist perspective first, quoting the report printed in *La Antorcha*:

They began by identifying the leaders, based on lists they carried with them, and took them aside. That night, ten of them were stripped naked[16] and tied to a barbed wire fence. Some thirty of them were shot the next morning. Only Comrade Camporro[17] was spared, though Varela had other horrors in mind for him. They made him gather a good deal of *mata negra* and pile it around a post. Then they stripped him naked, tied him to the post, pistol whipped him, and set fire to the mata negra. Let us honor his memory by undertaking our struggles with more enthusiasm, more unity, and more resolve!

To avoid wasting time in digging graves—there was an almost total lack of tools—Varela decided to cremate the bodies. He forced all those condemned to death to gather mata negra (the only firewood on hand) and then shot them en masse. Then their bodies were covered with the mata negra, doused with gasoline, and lit on fire. But first they were searched for any money or objects of value they may have been carrying, and all of their personal correspondence, certificates of ownership for horses and other documents were destroyed. Their clothing was given to the soldiers, chauffeurs, and guides. Only 196 workers escaped the slaughter.

Let's now examine the contradictions between the different press reports. This is how *La Unión* of Río Gallegos describes the events at Bella Vista:

Santa Cruz, December 7th—Following up on my previous report, allow me to inform you that Varela, with thirty soldiers under his command and accompanied by the civilian volunteers Helmich, Saller, Dobreé, and Raso, ambushed the bulk of the rebels as they were setting up camp. The first of the rebels to be captured was the ringleader Outerelo, the former secretary of the Workers' Federation in Puerto Santa Cruz and one of the main organizers of the strike. He was accompanied by a Russian. Commander Varela advanced boldly and, after a brief exchange of gunfire, captured five hundred rebels and seized 140 guns, including several Mausers, eighty revolvers, more than 100,000 bullets and five thousand horses, as well as cars, trucks and other goods that had been stolen by the strikers.

The newspaper states that Outerelo was taken prisoner. So how is it that Varela and Anaya will later say that he died in the "fighting"? The newspaper goes on to state:

> We would like to take the time to warmly praise Commander Varela, who has proven his integrity, zeal, expertise, and bravery. He has surpassed all of the expectations of the populace, who, appeased, applaud his actions. Commander Varela's recent actions have convinced them that the man responsible for the current movement is Governor Yza, whose tolerance towards the rebels last year has given their leaders a free hand in the current movement. Public opinion unanimously condemns Governor Yza, who has made the army's presence in the territory indispensable if further travesties are to be avoided.

And there you have it. The mouthpiece of the Rural Society says it quite clearly: Varela has surpassed the expectations of the populace. Those most surprised by the incredible severity with which Varela crushes anything that smells of organized labor are the ranchers themselves, who elevate him from suspect to hero. With Varela's change of heart, they begin to blame everything on Yza, who remains in Buenos Aires.

In my conversations with Edelmiro Correa Falcón (which occurred over the course of the years 1969 and 1970), I was told again and again that the ranchers never would have believed that Varela and his troops would act as uncompromisingly as they did during the second strike.

We have collected valuable testimony on the Bella Vista massacre. The first two accounts, of course, are not from the perspective of the workers—these witnesses continue defending the repression to this day, arguing that it was regretfully necessary—but they nevertheless maintain a laudable objectivity. The first is from Commissioner Isido Guadarrama, a man who witnessed the action hour by hour as part of Varela's column. He recalls the incident with a remarkable clarity and maintains that there were approximately forty peons shot at Bella Vista, a figure that matches that given by the rancher Augusto Moy, who had been taken hostage by Outerelo's group and was rescued by Varela. According to Guadarrama, the only rape during the strike that he was able to confirm occurred at Bella Vista. Two Chilean peons attacked the daughter of a Basque named Victoria, who was the ranch's caretaker. The two Chileans drunkenly entered the manor house while the soldiers were "assigning responsibilities." The caretaker's son reported the rape, and the two Chileans were shot without a second thought.[18] Our second witness is Luis Urbina, the son of one of the richest landowners in Chilean and Argentine Patagonia. In 1971, Urbina was seventy-five years old and lived on Clark's El Tero ranch. He was very close friends with the officers Campos, Correa Morales, Frugoni, and Anello. He informed us that the number of strikers executed at Bella Vista and Cañadón León (an Anaya operation we will examine shortly) added up to seventy—fifty-five at Bella Vista and the rest at Cañadón León.

Following the mass executions at Hospitaleche's Bella Vista ranch (now owned by Merelles), it falls on Captain Anaya to "assign responsibilities" among the strikers and locals. But as he must continue the pursuit of the Argüelles column that he began in San Julián, he leaves Lieutenant First Class Aguirre in command at Cañadón León, while Aguirre will in turn pass off his responsibilities to Sergeant Celestino Dapazo of the 2nd Cavalry Regiment.

Longtime residents of the region still remember the name of Sergeant Dapazo, who held the power of life or death over anyone who crossed his path for several weeks. We have conversed at length with Prudencio Moreno—the oldest resident of Gobernador Gregores—who told us his memories of those terrible days:

Nothing ever happened around here until Outerelo, Descoubiére, and their men arrived, fleeing from Paso Ibáñez (now known as Comandante Piedra Buena). They went to the Bella Vista ranch, which was then owned by the Hospitaleches and is now owned by the Merelles family. There they surrendered to Varela without a fight and there they were punished, with many of them shot. Juan Raso, who lived on the La Julia ranch and was acting as a guide for the troops, saved many of their lives by personally intervening on their behalf with Varela. He later insisted that fifty had been shot by Varela at Bella Vista—almost all of them Chileans, though six or seven were Spaniards. The first ones shot were identified by the ranchers as union members; then others were later because someone didn't like their looks or because their presence on the ranch was suspicious, which nobody ever talked about later. The prisoners were tied to the fence the entire time. After Varela, Anaya, and Lieutenant Aguirre left, Sergeant Dapazo was given command of the detachment. The ranchers acted as his spies, reporting on the behavior of the locals. There was, for example, the case of the Lerdo brothers,[19] who lived near Augusto Moy's ranch. Varela's troops went looking for the eldest of the two. When his wife asked why they were taking her husband away, they told her that he was being taken to Paso Ibáñez for further questioning. But he never made it to Paso Ibáñez. We later heard that he had been shot near Corpen.

In February 1922, the rancher Augusto Moy told Sergeant Dapazo that he had seen the younger Lerdo near his property, describing him and his brother—*who had already been shot*—as "bad neighbors." The day that Sergeant Dapazo went looking for the accused, he instead came across a "green" Chilean riding an emaciated pony.[20] He was very confused by everything that was going on around him and had gone to ask Lerdo for advice. He had bad luck. When the soldiers arrived, he was unable to produce the documentation that Varela was requiring of all farmworkers. They took Lerdo and the Chilean back to Cañadón León before noon. That evening, we saw Lerdo and the Chilean, guarded by soldiers, carrying cans of gasoline. The Chilean was crying. They were shot shortly afterwards on a hill facing the offices of La Anónima, next to a pepper tree. Then their bodies were doused with gasoline, from the same cans that they had been forced to carry, and set on fire. Their bodies burned for several hours and the fire could be seen from far off. This was the spot where Sergeant Dapazo always carried out his executions. Another time we saw them go off looking for a Chilean who had been accused by a certain Medina of having stolen a harness from the Molinari ranch. When Dapazo's detachment left, the locals climbed the hill out of pure curiosity. They found nine skeletons. Almost all of them still had pieces of darkening flesh, the color of burnt offal, hanging off their otherwise clean bones. Their work boots were still on their feet. They lay on a sort of sandy crust that seemed to be made up blood, ashes, and melted human fat.

When the ranchers Pedro Hospitaleche and Ezequiel Merelles showed us where the Bella Vista strikers were shot, cremated, and buried, they also spoke to us of the "crust" formed on the ground where the corpses were burnt.

Hospitaleche's account, which we heard on December 14th, 1972, has a special importance. Pedro Hospitaleche is the son of Tomás Hospitaleche, owner of the El Águila and El Cerrito ranches and administrator of Bella Vista. Tomás Hospitaleche provided unconditional support for the army, guiding Captain Anaya as far as Bella Vista and staying to witness the tragic events that unfolded there. Pedro's account is based on his memories—he was living at El Águila and was only twelve years old at the time—as well as on his conversations with his father:

Our first contact with the strikers was with Rubio Pichinanga's party at El Águila, where eleven peons threatened my mother with a Winchester. My father had already gone off to the south to accompany the troops. The peons seized food and weapons and then left. Then Armando Camporro's party arrived, bringing the rancher Augusto Moy with them as a hostage. Moy asked Camporro permission to enter El Águila and talk with my mother, who had been left all alone. Camporro allowed it and they spent two or three hours in conversation. María Concepción Victoria, the daughter of the Basque, Victoria, was in my house the entire time and the strikers never laid a finger on her. The rumor that she had been raped by two Chilean peons was entirely false and was spread by someone with an interest in making Commander Varela even angrier than he already was. I regret that those two Chileans paid the price; the entire Hospitaleche family is witness to the fact that nothing at all happened to that girl, who was in our care.

My father and Norberto Pedernera accompanied Elbio Carlos Anaya's forces, taking them to Bella Vista. There they found Varela weighing the guilt of the strikers, who had surrendered without firing a single shot. They were being held in the corral. Two Argentines—there were only a few shepherds—were kept apart. One of them was Gorra Blanca, the nickname of Telésforo Teves. They roughed him up enough to drive him crazy but imprisoned him instead of having him shot. They sentenced the strikers in the same corral where most of them were being held and then simply took them up a hill and shot them at a place that's now called Cañadón de los Muertos. They made them dig their own graves first. But not all them were killed there. Some of them were taken to another spot three kilometers away and they weren't buried but burnt with gasoline on top of heaps of *mata negra*. My father always said that around fifty strikers were shot there. He and Raso, the scout, saved many people they knew from the corral, begging Commander Varela for clemency. Rubio Pichinanga was caught in Sierra Ventana, brought back to Bella Vista, and shot without another word.

Pedro Hospitaleche has also described the death of the strike leader known as Vivillo for us:

I was at the La Osamenta tavern. A group of soldiers entered and there they ran into Vivillo, who pretended to be a stranger who was just passing through. Sergeant Dapazo—a clever and quick-witted man—suddenly asked him, "Are you the one they call Vivillo?" Taken off guard, he admitted that he was. Sergeant Dapazo immediately took out a *guacha*—a riding crop with a wide keeper and a short rod—and hit him in the face so deftly that it took out his eye. Without giving him time to catch his breath, they took him to a spot two hundred meters from the tavern and forced him to dig his own grave with a shovel they had borrowed from the tavern keeper. And then Dapozo personally finished him off with his revolver.

Pedro Hospitaleche, Prudencio Moreno, and Miguel Isla (who was among the strikers at Bella Vista and was saved by the army scout Juan Raso, who knew him) all confirmed a story about a Spaniard who was brought before the firing squad but was only wounded in the shoulder.[21] He was left for dead and was to be burned with gasoline the next day, but then he appeared several days later, badly wounded and completely naked, on a ranch owned by Ugarte. He was nursed back to health by Montenegro, the caretaker of Las Tunas, who gave him clothing and helped him escape across the high plains. He later worked for many years on Bricich's ranch in Río Chico.

Miguel Isla told us what happened at Bella Vista immediately before. According to him, "all of the speakers were Spaniards" and "they made a lot of noise about workers' rights and the equality of man." He adds that the workers surrendered without firing a single shot, believing that they would simply turn over their weapons and then go back to work on the basis of the Varela-Yza settlement.

We were also comforted by the fact that Tomás Hospitaleche, Norberto Pedernera, Juan Rosa, etc. accompanied the troops. The thought of executions never crossed our minds. Even still, the Spaniards didn't want to even hear talk of surrendering without first signing an agreement with Varela. But everything was very confusing because there were ten people speaking at the same time and they all disagreed with each other. And we had the troops standing by. Then came the time for weeping: they treated us very roughly. They held us in the corral without food or water, like sheep for the slaughter. Juan Raso saved me by saying that I was a good worker. There were many executions, but those who say that there were more than one hundred are exaggerating. According to the soldiers and the workers who were taken as prisoners to Río Gallegos but who were at Bella Vista up until the end, fifty people were killed, almost all of them Chileans, though there were some Spaniards and three or four gringos, by which I mean Poles or Russians. I'm only talking about those killed at Bella Vista—this is separate from the purges carried out by Sergeant Dapazo of the 2nd Cavalry Regiment at Cañadón León.

Once again, we have to settle for rough estimates. According to Varela, twelve workers were killed in combat at Bella Vista; according to Loza, the exact same figure; according to Captain Anaya, between twelve and fifteen strikers were killed; the anarchists speak of two hundred executions (they also say that 196 people survived); Commissioner Guadarrama, forty; Luis Urbina, fifty-five; Artemio Moreno, fifty executions; Miguel Isla, fifty executions. One final figure is provided by Edelmiro Correa Falcón. He told us that, based on his conversations with the ranchers of the Cañadón León area in the months following these bloody events, the approximate number of executions was between forty and fifty and that most of the victims were Chileans, although there was the odd European.

Before telling the story of Antonio Soto's utter defeat in the southern cordillera of Santa Cruz, we will examine the masterful military exploits of Captain Anaya to the north of the Río Santa Cruz. And if we describe it as a mopping-up operation, it is surely only in the loosest sense of the word. The Argentine Cavalry knew no sacrifices. It was a true manhunt, kilometer after kilometer, league upon league. Our boys in uniform knew how to handle those disorganized chilotes, who were already frightened to death, those Spanish anarchists and those pale Europeans, be they Germans, Poles, or Russians.

Anaya's dispatches mention that the strike leaders Juan Nayn (Chilean) and Juan Olazán (known as Rubio Pichinanga) were arrested by an army patrol on December 3rd. That the latter was killed "while resisting"—Hospitaleche has already told us that he was executed—and that Juan Nyan was mortally wounded "while trying to escape." On the 4th, Captain Anaya wrote that a strike leader known as El Mayor also tried to resist arrest and had to be killed.

It's clear that, whenever the death of a strike leader had to be explained, it was said that they had been trying to escape or that the soldiers were acting in self-defense. El Mayor was killed with a bullet to the brain. This was one of the methods most favored by officers and NCOs to eliminate troublemakers: a bullet to the temple avoided the need for firing squads, which could sometimes be a hassle. Commissioner Guadarrama told us that one of the men who showed the most bravery and skill in dispatching Chileans was Sub-lieutenant Frugoni Miranda, whom we will see in action at Lago Argentino, during the La Anita massacre.

On December 5th, Anaya states that:

> We resumed assigning responsibilities and identifying the origin of the stolen horses, ranch by ranch, so that they could be returned to their owners.

Here is an interesting paragraph—the horses belonging to the peons were given to the soldiers:

> Some two hundred horses from among those belonging to the rebels were set aside for the use of the troops. Which horses

belonged to the rebels was easy to determine because they had collars made from capon leather and also because they were better groomed and better fed.

This is what's called the spoils of war. The looting of a defeated enemy. Not only were the strikers relieved of their horses but all of their belongings, as we shall see when we get to the judicial proceedings. At no point did the army turn over the belongings of those executed or killed in action to their next of kin. What became of it all?

Captain Anaya and his column will continue purging central Santa Cruz of strikers. His dispatches will repeatedly state that the strikers attacked the troops and that they died in the combat that followed. The soldiers, oddly enough, were only ever "grazed" by bullets.

Anaya will then be ordered to fight the San Julián group, commanded by the socialist labor leader Albino Argüelles, who spread the strike throughout all the ranches of central Santa Cruz, from the coast to the cordillera. Albino Argüelles was the secretary general of the San Julián Workers' Society.

Argüelles's tactics were aimed at disorienting the enemy. He and a group of several hundred agricultural workers remained constantly on the move, thus evading Anaya's troops. Anaya then began a strict system of interrogating all residents and merchants whom he suspected of helping the strikers in any way. A typical example of this was the treatment of a Spanish merchant named Martense. The method used to extract information from him was very original. Responsibility for the interrogations fell on the shoulders of one Sergeant Espíndola, a man the Buenos Aires press will later describe as "the most bloodthirsty of jackals." Anaya's dispatches report the following:

> Sergeant Espíndola, who was keeping watch that night, told us that he heard our prisoner Martense talk in his sleep, mentioning an automobile part that he had hidden so that it wouldn't

fall into the hands of the police or the army and so that he could faithfully keep his promise to pass on any news that would be of interest to Albino Argüelles.

Evidently, Sergeant Espíndola was one of the pioneers of the Freudian technique of dream interpretation in the far south. He overheard this information at 2345 hours on the 15th. Five hours later, at 0500 hours on the 16th, the Spaniard had already been broken. Anaya continues: "After Martense confessed to his involvement in the movement, serving as a spy for the strikers, he was sent off with strict orders to locate his automobile." We will later see how Martense was made to confess before being shot.

The squadron headed towards the Los Granaderos ranch, owned by Juan B. Tirachini. This was where Anaya first heard the name José Font, alias Facón Grande, who had just arrived in the area to make contact with the strikers operating near Cañadón León and San Julián. He had been brought there by fate, as his carts were in Cañadón León. His job was transporting wool and leather. Because of his honesty and generosity, the landowners esteemed him far above the rest of the region's carters. He was never fixated on money and always gave to those in need. Every witness we have spoken with agrees that he was a good man, one who was humble, trustworthy, and upright. There's not a single long-term resident of Puerto Deseado that knew him who would hesitate to describe him as a decent and well-loved person. He dressed like a farmer, with baggy trousers, sandals, and a large black belt with a long gaucho knife, which he never used against people. He had come to Santa Cruz from Entre Ríos to work as a horse trainer for a rancher named Iriarte and then later went independent; he liked to live freely and work for himself. He was a man who always forgave slights, with only one exception. León Soto, the dean of Puerto Deseado's journalists and a living library of history from the turn of the century onwards, has told us that José Font settled on a few hectares of land near Bahía Laura and the infamous Commissioner Lopresti decided to evict him. José

Font ignored the police officer and continued with his labors. And so he was arrested, tied up, and beaten while the police destroyed everything they found at his camp.

It's difficult for an upright man to forgive an insult of this nature. But José Font, though quarrelsome, did not seek vengeance. After being freed, he returned to his old profession as a carter, but something changed deep within him. It became a rare sight to see him in the company of ranchers or authority figures. Instead, he spent almost all of his free time in the boarding houses catering to chilotes, the campsites of simple folk, or the ranches of his horse trainer friends.

When the great strike of 1921 erupted, the peons sought him out. He was the only man who had won moral authority over them through his conduct. He refused their requests time and again, perhaps foreseeing the coming tragedy and understanding the strength of the mighty. But he finally gave in. His blood still boiled from the beating he had received from the police, who were but the tools of those who already had everything and still wanted more.

To shed more light on the figure of Facón Grande, allow me to transcribe the testimony (recorded by the Adolfo González Chávez Permanent History Center) of Kuno Tschamler, a Czechoslovakian, who for many years—including during the strike—was the administrator of Mateo Martinovich's Santa María ranch, located between San Julián and Puerto Deseado. Tschamler sides with the bosses, which makes his declarations regarding José Font all the more interesting:

> First of all, I must clarify that most of the peons had been forced into action by seditious elements, and so their responsibility for those tragic events was very relative and the bosses understood this. The bosses had a terrible hatred for the strike leaders, however. What happened is that the labor leaders and ranch delegates wanted to redistribute the land amongst themselves. I never shared their ideas and considered them to be nothing more than highwaymen. But I did sympathize with a gaucho

known as Facón Grande, the owner of a fleet of carts, who was one of the leaders of the rebellion. I could never understand how he ended up coming to terms with the strikers. He had a heart of gold and was always there to help anyone in need, including myself—he once lent me a horse.

After describing the execution of Facón Grande—testimony we will transcribe later on—he adds:

> Many people regretted the death of this great man, who was respected by his rivals for his skill as a horseman: there wasn't a single wild horse capable of throwing him. Whenever someone mentioned an especially spirited horse around him, he simply said, "Bring me that nag." And each time, he broke it in.

Let's return to Juan Tirachini's Los Granaderos ranch. Tirachini was a self-made man who had built his business through enormous sacrifice. And like many men who start with nothing and then get accustomed to comfortable living, he was a friend to the authorities and respected the law. He named his ranch "the Grenadiers" after the regiment in which he had served. And he was a close friend of Colonel Martínez, his former commanding officer, who had helped him secure the land concession for his ranch.

Tirachini is perhaps the only person in Santa Cruz to ever speak ill of Facón Grande. In his book, *My Half-Century of Labor in Patagonia*, Tirachini says that Facón Grande "tried to pass himself off as a thug." But he wasn't an objective witness. After Commissioner Lopresti, Tirachini was the second and final person to have problems with Font. José Font went to settle a field that Tirachini wanted to sell to a company owned by a Buenos Aires capitalist named Casterán. Font, of course, was arrested and evicted a second time.

Nevertheless, Facón Grande did not hold a grudge against Tirachini. In his book, the rancher admits that Font acted nobly when, out of desperation, he had to turn to him for help. Despite Tirachini's pejorative tone, anyone who reads those pages can glimpse the nobility of Font's attitude, a nobility that was repaid with four gunshots.

On December 21st, before Captain Anaya reaches Los Granaderos, Facón Grande—on his way to Cañadón León—visits Tirachini to track down some milk cans he owned. Though invited to spend the night, he continued on. On his return trip, he leads the column of strikers that had been camped out at Boca del Tigre. At this time, Tirachini—whose ranch, on Facón Grande's orders, had been saved from attack—begs him to spare the life of Commissioner Albornoz, a friend of his.

Albornoz is none other than the founder of the San Julián Patriotic League, as well as the former police chief appointed by Correa Falcón who had been forced to resign because of his brutality. For union members, he was one of the most hated men in Santa Cruz. And there he was on his ranch, just a few kilometers away from Tirachini.

The owner of Los Granaderos asks his former friend to delay his departure as much as possible, so as to give him time to warn Albornoz of their approach. In spite of the strikers' hatred for the commissioner, Font agrees to his request. Tirachini sends a messenger to Albornoz, who hides himself and his two daughters in a cave two hundred meters from their house, along with a long range precision firearm and a large stock of ammunition. Tirachini writes:

> It was around four in the afternoon when the group of strikers appeared on the high ground surrounding Albornoz's ranch. Leading them was José Font, accompanied by two aides. After the group arrives within two hundred meters of the ranch, he orders them to halt. He and his two companions approach on their own. Albornoz's wife was waiting for them and, when questioned about her husband's whereabouts, she pretended to miss him, replying that he had left for San Julián two days

beforehand. Font and his companions then returned to the group without causing any damage to the property, without demanding weapons or horses. And so José Font kept the promise he had made me...

We shall see how Commissioner Albornoz will repay this noble gesture. From the moment Anaya arrives, he will be the fiercest persecutor of the strikers. He was not a tactful man. And he will repay Font's favor in counterfeit coin.

Three days after Facón Grande and his men pass through Los Granaderos, Anaya and his troops arrive. Facón Grande never returns to the area, leaving Albino Argüelles and Pastor Aranda in charge of carrying on with the strike.

In the dispatch dated December 15th, Anaya writes that the Los Granaderos ranch,

> ...owned by Tirachini, had been attacked three days earlier by around twenty armed bandits. They demanded that he gave them all of his weapons, ammunition, supplies, and horses, which he had to go out to the pasture and round up himself. They did not take him hostage, ceding to the pleas of his wife to not be left on her own.

All of this is quite different from what Tirachini himself relayed in his book. Font's men not only didn't touch his property, but he even invited Font to spend the night during his first visit to the ranch. On his return trip, they discuss Albornoz. The only thing that Tirachini says is that the strikers "kept their horses in the corral next to the shearing shed, 150 feet from our house."

Let's continue with Anaya's report:

> As we required news from the surrounding area, it was brought to our attention that Juan J. Albornoz, who lived with his wife only four leagues away on the La Aída ranch, was being threatened by a rebel attack that would be carried out in the coming

days. This was highly likely, as the gentleman's previous position as the territory's police chief had earned him a great deal of enemies among the criminal element. Meeting with him would also be of great service to the troops.

As we can see, Anaya's dispatches refer to the strikers as "criminals." Furthermore, Anaya neglects to mention that, despite Albornoz's reputation as a thug, the strikers passed over his ranch without touching anything.

The military column will continue onward until they find the strikers. Anaya writes the following on December 17th:

1015 hours. A group of barking dogs alerts the patrol from the right flank to the presence of a campsite at the bottom of a steep ravine, which they then bring to my attention. As they approached, they were greeted with gunshots spread across a five-hundred-meter front, while other armed individuals attempted to scale the slopes behind them. While taking all the necessary measures to return fire, further detonations were observed from a group of large rocks to the west, about two kilometers from the camp. The detonations increased in frequency until they became generalized across that new front. At this time, Corporal First Class Landa was shot twice, just fifty meters from the front. He dismounts to save his life and runs to a position that had just been taken by the machine gun detail, who were ordered to open fire in the direction of the rocks in order to intimidate the enemy and prevent them from scattering further. The troops under the command of Lieutenant Correa Morales, who were bringing up the rear, assessed the difficulty of the situation from the intensity of the gunfire and ignored the horses, instead aiming to circle around the camp from the north. They were fired upon by another group that was hidden in a gully. The shooting dragged on for an hour, ending only when so ordered by the squadron's commander, who saw the rebels wave the white flag from the edge of the ravine.

1230 hours: Lieutenant Correa Morales orders his men to chase down two fugitives while the rest of the troops proceed to round up, disarm, and interrogate the rebels scattered among the rocks. They are separated according to their degree of guilt and the rancher they worked for. *This last task took a total of three hours, during which time the occasional gunshot could still be heard. These were assumed to have been fired by the fugitives.*

This final passage is key to understanding what happened. What in times past was known as *degollina*, slitting the throats of one's prisoners. We Argentines were masters of the art of slitting throats. You could take a knife to your prisoner's throat or to the nape of their neck. Either a sharp or a dull blade could be used. When using a dull blade, you needed to press hard against your prisoner's throat until blood spurted out. The nape of the neck was more entertaining because, without tendons, the victim's head and limbs danced about comically before they died.[22] Slitting throats was something authentically national, there was nothing foreign about it, no damaging influences from abroad.

But now we're in 1921 and our traditions were already being lost. Here, on the San José ranch, there's no throat slitting in the proper sense, but prisoners were shot. And that's something else that we can see repeated time and again throughout our history, no matter the era.

But Anaya's dispatch doesn't immediately mention the dead, he will save that for later. He's more interested in other matters:

1600 hours. The prisoners, split up according to the three groups in which they had been organized, were escorted back to their campsites to collect their equipment and turn over their weapons, which they had hidden. The same was done with the ringleaders, who were exposed as such by the majority of the prisoners and especially by the ranchers and foremen who had been taken hostage by the rebels.

And so the commanding military officer himself admits that the judgments as to who was guilty and who was innocent were made by the "ranchers and foremen." This was the conduct of Varela and his officers, as admitted in their own reports; survivors and neutral witnesses will make the same accusation. Many accounts state that the ranchers didn't just point out the "ringleaders" but also any peons who had been slightly insubordinate or to whom they owed wages. For some, it was very simple—you had to take advantage of the circumstances and rid yourself of anyone who could cause you trouble.

Let's continue with Anaya's dispatch until he mentions the cadavers, which is the furthest detail from his mind:

1700 hours: Horses were distributed to the prisoners and they were ordered to saddle them up, which they did with an astonishing slowness, giving an idea of how difficult their frequent changes of camp must have been with all of these hindrances and their large number of foreigners, who confessed to having no experience in rural living.

1900 hours: The march towards the San José ranch finally got underway. Despite being located only fifteen kilometers away, it took a full three hours to arrive due to the rebels' poorly secured packs.

2200 hours: We finally arrived at San José. The troops took the best of the accommodations and the rebels were imprisoned in a sheep pen located next to the shearing shed. The horses were taken to a nearby paddock and the men were allowed to rest, as they had been overworked and had gone the entire day without eating.

On December 18th, reveille sounds at 4:30 a.m.:

0500 hours: The prisoners were carefully identified, registered, and classified by the squadron commander, assisted by Sub-lieutenant Sidders. Lieutenant Correa Morales, who had just entered the service, was in charge of sorting the weapons, equipment, and clothing taken from the prisoners to prove that they were stolen goods.

Here we must stress the number of accounts reporting that the peons were stripped of their quillangos, their ponchos, and their money, which were shared as booty among the soldiers and the police that accompanied them. The peons who managed to survive were left half naked, wearing only their ragged baggy trousers without a belt to hold them up and trying to cover themselves with their slouch hats for lack of a poncho.

And finally we get to the cadavers:

0530 hours: Accompanied by ten soldiers, Sergeant Baigorria headed out to Tapera de Casterán to resume the task of collecting weapons that began the previous afternoon and to identify and bury the cadavers that had been left on the battlefield.

So far, Anaya does not mention the number of prisoners nor the number of dead. The first figure will be given when he describes what happens when these soldiers return:

1700 hours: Sergeant Baigorria's patrol returned, bringing with them seven prisoners, five Winchesters, and two ammunition clips, along with other supplies. They reported that they had buried two bodies, which belonged to the Paraguayan, Jara, alias Tres Dedos, and Albino Argüelles, the ringleader.

That is, the two leaders of the column.

But another casualty appears in the telegram that Anaya sends to Varela and the War Ministry. (The telegram is sent on the 20th, or two days after the return of Baigorria's men. What happened on the 19th, surprisingly, doesn't figure into Anaya's collected dispatches—the only day unmentioned since the beginning of the campaign). The telegram reads as follows:

Day 17: I stumbled upon the rebel camp at De La Mata Tapera de Casterán. The rebels put up resistance. The fighting lasted for three hours and resulted in the deaths of the infamous ringleaders Albino Argüelles, Jara Tres Dedos, and Ledezma. There were also several wounded. We seized two thousand horses, 140 mules, rations, fifty-five rifles, sixty-one revolvers, 129 bladed weapons, clothing, and abundant supplies and ammunition. We took 193 prisoners, who were identified, judged, and then released upon the recommendation of the ranchers. In accordance with the instructions I have been given, I will send the guilty to San Julián. The horses have already begun to be returned to their owners.

Now we have three dead, but the telegram never says how many prisoners there are. It only mentions the number that were released (193). Anaya says that he will send the guilty to San Julián but he never provides a number. He also contradicts what he always maintained in his dispatches: that the strikers were well armed and supplied with ammunition. They had fifty-five rifles (which had to be shared among a presumed total of three-hundred people), sixty-one revolvers, and…129 "bladed weapons"! (They're called knives.) There wasn't even one knife per person.

Attending historical conferences or reading academic articles stating that the Chilean government armed the strikers is enough to make you laugh through your tears. Well then, if the Chileans did arm them, then they did a pretty bad job. And here we're citing official military sources. As we can see, the myths collapse on their own when the facts come to light.

Before continuing our account of Anaya's mopping-up campaign, let's pause for a moment at the San José ranch. There, at Tapera de Casterán—near the María Esther ranch—the only casualties, according to Anaya, were Albino Argüelles, Jara, and Ledezma.[23]

Erasmo Campos, retired and currently living in Río Gallegos, is a reserved man, but a man of integrity, hardened by the

Patagonian winds. He has told us of the plight of the peons taken prisoner at San José:

> They were all Chileans or Spaniards, with the exception of a few blond Europeans and three or four Argentines. They were starved and pistol-whipped in the livestock crush. It was terrible to see how these men were treated, much worse than on the hacienda. They were simple peasants, all of them quite poor, corralled like animals and expecting to be sacrificed at any moment. By my reckoning, around fifty of them were killed: either the bosses identified them as activists or their new clothes made them stand out.

The information collected by Commissioner Guadarrama in the months following the end of Varela's campaign tells us that the number of strikers executed on the San José ranch could be anywhere between forty-five and fifty-five.

Former governor Correa Falcón declined to provide an exact number of the dead, but he did tell us that there were "less than at Hospitaleche's ranch."

La Unión of Río Gallegos reports on December 24th, 1921 that:

> The machine guns went into action and so the number of dead and wounded was therefore quite high. (...) Twenty bandits were killed and a considerable number were wounded. The famous ringleaders El Paraguayo Jara and Argüelles have been killed.

Anaya never mentions any wounded, which makes his claims of a battle that much more implausible. What sort of battle leaves no wounded and kills only the leaders? And if some of the strikers were wounded, what became of them? Were they finished off or were they sent somewhere? This question remains unanswered in every army dispatch, and the wounded make no appearance elsewhere.

Yet again, there's an enormous doubt regarding the number of strikers who were either executed or "killed in combat." Numbers, nothing more. And only three names: Argüelles, Jara, and Ledezma.

Months later, the Maritime Workers' Federation will manage to discover the names of fourteen people who were executed at San José (among them only one Chilean—nothing is known of the others, not even their names). This list published in *La Unión del Marino* on May 1st, 1922 is as follows: Albino Argüelles, Argentine; Alfredo Vázquez, Argentine; Manuel Alba, Argentine; Francisco X., Argentine; Zenón Ledezma, Argentine; X. Díaz, Argentine; Ramón Martense, Spaniard; Maximiliano Almeira, Spaniard; X. Juaner, Spaniard; Estanislao Schuger, Pole; Miguel X., Turk; Bautista Oyarzún, Chilean; Manuel Jara, Paraguayan; and Machesky, Pole.

In his dispatches, Anaya will later admit that many strikers were shot while trying to escape, and an attentive reader will see him mention some of the names listed above:

On the night of December 21st, at approximately 2300 hours, eight prisoners who had been classified as dangerous attempted to escape, taking advantage of a sentry's momentary inattention. The sentry opened fire the moment he noticed their escape. The guards, under the command of Corporal Díaz, pursued the fugitives, managing to capture three of them and killing the other five, whose names were Alfredo Vázquez, Orencio Alba, Pancho or Francisco Depán, Martense, and Bautista Oyarzún. This incident occurred in the presence of the author of this report, who arrived after hearing the first gunshots.

We have interviewed Antonio Tiznao, a former resident of the area who now resides in Jaramillo. He was presented to us by José García, the owner of the Hotel España. Tiznao was a shepherd on Miguel Iriarte's San José ranch in December 1921, during the second strike, and was an eyewitness to these events. Serapio García was the ranch administrator. Tizano says:

One morning at about 7 o'clock, one of Argüelles's columns arrived and took us, the staff, to their base camp at Bajo Tigre, and from Bajo Tigre they took us to La Mata, a place on the San José ranch known as Bajo Casterán. We were all there at the camp when the army arrived and surrounded us. Some ran to the rocks for cover and fired a few shots but nothing else happened because the group surrendered easily. They immediately took Argüelles and Jara aside. We were almost all on foot, which made it easy to catch us because no one had readied their horses. Some of us were asleep and others were relaxing and talking amongst themselves. We had sentries but they didn't warn us because they were captured before we were. The sentinels had been posted far off, on a hill near the ranch, and they had distracted themselves by racing their horses in a nearby meadow. When they remembered their duty, it was already too late.

Argüelles and Jara did not survive long. They were executed on the spot, gunned down before us after being beaten with the flats of the officers' sabers. They died bravely, without begging for mercy. I felt it deeply, as we were very close to them. A lieutenant approached and asked Jara, "Are you the famous Paraguayan?" And he replied, "That I am. I know my fate. My only regret is not having made things harder for you." Argüelles said nothing, the poor man. Before they were shot, the officer asked them if they were married. Neither one was. Argüelles fainted as the soldiers took aim, probably from the blows he had received. He had good intentions, he was a good criollo. After they were given the coup de grace, the soldiers threw them on the mata negra and tried to burn their bodies, but they botched the job.

Next we were taken to the San José ranch and they held us in the horse corral. They took away seven or eight men suspected of being leaders and shot them about three hundred meters from the shearing shed, behind a boulder. There they remain. The shearers erected a cross to mark their graves, which they still maintain to this day. They are buried in twos and threes, as they were executed. There lies, Ratif, a Turkish boy; the Russian

Estinslao, who was Cobos's cook; several Chileans; Argentines, such as Orencio Alba. There they also shot Martense, an elderly Spaniard who lived near Feijóo and ran a tavern, a very good man. They shot him because they said he had helped the strikers, but it wasn't true. When we were at Cerro Mirador, Bajo Tigre, the poor man was passing through on business and the boys stopped him and brought him back to our camp. Everyone knew him and knew he was a good man who wouldn't hurt a fly, so they immediately released him and sent him on his way, but then he was captured by the army. They refused to believe his story and executed him after leaving him hogtied in the corral for several days, humiliating him in an attempt to get him to talk. They also executed Orencio Alba. I would have set my own hands on fire for him. They said they shot him because he was one of the leaders, but who knows the real reason. Look, the only important thing was the word of the ranchers, nothing the poor said mattered. The ranchers decided whose lives were to be saved, and if nobody claimed them, they were executed or taken to prison. The same thing happened to the men nobody knew, the migrant workers. And then there was the punishment they gave us. They beat the prisoners with whatever they had on hand, with their sabers or even wire. Since I worked at San José, the ranch administrator Serapio García selected me to accompany six soldiers to look for the equipment that had been left at the strikers' camp. It took several trips to bring it all back and the soldiers kept it all. They took it with them when they left the ranch.

I have fond memories of Serapio García, the ranch administrator. He saved many people's lives. Whenever he saw a peon he knew, he approached Captain Anaya and said, "Captain, this poor boy didn't understand what he was getting mixed up in" or something like that, which saved many peoples lives. He was a highly regarded man.

But my foulest memory is of Sergeant Espíndola, who was merciless with the prisoners. And there were many like him among the troops. I don't want to say for certain, but I believe he shot many of the prisoners along the way just to take their belongings. For example, there's the fate of the Italian Ángel Paladino, which was completely unjust. He and several other prisoners were being taken to Helmich's ranch, two to a horse. They suddenly made Paladino dismount, gave his horse to someone else, had him sit down on a rock and shot him. The exact spot was at a place called El Contreras on what's now Zapata's Los Manatieles ranch, on the road from Ruiz's ranch to Truncado. I worked there as a shepherd and always visited him, as if he were a friend. His bones are still there, and so are the remains of his cap. His body was simply left on the ground next to the rock they made him sit on. We covered his bones with some branches as we passed.

At San José, the shooting was done at night. The first time they took three of us away. We personally felt each shot. Then they came for others.

The remains of the Argentine Ramón Medina are also in the area, out on the Maymo plateau near La Sierra police station. He was fleeing north with his men. The soldiers spotted them, waited for them to approach, and then took them down like game. Maybe that was his fate as a man, to die with his horses.

It was terrible. The next summer, Orencio Alba's brother visited the ranch. He was tracking down his brother's cart and thirty of his horses, beautiful horses that had disappeared after the executions. He came to San José to see where his brother was buried. At first, none of us dared to tell him. Finally we gave in. Imagine: when we reached the spot, he covered his face and started to cry. We had never seen a man, a great criollo like him, cry like that. It's because they killed Orencio in the foulest way. And if I ever come across Captain Anaya, I will ask him, "What crime did that man commit to be killed like that?" But… of course, that's man's fate, nothing more. What can you do?

Here ends the account of Antonio Tiznao. A typical working man of our Patagonia. A man of the land, frugal and attentive.

At San José, we also met Juan Andeado, a sixty-seven-year-old shearer from Pichileufú, Río Negro:

I was still a young boy when I ended up in Argüelles's group, which ended up here, on this ranch where I now work. I knew Orencio Alba well, he was a very hard worker despite his forty years. Captain Anaya took him aside and shot him on the spot. Orencio was from Chimpay, Río Negro and I believe his family was from Médanos in Buenos Aires province. Another acquaintance of mine, Oyarzún, is also buried here, executed on Anaya's orders as well, as was Martense, who owned a tavern out in Cerro Gorro and who never refused anything to anyone who was down on their luck. He was executed because there was a rancher who claimed that the tavern was on his land. He made Anaya believe that Martense was helping the strikers. They hogtied the poor man and left him in the horse corral. They refused him water and punished him like a beast. And then, on top of that, they shot him because they wouldn't be able to justify what they had done. The poor old man's legs had been broken and he couldn't stand up when they took him out to be shot.

After touring the big house and the shearing shed on the San José ranch, we headed out to visit the graves of the strikers, which were located some four hundred meters away in the direction of an enormous boulder that dominates the landscape. As we found a skull bearing the marks of a coup de grace, we decided to draft the following affidavit:

On January 14th, 1974, in the municipality of Puerto Deseado, we the undersigned—Leandro Manzo, cultural director of the government of Santa Cruz; Norberto Silvio Duran, employee of the aforementioned institution; Mario Echeverría, professor at the Río Gallegos Salesian School; Héctor Alberto Fente, employee of the Santa Cruz Provincial Farming Council; Osvaldo Bayer, historian—attest to the following:

On Thursday, the 10th day of the present month, we were on the San José ranch on Provincial Route 501 in the southwest area of the Deseado department. On the side of a hill next to the shearing shed, there is a rural cemetery identified by the locals as "the graveyard of the executed" and marked by a cross above an inscription reading: "1921. To those who perished for Liverty" (sic). Two hundred meters away, there are three crosses marking another burial site where we found a human skull on the ground, lying under some rocks. The skull showed clear signs of having received the coup de grace, with the entry wound on the left temple and the exit wound in the occipital bone. The wounds appear to have been caused by a heavy caliber weapon. We took the skull with us to be turned over to the Santa Cruz Provincial Museum. This discovery occurred at approximately 1600 hours. The following have affixed their signatures in witness there of: Leandro Manzo (I.D. 5.404.448), Norberto Silvio Duran (I.D. 8.247.946), Alberto Fente (I.D. 5.449.074), Osvaldo Bayer (I.D. 2.498.806), and Mario Echeverría (I.D. 7.318.525).

According to the information we received from Juan Andreado, the place in which the skull was found—together with broken human bones—was Martense's grave. Furthermore, the skull's teeth are worn down, as if belonging to an elderly man of roughly the same age as the Spanish businessman, while the rest of those executed were young or comparatively young.

We should note that the graves on the San José ranch—plus Elizondo's grave on the Alma Gaucha ranch—are the only ones still marked with crosses half a century later. This is a credit to the agricultural workers who have kept the memory of their fallen comrades alive. It is particularly moving to read the inscription on the enormous rock against which the workers had been executed: "1921. To those who perished for Liverty." How symbolic! It doesn't say that they died for higher wages or better working conditions, but for liberty. How different was the philosophy of our labor movement back then! "Liverty," as inscribed by the cal-loused hands of an uneducated worker.

Behind the cross is an enormous rock wall pockmarked with the bullets of the Argentine Army. This is a historic site, a natural monument commemorating those poor gauchos executed in the fight for "liverty," but also a reminder for us never to forget the name of General Elbio Carlos Anaya, who gave the order to take the lives of these men of the soil.

From there we headed to the Alma Gaucha ranch, which at the time was owned by the engineer Puchulú. The grave of the strike leader Elizondo, executed on January 1st, 1922, can still be found there. There were clearly no holidays for the executioners, not even New Years' Day. This execution was mentioned in one of Sub-lieutenant Loza's dispatches, although he attributes it to the Navy.

To finish our examination of Anaya's campaign, we only need to deal with the events at Tres Cerros, where he confronted a group of strikers under the command of the Uruguayan gaucho Pastor Aranda. The laurels here will go to Commissioner Albor-noz, a tough and courageous man who advocated immediately silencing anyone who dared to speak of strikes.

On December 20th, Anaya is still at the San José ranch, judg-ing his unhappy prisoners and organizing reconnaissance patrols to track down Facón Grande. At five o'clock that afternoon, a rancher named Doymo Duglesich brings news that a column of strikers has been spotted approaching Commissioner Albornoz's La Aída ranch, near Cerro Madre e Hija. The squadron hurries off in that direction at seven o'clock.

Here we will return to the testimony of Kuno Tschamler, the administrator of Mateo Martinovich's Santa María ranch. Recorded on May 8th, 1971 at the Adolfo González Chávez Per-manent History Center, this invaluable testimony coincides to a surprising degree with the troop movements and the events at Tres Cerros as mentioned in Anaya's military dispatches, which were written fifty years earlier.

Slowly and deliberately, Kuno sorts through his memories:

I was in charge of Mateo Martinovich's Santa María ranch, located between Puerto Deseado and San Julián. It was 1921 and Hipólito Yrigoyen was president. Patagonia's unions, confused by Spanish anarchists who were drunk on the outcome of the previous year's strike, thought to seize all the land for themselves. "We won't stop until Chaco" was their slogan. I never agreed with their demands. Life was better than anywhere else in the country. My boss had accepted all of the union's demands after the 1920 strike. Then they demanded even more and declared a general strike. Groups of up to two hundred strikers took the ranchers prisoner. They left one man in charge on each ranch and then took everyone and everything else with them: peons to swell their ranks, landowners as hostages, and whatever weapons they could find. It was a revolution of sorts. Pastor Aranda, a Uruguayan trade unionist, showed up at Santa María with thirty men. It was Sunday, December 18th, 1921. I went out to meet them at the gates. They aimed their rifles at me and asked for the boss. I asked them to come with me, on foot. While twenty-seven riders surrounded the ranch, all of them armed to the teeth, the other three dismounted. Mateo Martinovich ushered the delegation into his dining room. Pastor Aranda looked around cautiously and issued a stern warning about the consequences of resistance. "We will take all of your weapons, workers, horses and supplies," he said decisively. "You, Martinovich, will be coming with us, once you have selected someone to watch over your ranch." Mateo insisted on remaining, but they told him that it was Soto's decision and that the order was to take him away. Seeing that the strikers were unwavering, the boss decided to leave me in charge of his property. After looting the place, they left in a northwesterly direction. I still don't understand why those people acted the way they did. Two years of work were enough for me to afford a trip to Europe and indulge myself. And keep in mind that whenever landowners went to bars or restaurants frequented by workers, they weren't served until everyone had finished playing Truco, Mus, or some other card game. Well, let's get back to the strikers: two days after I had been left in charge of the ranch, an automobile stopped by. Its passengers included Lieutenant First Class Correa Morales, Commissioner Juan Albornoz, and Basilio Aranda, a local.

I ask Kuno if this Aranda was in any way related to Pastor Aranda:

They weren't related and they thought very differently. Pastor defended the idea that the land should belong to the workers, to the point of taking up arms, while Basilio was a fierce defender of private property.

Lieutenant First Class Correa Morales asked me which direction the strikers had headed and I replied that it was very probable that they had gone to the Laguna Chica ranch. I asked about the general state of the strike and he replied, "We're going to wipe them all out." Then he and his men left, I don't know where to.

Captain Anaya showed up the next day, accompanied by twenty soldiers, among them two machine gunners. He said that he knew where the subversives were. Basilio Aranda arrived early the next morning, this time accompanied by Albornoz and a sergeant named Baigorria. Albornoz, if I remember correctly, was a police commissioner or he had some other position with the police. He said that he knew the location of the group led by Pastor Aranda. I don't know how they found out about the position of the subversives but they headed in that direction, independently of Captain Anaya's troops. They came across one of the workers' sentries, who was sleeping at his post, and found out from him that the workers were getting ready to move on. Taking a gamble, Juan Albornoz sent the sentry ahead to tell the workers that they were completely surrounded by the army, asking them to surrender. It paid off brilliantly. The rebel workers debated their course of action for almost an hour and then surrendered. Then they were taken back to Santa María. There were around four hundred prisoners and five thousand horses. The hostages were freed and the strikers were disarmed and held in the corral. Their leaders were bound hand and foot. One of the machine gunners, or maybe it was a non-commissioned officer, I don't quite remember, formed part of the guard detail. He showed the prisoners the machine gun and asked them if they knew what it was. "Some sort of camera!" answered an Andalusian worker, who would later be shot. The interrogations lasted from December 25th to the 28th. During those days, I heard one of the officers say at dinner that they needed to shoot at least 10 percent of the prisoners to teach the rest a lesson, and that their deaths would be recorded as combat casualties. Mateo Martinovich was opposed to the executions, especially if they were to be carried out on his land. Martinovich thought that this was an excessive punishment for those poor wretches and suggested that they be handed over to the judge for sentencing. Captain Anaya then ordered Sergeant Espíndola to take eight of the leaders to San Julián, or to hand them over to any police officers he may encounter along the way, and then return. I later learned that this was done to deceive Martinovich, that they were taken to a ranch owned by Albornoz and executed. I don't remember their names, but I do know that the Andalusian who made the joke about the camera was among them. I remember that there were two Argentines, two Chileans, two Spaniards, one Uruguayan, and one Russian. Their bodies were burned with kerosene, which the troops had brought with them especially for this purpose.

When the peons were interrogated, if they said they didn't know or didn't remember the answer to the question, I remember that they were given twenty lashes "to help them remember." I asked Sergeant Espíndola, who slept in my room on the ranch, if he had shot many strikers. "One more and it'll be a hundred," he replied. The arrival of the naval troops put an end to the executions. I'm certain that many people would have survived if they had arrived before the army, but there was no such luck. These events affected me deeply and I lost fifteen kilos from nervous tension. I decided to go to Europe when the strike ended, and I returned in 1922.

Let's continue following the events at Tres Cerros. Captain Anaya's luck was running low in those days. A corporal—a conscript—who had died the day before was one of his most fanatical anarchist hunters, to the extent that he had been held up to the troops as a model for his outstanding ability to capture and punish the strikers. Anaya's dispatch reads as follows:

> Day 23, 2400 hours. While the troops were getting ready to sleep, the entire camp was startled by a shot fired from the revolver of a soldier named Peralta Eusebio who had dropped his gun while preparing to relieve the guards on duty. The shot fatally wounded Montenegro Domingo, a conscripted corporal. The acting commander was immediately alerted and proceeded to confirm the corporal's death, isolating Peralta and all eyewitnesses to the incident from the rest of the troops pending a preliminary inquiry.

An ex-servicemen named Saturnio Tapia, who lived in Morón until his death in 1969, had a very different story to tell. He told us that Montenegro was an argumentative and meddling individual who had driven Peralta crazy, though the latter was admittedly rather slow and provincial. Montenegro, abusing his stripes, played cruel jokes on him and forced him to clean up spittle and other disgusting things with his bare hands. This went on until Eusebio Peralta finally snapped and killed him with a single shot.

But Captain Anaya will correctly blame the imprisoned strikers. Because, in the end, they were guilty. If it hadn't been for the strike, Montenegro wouldn't have died. It's only logical. And with all the indignation that an Argentine officer can muster, Anaya writes in his dispatch:

Day 25, 1900 hours. The imprisoned strikers reached the camp on the Santa María ranch just as the convoy transporting Corporal Montenegro's remains was preparing to leave. The convoy delayed its departure several minutes to allow the squadron's commander to line up the prisoners to witness this imposing spectacle while giving them a speech about their responsibility for the officer's untimely death.

Captain Anaya was right. And his logic was felt by all the wretched chilotes who were forced to honor an Argentine soldier who admittedly hadn't fallen on the field of battle but had nevertheless given his life for his fatherland and its flag. And for the Argentines, it was a pleasure comparable only to the *droit du seigneur*.[24]

And again the official figures refute those rumors that the strikers were "well armed and supplied with ammunition" or "perfectly trained and commanded by officers of the Chilean Army." Anaya's dispatch on the Tres Cerros incident states:

2400 hours, December 25: Operational summary: Prisoners, 223; horses seized, 540; rifles seized, 47; revolvers and pistols, 53; abundant ammunition and assorted supplies.

And so it seems that this "armed revolution" had only one rifle for every five revolutionaries and a similar proportion of pistols. And this in a region where it was no secret that everybody, truly everybody, was armed in peacetime.

At Tres Cerros, Cavalry Captain Elbio Carlos Anaya's exemplary mopping-up campaign ended. In all the "fighting," his only loss was Corporal First Class Montenegro, killed by Peralta in an "accident."

In a telegram addressed to the War Ministry, Anaya states his four officers, sixty-three soldiers, and one machine gun detail were able to capture eleven prisoners at Hospitaleche's El Cerrito ranch, nine at Hospitaleche's Bella Vista ranch, seven at Osamenta, five at La Alianza, 250 at Tapera de Casterán, five at Vaga de Zaino, 204 at Tres Cerros, and twenty-seven at Martinovich's ranch.

He mentions prisoners but never clearly specifies the number of dead.

Regarding the events that occurred on the 26th, 27th, and 28th, Anaya says, "These days were spent registering prisoners and classifying them according to their degree of guilt."

But as Anaya's clean saber blows cut down the hopes of the strikers in north central Santa Cruz, in the south, near the cordillera, Varela's other captain was doing an exemplary job of ensuring that the peons of Santa Cruz would never again dare to raise their heads. Viñas Ibarra's actions, smelling of death, have a bloody halo of tragedy about them. And so that no one would doubt who was in the right and who had God on their side, this stark, brutal, and extremely craven action—though perhaps necessary as a patriotic holocaust—occurred on the largest ranch owned by the Menéndez Behety family, the descendants of that Asturian, José Menéndez, who allegedly massacred Indians but built temples as a sign of his humility before the Lord.

There, on the La Anita ranch, surrounded by the world's most breathtaking landscape, the foreign anarchists and Chilean wretches would be defeated once and for all.

Commander Varela's "Now they'll see" would be implemented in all its severeness, without hesitation, like machos, with orders given in a resounding military voice and obeyed with criollo boldness, with no qualms about who would be held responsible. After all, shooting a dirty Chilean in the head is not ladies' work. You have to get your hands dirty, you have to wade through warm blood—though the blood of the chilotes wasn't even that warm after centuries of hunger—you have to feel the true weight of your testicles and know exactly when to say "Chilean wretch" or "piece of shit Russian." No second thoughts, no ironic smiles. This was Commander Varela's duty and his hand would remain firm. Meanwhile, there were others, far off, who were incapable of acting but liked to read the newspaper and were pleased to see that somebody was able to do away with the rebels, ensuring that their immense fortunes had been made safe for generations to come.

But there's something Biblical in the idea that some must be sacrificed for the enjoyment of others. And this handful of young Argentine soldiers had indeed sacrificed themselves. In their dispatches, we shall see a story of forced marches day and night as they pursued the strikers through an inhospitable landscape.

After Punta Alta, Laguna Salada, and Fuentes del Coyle, where the strikers physically endured the brunt of Captain Viñas Ibarra's passions, the latter's troops set out to clean up all the ranches in the area known as the Cordillera Chica. But both Viñas Ibarra and Varela knew well that the southern region wouldn't be definitively pacified until Antonio Soto was captured. Soto had heard of the total defeat suffered by Outerelo and knew that he had been cut off from the rest of the strikers. He was also well aware that, under no circumstances, should the military forces be engaged in combat. Why? Because there weren't enough weapons, because the peons didn't have the least idea as to what combat meant. At best, they could prepare an ambush, but this would generate a tremendous backlash from the Argentine government and the army. Even if they managed to defeat Varela, what would happen next? Without any contacts in Buenos Aires, Punta Arenas, or even Río Gallegos, what could they expect?

In spite of it all, Soto hoped to come to some sort of arrangement with the army, although the news he received from Paso Ibáñez, which spoke of the deaths of Outerelo and Avendaño, dissuaded him from making overtures to Varela to repeat the previous year's achievements on the El Tero ranch.

Until early December, Soto dominated Lago Argentino, Lago Viedma, and their surroundings. His contingent had swollen to be the largest group of strikers: it contained more than six hundred workers. Many of those who had fled from Paso Ibáñez, Río Chico, or the Bella Vista ranch joined Soto. A very intelligent man named Pablo Schulz had arrived from Río Chico. A Chilean of German descent, he grew up in Punta Arenas, where his parents owned a hotel on Calle Borries. He was twenty-five years old and devoted to anarchist ideals. Erasmo Campos—whose testimony we have already examined—tells us that Pablo Schulz was constantly reading and considered the resolutions of strike assemblies to be sacred. This disciplined spirit would be the death of him.

Soto did quite a good job of organizing this motley crew. He took the Menéndez's La Anita ranch as his base of operations and from there he organized teams of twelve to twenty strikers who showed up on ranches unannounced, taking hostages, weapons, food and horses with them. They left promissory notes signed by Antonio Soto at each ranch, made out for the value of the "commandeered" goods, to be repaid by the Workers' Society following the end of the conflict. Another sign of Antonio Soto's influence over the strikers was the prohibition of alcohol consumption, though it was difficult to ensure compliance among the Chilean peons, especially in the middle of an uprising. Walter Knoll, the current administrator of the El Tero ranch and then a hostage of Soto's men, told us that when they arrived at La Anita, the first thing Soto did was order the destruction of all the alcohol on the ranch.

Soto tried to impose high moral standards. Jerónimo Berberena, who had a warehouse near Lago Argentino in Charles Fuhr and who later became an agent for La Anónima, told us the following anecdote about when Antonio Soto and his men arrived at his business.

It was a group of about twenty men. Among them, Soto stood out due to his blond hair, white skin, and great height. The rest were short, pallid chilotes, accompanied by a few Argentines. Among them were a few whose appearance was truly frightening, true gauchos with sinister faces and fierce glares. The first thing that Berberena did upon seeing the group arrive was to usher the women of his family into a locked room. While Berberena filled Soto's order for salt, sugar, and other trifles, two of the gauchos slipped away to the rear of the house, evidently looking for the women. Berberena, greatly concerned about something irreparable occurring in front of so many people, begged Soto to intervene. Soto flew into a rage and searched the house until he found the men, severely reproaching them for their conduct.

To this day, Berberena is still unable to understand how Soto, a Spaniard, managed to exercise so much authority over these unruly people, who generally didn't accept orders from anyone— much less from foreigners.

Experience will prove Soto's strategy of not confronting the army to be correct. During the first skirmish, which was not sought out by the strikers but only occurred due to an accidental encounter, they were routed by the soldiers. Here we will allow *La Unión* of Río Gallegos to speak, giving us the military's version of the events. The newspaper prints the following on December 3rd, 1921:

According to our special correspondent in Lago Argentino, there was an engagement on November 29th between the troops under the command of Captain Viñas Ibarra and the bandits on the grounds of William Dickie's Bon Accord ranch, near the El Perro police station.

A scouting patrol of ten soldiers from the 10th Cavalry Regiment had been sent one kilometer ahead of the bulk of the troops to explore the terrain by truck. They observed a group of more than twenty riders arrive from near El Perro, all of them armed with carbines and Winchesters and heavily laden with cargo. When the bulk of the troops arrived and the rebels were ordered to halt, many of the latter dismounted and dug in behind the large rocks scattered throughout those parts, opening fire on our nation's troops, while others fired from horseback. In light of this unexpected attack, the commanding officer ordered his men into formation to return fire with all the rapidity that the situation required. At that time, a rather large group emerged from the hollow in which they had been hiding, opening intense fire on the troops. As the fighting spread, many other rebels could be observed firing on horseback while another group, equally numerous, tried to surround the troops using elementary tactics.

A soldier named Alfredo Pereyra was wounded during the first minutes of the battle, taking two bullets in his left arm, though he continued fighting until the loss of blood kept him from standing his ground.

The bandits, who were well supplied with horses, abandoned the battlefield after two hours. They left behind five dead and a sizable number of wounded, as could be seen from the many large pools of blood staining the ground. But the numbers could not be confirmed as many of them managed to escape during the fighting.

This was the encounter at El Perro that was so demoralizing for Antonio Soto's men. The official story tells us of confrontation and combat. But historians get suspicious when all the casualties fall on the same side. Commissioner Guadarrama (who, as we have stated, was involved in many incidents throughout Varela's campaign and heard a great deal of eyewitness testimony, both from imprisoned chilotes as well as from officers, NCOs, and soldiers) states that the Battle of El Perro was nothing more than a chance encounter and that it occurred as follows: Antonio Soto and his men were returning from Charles Fuhr, where they had "borrowed" a great deal of merchandise, particularly tobacco. Their horses were heavily laden down. When they came to the crossroads, they had the bad luck of running into the truck carrying the soldiers under the command of Sergeant Sánchez, the advance party of the Viñas Ibarra column. Sánchez ordered them to halt. Antonio Soto immediately understood the situation they were in and ordered his men to disperse, knowing that if they dismounted and tried to resist they would be shot without mercy, which is exactly what happened. Soto was aware that the Winchesters and revolvers they carried could do nothing against the precision, long-range Mausers used by the army, never mind the difficulty of having to shoot from the saddle. And so they tried to flee.

Then the soldiers calmly took aim from their truck, as if at target practice. The chilotes who fell from their horses were dragged to the rocks and shot, even if they put their hands up. A few fought back, one of them wounding Pereyra, but they were all killed. It was almost fun, like a fairground shooting gallery, making mincemeat of the chilotes trying to hide behind rocks that were in some cases little more than rubble. It was like killing weasels as they try to burrow underground.

The pack horses were abandoned. The army will report that five workers were killed, but Commissioner Guadarrama will tell us that the inspection he conducted with Lieutenant Anello after the fact—which we will discuss later on—uncovered the existence of twenty bodies that remained out in the open several weeks later. Instead of being buried, the bodies were piled against the slope of a hill and covered with a thin layer of dirt. It took the wind and rain little time to unearth them, leaving the putrid flesh of the poor, half-naked wretches once again exposed to the elements.[25]

Viñas Ibarra's official report on the "Battle" of El Perro coincides with the version published in *La Unión*. But let's back up to the moment in which Viñas Ibarra cleanses the Cordillera Chica of strikers, teaching them a lesson at Fuentes de Coyle. Work resumes at each ranch visited by Viñas Ibarra. The Chileans are beaten into submission for half a century, perhaps more. Their backs bear the indelible marks of the Argentine Army.

There's no escape. Viñas Ibarra says it well in the dispatch dated November 17th:

I order ten men to head with me towards the Chilean border by way of Cancha Carrera. Upon arriving, I make contact with Chilean officers of the Magallanes Battalion and the carabinieri, who have stationed one hundred men and four machine guns along the border and have offered to cooperate with us. I thank them for the offer and we agree to close the passes along the cordillera from its southern limit up to Lago Argentino and

THE LONG MARCH TOWARDS DEATH

Lago Viedma. We mutually agree to hand over any dangerous individuals we apprehend, as well as to advise each other of any seditious movements that come to our attention; anyone who does not have my express written permission to cross the border will be prohibited from doing so.

La Unión of Río Gallegos will have this to say about the attitude of the Chilean armed forces: "Early this morning—December 12th—Commander Varela left in the direction of Lago Viedma, having stated that he is certain that the ringleaders will be captured as it will be impossible for them to cross the border, which is being closely watched by the Chilean carabinieri, who won't let the rebels pass." These are Varela's own offhand statements, made at the height of the campaign. It was later, when the executions needed to be justified in some way, that the conduct of the Chilean armed forces began to be questioned.

Captain Viñas Ibarra had done such a good job of teaching the defeated peons a lesson that he proudly writes the following in the dispatch dated November 21st:

> Most of the region's ranches have resumed work, which I have verified for myself. When I ask the workers if they have any complaints or demands, they reply that they can work peacefully so long as the army patrols the area, explaining that this is the only way to ensure that labor leaders don't bother them or shake them down for union dues or benefits that they will never receive.

The real advocate for the workers, in other words, is none other than Captain Viñas Ibarra himself. And the Argentine Army has become a supplier of cheap manual labor to the ranches—we shall examine the wages they pay later on. Viñas Ibarra himself explains the process in his dispatches:

> November 23: As this immense zone has already been pacified, I have been asked to supply peons. I divide up the prisoners at my

disposal and, after having returned their horses, I give them safe conduct passes for the Paile Aike, Esperanza Douglas, and San Elías ranches, along with several others in the territory's central and eastern regions.

But the most important part of Viñas Ibarra's punitive expedition is still to come. Before receiving orders from Commander Varela, he makes the following entry in his war diary, dated November 23rd: "Chilean officers have congratulated me on the squadron's performance and have repeated their offer to cooperate with us. I thank them and we agree, as before, to keep the passes closed." On the 24th, resupplied with gasoline, he receives Varela's orders to head to Lago Argentino. He leaves by truck that same day, bringing thirty-nine soldiers with him. He receives another message from Varela on the 25th that repeated the order to head to Lago Argentino, this time adding that Captain Campos would also be on the scene to provide support. Varela ends his message to Viñas Ibarra with a very suggestive phrase: "I recommend that you proceed with the greatest vigor."

On November 29th at 1:30 p.m., the encounter at El Perro occurs, which we have already described and whose outcome will be judged by Viñas Ibarra as follows:

The enemy has left behind five dead, along with some weapons, many dum-dum bullets and some horses, many of them loaded down with goods and supplies. On our side, we had one wounded soldier (Alfredo Pereyra, who had enough strength to shout, "Long live the 10th Cavalry!" as he fell, passing his ammunition to his fellow soldiers) and a great deal of losses in terms of clothing and state property. This battle on the Río Perro, near Lago Argentino, showed the mettle of our soldiers: sixteen days of continuous campaigning day and night with no time to rest, always on the alert with weapons drawn and often engaging in combat in an unfamiliar land whose inhabitants were mostly Chileans. We can rightly say, without a hint of egoism, that this is a heroic feat that our nation cannot forget. We must honor this handful of soldiers who, after finishing their term of service, returned to their ranks, thus showing the bravery and selflessness that the Argentine soldier is capable of when asked to give his all for the good of the fatherland.

These patriotic soldiers will find themselves surrounded by a marvelous landscape: Lago Argentino. A beauteous paradise. The perfect setting for heroic deeds.

But the story we have to tell is significantly sadder. An unwanted story of needless cruelty. In the midst of such natural beauty, man's egoism and intolerance will be all the clearer. Here, in front of this shimmering lake, many men died petty, absurd deaths. Killed for being chilotes, for being poor, for going on strike, for having wanted to one day be free, for having stolen the odd article of clothing, for having burned down the odd shed, as if out of a ritual from their indigenous past. Or for being Russians, for being anarchists, for believing in unachievable utopias. Killed. Killed on the shores of a lake named after Argentina, so there would be no room for doubt.

On December 2nd, Viñas Ibarra and twenty of his soldiers row across the Río Santa Cruz. Thirty kilometers from the lake, they come across a group of ten strikers near the Río Leona and overpower them. This is enough for the group of workers operating near Río Leona to completely lose hope. Without leaders—Antonio Soto is back at La Anita—without supplies and, above all, still believing that the army will provide the solution, they decide to send two delegates to Viñas Ibarra and negotiate a settlement. This will be convenient for the officer, who is facing an outbreak of mumps among the troops, but he doesn't waver. Like Commander Varela, he rattles his saber and scares them off. When the delegates offer to surrender if the federal government releases its political prisoners (Viñas Ibarra will mention in his report that they also demand to be "left at liberty so as to return to work, retaining their weapons"), the captain responds by saying, "If you don't unconditionally surrender within the next twenty-four hours, handing over all horses, weapons, and prisoners, then we will ford the river and take you by force."

His uncompromising stance has the intended effect, but Soto makes one last effort. He crosses the lake and speaks in the assembly that night. There are two options on the table: surrender or resistance. The La Leona group is entirely made up of Chileans, peons who lack even a basic understanding of unionism and class struggle. Antonio Soto tells them that there's a third option: going to Puerto Irma or Centinela by steamboat and joining the La Anita group. Antonio Soto's proposal is approved, but of the 180 men who voted in the assembly, only eighty follow him. The rest, one hundred strikers, decide to inform Viñas Ibarra that they will unconditionally surrender, traveling by steamboat to Puerto Irma on December 6th and driving their horses through Charles Fuhr.

And so they do. They are there at dawn on December 6th, waiting for Viñas Ibarra to give the order to disembark. The first to come ashore are the ranchers and administrators who had been taken hostage. Then come the peons. They hand over everything they have: thirty Winchesters, plenty of ammunition and provisions, and (according to Viñas Ibarra) the steamboats, intact. The hostages, all eighty of them, are each individually saluted by the officer.

And then, just after disembarking, a wretched-looking Chilean is shot without warning. This is witnessed by Berberena, a local businessman and a long-serving justice of the peace.

A few hours later, Viñas Ibarra will receive crucial support: Captain Campos arrives, accompanied by thirty-three men and enough ammunition to finish Antonio Soto off, once and for all. This gives him the courage to head out and immediately crush the anarchist who was hiding with his men at La Anita. Viñas is briefed by a man named Amador Álvarez who had managed to pry information out of the strikers. This is the man who claimed that the Chileans were tired of always wandering from ranch to ranch and could be persuaded to surrender.

The night of December 6th–7th would be the most terrible of Antonio Soto's life. He knows that the army is on his trail. He knows that his men are tired; they have been wandering across the vast plains of Patagonia for sixty days now, and he knows that he can't offer them any other solutions than to flee once more.

The presence of army patrols, which appear suddenly and then disappear just as suddenly, has utterly demoralized the strikers. They don't understand what's going on and think that things would play out the way they did during the previous strike, when the police were bad but the army was the only institution that could negotiate a settlement and keep the landowners in check. Neither Antonio Soto's arguments that no nation's armed forces could be trusted, nor Pablo Schulz's tales of firing squads and fallen comrades, can convince the peons otherwise.

The fair-haired Pablo Schulz is another whom Soto was unable to convince, despite their long conversations around the campfire. As a good anarchist, Schulz believes in direct action and holds that their only option is to confront the troops. "They'll scatter like rats at the first shot," he says. Soto disagrees. Despite having proved his bravery time and again, he's not enough of a fanatic to believe that they could triumph in a direct confrontation with the army: they don't have enough weapons, and the ones they do have—Winchesters and Savages—have a shorter range than Viñas Ibarra's Mausers. Furthermore, the peons lack military experience and the will to fight. As far as they are concerned, the real enemies are the police officers who beat them and shake them down for the few pesos they have. But fighting the army, no, they don't want to get involved in that. This is the moment when Antonio Soto realizes his biggest mistake: organizing a strike that is absolutely anarchist in form—authentic, sudden, unexpected, impulsive—without the support of a rank and file that understands the basic notions of human freedom and its enemies. And this will be seen that night, one that is perhaps more dramatic than the bloody day that follows. And sadder, because the sentiments that prevailed throughout this incredible adventure have faded. Here is where words like solidarity, nobility, and courage begin to disappear.

Soto knows that the army is now quite close. He has seen the fate of the Río Leona group. There's no time left to lose. He calls an assembly. And here is his other great mistake. While the enemy moves on the orders of one man, an officer who shouts out his orders to soldiers who move like automatons, here they follow the anarchist method, where each individual is his own master and everyone has the right to express his opinion.

That night at Lago Argentino, while the soldiers ready their weapons and Viñas Ibarra and Campos study their maps, the strikers spend long hours in debate. The Spaniards rail against capitalist exploitation, priests, politicians, and the government in general. The Chileans are amused by these speakers who get red in the face as their denunciations of the powerful intensify. The assembly drags on indefinitely, but it amounts to little more than wind. At least until just before dawn, when the campfires burn low and the coming light of day warns them that danger is approaching, that things are getting serious. The time for play is done and reality takes over. A bright Chilean named Juan Farina says that they can't go on any longer, that they hadn't declared the strike to take on the army or to redistribute the land, that all they wanted was to be paid fairly and treated well, that they're no longer interested in moving from ranch to ranch, that they have to negotiate with the army, and that it will only make things worse to try and trick them. The peons support him. Then it's Pablo Schulz's turn to speak. He's a far-from-talented orator, but his words nevertheless fall like hammer blows: he argues that the only way to win is to fight, that it's not possible to return to slavery after showing the mighty that they were capable of rising up, that they can't negotiate with the officers who murdered their comrades at Punta Alta and Paso Ibáñez, that the strike was declared to secure the freedom of their comrades in Río Gallegos, and that they can't abandon them now, that there's only one option left: to fight. They must ready their weapons and organize themselves, putting Comrade Otto in charge of the defense and using bales of wool to set up barricades. They need to dig in at La Anita and fight to the last man.

This dramatic assembly was described to us by Walter Knoll, the current administrator of the El Tero ranch, who was then a hostage of the strikers; Antonio Fernández, a striker who played a role in every dramatic moment at La Anita but still managed to survive; and Alberto Francisco Lada,[26] whose detailed testimony regarding the executions at Lago Argentino is key to understanding the tragedy that occurred there.

Pablo Schulz had named Otto as the commander of the strikers. Otto was a character who would have been unbelievable in any other circumstances. One of those beings who seem to be created for extreme situations, which magnetically attract them and place them in position to act, as if on a stage. And then history often passes by without even recording their names. It's as if fate ironically added dramatic touches to make reality more theatrical, stranger than the work of the imagination, than any illusion. And of German Otto, as he was called in the police reports, we have been unable to learn even so much as his last name.[27]

Not even our witness Walter Knoll—who talked to him in German—can remember his last name. "I never asked him," he tells us. Everyone called him Otto. He was a tall, thin man with blond, almost reddish hair. He was close to forty years old, had a long-suffering face and a receding hairline that made his forehead look bigger than it really was. He dressed like a sailor and his accent was that of a Rhinelander. After the war—he had fought for four years on the western front—he set out on his own to explore the world. When he arrived in Patagonia, he worked his way from ranch to ranch on foot, as he lacked a horse—a typical German *landstreicher*.[28]

Contrary to the false claims made by modern historians, lecturers and "strategists" who insist that the strikers were assisted by the Chilean Army, the absolute truth is that the only "instructor" that the rebel peons had at their disposal was German Otto, who was never promoted past the rank of private during all four years of the war in Europe.

The strikers obtained their first Mauser when they took Officer Pucheta prisoner, and since none of them knew how to use it, they gave it to German Otto. Whenever they had a moment to spare, he would satisfy the curiosity of the strikers by showing them how to load it, how to handle the bolt, how to aim it, and what the sight was for. He also showed them how German soldiers used to storm enemy trenches, etc. This was the entirety of the "military training" received by the strikers.

Pablo Schulz's dramatic harangue ends amid complete silence. Nobody wants to fight, nobody wants to take on the army that they all believe is invincible, solid, and—so they believe—not to be provoked.

Antonio Soto believes that his moment has arrived. After the failure of Pablo Schulz, he feels that it's time to exercise his moral authority and his powers of persuasion, which have proven so influential in the past. He tells them that the army cannot be trusted, that soldiers have executed their comrades at Punta Alta and Paso Ibáñez, severely punishing all those who surrendered. We shouldn't play their game, he says, we can't surrender, we must triumph. We called the strike on behalf of our imprisoned comrades and we will return to work with dignity after we have secured their freedom. But none of this will occur without sacrifice. We should remain in hiding. We should continue taking hostages from among the bosses and their agents. When we see the army coming, then it's time for us to leave. We should split into smaller groups and disappear, regrouping later. We should hide in the forests and in the cordillera until the government, the military, and the ranchers realize that they have to negotiate with us and settle, because if they don't, Patagonia will become a wasteland.

Pablo Schulz interrupts him. He doesn't believe it. His blood is boiling. He says that the time has come to go for broke. He cites the example of the Russian Revolution. This might be the last time they would all be together, and they needed to think of their imprisoned and fallen comrades. They have to do it for them, to free the prisoners and avenge the fallen. There is no excuse for continuing to run. Their ranks will continue to thin, their supplies are running low, the land has nothing to offer but more mutton, and there is no better place to dig in and resist than La Anita. There they could remain one month, two, a whole year and the army wouldn't dare enter. And this would show the world what they could accomplish and they would earn everyone's respect.

Unwittingly, Schulz's attack on Antonio Soto plays right into the hands of Farina, who speaks up and says that there's no point in running any longer, that they're backing themselves into a corner, and that the forces arrayed against them are growing stronger each day. The government is powerful and if they see that they can't destroy us with one regiment, they'll send another. There isn't enough weaponry or ammunition. If they stay the course they'll only irritate the army even more. It's better to open negotiations and settle, like during the previous strike.

Soto speaks, desperately striving to convince the chilotes, who evidently want no more confrontations. He plays his trump card, proposing that they send two men to speak with the troops under the cover of a white flag, and ask the officers about the conditions for the release of their comrades in Río Gallegos and the implementation of last year's settlement. He hopes that this will buy him enough time to convince the strikers, one by one, to continue the strike. And if the army accepts, he would have to go to Río Gallegos first to verify that the men of the Workers' Society had indeed been released.

But Soto is a dreamer, he has lost touch with reality. He doesn't know that he's facing captains Viñas Ibarra and Campos, worthy sons of Commander Varela. Free the prisoners? A joke, surely. This is between men, not ladies. There will be neither negotiations nor settlements. There will only be yea or nay. Nothing else.

The assembly approves Soto's suggestion and names two delegates, tough Chileans who won't frighten easily. They go to Viñas Ibarra's camp to open negotiations as instructed.

And so it goes. Neither Viñas Ibarra nor Campos can be reproached. They're not afraid of shadows. In this completely unfamiliar landscape, while their soldiers face an outbreak of mumps, they set out for La Anita to end things once and for all. While the Spaniards carry on shouting and the somnambulant Chileans stare on, the army advances. Viñas Ibarra's dispatch uses precise language and contains no rhetorical flourishes, leaving no room for doubt. Reality advances with clips filled with lead, lead that will neither forgive nor ask for permission:

> December 7: I set off with all of my troops in the direction of La Anita, located eleven leagues away, where the groups operating in the lake region have gathered and are preparing to resist. Upon arriving at the Quién Sabe ranch, I order Sub-lieutenant Frugoni Miranda and twenty-five soldiers to head in the direction of La Anita. This group will cut across the mountains via Calafate, Quebrada del Cerro Comisión, and Quebrada del Cerro Centinela to take the hills behind La Anita, where they will await my frontal assault and either cooperate or hold the rear in case the enemy retreats or flees.

When Viñas Ibarra reaches Cerro Comisión, the two Chilean delegates take him by surprise. A veteran named Moran who was a witness to the encounter provided us with the details. Two rather arrogant chilotes demand to speak with the commanding officer—as equals—so as to negotiate the terms of a settlement. Viñas Ibarra shakes with indignation upon seeing that these foreigners, these two wretched, stinking Chileans, have the nerve to come to him and speak of terms. What terms, if they are but rebels, bandits, foreigners who have no business in Argentina besides working and keeping their mouths shut? What terms?

His holy indignation, the authentic indignation of an Argentine, is limitless. He forces them to dismount, binds their hands behind their backs, and whips them all the way to the river, asking them where it can be forded. Once they show him the spot, he has them shot without another word so that they can go and talk terms with Jesus Christ.

You need to have red blood in your veins for such an act and Viñas Ibarra has it. He can't stand the idea that Chileans could so insolently demand to talk terms with an Argentine officer in the field.[29]

But despite his rage, Viñas Ibarra doesn't lose his head. He sends an NCO and two soldiers to La Anita with a white flag. His strategy will prove effective: his only offer is unconditional surrender, but he assures them that they will all be respected and treated well.

The NCO arrives at La Anita and speaks with Antonio Soto, Juan Farina, and Pablo Schulz. They will have to surrender unconditionally but they will be treated with respect and allowed to return to work without being harassed. And Commander Varela himself will take personal responsibility for freeing the prisoners in Río Gallegos. (Alberto Lada remembers the NCO's first words upon arriving: "We haven't come with the intention of doing anyone harm.")

The leaders ask for an hour and call an assembly. Farina argues in favor of accepting. Schulz, more than ever, wants to resist. Soto gives the speech of his life. Shouting dramatically, he commands everyone's attention. As he speaks, his Spanish blood comes to the fore:

They will shoot every single one of you, no one will be left alive. Let's flee, comrades, let's continue with the strike until we win. Don't trust the military, they're the most despicable, treacherous, and cowardly pack of dogs on the planet. They are professional cowards, resentful because they are forced to wear uniforms and obey orders their entire lives. They don't know the meaning of work and hate free thinkers. Don't surrender, comrades, await the coming dawn of social redemption, which will bring freedom for all. Let's fight for this dawn, let's hide in the forest. Do not surrender.

He beats his fists against his breast, shouts, and even sheds a tear when nobody responds. He tries to raise his men's irreparably fallen spirits, but they are already resigned to their fate. But Soto doesn't want to give up and so he gives his all in this final assembly, surrounded by the marvelous landscape of Lago Argentino:

> You are workers, you are laborers! See this strike through until our definitive triumph, when we will create a new society where there are neither poor nor rich, where there are neither weapons nor uniforms nor soldiers, where there is happiness and respect for human life and nobody will have to kneel before a priest or a boss.

Schulz says that they need to begin putting up barricades with bales of wool at once, right under the nose of the NCO. He says that there's still time, that their only salvation lies in fighting. But the die has already been cast. The NCO kindly tells them that they've run out of time and that the army will consider a failure to reply as an act of aggression.

The assembly votes, approving Farina's motion in favor of unconditional surrender by an overwhelming majority. Schulz says that he's completely opposed to the idea but will bow to the will of the majority (the hereditary disease of German discipline will be his downfall). Soto, however, rebels against the decision. He says that he doesn't plan to fall into the hands of the soldiers and that he refuses to meet such a miserable end. One last time, he calls on everyone to follow him. Schulz reprimands him, saying that the will of the majority must be respected and that everyone must share the same fate. Soto bids farewell with the words, "I am not meat to be thrown to the dogs—if my comrades are staying to fight then I'll stay, but my comrades don't want to fight" (as witnessed by Fernández and Lada). So, in the end, Soto would have accepted Schulz's proposal, but surrender never.

Barely a dozen men follow him.[30] They mount their horses as night falls. They disappear like ghosts. They don't know what fate awaits them, but they still have one final spark of rebellion: they won't tolerate humiliation. Theirs is to be a troubled path. Except for Antonio Soto, they are all experienced horsemen. And so they depart. Soto had tried talking Pablo Schulz into joining them again and again, but the blond man refused. He's stubborn. He knows that he's going to be executed, but it seems that dying is the only way for him to prove that the rest of the strikers were wrong in not supporting his proposal.

The riders head towards the cordillera. They have nothing but what they carry with them, but that does include good weapons—Winchesters, revolvers, and ammunition. It won't be easy to catch them. They are fierce, determined people. Their guide is José Luna, alias Guatón Luna: a chubby Chilean who knows the cordillera well and has been riding horses he was a small boy. Guatón Luna is followed by Florentino Macayo, Antonio Soto, José Ramos, Ángel Perdomo, Pedro Marín, Galindo Villalón, José Cárdenas, Rosas, Mena, Cuadrado, Martínez the Spaniard, and Miguel Zurutusa.

This list of names and nicknames is included in the official statement released by the government of Santa Cruz asking the Chilean carabinieri to hunt them down, arrest them, and turn them over to the Argentine police.

The decision made during the assembly at La Anita spelled the end of the strike. With Soto gone, the Workers' Society ceased to exist. Facón Grande, in northern Santa Cruz, was the only leader left.

But before we get to him, we will see how the army makes an example out of the strikers captured at La Anita. When the NCO is told that the workers have agreed to surrender, he orders them to pile up all their possessions—whether weapons, quillangos, or saddles—and then line up to await the soldiers. The hostage ranchers, administrators, butlers, and foremen are left in the shearing shed that the strikers were using to hold them. One of the soldiers rides off and notifies Viñas Ibarra of the surrender. And when Viñas Ibarra arrives at La Anita, he is greeted with a spectacle worthy of a victorious soldier. There are the famous red strikers of Patagonia, the feared bandits, lined up in a gesture of total submission to Argentina's armed forces.

The first thing he does is review the prisoners, intimidating them and shouting, "Where is Antonio Soto? Where is Antonio Soto, you bastards?"

Soto was not wrong about the fate that would await him if he had stayed. He would be punished, manhandled, and then finally shot in front of the rest of the strikers as a demonstration of what happens to subversive and anti-patriotic foreigners in Argentina. They would have left him gasping on the ground before the lascivious gaze of the victors and the vanquished, dying like a wounded weasel or a beaten dog. The necessary punishment.

But neither Viñas Ibarra nor Campos nor Varela will ever find Antonio Soto. Worse for those who remained, they would be the ones to pay the price. Idiots. You can't act a fool and then ask for forgiveness. Here at La Anita, the peons will be disabused of the idea of going on strike for centuries to come. The soldiers will ensure that, from this moment on, the peons will simply bend down and focus on their work, thinking of nothing more. The red flag, trade unions, petitions, songs of social revolution—that has all ended. The Argentine Army has arrived to clean up the region once and for all, just as the landowners had done years earlier when they ensured that the Indians would never again trespass on their pasture land.

Antonio Soto's disappearance greatly disappoints Viñas Ibarra, who frees the ranchers and their employees, asking them to point out the ringleaders.

Officer Pucheta is the most insistent, singling out Pablo Schulz and German Otto. He tells Viñas Ibarra that German Otto was the one who taught the Chileans how to fire his Mauser. When they take Schulz and Otto two hundred meters off to the side to execute them, Otto shouts at Viñas Ibarra in his broken Spanish, "This is not how you kill people! Not even in the European war, where I fought for four years, did they ever execute unarmed prisoners!"[31]

This same argument will be employed weeks later in parliament by a deputy criticizing Lieutenant Colonel Varela's conduct.

They execute another seven strikers that night, just to make things clear. Then Viñas Ibarra begins to apportion blame. Terror spreads among the chilotes, who are packed tight in the sheds. Each striker is given a candle, which they must keep lit throughout the night. This is evidently a means of keeping the place illuminated.

In the meantime, the rest of the hostages are released. At this time, a Chilean named Mansilla gets an idea that will end up saving his life. He and a group of eight other Chileans ask to speak with Viñas Ibarra, saying that they know where Antonio Soto is hiding and that they can bring him back to camp. The captain believes them because he has noted so much fear among the prisoners that he doesn't suspect that they could be capable of trickery. And so he allows them to ride off. That was the last he ever saw of Mansilla and his comrades, of course. It was as if the earth had swallowed them up.

This story was confirmed by Walter Knoll, Fernández, and Lada. And to this day, Chilean peons still laughingly pay tribute to Mansilla's audacity as they retell the story around their campfires on the ranches of Santa Cruz. It is, perhaps, the only revenge this simple people has had over the years for the deaths of so many of their own.

Viñas Ibarra and Campos don't sleep that night; they're too busy separating the wheat from the chaff, the righteous from the sinners. They are quite strict. The ranchers participate in the selection process. Helmich, Bond, and Willy Rintelmann (the administrator of Liniers's El Rincón ranch) are the most active, as is Cabeza de Cobre, the nickname given to La Anita's administrator, the man most trusted by Menéndez Behety.[32]

Walter Knoll, the current administrator of El Tero and an eyewitness to the massacre, has told us that the night following the surrender was a terrible one. The Chileans were "taken for a stroll" one by one. (This is the same expression used by Edelmiro

Correa Falcón to describe what happened at La Anita.) Knoll clashed with Viñas, who he said was unbending, refusing to listen to his pleas. He would only save a peon's life if they were claimed by their boss, and even then only if their boss provided the most glowing references. Clark, the owner of El Tero, hadn't arrived that night and the police had accused Walter Knoll of being a "labor delegate." Which was a true, but Knoll hadn't sought out the position. Clark had appointed him—a trusted man—as the ranch's labor delegate following the first strike, in compliance with the settlement arranged with the Workers' Society. The ranch's peons didn't oppose the decision because Knoll always listened to their concerns and worked impartially to solve their problems. The El Tero ranch had a somewhat paternalistic system but few major problems. But when Antonio Soto showed up during the second strike, Knoll opposed the use of force and was taken hostage.

Viñas Ibarra dismissed Knoll's explanations and ordered two non-commissioned officers to "take him for a stroll":

Two non-commissioned officers made a Chilean peon and I grab shovels and then took us away, saying, "Don't get upset, you're not going to be shot, you're just going to bury the ones we've already executed." But I had overheard the orders given to Viñas Ibarra and knew that I was done for. Everything was clear to me. As we walked away, I spent a lot of time thinking about having come so far just to die without even having committed a crime—I wasn't even a striker. After we had gone about four hundred meters, they told us to stop and dig and to do it as quickly as possible so that we could go back to the ranches where we worked. My despair was total but there was nothing I could do. The sergeant and the corporal were ready for anything. Even if we worked slow, we couldn't delay too long because we were afraid of making them angry and being shot on the spot.

It was something indescribable. We knew that we were going to die but we still wanted to delay our deaths for a few minutes more, just in case there was a miracle. Then a soldier rode up and spoke with the sergeant. They looked at me and said, "You're saved, German. Your boss is here." As it turned out, Clark had just arrived and immediately asked where I was. When they took me to him, he hugged me and burst into tears. Then he praised my character in front of Viñas Ibarra. I will never forget this. My life was saved by chance. Then the boss rescued several peons he knew from among the prisoners and we returned to El Tero that same morning, leaving that tragic place as soon as possible. I know that the executions continued without interruption and that they killed all the Chileans who weren't claimed by their bosses.

Ranchers who know Knoll have told us that his personality underwent a change after Clark saved his life. He remained unshakably loyal to his boss the rest of his life and refused to leave El Tero, turning down every job offer he received and ignoring the pleas of his family to return to Germany. Aside from sporadic trips to Río Gallegos or Punta Arenas, he never left the ranch and he's still in charge of everything at El Tero at the age of seventy-five. He was deeply grieved by the death of his boss—which occurred many years later—but he never left the ranch. After finishing his tale, he told us:

> I was always against the strike. Given the circumstances, I think you had to be crazy to think it was a good idea. But no matter how guilty the strikers were, there was no reason for them to be executed like that. It was a crime, a horrible crime to kill unarmed people like that without even asking their names. I don't understand how the Argentine Army could have done such a thing.

And once again he repeats the last words of German Otto: "Not even in the European war, where I fought for four years, did they ever execute unarmed prisoners!"

Antonio Fernández, a seventy-seven-year-old Spaniard living on a farm near Río Gallegos, has told us a very similar story. He added that the Chileans who weren't rescued by their bosses were subjected to a rushed screening process. A chilote wearing new clothes would be accused of having stolen them and was then promptly sent off to explain himself to St. Peter. He would have to hand over this new clothing before washing away his sins in Argentine lead, of course. But things weren't any better for those chilotes who were a bit too beaten down by life—they were taken for rabble, the scum of the earth. What purpose did these wretched people serve, with their fierce glares? There was clearly no reason to let them live, much less if they were going to cause problems in Argentina. These were the ones who perhaps suffered the most as they were left for last, swept up like refuse after a hard day's work. Or perhaps they didn't suffer, because it's hard to imagine God endowing such filth with the capacity for suffering. They resembled broken-down Buddhas waiting patiently for death or a whipping or a few blows from behind. Maybe it was all the same to them.

Edelmiro Correa Falcón calculates that there were roughly 120 executions at La Anita. Commissioner Isidro Guadarrama tells us that the total number must have been between 140 and 150, but takes Correa Falcón's figure seriously. He has also told us that it was Captain Campos whose cold-bloodedness ensured that none of the soldiers wavered. Commissioner Guadarrama was sincerely objective in remembering Sub-lieutenant Frugoni Miranda's feelings about personally executing his Chilean prisoners. "He shot them in the head," he said, "with a truly astonishing serenity."

Now let's examine the statements made by Octavio Ramón Vallejos, a cavalry soldier who served in Viñas Ibarra's squadron. He recounted what happened at La Anita on the night of December 7th, 1921 to the historians of the Adolfo González Chávez Permanent History Center:

That night they shot many of the workers who were thought to be the leaders. I was part of the firing squad. Generally speaking, the workers were lined up, elbow to elbow, in front of a ditch. Some of them fell in, others fell along the ledge or lay with only half their body in the ditch. We never buried them.

Vallejos goes on to tell us of the execution of an adolescent, one of the incidents that the anarchists made such a fuss about later and that can now be confirmed by the declarations of Viñas Ibarra's soldier:

On our way to some ranch, I don't remember which, we came across a fifteen-year-old boy who said he was looking for work. The captain let him go but then we came across him a second time and then a third. We discovered that he was a messenger for the strikers. He was shot alongside two other men. I remember the boy's bravery. When we took him before the firing squad, he shouted "Murderer!" to our commander and then he fell. One of the bullets severed his tongue. The truth is that when you're a soldier you're not afraid of death, you don't feel a thing when you're getting ready to kill, but I deeply regretted the death of this boy. I had to hide it from my superiors, though. When we were on La Anita ranch, one of the leaders slipped away from us, a Spaniard named Soto. Once, after an execution, I saw Corporal Sosa spit on the dead. I asked him angrily, "Why are you spitting on the dead?" He didn't answer, nor did he pull rank and punish me.

If the strikers were courageous, then the soldiers were equally so. No one shirked their duty. The deaths of Pablo Schulz and German Otto show us how human beings can face their destiny with serenity and stoicism. Walter Knoll told us that when they took Otto away, he nostalgically shouted, "*Grüsse an die alte Heimat!*" ("Send my regards to the old country!"), realizing that he would never again see the land of his youth. We also have the testimony of Captain Viñas Ibarra's own assistant, as recorded by the Adolfo González Chávez Permanent History Center. His name is Juan Faure. He is one of the oldest members of the Rural Workers and Stevedores' Union of Adolfo González Chávez and he did his military service in the 10th Cavalry:

> I was at La Anita, where I was put in charge of executing the first batch of strike leaders, me and five other soldiers. The prisoners, who were held together after the surrender, sat on the ground as they waited to be classified by the ranchers so that those who committed crimes during the strike or acted as labor organizers could be executed. We were told to execute a group of seven prisoners. Two of them, both Germans, asked the sub-lieutenant for permission to embrace before dying, as they were old traveling partners and death would be a small price to pay for everything they had done together. The shot I fired at one of the Germans only wounded him in the chest. He unbuttoned his shirt and, pointing to his heart, told me, "Fire another one so I can die quickly." But the sub-lieutenant [Frugoni Miranda, as named elsewhere by Faure] said, "Let him suffer a bit so he can pay for what he's done." He died after the second shot. There was another group of soldiers behind the firing line. They were armed with carbines and had been given orders to shoot anyone who refused to execute the strikers. We had orders to bury the corpses, but to save themselves the trouble of digging graves, some of the soldiers disobeyed and burned the bodies with kerosene. They were later arrested for this. The soldiers also always searched the pockets of the dead before burning them or burying them, keeping a little bit of money (in Chilean currency) for themselves.

Strange. It must be hard for those Argentines who are used to trusting the nation's institutions to believe that our soldiers could have done this. Stealing from the corpses of workers who were executed for going on strike. Taking the few pesos they had earned herding sheep, riding all day with calloused backsides and braving the cold and the snow, with no women to keep them company, no affection, no children, no books, and no schools. Always with the dumb grin of a Chilean peon, humble and evasive, on their faces.

Men with unwashed faces. Nameless, long-suffering men with glassy stares, as if the mutton of the sheep they slaughtered had reincarnated itself in their lifeless faces, in their shapeless bodies, in the clothing they only wore to hide their shame, as it did nothing to protect them from the cold. Chileans. Or perhaps not even that. Chilotes, nothing more than chilotes.

And even as these men were gasping their last breaths after facing the firing squad, like dogs rolling on the ground, there was someone going through their pockets. A shameless, obscene act.

More valuable testimony regarding the executions ordered by Captain Viñas Ibarra at La Anita has been provided by Juan Radrizzani, a veteran of the 10th Cavalry Regiment who lives on Calle Sebastián Costa in Tres Arroyos.

Juan Radrizzani tells us that he was born in Tres Arroyos on April 6th, 1900. A blacksmith by trade, he and several other young men from his town were assigned to the 10th Cavalry in March 1921 and were stationed at Campo de Mayo.

We ask him if he remembers the names of the other soldiers, and he tells us:

> Yes sir. There was Ceriani from Tres Arroyos, now deceased; Ulises Coman, who's still alive, you can go visit him if you want; Ramón Errea, who's also from Tres Arroyos but who's very sick right now; Francisco Pardiñas, who currently lives in Barrow, having retired from the municipal government; Juan Napolitano, from Aparicio; and Juan Saur, from Coronel Suárez.

They sailed south that November on the *Guardia Nacional*, disembarking in Río Gallegos on the 10th or 11th of that month. He remained in Río Gallegos to watch over the regiment's belongings—thank God, he says—but he had the bad luck to be ordered to drive seventy cans of gasoline out to La Anita, near Lago Argentino. By the time his truck reached the ranch, the strikers had already surrendered and their leaders were being executed.

When we realized what was going on, those of us who had just arrived at the ranch hid behind the shearing shed to avoid taking part in that terrible mission. But Saur the Russian stuck out his head to see what was going on and he was spotted by an NCO. They ordered us to form a firing squad. It was disgraceful. I was very afraid. When they ordered us to fire, my arms were trembling so much that my shots were twenty centimeters off. I had to fire and I remember I shot a Chilean in the groin. The poor man doubled over...

Radrizzani is so overcome that, after a long pause, he waves his hand as if to express the finality of something that he hadn't sought out.

And then he repeats, "Look, if Saur the Russian hadn't stuck out his head, then we wouldn't have had to shoot anybody..."

Later, after he calms down, he tells us about Lieutenant Colonel Varela's arrival several hours later:

He gave us a speech, trying to lift our spirits and explain why we needed to proceed in such a way. The strikers that were to be executed were being kept in a closely guarded shed. The firing squads were under the direct command of two corporals, and Sub-lieutenant Juan C. Frugoni Miranda supervised everything. Those of us who were on the firing squads also had to dig graves for the strikers, but we were barely able to cover up all the bodies. I remember that none of us could sleep afterwards; we spent the night telling each other stories. None of us said a word about what we had just done, except for one soldier who told us admiringly of the attitude of a German anarchist who told the firing squad that if they were going to kill him anyways, they could at least shoot right.

One of the condemned men tried to escape, making a break for it across open ground. He was felled by an unbelievably well-aimed shot by Sergeant Julio Moran. We left in the truck at 10 the next morning. By that time, thirty-three strikers had been executed.

And here we have Radrizzani's testimony. It's clear that his story makes him very uneasy. These are the dead ends that life has reserved for people who never expect to play a role in such dramas.

But not all men are alike. Let's leave Radrizzani behind and visit another veteran of the 10th Cavalry Regiment who also lives in Tres Arroyos: Ulises D. Comán. We visit him on a very cold day. Comán meets us on the street:

> Yes, I did my military service with Radrizzani in the 10th Cavalry, but I don't remember anything about the Patagonia campaign. I only remember that we went by ship and we returned by ship.

That's all. We ask him if he took orders from Captain Viñas Ibarra. "Yes, and Sergeant Esperguín, both remarkable men for whom I have the highest regard." All further questions are met by silence. He repeats that he doesn't remember the repression. We ask him if he was at Punta Alta and if there were executions there. He replies that the wounded were given the *coup de grace*. We repeat the question for La Anita:

> Look, they finished off a lot of men because they didn't have their papers. But I wasn't in the firing squads...they sent me off to look for meat so I didn't see anything. And I've forgotten what little I knew. But if you want to hear about my time at Campo de Mayo, I remember those days well.

A former soldier named Emilio Gamondi stated on a program broadcast on LU 32 Radio Olavarría that "the actions taken by the army were proper and necessary in the face of subversion" and admitted that there were executions.

Three soldiers, three different reactions. The first remembers the tragedy painfully. The second hardly speaks and only makes excuses when he does ("the wounded were given the *coup de grace*" and "they finished off a lot of men because they didn't have their papers"). The third—Emilio Gamondi—is proud of himself and still refers to the men who were his commanding officers fifty-two years earlier as "my superiors."

Radrizzani's hands trembled as he aimed. But what about the other two? It seems that the answer is no, but that's only human. If it wasn't there would be neither executioners nor torturers and their victims, nor riot police cracking the skulls of students and firing tear gas in the middle of cities, nor monsters who fire fifty shots into the bodies of people whose hands are bound.

Let's examine Viñas Ibarra's official report of the events at La Anita. It only acknowledges the death of "some seven strikers"—apparently those executed on the night of December 7th—credited, as always, to their resistance. Killed while resisting—the dull, repetitive language of police reports and military dispatches that we Argentines always see in our newspapers. Here is his account of the surrender:

> The rain is on our side, helping hide our approach from the enemy. I am thus able to get within three kilometers of the ranch. I order it to be surrounded by sharpshooters, with the left flank under my direct command. They advance at 2030 hours, but after five hundred meters I spot a group of between five hundred and six hundred men waving at us, indicating that they wish to surrender. As I advance, I hear rapid, sustained gunfire coming from behind the rebel position. I order my men to circle around to the back of the ranch and find that Sub-lieutenant Frugoni Miranda's troops are engaged in combat with a large group of men that refuses to surrender and is trying to make for Chile. I give the order to pursue them as far as the border and then return to take charge of those rebels who had surrendered.

According to the witnesses we have interviewed, Frugoni Miranda commanded the firing squad that killed the seven strike leaders. And now we will see that Viñas Ibarra's dispatch cites that same figure: seven.

Result: 420 rebels taken prisoner; one hundred ranchers, administrators, foremen and police officers rescued; 180 rifles, seven hundred knives, fifteen thousand rifle bullets, various revolvers and three thousand revolver bullets seized; three thousand horses; and a large quantity of food and other goods seized. Bickford fuses and various sticks of dynamite were also found. Some seven strikers were killed while trying to fight their way out. Many others were wounded but managed to escape under the cover of night.

If we analyze these figures, we can find support for our eyewitness testimony. Viñas Ibarra starts out by saying that a group of "between five hundred and six hundred men" surrendered, but then mentions only 420 prisoners. As we can see, the number of strikers remains fluid and approximate. Strange. There are between eighty and 180 men missing—dead or executed—depending on whether we started out with five hundred or six hundred. This is close to the number of dead reported by Correa Falcón and by Commissioner Guadarrama (between 120 and 140). And while the captain states that his troops seized 180 rifles, his report only mentioned that "some seven strikers" were killed. This imprecision is suspicious: you either find seven bodies, or less, or perhaps more, but never "some seven." It's also clearly deliberate; numbers needed to remain elastic in case another body or two showed up later...

With regard to the weapons, we can once again disprove all the literature that goes on and on about bandits who were armed and supplied by Chile. The official military report provides the numbers: 420 prisoners (there should have been five hundred or six hundred) and only 180 rifles. If we recognize that everyone in Patagonia owned weapons—as Varela's report repeats over and over again—then this doesn't seem to be proof of military organization among the rebel workers. And Viñas Ibarra can only mention "various revolvers." Why this imprecision, when he goes on to mention three thousand revolver bullets? Why is there a specific number for bullets but not for revolvers, which are much easier to count? We can imagine that Antonio Soto's group was the most disciplined and the best trained. But, according to the figures provided by the military itself, over half the peons lacked firearms.

Now we'll see how Viñas Ibarra tries to justify the events at La Anita by telling a hair-raising tale:

> I must repeat that the rebels had made plans to resist and it was only the timely intervention by the army that spared their hostages from their deadly fate. They were scheduled to have been shot at 2000 hours, the time at which my troops appeared, saving hundreds of households from misery and ruin.[33] And when the rebels saw that resistance was impossible, they decided to surrender, though not before attempting the lowest and most vile methods of doing away with us, such as poisoning all their provisions with strychnine, especially the flour and sugar. A letter in my possession that was signed by all of the ranchers, as well as the testimony from prudent individuals and those workers who were aware of the monstrosity of the plan, will stand as a testament to these unspeakable deeds, which constitute an assault on Argentine sovereignty as embodied by its servants. Dynamite, readied with Bickford wicks, was also found below many of the ranch's buildings, further proving their sinister intentions.

The special correspondent from the Buenos Aires newspaper *La Razón*—then considered to be the unofficial newspaper of the Patriotic League due to its conservative, anti-labor stance and its bias towards the ranchers—tells us of the living conditions of Antonio Soto's hostages. The article in question, which also appeared in Puerto Deseado's *El Orden*, ran on January 12th, 1922 under the title, "Events in the South: What Mr. Patroni Heard from the Ranchers During a 300-League Journey South of the Río Santa Cruz." The section dealing with the events at La Anita reads as follows:

Miguel E. Grigera, general manager of the Las Vegas Live-stock Company, was one of the victims of the bandits, or rather one of their hostages. We had the chance to speak with him at the Rubén Aike ranch. As a hostage, he and his fellow ranchers were forced to traverse the vast region between Río Gallegos and Lago Argentino, escorted by the large column led by Antonio Soto, the chief ringleader. This odyssey lasted for more than a month, during which time they moved camp on a daily basis. Their path took them far from the main road, which is why they cut through all the fences they came across. "In general, we weren't mistreated by the strikers, and we were given generous rations," Grigera tells us. "It is true that we were being closely watched, but we were given a certain free-dom to move about the camp as long as we had an escort." According to Grigera, the bulk of the group operating in the Río Gallegos watershed under Antonio Soto's orders was made up of agricultural workers who met in daily assemblies to dis-cuss and decide on the issues they were facing. He also tells us that Soto was constantly giving his men updates on the strike's progress, but leading them to believe that everything was going well and encouraging them to keep up their morale until the day they triumphed, a day that he assured them would not be long in coming.

It never took long for Soto to receive news of the setbacks suffered by the other groups of strikers, especially the one at Paso Ibáñez, but he always played down these defeats so as to keep up his men's spirits, otherwise they would have immediately become discouraged. Grigera feels—or rather insists—that the rebels had a well-organized courier service at their disposal. He himself made use of their couriers to deliver a letter to his wife, telling her that he was doing well, which gave her the strength to survive this situation. Grigera says that the march to Lago Argentino and over the mountains running parallel to the border was even interesting for many of the prisoners, especially for those, like him, who were unfamiliar with the area's natural beauty. Once they reached La Anita, the prisoners immediately took notice of the anxiety of the rebels, who had sensed that their defeat would not be long in coming. Their only hope was that Governor Yza would arrive with the soldiers and that they could surrender as they had in January 1921, but with the promise that their list of demands would be accepted: freedom for political prisoners, implementation of the agreement that the ranchers had signed following the previous strike, and a commitment to refrain from persecuting those accused of being agitators. But their hopes for a favorable solution evaporated when they learned that the 10th Cavalry regiment was approaching Lago Argentino. The leaders decided to lock their prisoners in a shed and spread rumors that their throats would be slit if the army attacked. If we believe the story told to us at D'Hunval's ranch, some of this must be true—two of the rancher's nephews, minors, had been taken hostage. They told us that the strikers separated them from the rest of the hostages, saying that the boys shouldn't suffer the same fate as their adult prisoners.

There's no need to report what happened after the rebels surrendered. According to the freed hostages, they were lined up two by two with their weapons on the ground and their arms crossed. We are reluctant to repeat what we have been told happened next, as these matters are over and done with. In general, if a landowner, administrator, or foreman vouched for a peon, they were allowed to leave La Anita. The exact number of those killed at Lago Argentino is unknown.

"We are reluctant to repeat what we have been told happened next, as these matters are over and done with"—this sentence says it all. The journalist doesn't even want to report what the ranchers have told him. And what they have told him is that there were executions.

"The exact number of those killed at Lago Argentino is unknown," reports *La Razón* of Buenos Aires and *El Orden* of Puerto Deseado. Both of these newspapers took the side of the ranchers. And they say it just days after the events at La Anita. If the number of dead was already being covered up back then, how are we supposed to learn the truth decades later?

The example that was made out of the La Anita strikers is easy to understand—in Varela's view, they were the most dangerous group, and besides, they were directly led by Antonio Soto. There was to be neither mercy nor wasted breath. As Correa Falcón will tell us fifty years later:

> The ranchers were the first to be surprised by the harshness of Varela and his officials, but there's no denying that it was perhaps worth it: anarchy was banished from the territory and none of these events were ever repeated.

Menéndez Behety's La Anita ranch still exists, with its beautiful name and its tragic shadow. Almost all of those killed were Chileans; there were also two or three Argentines, two Germans, and a handful of Spaniards. They were killed in paradise, facing one of the world's most beautiful landscapes. So God willed, and so Argentina's men-at-arms acted. Not even their names were recorded.

From a legal standpoint, this was the execution of unarmed prisoners. There can be no discussion of the matter nor any other legal description. Any elderly resident can show travelers the mass graves at La Anita.

Neither the army nor the Yrigoyen administration responded to these charges by denying that there had been a massacre. Varela never suggested opening an investigation into whether or not a massacre had taken place. The only one who defended himself was Viñas Ibarra, always using the same argument. Even in 1970, fifty years later, he continues insisting:

> We killed them in combat. This is what happened: each time there was a shootout, there was always one group of strikers who surrendered while the others continued firing. The Patagonian winds prevented us from distinguishing voices. We couldn't even

hear the gunshots except for when a bullet whistled past our ears. It was hard for us to understand the situation we were in and it seemed we had walked into an ambush. And so the conscripts fired at anything that moved. [Declaration made on December 18th, 1970.][34]

Another piece of evidence—aside from the statements made by eyewitnesses—that the dead were executed and not killed in combat can be found in Viñas Ibarra's own dispatches, which mention that many were wounded during the La Anita incident but that they all managed to escape. Firing squads leave no wounded, of course, only dead, but experience shows that the wounded outnumber the dead in a battle by a factor of two or three. But at La Anita, as elsewhere in this campaign, there's no record of wounded prisoners. It's the first time in military history when all of the wounded managed to escape the battlefield.

Let's look at the version of the events at La Anita offered by *La Unión*. It more or less faithfully follows Viñas Ibarra's dispatches, but with one meaningful difference. While Viñas Ibarra mentions that "some seven strikers" were killed in the "battle," the correspondent for *La Unión*—who was embedded with the troops—says that twenty-six were killed while resisting. Let's examine their article, which shows the author's complete satisfaction with the army's actions:

The army's efforts in the campaign against the rebels have been marked by the greatest success. They have managed to subdue the majority of the strikers, punishing them with the firm hand that the leaders and agitators responsible for this irreparably harmful situation had been spared. The first attack managed to destroy their resistance in a matter of minutes. Twenty-six bandits were killed and a large number were wounded in the battle, while four hundred individuals surrendered and were taken prisoner.

Here we see another mention of the wounded: "a large number were wounded."[35] Here it doesn't say that they escaped, but it doesn't say what happened to them, either. The battle turns out to have been a curious one: twenty-six dead on one side and not even so much as a bruise on the other.

The ranchers and the Rural Society are overcome with enthusiasm. Those who scorned Commander Varela now begin to sing his praises:

> Commander Varela's attitude in the present campaign has made an excellent impression on public opinion, which has instead harshly criticized Governor Yza. The governor had recently made statements to the press in Buenos Aires suggesting that the events of last January were incapable of being repeated. He considered any signs of unrest to be acts of isolated banditry, to which he attributed little importance. This shows either his complete unfamiliarity with the territory he governs or his tolerance for subversion.
>
> The region's ranchers and their families remain in Río Gallegos, where they plan to remain until their safety can be permanently guaranteed. They feel this can only occur in the presence of the military. Some ranches have already resumed operations under the supervision of soldiers.

In the meantime, Varela arrives at Lago Argentino. He arrives at 8 p.m. on December 8th, 1921—twenty-four hours after Viñas Ibarra began "assigning responsibilities." Varela's dispatch doesn't mention a word about what occurred there:

> I arrive at La Anita ranch at 2000 hours that day [December 8th], where I find that captains Viñas Ibarra and Campos have already restored order following a clash with the strikers, who represented the region's final remaining group of rebels. Their dispatches can provide details on the actions they have taken.

He merely refers us to the dispatches written by Viñas Ibarra and Campos. We have already examined the first; the second strictly follows its line, point by point. Varela only adds the following lines:

> Given the manner in which Captain Viñas conducted his campaign and his successful pacification of each region his squadron visited, as well as the guarantees provided both to the ranchers and the workers and the universal satisfaction with his actions, I am convinced that the cordillera region, from the southern border with Chile up to Lago Argentino and Lago Viedma, can be considered to have returned to normal. Most of the region's ranchers have resumed routine tasks such as branding and shearing.

But neither Varela nor Viñas Ibarra is at ease. Antonio Soto has escaped. The men of the 10th Cavalry are not used to such embarrassments. Everything had gone so well; not one of the anarchist ringleaders had survived. They couldn't let the biggest fish escape their net. And so Viñas Ibarra himself sets out for Cerro Centinela, accompanied by twenty soldiers, hoping to either pick up Soto's trail or hear that the Chilean carabinieri had captured him.

But Guatón Luna has guided his men well. Although he is no horseman, Antonio Soto endures the hardships of the trail that will lead him and his little group to safety. They ride by night and hide during the day. In Argentina, they travel far from the ranches to avoid police and army patrols. They know that there's not a bone in their bodies that will be left unbroken if they are caught. Soto carries tragedy with him: he has been utterly defeated. The struggle begun two years earlier, which demanded so many sacrifices from his comrades, has ended in the starkest defeat, in the most pitiless repression. It has been easy to crush the rabble. The punishment has been so cruel and disproportionate that not even tears of rage are enough. Everything that the Workers' Society had accomplished will be thrown on the rubbish heap. One kick from the boot of a lieutenant colonel was enough to destroy the beautiful sandcastles raised by the clumsy hands of workers who wanted to think for themselves and share their ideas with others.

Soto feels devastated. They have annihilated him. A few Mausers spitting live ammunition and a handful of young, eager soldiers were enough to destroy the ideas of Proudhon and Bakunin. There is nothing fainter and more ephemeral than thought, than books, when faced with a machine gun or a regiment under the command of a manly officer.

The fugitives cross the border near Cerro Centinela on the night of December 9th. They lead their horses by their bridles, far from the eyes of the carabinieri. They have been following the Río Centinela since they left La Anita. Now on Chilean soil, they will follow the banks of the Río Baguales until they reach Cerro Guido. From there they will head right towards Lago Sarmiento at the foot of Sierra del Toro, skirting around the shores of Lago del Toro and Lago Porteño and reach Río Prats by way of Cerro Campanillas. From Puerto Consuelo, they will gaze upon the waters of Última Esperanza, an ominous name for these men who have ridden for days without eating or sleeping. There they split up and make their separate ways to Puerto Natales, where their comrades in the Chilean labor movement offer them shelter. Though he may have saved his skin for the time being, Soto knows very well that the true manhunt has yet to begin, that Chile wants nothing to do with the man who disturbed the *pax latifundia*.

Viñas Ibarra reaches the border. He suspects that Soto has passed through Cerro Centinela, but nobody has seen the fugitive with their own eyes, nobody can provide concrete proof. Viñas Ibarra feels responsible for having let the anarchist escape. His sort must be eliminated—you never know when they might be back. And Soto has managed to create an aura around himself.

But there's nothing he can do. The fugitives have disappeared; it's as if the earth has swallowed them up. Viñas Ibarra returns with his hands empty, unable to hide his rage. In the dispatch dated December 12th, he writes:

With twenty soldiers under my command, I reach Cerro Centinela and head towards the border with Chile. There I hear the provocative news that the Chilean troops not only didn't close the passes over the cordillera but have been ordered to retreat so as to allow the fugitives to freely cross over the border. Remember that several officers of the Magallanes Battalion—including Captain Robles, Lieutenant Villafranca, and another whose name I don't remember—insisted that I accept their unsolicited help, promising that they would close all the passes as far as Lago Argentino and Lago Viedma.

A question arises. Who was responsible for allowing Antonio Soto to escape? The Chileans or the Argentines? Viñas Ibarra blames the Chileans for not watching the border. Were the Argentine border guards asleep at their posts?

We will examine the persecution of Antonio Soto by the Chilean authorities and his flight from Puerto Natales later on. But Viñas Ibarra felt ashamed; he had let Varela down by allowing the big fish to escape. A man that the press loved to use to scare their readers, painting a shadowy portrait of a foreign agitator, a dangerous subversive, a demagogue with a monstrous mindset. And he managed to escape by the skin of his teeth. He had refused to believe the army and he had refused to surrender. Viñas Ibarra was enraged, Varela was enraged, the Argentine conscripts were enraged. They were so close to capturing the author of these historically unprecedented events, the man who had kept them awake so many nights, forcing them to ride so many leagues and pass so many cold nights out in the open when they could have been back home, drinking mate with their friends or spending time with their girls. But thanks to that filthy Spaniard—an anarchist besides—they had to go around killing Chileans.

But while they couldn't physically eliminate him, there was another way: with the press on their side, they could say whatever they wanted. And so they began to say that Antonio Soto, the anarchist leader, had lost his nerve and fled, abandoning his men to their fate. And even worse, he had fled "with union funds." Antonio Soto's name was blackened and dragged through the mud for more than a decade. Until he reappeared on the streets of Río Gallegos to settle a few scores...

From December 12th to December 20th, the day he ends his campaign, Viñas Ibarra spends his time purging the countryside of strikers:

> With the entire region from the southern border with Chile to Lago Viedma under control, I have positioned detachments of soldiers in a semicircle centering on Los Baguales: Rospenteck–Fuentes de Coyle–Tapi-Aike–El Tero–Cerro Fortaleza–El Perro–La Anita. Couriers can bring news from one end of this 140-league expanse to the other in only two days. On ranches throughout the region, people were hard at work rebuilding what had been destroyed. The workers themselves seemed happy to get back to work amidst a calm that could only be guaranteed by the army. At the end of the day, I receive orders to return to Río Gallegos and I hand over command of the squadron to Sub-lieutenant Frugoni Miranda. I set out on the 21st and stop at various ranches along the way, where I am welcomed by both bosses and workers, the latter of whom show unmistakable gratitude for the army's recent actions and the rapid normalization of the situation, which saved the territory from complete ruin and depopulation.

The south had been completely cleansed of red flags. Soto had escaped, it's true, but there was not a single trace left of the Río Gallegos Workers' Society.[36] Viñas Ibarra had proven himself to be Varela's most valuable man.

But Santa Cruz had yet to be completely pacified. Facón Grande was still at large in the area surrounding the Puerto Deseado–Colonia Las Heras railway line. Despite being left to his own devices, as the defeat of the columns commanded by Soto, Outerelo, and Albino Argüelles had left him without support,

Facón Grande continued organizing the peons for an indefinite general strike.

Lieutenant Colonel Varela will handle the matter himself:

> Accompanied by Lieutenant Schwiezer and his troops, I headed back to San Julián on December 13th after first visiting Lago Tar and Lago San Martín. We then continued in the direction of Lago Posadas and Colonia Las Heras, as I had received some rather disquieting news about large groups of rebels who were carrying out all manner of predations in the region, terrorizing the residents of northern Santa Cruz. This led me to believe, as I was later able to corroborate, that the subversive movement was rapidly spreading north, seeking the support of Chubut's labor federations. Their purpose was to terrorize the population into submission and spark an uprising by the workers in Comodoro Rivadavia, as had been their goal since the beginning, followed by a march on the nation's capital, where other workers' societies were making their preparations to deliver the final blow to the established authorities.

We have been unable to find any proof for Lieutenant Colonel Varela's tremendous assertions. The syndicalist FORA hadn't even taken sides in the conflict, even though news of the executions had already reached Buenos Aires. The anarchists of the FORA V were shouting to high heaven, desperate to help their persecuted comrades in Patagonia, but they were powerless. What could they do? Nothing but protest. They were too far away, and there were more than enough problems in Buenos Aires to keep them busy without concerning themselves with events occurring elsewhere, in the practically unknown regions to the south. But it has to be admitted that it is the anarchist newspapers that will be the first to denounce the massacres. The Maritime Workers' Federation, which was enamored of Yrigoyen, will continue to wash its hands of the situation. And there is no evidence that the workers of Comodoro Rivadavia had organized in solidarity with the strikers of Santa Cruz. Quite to the contrary. As we shall see, the governor of Chubut will send nearly all of the police at his disposal to Colonia Las Heras, which indicates that he did not fear an uprising in his own province.

It can't be denied that Facón Grande realizes that the railway line between Puerto Deseado and Colonia Las Heras might be the key to victory, but he never quite manages to take control of it. The multitudinous nature of the movement prevented this. The workers wander back and forth en masse. Besides, José Font has neither the gift of command nor any sense of strategy and tactics. He does have unlimited authority over his men, it's true, but he never abuses it. He prefers to talk things over and ask for their advice. He never shows weakness, but is afraid that those who elected him as their leader will begin to suspect that he wants to benefit from his position.

But that's not the way to do things. Especially not when facing a man like Lieutenant Colonel Varela, who doesn't waste time and knows that when the hour comes, it's better to shoot first and ask questions later.

But let's continue with Lieutenant Colonel Varela's dispatches: "The group operating in the north is commanded by a certain Font, alias Facón Grande, and is comprised of between 350 and four hundred well-armed and well-supplied men."

As we shall see later on, in Varela's own dispatches, Font's men were neither well-armed nor well-supplied. Varela writes:

Having taken possession of every station on the Deseado–Las Heras line, which lies on the border with Chubut, they have been constantly harassing the population near the railway. It was necessary to act quickly and decisively to prevent the group from reaching Comodoro Rivadavia and organizing an uprising among the city's workers.

At no time did Facón Grande's column attempt to reach Comodoro Rivadavia. They instead remained close to the railway, making no attempt to press north or south. It was clear that they were trying to keep the strike going as long as possible to improve their negotiating position with the army.

Lieutenant Colonel Varela heads towards the Jaramillo railway station, and that's where the trouble will really start. Things will turn out nicely in this campaign. There's even real combat with Facón Grande's men! They even force the 10th Cavalry regiment, fighting under the blue and white banner, to retreat. And so there can never be forgiveness for the brave gaucho Facón Grande. Varela can't forgive him. A civilian, no matter how much of a criollo he may be, can't be forgiven for firing on the Argentine Army, especially if he has chilotes under his command. It's a matter of prestige. It would have been a different matter if it had only been Argentines versus Argentines. But this is Argentines versus chilotes commanded by an Argentine. José Font may be a gaucho, it's true, but he flies the red flag.

But let's start at the beginning, because Facón Grande's feats will fill many pages.

One of Facón Grande's columns headed towards Colonia Las Heras, the final stop on the Puerto Deseado railway line. There the men of the Patriotic League had organized their defense while the women and children left for Comodoro Rivadavia.

In Colonia Las Heras, the strike leader Antonio Echeverría will await Facón Grande's orders.

Regarding the fall of Colonia Las Heras and the death of Antonio Echeverría, we have the testimony of former Lieutenant Federico S. Jonas, who actively participated in the events in Las Heras and Deseado:

On December 15th, 1921, immediately after the events at Bajo del Tigre, I was stationed at San Julián with a corporal and eleven gendarmes under my command. From there, I received orders to provide security for the ranches near Bahía Laura. After three or four days in the area, which was in a state of perfect calm (work never stopped on those ranches), I met with Commander

Varela, who was on his way to Puerto Deseado, accompanied by just one official and two civilians. Upon learning that there were no threats to the peace where I was stationed, he ordered me to immediately move my detachment to Deseado.

I arrived in Deseado the following day. Immediately after reporting to Varela, he ordered me to leave seven of my men with him and then take the remaining four (I selected Juan Rodríguez, Alejo Duarte, and Ramón Valdivieso, all of them from Corrientes, and Juan Rugestein, from Azul), plus a small group of volunteers, to Las Heras. A train was immediately prepared for us and we left at 8 a.m. on the 18th. The journey passed by very slowly and we didn't arrive at the Pico Truncado station until evening. We spent the night there. The next day we came across a truck that was traveling parallel to the tracks, but in the opposite direction. Seeing that its occupants were armed, I ordered my soldiers to fire into the air. The men in the truck put their hands up to show that they weren't resisting. We realized that there were two strikers in the truck—one of them was Echeverría, the leader of the group camped out at Las Heras—and the rest were locals. They had been heading to Facón Grande's camp, where they were to discuss the organization of supply lines. As Las Heras had been cut off from the coast, goods were in short supply and merchants were trying to find a way to alleviate the situation. The people in the truck didn't return fire but instead approached the train and told us who they were. When our warning shots told them that the train was carrying soldiers, the attitude of the locals towards Echeverría changed. We arrested him and took him with us to Las Heras, where we arrived early the next day. At the Las Heras station, we met with several locals (Dr. O'Connor, Juan Pedmonte, Antonio Capagli, the local manager of La Anónima, Rodríguez, and others, who jointly signed a police report). Assisted by Officer Sureda, I proceeded to arrest the workers they accused of being strike leaders. None of them offered any resistance and simply asked that I spare their lives. I told them that they had nothing to fear from me and that my only mission was to hand them over to Commander

Varela in Deseado. Despite the clear animosity displayed towards the strikers by many of the town's residents, none of them accused the workers of any crimes more serious than requisitioning clothing and other supplies from a few stores and forcing innkeepers to take them in as guests. A lot has been said about looting and other outrages in Las Heras, but none of it is true except for the looting of the warehouses owned by the hated Patagonia Import and Export Company, which lost between 4,000 and 5,000 pesos worth of merchandise. That same night, I put the prisoners—twelve in all—aboard a freight car and returned with them to Deseado. Once we arrived in Deseado, I turned them over to the local police chief, Commissioner Barloa, who then turned them over to Commander Varela. Nothing occurred while I remained in Deseado, but three or four days later I was once again ordered away, this time to Lago Buenos Aires. I later learned that my departure from Deseado coincided, or rather preceded the violent deaths of three of those arrested in Las Heras: Antonio Echeverría, Maximiliano Pérez, and R. Diachenko (Russian). Late that night, they were removed from their cells and taken to the outskirts of town, along the banks of the Río Deseado, where they were shot to death in the usual manner.[37] The other nine prisoners were put aboard a steamship to Río Gallegos. After my return from Lago Buenos Aires, I tried to discover what happened to those nine unfortunates but was unable to confirm anything.

We have already provided more than enough testimony regarding the excessive cruelty shown to the vanquished. Before being shot, their flesh was softened up by beatings. But let's hear from one more witness: Víctor S. Rodrigo, the local administrator of the Patagonia Import and Export Company. As we shall see, his perspective isn't exactly friendly to the workers. Quite the opposite: he's a man who defends his company, which is owned by Braun and Menéndez Behety. Nevertheless, his account clarifies everything that happened in Las Heras. We are indebted to his granddaughter María de los Angeles Rodrigo for providing us

with a copy of his memoirs, which were published by the Comodoro Rivadavia newspaper *El Patagónico* under the title "Difficult
Times." In them, he tells of the following events at Pico Truncado,
near where he was living:

> (The strikers) committed all sorts of atrocities: upon entering
> the offices of La Anónima, they stripped naked and changed
> their clothes, leaving their dirty clothing on the floor, even their
> underwear. You can imagine the smell, as they only ever changed
> their clothes when they attacked a business. A few days later,
> a man arrived who had the look of a peon about him. When I
> met with him, he told me, "I am Antonio Echeverría, a delegate
> from Facón Grande's column. Three hundred men will come
> into town tomorrow and we need to prepare for their arrival."
> I then told him, "Look, Echeverría, your request is irrelevant. I
> know how you people operate and it would be useless to refuse,
> because you're simply going to take whatever you want." He then
> told me, "You're right, and I admit that many of my men have
> acted badly, but I won't allow them to commit any crimes."
>
> As he seemed to be a poor man who was simply follow-
> ing orders, I asked him, "What are your aims? Don't you
> realize that you will be severely punished?" He paused for a
> moment and then said, "We're not afraid, we're being protected
> by high-ranking authorities in the territory and are only fol-
> lowing orders." And so I said, "I'm all for forming a union of
> rural workers, but not like this." The interview was over. As
> the group of men he was expecting never arrived, Echeverría
> decided to form a new group.
>
> This new group looted La Anónima's warehouses, dividing
> up clothing and provisions not only among themselves but also
> among the townspeople as well. Echeverría signed an order form
> that we had to fill, as if they were proper customers.
>
> He drove off to meet with Facón Grande a few days later,
> but was arrested along the way by a group of gendarmes and
> White Guards.

As the administrator of La Anónima, it was my duty to meet with the lieutenant and inform him of what had been going on in Las Heras. It was a terrible, inhumane, and degrading spectacle. He ordered the prisoners to be lined up at the station and offered me his saber, which I refused. I saw Echeverría be beaten bloody by their saber blows and then walked away, outraged.

The punishment didn't end there. From my house, I heard the cries of the prisoners who were being held in the train car. I couldn't stop myself from telling the lieutenant that he was being unjust and was providing the neighborhood with a poor moral example. The train left a few days later to turn the prisoners over to Varela, who had them shot.

Here we have the declarations of the administrator of the Patagonia Import and Export Company. If we compare this statement with that made by Sub-lieutenant Federico Jonas, we can see that they coincide on the details regarding Echeverría's fate.

We have further testimony on the events in Las Heras from Enrique Salgot Morell of Haedo. Now seventy-nine years old, he was a member of the White Guard during the second strike. Salgot Morell was employed by La Anónima and later by La Mercantil. He then worked as an administrator on Carlos Helmich's ranches and as an independent rancher. He was a justice of the peace in Las Heras and managed the Las Heras Ranchers' Cooperative and the Rural Hospital. He tells us that when Facón Grande's column approached Las Heras in the summer of 1921, they formed a White Guard to protect the town:

In all honesty, nothing happened in Las Heras. A small group arrived, under the orders of an agricultural worker named Echeverría. He was very slow, but he wasn't a bad gaucho. I know for a fact that he didn't order the looting of La Anónima's warehouse—that was the work of the townspeople, who were taking advantage of the situation. But everyone blamed Echeverría. In the White Guard, we were waiting for a flood of strikers that never arrived. As one of the few people who knew how to drive, I had to take all of the important people of Las Heras to Comodoro Rivadavia. I took my wife and my three-month-old daughter to a nearby ranch. But nothing happened to anyone in the area. To get their hands on Echeverría, they used the same trick that they used on Facón Grande. They told him that they would take him to meet with Commander Varela, who wanted to negotiate with him. And this poor, gullible man, who couldn't imagine that they would deceive him, accepted. How else can you explain their surrender to the first soldiers that came along? Or that Echeverría, a striker, would head to Puerto Deseado in the company of a group of ranchers? Echeverría was shot and everyone in Las Heras heard that it wasn't a simple execution, but that he was beaten first by the soldiers. I often think about what happened and still can't understand why you would take out your anger on a defeated man. If you have to shoot him then shoot him, but don't punish him like that first. Though I was a member of the White Guard, my conscience is clear. There's no excuse for what happened in Jaramillo, where they executed Facón Grande and his men. There was no need for such severity. I should add that the persecution ended when the navy arrived. They behaved themselves like gentlemen who had come to restore order, they were not murderers. That was how the crack-down should have been conducted, following the navy's lead. Look, I met with many ranchers afterwards and heard them criticize the executions and Varela's use of corporal punishment on those poor unfortunates. I've heard people say things like, "Those soldiers from Buenos Aires turned out to be nothing more than murderers!"

There are contradictory reports as to how Facón Grande's column was defeated. Reconstructing these events by comparing dates, documents and witness statements was a very difficult task. But let's begin with Varela's report to the War Ministry:

I learned from the prisoners captured in Jaramillo that the rebels had set up their main camp near the Tehuelches station, which was the heart of the rebellion. Upon returning to Jaramillo, I immediately set out for Tehuelches, arriving at 1600 hours that same day (December 20, 1921). Just as I was trying to learn where the rebels had their camp, I saw five cars and a truck approaching. They came to a stop eight hundred meters away. About fifty individuals climbed out of the vehicles and started firing on our troops. I immediately ordered my men to return fire and battle commenced all along the line.

The shooting lasted forty minutes, after which time the rebels withdrew, taking their dead and wounded with them. We were unable to pursue as we lacked a means of transportation, never mind that we had exhausted all our ammunition. The lay of the land also allowed them to quickly vanish into the deep ravines that dotted the land. On our side, Salvi and Fischer were wounded, and the latter died later from his wounds. When the rebels retreated, we only had ten bullets left.

But it was actually Varela who is the one to retreat from the "battlefield," as he himself later admits, albeit indirectly, when describing the negotiations at the Jaramillo ranch. From Tehuelches, Varela retreats to Jaramillo, taking the two wounded soldiers with him. Fischer dies several hours later from the wound in his throat. "When he felt the death blow," Varela's dispatch reads, "Fischer, with typical Argentine bravery, still had the strength to shout, 'Long Live the 10th Cavalry!'"

The Puerto Deseado journalist León Soto, who served as the director of the newspaper *El Orden* for many years and played a role in all of the most important events of that chaotic period of Patagonian history, told us that the so-called Battle of Tehuelches occurred as follows: Facón Grande was unaware of Varela's arrival in Puerto Deseado and his push nouth—he thought that Varela would instead head towards Colonia Las Heras.

As we have seen, Varela arrives in Jaramillo and then heads to the Tehuelches railway station. He remains there while several cars and one truck approach. Facón Grande is riding in the first car—a double phaeton seized from a rancher—with his closest collaborators following in the other vehicles. When he sees them coming, Varela—whose troops are outnumbered—greets them with a round of gunfire, believing that this would be enough to get the strikers to surrender. But this doesn't work, to his surprise. Though the army's first volley takes the lives of three strikers, they take up positions and return fire. When Varela sees Fischer and Salvi fall, he orders his men retreat to Jaramillo. It's only now that Facón Grande realizes that he has been fighting against the army and not the police.

Mario Mesa—the local manager of La Anónima in Pico Truncado, who had been taken hostage by Facón Grande's men—then offers to mediate. Facón Grande accepts because the situation has become critical: he had fired on the army, which was something he had not been expecting—he was actually waiting for Varela to arrive so that they could negotiate. Mesa, accompanied by three labor delegates, heads towards Jaramillo to propose a new settlement and the release of all imprisoned workers in exchange for lifting the strike.

Varela converses at length with Mesa. We know nothing of what was said, as Mesa has chosen not to speak on the matter. What we do know is that he returns to Tehuelches and tells Facón Grande that Varela is open to the proposal, but that the strikers must surrender and hand over their weapons before negotiations can begin. Mesa offers his words that nobody will lose their life.

In the assembly held that day, Facón Grande encourages his comrades to accept Varela's proposal. And on December 22nd— after Mesa returns to Jaramillo and meets with Varela—the strikers turn themselves in at the Jaramillo railway station.

Let's take a look at Varela's surprising report to the War Ministry—why it's surprising should be clear:

At 0200 hours on December 21, two labor delegates show up at the Jaramillo ranch, asking me to accept the unconditional surrender that would occur the following day, during which the strikers would hand over all of their firearms, ammunition, and horses. The group decided to surrender because they had lost some of their most feared leaders during the fighting on December 20: a certain Font, alias Facón Grande, Leiva, and several others whose names remain unknown, as they were not from the region.

It is surprising that Varela mentions that Facón Grande, Leiva, and "others"—not even so much as a number—were killed in combat at Tehuelches while there is a photographic record of Facón Grande's surrender at the Jaramillo railway station two days later. And if Facón Grande appears alongside the soldiers of the 10th Calvary in photographs taken in Jaramillo, then he couldn't have died in Tehuelches two days earlier.

But let's return to events as they unfold. Facón Grande's position is to accept Mesa's offer to mediate and then accede to the demands imposed by Varela, even though the latter had been defeated by the strikers at Tehuelches. This shows once more, and even more clearly this time, that the movement's leaders only sought to attract the attention of the federal government, here represented by Varela, and ensure the implementation of the settlement negotiated during the previous strike. They were aware of the weakness of their position and clearly understood that they couldn't launch a revolutionary strike with the men and arms at their disposal.

When Facón Grande agrees to the proposal made by Mesa, a man in the employ of Menéndez and Braun, he's unaware that he will be negotiating with Varela, a lieutenant colonel whose pride as an Argentine military officer has been deeply wounded. Those dirty chilotes, those anti-Argentine anarchists, had killed his favorite soldier and forced his regiment, the glorious Hussars of Pueyrredón, to retreat. A gaucho bandit and the rabble that followed him had turned back the fatherland's armed forces, killing a soldier in the process. They will pay. They'll get their safe conduct passes, labor settlements, and the release of their imprisoned comrades. Commander Varela is a man of boundless rage, of boundless fury—and even more so when someone lays a hand on one of his whelps. These vagabonds, who had declared themselves to be their own lords and masters when they should have been working, killed a young man wearing the Argentine uniform. They will get what's coming to them and they will be made to kiss Argentine soil. They'll get their red flag, their Russian Revolution, their equality of man, and all that nonsense.

As a gesture of goodwill, the strikers put all their possessions on the ground and hand over their horses. Facón Grande is separated from the rest of the men and held near the station house. He's far from naïve and immediately realizes what's going on—not only have they imprisoned him, refusing to respond to his requests to speak with Varela, they've even taken away the famous knife that gave him his nickname. Facón Grande is now merely José Font, but he remains arrogant enough to demand that they stick to the agreement. It's no use. The soldiers abuse him. They have to be held back or they'll beat him to death. He's the one responsible for the death of Fischer and each one of the conscripts wants to make him pay dearly for what he's done.

When José Font realizes that he's fallen into a trap and that these men won't show the least mercy, he shouts at the soldiers that he's challenging Varela to a knife fight in front of all his men to see if he's as brave as they say. Varela's only response is to have him bound hand and foot. They leave him alone to let him chew on his rage, the veins on his neck swollen as if ready to burst from pure indignation. There is the famous Facón Grande, the chief of the Puerto Deseado strikers, lying on the ground. All of the soldiers, who share his criollo blood, come to take a look.

Varela is a practical, quick-thinking man. He has no time for reflection or intrigue. Two NCOs and two soldiers carry José Font and toss him in the back of a truck like a sack of potatoes. They drive him over to the livestock chute and untie his bonds. There he stands, waiting to be shot. Without a knife, without his slouch hat, and without the black sash he used as a belt. The bullets pierce his body as he struggles to keep his pants from falling down.

The testimony of the Puerto Deseado rancher Pedro Jenkins largely coincides with that of the journalist León Soto on all these points, as does that of Kuno Tschamler, the former administrator of Martinovich's Santa María ranch:

> Facón Grande turned himself in and, in accordance with the agreed upon conditions, he wanted to shake hands with his counterpart, Héctor Benigno Varela, who refused the gesture and ordered him to be bound hand and food. Facón Grande, brimming with rage, said that this was no way to treat a man and that he would take them all on, even with his hands tied. They shot him in Jaramillo. The first round didn't even make him flinch. The second brought him to his knees.

In 1924, Sub-lieutenant Jonas writes the following on the shootout in Tehuelches:

> Fischer had been imprudently positioned by his commander in the middle of the road, where his silhouette was clearly visible, making him all too easy of a target. He was shot in the mouth, a wound that killed him two hours later.

After stating that Facón Grande was shot in Jaramillo along with "thirty or forty of his men," he makes the following accusation:

> As I was at the Puerto Deseado police station the next day, I saw Commissioner Barloa and his subordinates dividing up the clothing and other personal possessions of Facón Grande and Leiva. I have seen few spectacles as repellent as the behavior of Varela's soldiers and their public ostentation of the money and

clothing stolen from the men who surrendered to them, some of whose wallets were full of money.

After describing the execution of Facón Grande, Kuno Tschamler says that he had between 2,000 and 3,000 pesos on him when he was shot, but that nobody knows what happened to his money.

Sub-lieutenant Jonas will later write that Facón Grande approached Varela as he surrendered, reaching out his hand and saying, "Do I have the honor of speaking with Commander Varela? I am Facón Grande." Varela only glared at him, refusing his hand, and gave the order to disarm him and separate him from the rest of the prisoners.

Jonas also states that Antonio Leiva, Facón Grande's second-in-command, was shot in the head by "a sergeant with Indian features" for not immediately dismounting. Leiva was a quiet Chilean, short and skinny, between twenty-eight and thirty years old. He was a peon on Iglesias's La Sofía ranch. He was a hard worker but drank frequently. They say he had been drinking that day, which is why he ignored the order to dismount.

Jonas insists that all of the executions took place near Jaramillo rather than in Tehuelches or Pico Truncado. He also says that the corpses were left next to the station, unburied, until the end of December:

> Several days after the massacre, Facón Grande's body was still out in the open, holding a jar of pickles that somebody had placed in his hand for a laugh. His other hand had been cut off. They say that it had been preserved in formaldehyde by a rancher or a friend.

The corpses were later burned using gasoline brought in from Comodoro Rivadavia.

La Unión del Marino, the official newspaper of the Maritime Workers' Federation, includes precise details on the number of people executed in Jaramillo in the special issue printed on May 1st, 1922:

> Jaramillo: Six people were shot on Baldomero Cimadevilla's land, located five hundred meters from the railway station on the Puerto Deseado side. Antonio Leiva's body was left unburied near the railway tracks on the south side. Another three were shot on the north side. Fifty were shot south of the tracks on the Puerto Deseado side, three hundred meters from town.

All of the reports disagree on the number of people executed. Curiously, Varela makes no mentions of the number of weapons seized from Facón Grande's group and only mentions that "Font, Leiva, and others were killed in combat"—a suspicious lack of information in a military dispatch where he had the obligation to be precise.

The only accounts that seem to be reliable are those of Sub-lieutenant Jonas (who mentions between thirty and forty executions, not including Font and Leiva) and that of the Maritime Workers' Federation, which places the number of executions at sixty and mentions where their bodies could still be found. The Maritime Workers' Federation's newspaper even prints the names of some of those killed:

> José Font, Argentine; Guzmán, Argentine; Alejo López, Argentine; Servando Romero, Argentine; Balcarce, Chilean; Ramón Elizondo, Uruguayan; a Spanish tavern keeper; two Greeks; a Russian; (and) ... Antonio Leiva (...). Mario Mesa (Italian) and the rancher Guillermo Bain (British) told Varela who the most dangerous workers were so they could be executed.

The newspaper also reports that "José Font received perhaps the worst treatment. He was left alive and half buried for several hours, during which time they forced him to watch the executions."

The arrival of the naval troops was crucial in stopping the executions—there had been disagreements between Lieutenant Colonel Varela and the naval officers regarding the use of drastic repressive measures since the beginning of the campaign.

In his writings, Sub-lieutenant Jonas emphasizes that it was the naval troops who cremated and respectfully buried the corpses they found in Jaramillo. He also quotes Naval Lieutenant Dacharry, who came to Las Heras from Comodoro Rivadavia (his troops had arrived in the General Belgrano, commanded by Captain Lan). "I heard Officer Dacharry forcefully reproach Varela for the way he had exterminated the strikers in Las Heras," Jonas says.

Two days after the execution of Facón Grande, Frigate Captain Julio Ayala Torales arrives from the coast, bringing heavy artillery to defend the Puerto Deseado–Colonia Las Heras railway line. He has a stormy telephone conversation with Lieutenant Colonel Varela, who points out that the naval troops always arrive "when everything is already over." Once again, the army has pulled the chestnuts out of the fire. Captain Ayala Torales disapproves of the army's actions, especially the execution of chilotes. The doctor who accompanied the naval troops, Dr. Ramírez, confirms the executions of agricultural workers, among them Facón Grande. And the orders that Captain Ayala Torales received from the Naval Ministry simply said, "Act on a war footing."

On the basis of my own lengthy conversations with Captain Ayala Torales in his home in Martínez, I have come to the conclusion that the former officer was deeply embittered by the events in Patagonia, which he interpreted as something unavoidable, something that was fated to happen. And the question he asked himself was whether man loses his sense of proportion when given the chance to dominate and punish another. His troops, anxious to shoot Chileans, had to be repeatedly told, "He who has not fought cannot carry out executions." This was the code of conduct that was so difficult to instill among his subordinates. According to Captain Ayala Torales, Facón Grande was buried in Jaramillo.

Our research into the fate of the famed Facón Grande has led us, time and again, to Tehuelches, Jaramillo, and Puerto Deseado.

The ranchers who knew Facón Grande have served as his character witnesses. There's Victorino Basterra, owner of La Navarra ranch, and José Turcato, owner of the San Marcos ranch near the Tehuelches railway station, where José Font and his men forced Varela and his Hussars of Pueyrredón to retreat. Let's examine Victorino Basterra's account first:

> José Font was born in Montiel, Entre Ríos. They say that he was brought here by a rancher named Iriarte, but the truth is that he came to Santa Cruz in 1904 or 1905 to cull foxes in the Cabo Blanco salt marshes, north of Puerto Deseado. As he was an honest man and a hard worker, he quickly started working for himself and obtained five horse carts for making deliveries along the route between San Julián, Lago Posadas, and Lago Puey-rredón, which is a long and dangerous journey. He was a skilled horse-tamer and could build houses out of whatever materials he had on hand; people always came to him for advice. There's no doubt that he was the best horse-tamer in the region. People always came around to watch him break in a horse. I myself saw him break in a horse that had killed an Indian who tried to ride it. Font looked and the horse and said, "He'll throw me if I break him by force."

To this day, Basterra still has a silver belt buckle given to him by Facón Grande:

> Above all, he was generous. He was always there if someone needed help. He once gave 1,000 pesos to the Lavatelli family of Puerto Deseado, who needed to send their son to Buenos Aires for treatment. The family was eternally grateful. And when Elve-ria de Lavatelli heard that he had been shot in Jaramillo, I recall that she said, "He would be any mother's favorite son."

Font had never gone to school and could barely read and write. He never lost his Entre Ríos accent. Francisco Gómez gave him the nickname Facón Grande, which he took to kindly. He liked everything big, maybe because he was so short himself. His stirrups where the size of wagon wheels and his bolas were very heavy. He treated his friends like family. You could see this in his friendship with the Chilean Leiva, whom Varela had killed in Jaramillo. The Chilean, who was also a horse-tamer, was a hard worker but had a weakness for drink. He was also a fugitive: he had once fired two shots at a police officer who had cheated him at the horse track. He had been hiding out in the wilderness ever since. Facón Grande never abandoned him and was always bringing him supplies. Leiva was a sickly man and carried three bullets in his body, which were given to him by Eusebio Martínez of Entre Ríos during a fight. Martínez was arrested in Río Gallegos. After he served out his sentence, he went looking for Leiva. He went directly to the San José ranch, where he knew that José Font was working as the ranch administrator. He thought that if he found Font, Leiva would be nearby. Font had gone to get some oxen from the Buenos Aires ranch and found Eusebio Martínez waiting for him when he returned. Martínez asked him coarsely where he could find Leiva. Words were exchanged, and the two men from Entre Ríos confronted each other face to face. At nearly two meters, Eusebio Martínez towered over José Font. "Don't talk to me like that," Font told him slowly. "We're both sons of Urquiza." Martínez drew his knife, but Font's hand was already on his whip and he struck his opponent on the shoulder. Despite his size, Martínez backed off and agreed to talk things over. In the end, he decided to leave Leiva alone. Font was neither a troublemaker nor a brute, but he still had that criollo attitude of settling differences with a fight.

He did much to help farmers who had just arrived in Patagonia or who were experiencing difficulties. He helped the Tirachinis, for example, by buying them groceries.

He was also involved in a much-discussed incident in which a certain Casterán, with the backing of the authorities, built a shack on some land owned by José Font. When he saw the building that had been erected in his absence, Font used a team of eighteen horses to pull it down. But he was arrested and taken to San Julián.

After that, something changed in Font. This is why the carters, who were looking to secure better haulage rates, elected him as their delegate during the second strike. They knew that Font was the only one who could stand up to the police. When the strike broke out in Cañadón León, Font headed to Las Heras. He was then shot in Jaramillo after the shootout in Tehuelches.

Here ends the testimony of the owner of the La Navarra ranch, which is located between San Julián and Puerto Deseado.

We have tried to reconstruct the final days of Facón Grande from the statements made by José Turcato, the owner of the ranch next to the Tehuelches railway station. Turcato also married the daughter of Guillermo Bain, an English landowner who had been taken hostage by Facón Grande's men. He received us in the company of his wife and his two adult sons. He started off by telling us that he supported the decision to send in the army to end the strike and declined to comment on the executions of Facón Grande and his men. He only agreed to tell us what happened. He was a young boy in 1921 and the ranch was run by his father. He showed us a massive old book that he had in his library, telling us:

This was a gift to my father from José Font, alias Facón Grande. It's a copy of the civil code of the Argentine Republic. My father knew him very well, so he wasn't taken hostage when the strike broke out. They only took some of his horses. They camped out on the ranch at a place known as Cañadón del Carro, where the two strikers killed at Tehuelches are buried. I still remember when he came to our ranch to tell my father that he was a strike leader. My father asked him why, since he was earning a good living from his carting business. Facón Grande looked in my direction—I was just a boy—and said, "I'm doing it for them."[38] He then thought for a minute and added, "Look, my mother raised me to be a man and I'm going to prove it; they've chosen me as their leader and I will do my duty."

And then he went back to his camp, which was quite close to here, in a little gully where there was a spring. From there, you have a clear view of the Tehuelches railway station. Through his binoculars, Font saw Varela arrive and thought they were the police. This is why he ordered his men to intercept them. They headed down the road (now Route 520) and Varela opened fire when he saw them. The soldiers, who took up positions behind the tavern that faced the station in those days, had longer range weapons. Three of the strikers were killed and one of their cars was set on fire, while one of Varela's soldiers was seriously wounded (he later died) and another was lightly injured. The shootout could be heard from our ranch. When the soldiers retreated, Facón Grande saw Fischer's army hat and realized that he hadn't been fighting the police. He then ordered his men to take the wounded—José Becerra, Armando Ríos, and another man nicknamed Oveja Negra—back to camp. The first two were in very bad shape. They asked for something to drink and died shortly thereafter. They're still buried out there, and up to a few years ago their graves were marked with a small wooden cross made from parts of a yerba mate barrel. They wanted to take Oveja Negra somewhere else, but he died on Gamarra's ranch.

José García, the owner of Jaramillo's Hotel España, showed us José Font's grave. García had come to town in 1921, just one month after the conflict ended. He still lives there with his wife, who was born in Jaramillo. If you leave town in the direction of Puerto Deseado, Font's grave can be found one kilometer down the road on the right hand side. You need to be accompanied by a local, as the site is not immediately obvious—it's located in a ravine that's entirely covered with vegetation. A typically Patagonian landscape with rocky outcrops and mata negra. There's no wooden cross, not even a pile of stones. Nothing. "Nobody wanted to speak of these things for a long time," García told us.

> Everybody was terrified. The bones of those unfortunates were left out in the open or were only partially buried for a long time. Then, as time went by, somebody anonymously buried them here. One of the men who was shot was Servando Romero of Puerto Deseado, the son of a barber. He was twenty-two years old and his father came to claim his body. His corpse had been piled up with the others. His father recognized his body from a handkerchief, as the skunks and armadillos had left him unrecognizable. He's now buried in the Puerto Deseado cemetery. The same thing happened with a boy named Alonso, who was shot five leagues from here. He was from a well-known Puerto Deseado family. His relatives came looking for him and gave him a Christian burial.

While in Jaramillo, we went to visit Lorenzo Jaramillo, whom everyone called El Indio Jaramillo. A Mapuche, his family had once owned all of these lands, but he lives with his sister in a humble, one-room cottage. In poor health, he smiles at us from his bed and respectfully bows his head. He is eighty-one years old and lived near Tehuelches during the strike. We ask him what he remembers and, grinning mischievously, he tells us:

> I know nothing, absolutely nothing. I fled to the hills when the strikers showed up and then fled to Barbucho when the army came. I stayed there until I heard that the naval troops had arrived and that the executions had ceased. Then I came back here. No, no, neither the strikers nor the soldiers could catch me.

El Indio Jaramillo smiles and repeats, "No, they couldn't catch me." We ask him if he lost any friends in those tragic events and he responds, smiling:

Yes, two good friends. Pichinanga was shot on Hospitaleche's ranch in Cañadón León and Antonio Leiva was shot off his horse here in Jaramillo.

Juan Melchor Michelena, the owner of the El Rambueyés ranch and an eyewitness to everything that occurred in Jaramillo following the arrival of the army, provides another piece of invaluable testimony:

Varela brought two strike leaders with him from the Jaramillo ranch. One of them, who had a birthmark on his face, was known as Ruso Manchado, and the other was named Peñaloza. They were tied up and transported by train. When Varela came back from Tehuelches after his defeat at the hands of Facón Grande, the soldiers and NCOs forced Ruso Manchado and Peñaloza off the train with their rifle butts. One soldier gave Ruso Manchado[39] a terrible blow that smashed his face in. After beating them with the flats of their sabers, the soldiers took them a couple hundred meters from the station and shot them. When Facón Grande came to negotiate with Varela, they didn't shoot him straight away. They held him here at the station all day and took photographs. When night fell, they drove him away from here and shot him. Antonio Leiva arrived much later than Facón Grande, riding in on an Arabian horse and all dressed in black. The first thing he did was ask where Facón Grande was. That was when they killed him.

We have two testimonies dealing with the hours just before Facón Grande's death. The first is taken from the Comodoro Rivadavia newspaper *El Patagónico*, which ran a letter on January 21st, 1974 from Félix Oruezábal, who lives at Pellegrini 890 in Comodoro Rivadavia:

I remember that when I was assigned to the Puerto Deseado—Las Heras railway line in 1938, Stationmaster Leoncio Cid told me all about what happened during those years. Once the strike broke out, Facón Grande went around organizing the men and rounding up horses. President Yrigoyen immediately sent in the army, which arrived in Puerto Deseado in a matter of days. They came to the interior by train and set up camp in Jaramillo. Meanwhile, Facón Grande and his men made a push for the coast, completely unaware of the arrival of the armed forces.

Elsa Minucci de Gamarra,[40] who lived with her family near the Tehuelches station, warned the army of the proximity of the strikers. A contingent arrived by train from Jaramillo and positioned themselves behind the stone boardinghouse.

Without expecting it, the strikers found themselves in the middle of an intense firefight. Winchesters against Mausers. As the soldiers were outnumbered by Facón Grande's men, they were pushed back to the train. One of their men died and another was wounded. As Facón Grande occupied the battlefield, he was astonished to see a soldier's cap. He thought he had been fighting the hated White Guard.

After that, he was determined to do whatever it took to reach a settlement with the armed forces and left for the Fitz Roy railway station. He was accompanied by all his men, who brought with them their horses and carts, loaded down with supplies. Contact with the army was established by means of the railway station's telephone and Leoncio Cid told Facón Grande all the news he had received from Jaramillo. Leoncio Cid insisted that Facón Grande had told him, "I can accept any settlement between equals" and that he was pacing up and down the platform until he got an answer. They left for Jaramillo on the basis of dubious promises and there they met their fate.

We have transcribed this account so it can be compared to that of Stationmaster Leoncio Cid's son, which is impossible to refute. Alberto Cid was born in 1907 and worked for the 24th Postal District in Río Gallegos from 1929 until he retired. He now lives in Bahía Blanca. At my request, Alberto Cid wrote down his memories—as we have said, his father was the station-master in 1921. The above testimony is from the father in 1938; the one we have transcribed below is the son's from February 1973. Though there are decades between them, they coincide on almost every detail:

> At the time, in 1921, I was living at the Fitz Roy station (kilo-meter 142 of the Puerto Deseado–Las Heras line), where my father was the stationmaster. When Varela stopped by on the way to Tehuelches, my father told him that he would encoun-ter a group of 150 to 200 people. "The strikers never resist the army," Varela responded, "only the police and the White Guard. I'll break up their group and send them home this very afternoon." He optimistically pressed on towards Tehuelches, which is twenty kilometers down the line. The sister of Tomás Minucci—who had been taken hostage after firing a few shots at the rebels—was at that station. This girl, Elsa Minucci, later Mrs. Gamarra, was in communication with Fitz Roy by telephone and telegraph. My father informed her of Varela's approach. When the troops arrived, she told Varela that the dust kicked up by their vehicles had tipped off the strikers and that Facón Grande himself had said, "Here come the police and the White Guard." Then he got ready to resist. They headed out by car and by horse, stopping just in front of the boardinghouse, while Varela stopped behind the tavern facing the station and took cover behind the ranch's fence (there were about two hun-dred meters separating the two). They held their position for a long time. Guillermo Bain, the administrator of the Josefina ranch who had been taken hostage and was being used by the strikers as a chauffeur, made a run for Varela's group. This was inexplicable, as he was a tall, thickly built Scotsman who must have weighed close to 110 kilos, but all the shots that the strik-ers were surely firing at him missed and he was able to reach the army lines. There was a strong wind that day. Fischer, who

had been crawling forward along the ground, was shot later on. Another soldier dragged him back to the vehicles and Varela decided to order a retreat. When they returned to Fitz Roy, my father asked about the solider who was lying in the back seat of their car. "They've killed this boy, but they're going to pay a very heavy price for it," Varela responded nervously. He was no longer the calm, optimistic man we had seen just a few hours beforehand.

After Varela left, Facón Grande scouted the area and found the dead soldier's cap. He was stunned to realize that he had been fighting the army and not the police. He put himself in contact with Varela, with the stationmaster's sister acting as an intermediary. He and his men decided to surrender to Varela the next day. I arrived in Fitz Roy in time to see Facón Grande's column arrive at the station. He drank his last mate with me. I had been brewing some to drink with my father when he showed up. He sat down to talk with us about the movement. This was around three or four in the afternoon. It was my father who passed on Commander Varela's request that his men stop five kilometers outside of Jaramillo and that only Facón Grande and the other strike leaders should meet with him. He agreed.

Facón Grande was shot in Jaramillo. In total, there must have been forty or fifty men who were executed in the area. The corpses were left out in the open for several days and were simply piled up instead of being buried. It seems that they tried to burn them with gasoline, but it didn't work. The locals ended up burying the bodies themselves after the soldiers left. One or two of the bodies were taken from the mass grave. One of them belonged to Servando Romero, who was reburied by his father, a Puerto Deseado barber, after Varela's departure.

I should also mention what Varela's troops did after passing through Fitz Roy on the way back from the shootout in Tehuelches. They entered the tavern owned by the Basque Azurmendi and the Englishman Smuler—which faced the station—and ordered everyone out at gunpoint. Then they stripped them of all their money and valuables, even their quillangos. The victims were all humble people. The naval troops behaved very differently and always tried to avoid any abuse of power.

Alberto Cid considers Facón Grande to have been an honest and simple man. And, regarding the strikers, he said, "You can't go around calling them bandits when most of them didn't even know why they were there."

We have no wish to tire our readers with too many details. But we believe that all testimony is valuable, especially in a drama such as this one, where the truth has been distorted and covered with a leaden silence. We can see, now, the fallacies, fabrications, and lies with which Lieutenant Colonel Varela, commander of the 10th Cavalry Regiment, the Hussars of Pueyrredón, tried to cover up the murder of Facón Grande. Remember: he reported to his superiors that Facón Grande died in combat in Tehuelches.

We have labeled Varela's reports "fallacies, fabrications, and lies." We could have said that they were merely "untrue," avoiding such harsh words, but when we're discussing a man's life we must be unafraid to be blunt. And Lieutenant Colonel Varela's own second-in-command, Elbio Carlos Anaya, confirms our position. In an interview published by the Buenos Aires magazine *Gente* on July 19th, 1974, Anaya says, "…and Varela ordered Facón Grande to be shot on the spot."

With the exception of Anaya, the only Argentine officer to have publicly admitted to the executions is Major Jorge Félix Gómez, who participated in the army's first intervention in Patagonia as part of Captain Laprida's column. Major Gómez—currently the owner of the Dora Elena, Tatá-Cuá, Saladas, and Corrientes ranches—served as a lieutenant in the 10th Cavalry Regiment, 3rd Squadron. In a letter addressed to Dr. Félix Luna, the editor of the magazine *Todo es Historia*, he refers to my work entitled *The Avengers of Tragic Patagonia* and states, "The good faith of the author is evident, as is that of all those who assisted him in his research. I congratulate them." And he referred to the dead strikers by saying, "It's true, some of them were given a hand in dying. They were outlaws." Later on he adds:

> Some corpses appeared in Punta Alta? Yes, the foxes of Patagonia were able to uncover them as they were very badly buried. There weren't any shovels on hand and digging in that soil was as difficult as digging a well on a macadam road. Of those killed, many of them had learned all they knew in prison and deserved to die. Others were killed by mistake.

After justifying the methods employed by the army, he states:

> Though I am not trying to defend the ranchers or the manner in which they settled those lands (a rancher by the name of Dickie told me that when he first arrived in Patagonia, they paid him one pound sterling for every Indian head he gave to Menéndez Behety), what's most unfortunate is that Santa Cruz has never erected a monument honoring Commander Varela.

We appreciate Major Gómez's sincerity, as well as his initiative in writing to us himself. Other officials who participated in the massacre have attempted to explain away the dead with ridiculous interpretations of wind speed, as Colonel Viñas Ibarra repeated towards the end of his life when asked about the executions at La Anita.

But let's get back to Jaramillo and Facón Grande. Another important piece of evidence refuting Varela's narrative can be seen in the testimony of Pedro A. Cittanti, an elderly resident of Puerto Deseado. He witnessed the events that transpired in Tehuelches, Jaramillo, and Puerto Deseado at the age of eighteen. Accompanied by Ricardo Roberts, the culture secretary of Puerto Deseado's municipal government, we visited Cittanti at his home. This is what he had to say:

I was eighteen years old in December 1921. I had a job with the Patagonia Import and Export Company, which was popularly known as La Anónima. They were the local distributors of the Ford Motor Company. When Varela arrived with the 10th Cavalry, they ordered us to load some vehicles on to a train for the use of the troops. It took us until midnight. We left for Jaramillo at dawn, taking the vehicles and the soldiers with us. The cars were unloaded in Jaramillo. There, Varela received news on the strikers from Miss Minucci, who behaved like a real heroine. The strikers left her at the Tehuelches station and she took advantage of this to inform the army about the location of Facón Grande's camp in Cañadón de Turcato. We were given orders to encircle his location. But the strikers came out to meet the army. That's when the shooting started. We drove off in the cars. I was with Patricio Mendeaga, Nagore, and a couple others whose names I can't remember. A bullet shattered the windshield of one of the cars. We were very frightened. Then Fischer was shot and another soldier received a bullet in the elbow. Varela had only twelve soldiers left, so he ordered his men to drive back to Jaramillo. Everything was calm after that. With the help of Mesa, La Anónima's representative in Pico Truncado, Varela and Facón Grande were able to reach an agreement. Mesa was the one who convinced Font and his men to give themselves up. When Font got to Jaramillo, he wasn't shot right away. He stayed there at the station for a while, there are photographs of him where you can see the houses of Jaramillo just as they are today. He even got impatient and said, "Let's go!" And then we got underway. We noticed that the vehicles behind us were carrying eighteen of the strikers, including Facón Grande and that Romero boy whose father was a barber in Puerto Deseado. The other vehicles went off in a different direction after we left Jaramillo. We stopped and heard gunfire. Then we saw two men running up the hill, but another round was fired off and they fell to the ground. They didn't bury any of the bodies. They were left out in the open on Cimadevilla's land, about three kilometers from the Jaramillo station. That area is fenced off now, but it wasn't back then. I saw it for myself a year later, when my father, my brother, and I went to visit Turcato on his ranch. We stopped to eat lunch at the hotel in Jaramillo and the waiter told us the exact location. We followed his directions and found the well, about ten meters in diameter, where the bodies were buried. This was the following year, in the summer. We found eighteen bodies.

It was a very unpleasant experience for all of us. We fell silent after hearing the gunfire and watching them shoot down those men who were trying to run away. We didn't speak again until we reached Puerto Deseado, where we were finally able to get away from the soldiers. What Lieutenant Colonel Varela said, that Facón Grande was killed in combat in Tehuelches, is nonsense.

It isn't nonsense, though, but a means of covering up a crime. Facón Grande surrendered under false pretenses. If the man responsible for such a trick had not been a military officer—and not just any officer, but the commander of the glorious Hussars of Pueyrredón—nobody would be ashamed to call him a traitor. But every military action can be explained away. Facón Grande had defeated Varela, the workers had defeated the army. This was very dangerous. If the problem wasn't definitively dealt with then and there, the tables could easily have been turned on Varela. That's why he acted the way he did, it was the only way to liquidate him. And so he invites him over. Facón Grande—naïve and simple-minded like all country folk—took the officer at his word. And in this harsh, egotistical world, naivety has its price. Derision, ridicule, four gunshots and then it's all over.

Ernesto Venditti of Puerto Deseado has provided us with an intriguing piece of testimony. He was introduced to us by the town's mayor, Martínez Lucea. Venditti, who was seventy-eight years old in August 1973, was born in Lujan, grew up in Avellaneda, did his military service at Campo de Mayo ("I was discharged with an impeccable record"), and moved first to La Pampa and then to Puerto Deseado. When the second strike was declared, Venditti was a delegate of the Workers' Society—but with Rogelio Lorenzo's men in the syndicalist FORA IX, the faction opposed to Soto. He speaks categorically:

> The workers were trying to act big, it was a foolish uprising. They were in the wrong. Going to ranches, stealing horses, and taking people like Guillermo Bain hostage isn't the way to ask for better wages or working conditions. Those ware not the methods of true syndicalism, as we stand for. When their first delegates arrived in Las Heras, all the railway workers fled to El Escorial. I stayed. One of Facón Grande's men approached me and said, "We want you to join the cause." "What cause?" I asked. "I'm a union member but I'm not one of you." "We're fighting for the good of the workers," he told me. I was curt. "What is the good of the workers? This isn't the way to fight for it. Union delegates should act properly and shouldn't endorse this kind of strike."

Venditti—who was an organizer for Hipólito Yrigoyen's Radical Civic Union in his hometown of Lujan—describes Facón Grande as:

> ...a fool and an innocent. Though it's true that he was a hard worker and a good person, he wasn't shrewd enough to be a union leader. This is why they were able to catch him so easily. Varela pretended to negotiate and Font walked right into the trap. And then they shot him and the strike was over. If he had called in the cavalry instead of agreeing to negotiate, things would have been very different.

He then tells us the following story, in which he played a key role:

> José Font was camped out at Cañadón del Cerro on Turcato's ranch. Elsa Minucci de Gamarra, who was then at the Tehuelches railway station, told me that the strikers were carrying out

military exercises in their nearby camp. That brave woman saved our lives. This is how it happened. While Facón Grande was at his camp, the railway director, Manuel Usandivaras, arrived to deal with a very serious problem: Puerto Deseado had run out of water. In those days, the town's drinking water was brought in by tank. When the strike broke out, the tanks were in Las Heras. They had to be brought in to Puerto Deseado by train, passing by Facón Grande's camp. Usandivaras asked me if I wanted to accompany him. I said yes. A small group of us set off for Deseado with the tanks, running the risk of being stopped by the strikers and being left to their mercy. I remember that our group included Usandivaras, a boilerman named Olguín, Pedemonte, and Father José, a priest from Puerto Deseado who wanted to join us on our difficult mission of slipping past the strikers. This is when that heroic young lady from Tehuelches saved our lives. The strikers had ripped up the tracks and we would have been derailed if that woman hadn't run out on to the tracks and signaled us to stop. She then filled us in on the situation. After repairing the tracks, we were able to arrive at our destination, safe and sound. Her actions were later memorialized by Usandivaras. This was the role I played during the strike. As I have said, the strike ended very badly because it was planned badly and handled badly. That doesn't make it right to shoot peasants, of course, especially because they joined the strike like it was a party. They could have just arrested the leaders and deported them. I didn't approve of them being shot like that.

Yet another piece of testimony regarding the events at Jaramillo has been provided by Faustino Peláez Villa, who was living in Colonia Las Heras in December 1921. He witnessed Facón Grande's final moments in the Jaramillo railway station and still recalls the sight of the gaucho and his comrades in misfortune riding off to their deaths in the truck provided by La Anónima.[41] He says that the place where the bodies were found was overrun with armadillos. "They burrowed into the bodies and came out covered in human hair," the seventy-five year old man tells us. "After that, I never ate armadillo again." He goes on:

> Vizcay, the administrator of La Anónima, was devastated when they told him that Varela had Facón Grande shot. The ones who had convinced Facón Grande to give himself up—insisting that Varela would be true to his word and free the prisoners in Río Gallegos—were Mesa and Núñez (we got their names from Sabino Urrutia of Puerto Deseado). Antonio Leiva, Facón Grande's second-in-command, rode in alone on a horse with a new saddle. Before Facón Grande arrived, Ruso Manchado and another man were shot next to the pile of scrap metal, where the first aid station is now. They had been tied up and were writhing around in desperation.[42] Before they were shot, the soldiers were making fun of them on the platform.

The mopping-up operations in the north were very calculated. As luck would have it, Captain Anaya was the one to organize these patrols. The crackdown was swift and rather dubious criteria was used: "Anyone suspected or accused by the ranchers of having participated in the movement was to be arrested and taken to the squadron's base of operations until things could be clarified." So reads Anaya's own report to the War Ministry.

Sub-lieutenant Loza's dispatches accuse the naval troops of being responsible for shooting the strike leader Elizondo. On January 1st, 1922, while he was on Florencio Puchulú's Alma Gaucha ranch, he reports the following:

> It had been raining since dawn. That morning, a truck under the command of Naval Lieutenant Menéndez arrived, bringing us prisoners that had been captured up north. As it was still raining, I spent the rest of the day inspecting the workers that had been brought in for the shearing by a contractor named Arcal, witnessing nothing of importance. Some of them had been issued safe conduct passes in San Julián and others in San José. I confiscated

the clothing they had received from the ringleaders, as well as an automatic pistol, also ill-gotten. At around 2000 hours, I heard a gunshot. A man named Elizondo, one of the ringleaders who had been turned over to us by Lieutenant Menéndez, had tried to steal a carbine from Private Pedrosa, who was on guard duty. Elizondo was shot for this by the naval troops.

Sub-lieutenant Loza brought in a good catch that day. His report on the death of four strikers reads so naively that it could have only been written by an officer of the Argentine Army:

More or less one league away from the Ruiz ranch, in some very rough country, I came across a small encampment of four men who resisted until they ran out of ammunition. They were killed while trying to escape. We later identified them as Gorra Colorada, Juan Campos, Juan Wenteleo, and an Italian named Ángel Paladino. The latter confessed that Gorra Colorada had been in the shootout at San José and that the others had fought at Tehuelches, where he himself had been one of the most bloodthirsty.

It's strange that Paladino was able to make a confession after dying, taking the time to accuse himself of being "one of the most bloodthirsty." It's clear that these four strikers were taken prisoner and then executed.

Loza concluded his mopping-up operation on January 10th, thus definitively bringing to a finish the "war" in Santa Cruz, which had been waged from the southern border with Chile all the way up to Caleta Olivia.

CHAPTER SIX

THE VICTORS
(FOR HE'S A JOLLY GOOD FELLOW)

> "The ranchers dearly wanted the revolt put down
> before the shearing began. The numerous executions
> sowed terror and allowed them to force their peons
> back to work for lower pay."
> (Frigate Captain Dalmiro Sáenz's report to the naval
> minister on the second strike.
> Confidential Document No. 443,
> January 14, 1922)

For Varela, the bitter part was over. There would be no more fighting and no more sleepless nights. Now it was time to celebrate his victory. The time had come for banquets, receptions, and the admiration of the mighty, which he had worked so hard to earn.

But even before the tables were set and the laudatory speeches written for the Liberator of Patagonia, the mighty had already begun to reap the benefits of Varela's actions. They had used him. Now everything was clear, the truth could finally be seen. Everything that has been written about whether or not strikers were executed, every argument that the Radical Civic Union and the military had used to defend themselves and all the theories about Chile's intervention in Argentine Patagonia can be disproven by analyzing the following document, drafted by the Río Gallegos Rural Society and printed on December 10th, 1921 in *La Unión*:

RANCHERS:
The Rural Society has decided to set the following prices for ranch employees:
Shearers, 12 pesos per 100 animals
Peons, in general, 80 pesos per month
Carters, 90 pesos
Day laborers, 5 pesos per day
Herders, 100 pesos per month
Cooks, 120 pesos
Balers (Ferrier press) 150 pesos per bale
Drovers with horses (per day, meals included) 12 pesos
Ranch herders, 5 extra pesos

These prices will be applicable as of the 15th of this month.
Río Gallegos, December 10, 1921.
—Ibón Noya, President; Edelmiro A. Correa Falcón,
Secretary General

The landowners, in other words, had taken advantage of the destruction of every labor organization in Santa Cruz and imposed a new labor arrangement, *motu proprio*, in the midst of Varela's campaign of persecution and extermination. They decided to slash wages in open defiance of the Yza settlement, which had been approved by the governor and ratified by the National Labor Department. Let's compare the new wages with those established by law:

Peons, 120 pesos (now 80)
Carters, 130 pesos (now 90)
Herders, 140 pesos (now 100)
Cooks, 160 pesos (now 120)
Drovers, 25 pesos per day (now 12)

For most workers, this meant that their wages were cut by a full third, while daily wages for drovers were cut in half. The other working conditions that the Workers' Society had fought so hard for are not even mentioned. The only victors in the dramatic events in Patagonia were the landowners, and their victory was total. They even overruled the decisions of the Argentine Army itself and nobody said a word. After the pacification campaign, every ranch in the region began to apply the new "prices," as the Rural Society called wages.

So, who was right? Should we believe the Workers' Society and Antonio Soto when they said that it was the bosses who had declared war on the workers and forced them into going on strike? The answer could be seen in the insolent reply of the ranchers, who didn't even wait for Varela and his troops to leave before slashing wages. No, the shearing season had already begun and the decree had to be issued immediately.

Nevertheless, it's true that the ranchers won't skimp on their tributes to the military. The receptions held in the cities of Santa Cruz will leave no eyes dry.

On January 1st, 1922, the Río Gallegos Rural Society holds a lavish banquet for Lieutenant Colonel Varela in the Hotel Argentino. "The hotel didn't have enough space for all the people who came out to celebrate the brilliant feats of the armed forces," *La Unión* reports, adding that only eighty people were able to get a seat at the tables:

> …but among them a frank sense of joy could be felt, which they celebrated with liquor and gourmet food. After the champagne was poured, Rural Society President Ibón Noya gave a toast: "My spirit has opened itself up to experiencing the sweet excitement of these times, in which gratitude mingles with the satisfaction of seeing such a noble mission accomplish all of its goals in our territory. It's enough to look around this room to be certain of the high regard you have earned through your crusade of liberation. And I say liberation because anachronistic hordes hiding in the folds of the red flag have spent the past year violating all the rights and freedoms secured by our heroic ancestors for the well-being of their children.

The ranchers are visibly moved as Ibón Noya speaks of the debt of gratitude that they all owe Varela:

> We have lived through trying times and we have all experienced the feeling that our forces, honed for no struggles other than our daily labors, have collapsed under the unprecedented attacks of a directionless, unscrupulous mob. Lieutenant Colonel Varela: you knew how to act in such a way that definitively guarantees our national sovereignty and the rule of law. Our gratitude will follow you wherever your destiny takes you, and the memory of your actions in our territory will endure in our memory as a lesson of what men can do when inspired by their patriotic duty and their love for the fatherland.

Varela will be brief. He says that his troops have been driven by their "noble inspiration" and that he had done nothing more than his duty "as a soldier of the nation."

Alberto Hamlich then spoke on behalf of the foreign-born ranchers and Captain Viñas Ibarra concluded by praising the gallantry of his soldiers.

But the end of the evening was genuinely moving. The officers, ranchers, merchants, and police all got to their feet and sang the national anthem. And then, to top it off, "the British subjects, who were quite numerous, sang 'For He's a Jolly Good Fellow' in honor of Varela." The sound of those foreign voices, hoarse with gratitude, was a worthy finale.[1]

But the men of the Río Gallegos Rural Society aren't the only ones to pay tribute to the victors. In Puerto Santa Cruz, the reception held in Varela's honor outdoes that of Río Gallegos. According to *La Unión*, the banquet reaches "extraordinary proportions." It is held in the spacious dining room of the Social Club, "which proved too small for the 120 diners, who were among the area's finest individuals."

A banquet is held to honor Anaya in Puerto Deseado, but the ranchers Esteban Martinovich and Pedro Fasioli refuse to attend as a protest against the execution of farmworkers. The newspaper *El Orden* describes their absence as "regrettable." Days later, the "leading families" of Puerto Deseado organize a dance paying homage to Captain Anaya and his officers. The article in *El Orden* pompously states:

> The sons of Mars paid tribute to Terpsichore throughout the party, which was also attended by the sailors of the *Belgrano*. The champagne was uncorked at midnight and Miss Rojas gave Anaya a scroll thanking him for his services. The dancing lasted until five o'clock Sunday morning. The scroll given by Miss Rojas read, "To Captain Elbio Carlos Anaya and the officers and soldiers under his command, whose effective campaign of repression against the enemies of social order has once again proven the traditional virtues of the Argentine soldier. The people of Puerto Deseado express their gratitude."

The time had come for the soldiers to rest. After so much tension they craved the freedom to do nothing at all, and above all they craved sex.

Shooting had been an exhausting task. Although everything had gone well and required little effort, over time it had become an unpleasant memory. Practically all of them remembered the look of fear in the faces of the chilotes as they were about to die, the furious expressions of the Spaniards and the tragically ironic looks of the German, Russian, and Polish anarchists facing the firing squads composed of Argentine soldiers.

But it was all over now and the soldiers were back in port, waiting for the ships that would bring them back to Buenos Aires. Lieutenant Colonel Varela had eased up on discipline. A good man, that Varela. And nobody's fool. In just a few short days, he had managed to break the strikers and give them what they deserved. His hand never trembled under the sheepish gaze of the chilotes. He didn't allow a single one of his soldiers to get weak in the knees. Instead, he dressed them down with only a few short shouts—that was enough for even timid men to become the finest of marksmen.

When it was all over, Varela adopted a fatherly approach to his soldiers. When they got back to town, for example, he gave them permission to visit the brothels and satisfy the desires that they had been bottling up for so long. Since they left to hunt chilotes and anarchists, they hadn't so much as seen a woman, not even a Chilean.

This whole historic episode—the cruelest of the first seventy-five years of the twentieth century and as cruel as the custom of slitting the throats of prisoners in the nineteenth century—has all the characteristics of the mischief that men engage in when they are amongst themselves for too long and feel the need to show that they are tough, strong, macho. The killings were carried out in cold blood. Silently. If there had been birds in the area, their songs would have been heard between each gunshot. But there was nothing, not even a woman's cries. Even the chilotes, with terrified expressions on their faces, remained silent. They neither begged nor pleaded. This was between men.

But now things were different. There were women in the cities, and that changed everything. The tough men in uniform softened up and giggled when they see a woman pass by.

The soldiers are gathered together, put at ease, and told that they will visit the town's brothels in small groups. In simple language so that everyone could understand, an NCO explained how to make use of a prostitute's services without catching gonorrhea or syphilis.

Everything had been organized well. The brothel owners had been told when to expect the first group of soldiers so that they could get their girls ready. In San Julián, this notice went out to Paulina Rovira, the Madame of the La Catalana brothel.

But when the first group of soldiers approaches the brothel, Paulina Rovira rushes out and speaks with the NCO in charge. It's clear that something's going on and the soldiers begin to get nervous. Their superior explains that something unexpected has happened: all five of the bordello's prostitutes have refused to sleep with them. And the madam insists that she cannot force them. The NCO and the conscripts take it as an insult, as an attack on the country they represent. Besides, they were also very aroused. They talk amongst themselves and spur each other on. They try and storm the doors of the brothel. But then the five girls come out, armed with brooms, and confront the soldiers with cries of "Murderers! Pigs!" and "We don't sleep with murderers!"

The word "murderers" sends a chill through the soldiers. Though they still reach for their sabers, they back away from the whores, who are swinging their brooms like women possessed. There's a terrible commotion. The soldiers give up but remain on the sidewalk in front of the brothel. The girls in the doorway don't hold their tongues. Aside from "murderers" and "pigs," they call them "sons of bitches" and—according to a later police report— "other obscene insults, as could be expected from such sluts."

But there's nothing that can be done. Being called murderers is enough for these seasoned soldiers to forget all about women. The itching between their legs turns into a bitter taste in their mouths. And the only desire they have left is to drown their rage in drink.

But it doesn't end there. The police commissioner of San Julián orders two of his officers to bring the five ingrates back to the station. Along the way, the men smirk and the town's honest women glare at them. The brothel's musicians—Hipólito Arregui, Leopoldo Napolitano, and Juan Acatto—are also arrested, but they are released shortly after being booked because they state their disapproval of the position taken by the girls. Besides, they always play for free on patriotic occasions.

The prostitutes are imprisoned. Here the commissioner has a serious responsibility. They have insulted the nation's soldiers and taken the side of the strikers. He consults asks the garrison commander, first Lieutenant David S. Aguirre, for advice. The officer doesn't want a scandal and doesn't want for things to drag out. After all, nobody cares what five whores think.

Patient research has allowed us to discover the names of these five whores, these five women who were the only ones brave enough to publicly say that the perpetrators of the bloodiest massacre of workers in our history were nothing more than murderers. Their names are reproduced here as a small tribute to the memory of these five women who closed their legs as a gesture of rebellion. Here are their names as they appeared on the yellowing pages of the police report: Consuelo García, twenty-nine years old, Argentine, single, prostitute at the La Catalana brothel; Angela Fortunato, thirty-one years old, Argentine, married, seamstress and prostitute; Amalia Rodríguez, twenty-six years old, Argentine, single, prostitute; María Juliache, Spaniard, twenty-eight years old, resident of Argentina for the past seven years, prostitute; Maud Foster, Englishwoman, thirty-one years old, single, resident of Argentina for the past ten years, a woman from a good family, prostitute.

No flower has ever been placed on the mass graves of the strikers, which have only ever been graced by stone, mata negra, and the eternal Patagonian wind. The only flower we have managed to find is the brave gesture of the prostitutes of the La Catalana brothel on February 17th, 1922.

A new era has begun in Santa Cruz. There would be no more troubles, strikes, assemblies, flyers, or red flags. Lead and blood have secured a peace that would last for over half a century. Power has returned to the powerful, to those who have always exercised it. The man responsible for this—and you need only count the number of leagues traversed by the 10th Cavalry to be convinced that it was a truly heroic feat—was Lieutenant Colonel Héctor Benigno Varela. His father had christened him Benigno to distinguish him from the "evil" Varela, the guerrilla.[2] Benigno means benevolent. But it also means peaceful, charitable. And while Varela may not have been very benevolent or peaceful, he was certainly charitable—at least to those who already controlled the country's wealth.

Manuel Carlés, the president of the Patriotic League, visits Patagonia to celebrate the triumph of the Argentine military. He is enthusiastically applauded as a beacon of freedom. Upon his return to Buenos Aires, Carlés makes bombastic statements to the press, praising the spirit of sacrifice shown by the ranchers and the troops of the 10th Cavalry, who together managed to defeat their stateless enemies. He says that the workers have been taught a lesson:

> In Puerto Santa Cruz, the first people to call for a monument to the 10th Cavalry in Cañadón Quemado were the workers themselves. In San Julián, the membership of the Workers' Society passed over *en masse* to the Patriotic League. And in Río Gallegos, a delegation of authentic workers proclaimed that they had accepted the moral standards and nationalist precepts of the Patriotic League.

But it won't remain this easy. Remote as Patagonia may have seemed in those days, it would nevertheless be difficult to keep things covered up. The dead were too many, as were those who benefited. The news managed to reach Buenos Aires. Anarchist groups were the first to speak out. What first seemed to be an exaggeration made by fanatics was later confirmed to be true. Suddenly everyone knew that something horrendous had occurred in the unfamiliar land of Patagonia. When *La Vanguardia*—the newspaper of the Socialist Party—learned that the dead included Albino Argüelles, secretary-general of the San Julián Workers' Society and a card-carrying party member, they began attacking Yrigoyen and Commander Varela day after day. The leaders of the Argentine Syndical Union (USA, formerly the FORA IX), who had sought to prevent a second strike at all costs, realized that they couldn't stay on the sidelines once they understood the scale of the massacre carried out by the 10th Cavalry in Santa Cruz. And so they joined the protests. They were soon followed by the newspapers *La Montaña* and *Crítica*.

And so Lieutenant Colonel Varela began his slow, delicate march towards his downfall, towards his pitiful death.

When the military commander departs for Buenos Aires, he is sent off in style by government officials and members of the Rural Society, the Commerce and Industry League, and the Patriotic League. But as he sets sail on the *Asturiano*, he learns of the welcome that is awaiting him back home. He hears that the repression has been criticized by the Radical Civic Union, by the population in general, and, as if it really needed to be said, by the working class.

As he disembarks in Buenos Aires, he sees that all of these rumors are true. There's nobody there to greet him. Absolutely nobody representing the federal government or the War Ministry. There's not even so much as a dog there to greet Commander Varela, the man who bravely restored order in Patagonia. The youth of the Patriotic League are the only exception; they form an invisible cordon behind the warehouses. Carlés tells Varela to remain calm and remember that he did his duty. In their meetings and assemblies, the anarchists denounce the massacre in the south and scream at the top of their lungs that they'll be waiting for Varela. They call him a murderer, a mercenary, a thief, a criminal. But Carlés's boys show up to defend the officer who taught the workers the harshest lesson in Argentine history.

What a contrast between his arrival in Buenos Aires and his departure from Río Gallegos! Important men slapped him on the back and were already calling him colonel, promoting him before his time and foreseeing his swift return as the territory's military governor.

But the truth could be seen on the docks in Buenos Aires. There was nobody representing his beloved president, as was his due. After all, discussions aside, he had managed to pacify Patagonia with just a handful of young soldiers. The Radicals weren't there to greet him, either. Only the sons of high society, the "forty families" who hated the Radical rabble. Varela isn't the sort of man to feel sorry for himself; he knows how to swallow his pride when the situation demands it. He goes to the War Ministry to request an audience with Minister Moreno. As he enters the ministry's offices, he's harassed by journalists. Their eyes show the same glimmer of curiosity as the pedestrians who turn around to stare at him on the street ("Look, it's Varela, the one who's responsible for the executions in Patagonia!"). When the minister declines to meet with him and sends Colonel Alfonso in his stead, Varela realizes that he's finished. There must be a plot against him—everyone is refusing to be seen with him for some reason. Varela insists that he wants to personally meet with the war minister to give him his verbal report. After a great deal of prevarication, Alfonso tells him to return the following day.

When Varela returns, he's more resolute than ever. He refuses to leave without seeing the minister. After a moderate wait, Moreno calls Varela into his office and listens silently. Varela speaks of the bravery of his men. Moreno tells him to prepare a written report so that he can study the matter in more detail. The commander asks the minister to help him arrange a meeting with Yrigoyen. He wants to tell him in person that he did his duty.

The journalists are waiting for him as he leaves the ministry. Varela understands that he has to respond, that he has to start defending himself. And so he does.[3] "Before anything else, I must speak of the performance of the troops under my command, as well as that of the civilians who accompanied us," he says. "They acted commendably at all times and their behavior was worthy of the highest praise." And then he makes the mistake of taking out a clipping from an English-language newspaper to back up his claim. The clipping is from *The Magellan Times* of Punta Arenas, a newspaper for Patagonia's British ranchers and merchants. It concludes by saying, "Patagonians should take off their hats to the 10th Argentine Cavalry and these very gallant gentlemen."

Varela defends himself with a newspaper for British landowners that he had to translate into Spanish himself. After describing the "fight" at Tehuelches and praising the commander in glowing terms, it ends by saying:

This brief account of the action would not be complete without mention of the scouts Robert Saller and Gerald Dobree, who in a two seater Ford always dashed ahead to explore the ground; Otto Hinsch, the genial inspector of the Sociedad Anónima; Robert Oerton, who joined us in Deseado to drive his own car and proved himself to be a stout fellow; Raul Kirchener, the Gallegos photographer, who discarded his camera for a Mauser; the two courageous chauffeurs Bosso and Argañaraz, who fought right through beside the soldiers.

As we can imagine, an article from an English-language newspaper published in Chile that refers to an inspector for La Anónima using the curious adjective "genial" is not likely to be interpreted as an accurate account of Varela's campaign by a public that has already begun to suspect that something very dirty had occurred in the far south.

In the days that follow, Varela continues to lobby for official recognition or, at the very least, a public statement from his friend Yrigoyen. *La Nación* announces that President Yrigoyen will meet with Varela, but days go by and the officer continues to wait. The attacks on Varela in the pages of *Crítica*, *La Vanguardia*, *La Montaña*, *La Internacional*, and the anarchist press are increasingly intense. And each ship that arrives from Patagonia brings someone who has another hair-raising tale to tell.

But in a certain sense, there's a true debate—subtle, without sensationalism—in the press. *La Prensa*, *La Nación*, and *La Razón* continue defending Varela's mission. So Argentina's three main anti-Yrigoyen newspapers defend a military officer closely allied with the president and, therefore, with the Yrigoyen administration itself. But the Radical government remains silent.

The army closely observes the press onslaught and the lack of a response from the government. And then comes the straw that breaks the camel's back. *La Protesta*, the mouthpiece of Argentina's orthodox anarchists, publishes the following article:

There seems to be no end to this infamy, this bloody war declared on the proletariat by all the forces of tyranny: capital, the press, and the army. In Santa Cruz, the iron boot of the militarist beast has destroyed everything, both the workers as well as their unions. Now there's nothing left but a pile of rubble lorded over by drunken soldiers, the Assassins' League and the bandit rulers of Patagonia. Atop the ashes of what once was, freedom perishes under the heel of raging barbarism.

The article is carefully cut out by the General Staff and forwarded to the war minister, accompanied by a note signed by Colonel Elías O. Álvarez:

Reading this article, it becomes clear that it represents a threat to those military personnel who are fighting tenaciously and at great cost in our nation's southern territories in defense of the constitutional authorities and the law of the land, as they have been ordered.

Articles of this nature are an abuse of the freedom of the press guaranteed by the Constitution. By attacking our national identity and inciting hatred between brothers, they are opening themselves up to the intervention of the authorities (Folio II 1922, No. 441, Interior Ministry).

As we can see, the General Staff is trying to silence its critics. But Yrigoyen isn't looking for trouble and, as always, takes an intermediate position. The war minister forwards the article to the interior minister, who then passes it on to the police. Police Chief Elpidio González, in turn, passes it on to the "appropriate" department, where it is buried. The Radicals are second to none in such maneuvers.

But the situation that so frightened the military becomes normal. Each passing day sheds more light on the massacre in Santa Cruz. The anarchists launch an enormous campaign of agitation, not just in their newspapers but also in unions and public meetings. Little by little, they manage to win over the "pure syndicalists," the socialists, and even the left-leaning liberals. And the silence of the Radicals leaves Varela increasingly isolated; the only defenders he has left are the nationalists and some small ultra-Catholic groups.

The mysterious word "Patagonia"—the unknown region, the forgotten region—now looms large on everyone's conscience. Public opinion is inflamed. What began as a heated complaint in the anarchist press has won over the street. The Socialist Party takes up the issue. On February 1st, 1922, a bomb goes off in Congress: a wise, insightful man by the name of Antonio de Tomaso places an item on the agenda that will cost the Radicals more than a few tears and more than a few votes.

With feigned detachment, as if he is going to speak on nothing more important than a pension for a widow whose husband died exploring the desert, Antonio de Tomaso takes the floor. The Radical bench is quite accustomed to listening to those Socialists: their fiery speeches always end in calls for moderation. De Tomaso speaks softly. He is barely audible over the other deputies, who talk amongst themselves. And then he raises his voice, his words like a punch to the ears: "Honorable deputies, a horrific tragedy has occurred in the territory of Santa Cruz."

He goes on, staring directly at the Radical leader:

All parties involved, particularly the nation's leading newspapers, have shrouded this affair in a heavy silence. But those of us who have accurate information about what has occurred, which now includes a large sector of the public, would become willing accomplices to this silence if we did not denounce these events within this chamber and if we did not demand the inquiry that our nation's honor requires. For many days now, our leading newspapers have accustomed us to reading headlines about banditry in Patagonia. They have led us to believe that the territory is home to an inexplicable horde of bandits, operating outside all laws and with no purpose other than pillage. These bandits allegedly roam the countryside, spreading terror, destroying the social order, and preparing for a far-reaching revolution that would radiate north through the interior and along the coast. Many people have believed this legend, but the truth is beginning to come out...

This is a deeply uncomfortable turn of events for the Radicals. They are not murderers, much less of the defenseless. But this sort of thing always seems to happen to them.

De Tomaso continues explaining how the truth came to be known. Among other reasons, he mentions that:

...those responsible at the highest levels, foreseeing the possible consequences, have begun to speak, albeit indirectly, in order to cover up their own responsibility or to shift the blame to other government agencies.

These insinuations from de Tomaso make the Radical bench extremely nervous. The problems presented by the Tragic Week have arisen again. Spilled blood is the worst thing that can happen to a government of peacemakers, as the Radicals wished to be. But before singling out those responsible, de Tomaso wants to provide accurate information:

Honorable deputies, the so-called banditry in Patagonia is actually a labor movement, and I am not saying this capriciously or out of sectarianism. We can find the proof of this in official documents. I know that official documents are not often read in this country, but sometimes they can provide you with interesting information. In this case, in order to avoid accusations of bias regarding the events that have occurred in Patagonia since 1920, I want to cite the governor of Santa Cruz himself. At the request of the National Labor Department, he produced a report that includes a great deal of information on the living conditions of the region's workers.

Here de Tomaso reads the words of Captain Yza, the Radical governor appointed by Yrigoyen, before continuing:

It can be seen from this report that the toiling masses of Santa Cruz suffer from an almost total isolation from the world and have no protection from the harsh climate. They lead some of the hardest lives imaginable and have been fighting since 1920 to secure basic concessions from the ranchers, many of whom are capitalists from Buenos Aires or London. Some of these concessions deserve the special attention of this chamber as they coincide with legislation that we socialists have consistently demanded and which has been approved by the Chamber of Deputies but died in the Senate: a requirement that all employers pay their workers in domestic currency.

De Tomaso's speech is quite lengthy. He plays with time in order to take advantage of the nervousness of the Radical bench. The Socialist legislator recounts the events of the first strike in Santa Cruz, adding:

On most of the territory's ranches, it was the custom not to pay workers in domestic currency. I can testify to this myself, as I have spoken with several peons in recent days. Workers were paid in scrip, in vouchers that could not be used in the shops and grocery stores of Santa Cruz without a great loss in value. Others, excusing themselves with their difficult financial situation, paid in checks that shops refused to accept because of their lack of deposits. And so many peons haven't been able to access the pay they are owed in any form since 1920. The November 1920 strike ended without bloody repression. The 10th Cavalry was ordered to Santa Cruz and the alleged rebels surrendered— they were, after all, nothing more than peons who had escaped into the hills to avoid the attacks of the local police and to have the freedom to hold their assemblies in peace. The strike ended with some mild concessions.

Mentioning the list of demands, de Tomaso states:

Honorable deputies, you can read this document for yourselves in the official bulletins of the Labor Department, where it is accompanied by the ruling of the governor, who takes the side of the workers and provides a report on the living and working conditions in that desolate region. In his report, the governor emphasizes the grave situation faced by peons who are paid in scrip or Chilean currency and argues that it is importance for men who earn their living solely through wage labor to be paid in a timely manner in domestic currency; he refers to the sheds that most ranches make available for lodging peons as pigsties; he speaks of the demanding nature of their work; he mentions the strain on the finances of these men, most of them single, caused by rising prices, which have not been compensated for with a parallel increase in their wages—even though, as the whole world knows, the region's ranchers have been making good money from the sale of wool and meat for quite a long time. The governor's arbitration was not sincerely accepted by most of the ranchers and harassment of the workers resumed soon after the settlement was signed. The local police—of whom I will have more to say later, always using the words of others so that no one can accuse me of bias—placed itself at the service of the ranchers and harassed the peons, particularly those affiliated with the Workers' Society. Deportations and violence began again. Fewer and fewer peons were able to exchange their vouchers for cash. And so they drafted a new list of demands and undertook to organize the workers throughout the territory. They resolved not to go back to work until they had secured the freedom of their imprisoned fellow workers, of whom they had received no word, as well as a ten to twenty percent increase in their daily wages and the right to exchange their vouchers (which represented the equivalent of nine to ten months' pay) for cash, plus assurances that all future pay would be in the form of cash or in checks that could be exchanged for their full value in cash at any bank.[4]

More moderate and less revolutionary demands could scarcely be formulated.

Given the region's characteristics and the impossibility of holding meetings in the coastal towns that could be attended by all the workers, who were dispersed in small groups with many leagues between them, the peons decided to travel from ranch to ranch and invite people to join the strike, as they had in November 1920. And so they organized large, determined groups of strikers and retreated to their Aventine Hill until those who needed their labor came to negotiate with them.

De Tomaso then comes to Varela's second intervention. With the chamber silent, the Socialist orator lowers his voice once more:

> At first, many believed that the military intervention would end as it did in 1920—that an unbiased outside force supported by the prestige of the federal government would work to their advantage. Instead, they carried out the massacre of which we have all heard. And to cover it up, they concocted a story of combat and tried to give the impression that there had been pitched battles, that there was a perfectly armed and well-supplied military force that attacked the nation's troops. ALL OF THIS IS UNTRUE. Of course, there is one key piece of information that all of the newspapers reported that would have been impossible to disprove: there were no casualties among the troops! It's incredible that a well-armed army of bandits, with fine sharpshooters fighting pitched battles, was unable to kill a single soldier while they died by the dozens.

De Tomaso has an abundance of facts and testimonies at his disposal, which he uses to reject the claims of the "serious" press of Buenos Aires:

> I have spoken with the administrators of one of the region's largest ranches, a man who was held hostage for several days

by a group of peons who planned to use him as a bargaining chip when negotiating the release of the imprisoned workers. He has described the mindset of the strikers and the customs of the peons who live in that harsh climate, isolated in the countryside, with entire months going by without a single visit to town. When the strikers approach commercial establishments, they left the alcoholic beverages intact and didn't allow the administrators or ranch employees who accompanied them to have even so much as a glass of wine. Issues such as the day's tasks, security measures for the prisoners, and order in the camp were resolved in assemblies, which shows that they had some degree of social education. During all their travels they never harassed a single woman, not even verbally. And this despite having encountered the wives of the region's most hated ranchers, some of whom hadn't paid their workers a single centavo for the previous nine months. They respected married men and ensured that they weren't separated from their wives and children. None of the prisoners were verbally or physically mistreated. If they were bandits, then it's clear that there would have been deaths, injuries, persecution, and mistreatment of the ranch administrators and employees that were temporarily taken hostage. And this alone is enough to clearly show that this was not a gang of murderers but a group of poor, desperate peons who believed that their actions—which, by the way, were in line with the harsh customs of the region—were the best way of coming to an understanding with the landowners and securing the minor concessions they demanded.

De Tomaso came prepared. He is unsparing with the Radical bench, which remains in silence, not daring to interrupt him:

Some time ago, I spoke with one of the peons who managed to survive the massacre. I will not repeat everything he told me, as his story has already been published in *La Vanguardia*, our party's official newspaper, but I will mention the most interesting points. This man—a Spaniard who has been working in Patagonia for the past fourteen years—told me that when the peons resolved to go on strike, they headed west from San Julián in small groups to organize the ranches. Their ranks swelled as they advanced. At a certain point, some fifty or sixty leagues from the coast, they gathered to hold their first assembly and drafted their list of demands, which they delivered to the Rural Society using a rancher as a messenger. Before reaching El Posadas—one of the more distant ranches, where there was a large group of peons who hadn't been paid for nine months—they were attacked by a cavalry regiment under the command of Captain Anaya. They negotiated, surrendered, and were forced to watch as one of their leaders—Albino Argüelles, secretary of the San Julián Workers' Society—was beaten with the flats of the soldiers' sabers. Moments later, when they were ordered to disperse, they heard gunshots. Argüelles had been shot—or, to use the language of military dispatches, "fell on the field of battle."

There were at least six other men executed at that place, with one aggravating circumstance: the men were being held in the corral, guarded by the troops, and the region's ranchers came and claimed them, securing their release by simply stating that they were known to be honest. Anyone who went unclaimed was to be punished. It was up to the ranchers if the workers were to live or die!

The tension in the chamber grows. The conservatives relish the sight of the Radical bench, whose deputies look like they have just stepped into a Turkish bath. What a mess they had gotten themselves into, and just weeks before the presidential elections! And de Tomaso doesn't let up:

People have been killed indiscriminately, honorable deputies! For no reason, for no motive and without the benefit of a trial. This should not have happened—the territory was not under martial law. Santa Cruz was not at war and the military authorities did not have the jurisdiction to declare a state of emergency. If they had followed the instructions that they must surely have been given—to restore order—they would have arrested any men who were committing crimes and then turned them over to the local authorities so they could be taken to trial and then sentenced. I will not recount everything that occurred elsewhere in Santa Cruz. So as to not take up too much time, I merely wish to give this chamber an impression of the reasons behind the strike, the true character of the strikers, and the behavior of the troops, which is the responsibility of their officers, chiefly Lieutenant Colonel Varela, who briefly became the region's supreme dictator.

Like my colleagues, I bear no particular animosity towards the army. But we do not want the army, which is an instrument of last resort, to bloodily, violently, and cruelly repress the aspirations of the multitude. We maintain that men who commit crimes should be subject to the civil authorities. This is why we have a penal code, from which no one should be exempt. But it's unacceptable that military force be blindly and harshly used to crush movements whose goals are so just and, I would say, so sacred as improving the living and working conditions of the poor.

If, due to outside pressure, excesses have been committed in the Santa Cruz labor movement, it is nevertheless not the job of the army to pass judgment, but the territory's civil authorities.

But it's not just the violence of the armed forces that inflames our sentiments, but also the excesses of the local police, who have a sinister reputation. When I use that adjective, I'm not being melodramatic. The crew of the *Almirante Brown* witnessed police brutality in Santa Cruz: one worker was beaten to death with clubs and sabers and the commissioner then had the nerve to ask Dr. Goya, the *Almirante Brown*'s doctor, to sign the death certificate. Dr. Goya said that he could not report anything but what was obvious from the most elementary inspection of the body: that the deceased had been beaten to death.[5] The administrator of one of the largest nearby ranches, who was taken prisoner at Paso Ibáñez, told me that, upon arriving in Santa

Cruz, he witnessed the edifying spectacle of a group of imprisoned workers cleaning the streets. The police had forced them to work all day, running from one end of town to the other. And when they stopped to catch their breath, on the point of collapsing from exhaustion, the commissioner—who was personally witnessing this small celebration—beat them himself to get them moving again.[6]

This, broadly speaking, is what happened in Santa Cruz. Here are the causes of the movement that was drowned in blood by the military authorities. As is my duty as a deputy, I accuse Lieutenant Colonel Varela of having abused his office and brought upon our armed forces a shame they do not deserve by having ordered—either directly or through his subordinates—the mass execution of men randomly captured by the army, many of them Argentines, on the suspicion of being strike leaders. I accuse him of having not confined himself to his sole duty: restoring order—if those were indeed the orders he was given—by arresting those men he encountered in the countryside and turning them over to the local authorities to undergo normal judicial proceedings. I accuse the local police—over whom the governor has no authority, as he neither appoints nor commands them—of having employed brutal tactics that contributed to the formation of a combative mindset in the laboring masses.

But de Tomaso doesn't want to stop at the virtually unknown Lieutenant Colonel Varela. He wants to get at Yrigoyen. And so he concludes his speech by saying:

Was Lieutenant Colonel Varela following orders when he committed these acts I deem to be so savage? It would be very interesting to know. It's hard for me to believe that there's an Argentine minister—much less a president—that would send in troops with the cruel and ungodly orders to have striking workers shot where they stood.

De Tomaso was straightforward in accusing Varela of having "brought upon our armed forces a shame they do not deserve." This is the worst offense that an officer can commit. And we know that military men do not allow these sorts of accusations to be made without protest. But Varela will remain silent.

What de Tomaso wants is for a committee to be formed to investigate the facts on the ground. But the debate will be tabled for a week. The Radicals feel disoriented and wounded and want to speak with Hipólito before making any decisions. There's only one possible solution: Somebody has to take responsibility for the dead to save the government from being discredited, somebody has to take responsibility for the dead. The Radicals can't have the entire working population turn against them. They need a scapegoat.

Varela is only too well aware of this and once again asks to meet with Yrigoyen. But his request falls on deaf ears. One day before the debate on Patagonia resumes in the Chamber of Deputies, he barges into the Casa Rosada in full dress uniform, greeting everyone like he lived there. He enters the president's office, ignoring the timid, desperate gestures of the secretaries swarming the hallways.

Yrigoyen greets him calmly: "You are precisely the man I wanted to see, Lieutenant Colonel…" Varela tells him of the attacks on him and his men and asks the president to issue a statement in support of the troops under his command, promoting all of his subordinates for their bravery. He doesn't ask for anything for himself. He only requests that Yrigoyen "meet with the Socialist deputies before the debate resumes." Yrigoyen listens to him in silence. After explaining Varela's request to the war minister, he sees him off with the words, "Don't worry, Lieutenant Colonel…"[7]

But no statement is issued. The performance of the 10th Cavalry Regiment is not commended and no one is promoted. There's not even so much as a press release from the War Ministry.

On February 8th, the Socialist Héctor González Iramáin calls for an immediate vote on the creation of a committee to investigate Varela's actions and the massacre in Patagonia. But the Radicals have finally decided on a strategy. Valentín Vergara, a Radical deputy representing Buenos Aires, asks to speak. His voice heavy, he demands, with agitated expressions, that the motion be rejected "not only out of respect for the army and its officers, but also in deference to the Republic's standards of culture and civilization."[8]

The Radical bench agrees, with a "very well" that scarcely rises above a whisper. The conservatives smile at the new fight between the Radicals and the Socialists.

Vergara does not stop there. Seething with indignation and repeatedly thumping the podium, he shouts at de Tomaso, "There was a genuine uprising in the south that threatened the lives and property of the region's peaceful inhabitants."

And to bring his point home, he quotes from nothing less than the report submitted to the Chamber of Deputies by Dr. Manuel Carlés, president of the Argentine Patriotic League:

Here I shall refer to the words of president of the Patriotic League, Dr. Manuel Carlés, who mentions social revolution, revolutionary strikes, rebels who have conspired against the peace and well-being of the region's inhabitants, committing excesses and acts of vandalism that bring shame upon our culture. But that's not all. Just today, I read a report from a special correspondent for *La Prensa* that confirms Dr. Carlés's account on all relevant points. I therefore believe it's clear that the army's mission was to restore order—a social mission, if you will, against the anarchist elements that raised the red flag in that territory.

As we can see, the Radical legislator defends his government by citing the testimony of staunchly anti-Radical sources: Dr. Carlés and *La Prensa*.

At this point, the debate takes a dramatic turn. De Tomaso interrupts Vergara to read Varela's proclamation instituting the death penalty, explaining, "This clearly shows that he took on powers not granted to him by the Constitution or existing laws."

And so there would be no room for doubt, he adds, "The truth is that there were executions, the truth is that the commanding officer on this mission acted with a severity and a cruelty that he had not been authorized to employ."

Vergara pretends not to hear and continues his arguments, unmoved. "The rebels who overran Santa Cruz and laid waste to the territory were bandits, most of them Chileans." And then he continues to read the Carlés report:

> In Santa Cruz, anarchists have risen up against the nation and proclaimed a general strike. And regardless of whether their ideas are right or wrong, combat operations were undertaken; foremen, administrators, and workers were taken prisoner; shops and ranches were attacked; machinery was destroyed; farmland was ruined; automobiles and weapons were stolen; women were raped; employers were shot; telegraph lines were cut; railway tracks were torn up; and the nation's armed forced were fired upon.

This is the extent of Vergara's arguments. Notice how he never tries to prove that executions did not take place. Instead, he tacitly justifies them by painting a Dantesque portrait of the crimes of the workers. He concludes by asking the chamber to vote against the creation of an investigatory committee. "I believe that we should vote against any investigatory committee," he says. "This chamber's job is to request official reports on these events."

In other words, the Radical bench rejects the creation of an investigatory committee and attempts to divert the issue into a mere request for more information from the president's office. But the Socialist González Iramáin, who is neither slow nor stupid, seizes the moment. Feigning innocence, he addresses the president of the Chamber of Deputies, a Radical named Goyeneche, and asks him:

> Mr. President, lest I speak out of turn, I would like to know if the chamber has received the reply of the executive branch to our

request for information regarding labor conflicts that was filed upon the motion of Deputy Mario Bravo. This request for information was originally made with the approval of a large number of Radical deputies and has since been repeated many times.

González Iramáin is rubbing salt in an open wound. He's referring to the request for information on the Tragic Week. The president of the chamber, understanding the impact of his words, clears his throat and, after nervously speaking with his secretary in private, responds, "Are you referring to the information request made by Deputy Bravo?"

"Yes, the one made in January 1919," González Iramáin insists with the same tone of apparent naivety. "It's been three years now and the request has been repeated several times since then."

The Radical bench has been painted into a corner. These Socialists are wolves when it comes to parliamentary debate: they've torpedoed the government's strategy with one innocent question. Whispers are overheard. The faces of the conservatives continue to glow. For them, this is a highly entertaining spectacle.

Goyeneche pulls himself together and answers nonchalantly, "No reply has been made to the information request you have mentioned."

This is the moment, then. Half-standing in his seat, González Iramáin brusquely addresses Vergara: If three years have gone by without a reply to a request for information on the massacre of workers in January 1919, how can the official response to a much more serious massacre be reduced to simply asking Yrigoyen to issue a statement?

An irrefutable argument. But the Radicals are experts at these political skirmishes and they are capable of getting back in the saddle in the middle of a race. Now their tactic will be to pretend to go over to the side of the Socialists. The Radical Leónidas Anastasi speaks. This is the moment in which Commander Varela, a fellow party member, will be offered up for sacrifice:

Honorable deputies, a proclamation issued by Commander Varela has been mentioned, a proclamation that I do not want to believe is authentic. I cannot imagine for a single moment that an Argentine officer could sign a proclamation stating that whoever fires on the army will be shot on the spot. No similar proclamation was ever issued by the Germans during the occupation of Belgium. To find a similar case, I confess that I took the time to read *Climet*, a French propaganda newspaper that printed many accusations during the war that later turned out to be exaggerated. And even here there's no reports of any Germans anywhere making similar threats. Needless to say, this would be highly illegal under Argentine law. It seems to be a truly gory irony that, just when we prohibit the death penalty in our civil code, we wake up to see threats of this nature. Another paragraph of Varela's proclamation states, "If it proves necessary for the army to resort to the use of force against the strikers, be warned that there will be neither negotiations nor suspensions of hostilities." This means war without quarter, and war without quarter ended with what we could call the Argentine Age of Barbarism. During the civilized period of our history, I believe that there is no evidence that war without quarter has even been threatened, even on the battlefield. I will even go so far as to say that we may have been dealing with bandits—but in no part of the world are bandits punished with death unless they have also committed murder, and it can be easily proven that no murders were committed in Santa Cruz. In the modern age, there is no penal code anywhere in the world that punishes the simple crime of banditry with the death penalty and, as I have said, no other crimes were committed that deserved such sentencing.

These charges are devastating to Varela. Leónides Ansastasi continues by criticizing the arguments of his colleague, Vergara:

The report cited was submitted to us by Manuel Carlés, president of the Patriotic League, who tours the country from one end to the other calling for the institutionalization of free labor, which was rightly called "free cannibalism" by none other than Cardinal Manning. The Carlés report simply shows that the Patriotic League thinks that any worker who insists on being paid and who demands better living conditions is an anarchist. The report actually demolishes the myth of Patagonian bandits because he himself admits that it was a strike, a strike that can be compared to those we have seen time and again in Buenos Aires, Entre Ríos, Córdoba, Mendoza, Tucumán, Chaco, and Misiones. "Rebels who have taken up arms against the nation do not die as soldiers," says Dr. Carlés. And here I must add one piece of news that I hope will not be confirmed: it is said that a large number of the two thousand workers who died in Santa Cruz were labor militants. What strange bullets could pick out, in the midst of a battle, the organizers of a movement standing up to the bosses?

Anastasi's arguments are conclusive—even better, perhaps, than those of his opponent, de Tomaso. But therein lies the danger. Anastasi plays to the Socialists but, in the end, votes against the creation of an investigatory committee. He says that people need to keep their heads cool and trust the decisions of the military courts and the war minister. In other words: we'll admit they're right, but fall back in line.

De Tomaso immediately catches on to the tactics of the Radicals and believes he can discern the hand of Hipólito Yrigoyen, who was not in the chamber but seemed to be manipulating the situation from behind the scenes, just as he manipulated Argentina's social movements from behind the Persian blinds of his house on Calle Brasil. The Socialist deputy asks to speak and denounces the bad faith of the Radicals:

> On the one hand, Deputy Vergara votes against the investigatory committee because he believes everything that Dr. Carlés says in his report as if it were the word of God. According to him, there

was an anarchist uprising in Santa Cruz and the red flag was raised. And on the other hand, Deputy Anastasi makes the same arguments as the Socialist deputies. Like us, he is shocked by the enormity of the repression, the truly cruel abuses of the military authorities, and he attacks the Patriotic League, arguing that most of the statements in the Carlés report are incorrect—but he still votes against the investigation. Deputy Vergara will appear before those who support the Patriotic League to receive their applause, while Anastasi will go before the victims, the workers who have raised their voices to condemn the massacre. But both of them will have contributed to preserving the official silence surrounding these crimes.

De Tomaso knows that the game is up. His motion to investigate the massacre will be swallowed up by the nays of the majority bench. But he still appeals to the conscience of his fellow deputies:

Let me repeat once again that we must examine this matter as legislators, without any prejudice.

But there's no response. The silence from the Radical bench is absolute. The only thing he has left is outrage, and so he continues with his devastating arguments:

The leaders of these labor organizations, labeled "ringleaders" by the military, have all disappeared. How could this have happened? They must have been executed. This is the best proof that executions occurred. The bullets of the army were specially destined for these men. How could this happen? These men were carefully selected from among the prisoners and then shot to make examples out of them, providing a cruel and barbarous spectacle for the conscripts. Even *La Nación*, which helped spread the myth of banditry, has printed the names of the dead, the purpose of which can readily be understood. As they could not deny the disappearance of a large number of men, and as they could not keep their readers from realizing that a large number of them were labor leaders and energetic organizers, they reported that they were killed while trying to escape.

And now de Tomaso turns to sarcasm to get a response from the Radicals:

> There's no need to take half measures, honorable deputies. Double dealing will not work here. The president, the friends of the workers, did not send troops south, he did not give the order that led to the executions. But these events have nevertheless occurred. So who gave Colonel Varela his orders?

The question resounds in the chamber like the crack of a whip. De Tomaso allows half a minute to go by, a minute, more. The Radical bench is silent. Some deputies read, others look at the ceiling and there are even a few who hang their heads.

"So who gave Colonel Varela his orders?" de Tomaso asks again. He then lowers his voice and adds, "Or did Lieutenant Colonel Varela act on his own initiative?"

They've all abandoned Varela. Not one voice speaks out to defend him. No one says, "No sir, Commander Varela followed the orders he was given by the president."

Sensing the momentary weakness of the Radical bench, de Tomaso continues with his verbal punishment. "The deputies from the ruling party are split," he says. "Some condemn banditry and others criticize the barbarous military repression. But none of them want an investigation. Where does that leave us?"

"It's how we see things." Leónidas Anastasi has spoken up.

And here de Tomaso utters some visionary words, foreseeing a situation that will be repeated over the following six decades precisely due to the indecisiveness of Argentina's politicians, their double dealing, their eternal calls for the military to save them and their classic gambit of avoiding responsibility. It's only 1921 and de Tomaso is already sounding the alarm about military dictatorship.

If an investigatory committee established the truth of what happened, we would gain much from it. It would mean that the Chamber of Deputies took the opportune measures needed to ensure that this country never again faces a military dictatorship! With these sorts of things, everything depends on the first step.

I have said and I will repeat—because we don't want this to occur again—that we cannot accept that the army be actively used to resolve social conflicts, or that cruel and barbarous repression be used to drown social movements in blood, because even if they include some excesses, they are nevertheless determined by deep social causes.

These words were spoken by de Tomaso more than eight years before Argentina's first military dictatorship of the twentieth century, that of Uriburu.

Without slowing down, the legislator continues to demand an investigation—an investigation and nothing else.

The Chamber of Deputies would be well advised to vote for an investigatory committee for a number of important reasons. It will be derelict in its duty if it does not. It would be extraordinary for such a serious upheaval to have taken place over the course of a month and a half in a territory that is directly under our custody, as it lacks self-government, and that we are the only institution in the entire country with nothing to say on the matter, even though some of these events have overturned the entire constitutional and legal framework of the republic and have placed an entire region of our nation outside any standard of civilization.

With emotion in his voice, de Tomaso concludes his speech:

Let's not fool ourselves. What has happened is that, in this case, the victims are poor devils, as the rich would say. They are peons, carters, shepherds. Deep down, many people realize that what has happened is a serious violation of our laws and our Constitution, but they're pleased that such a harsh lesson has been given. It means that there will be no more lists of demands, no more struggles for pay raises or such revolutionary and scandalous demands as prohibiting eight men from being housed in a room measuring three meters by three meters. We are asked for hard evidence, but what evidence can we provide? The bodies? I assure the chamber that many of them have been left on the ground, exposed to the elements. An investigatory committee could still arrive in time to see the remains of some of the bodies that were burned by the gasoline poured by our soldiers.

He adds that the committee could also "hear the testimony of hundreds of peons and other residents of Santa Cruz, San Julián, and Puerto Deseado." And once again he stresses something that Argentine society—especially the politicians—would increasingly forget:

The Chamber of Deputies should get to the bottom of this matter: it has the right to do so. And by doing so, the chamber will have done a service to our country's republican framework, as it is in our interest to separate the military sphere from the civilian sphere. The army is an institution of exception that can never be used in peacetime or in day-to-day civilian life. It cannot play so inglorious a role as it did in Santa Cruz. On whose orders I cannot say. Perhaps Colonel Varela acted on his own, or perhaps he was following orders from the war minister or the president. If you don't vote for this investigatory committee on the pretext of waiting for the war minister to issue a report, you will allow this enormous brutality to not only go unpunished, but also to go without being morally repudiated!

This touching conclusion isn't enough to change the final vote. But before the vote begins, the Radicals, stung by the direct accusations of the Socialists, take the floor. The first to speak is Deputy López Anaut, who uses a truly amusing pretext for voting against the formation of an investigatory committee. He says that the Socialist deputy spoke immoderately in arguing for his proposal: if de Tomaso "had spoken in moderation, then the Chamber might vote for his motion and we would be able to satisfy our common desire to learn the truth of the situation in Santa Cruz."

De Tomaso: "I couldn't have painted a rosy picture…"

López Anaut: "You could have spared us the details…"

Then López Anaut continues:

I would perhaps vote for the proposal because I believe that this committee could provide us with important facts—not so much in terms of the events that took place, but in terms of measures that could be taken to prevent their repetition in our southern territories. I therefore lean towards voting for a request for information.

When the Socialist González Iramáin insists that Yrigoyen hasn't even responded to a three-year-old request for information on the Tragic Week, the Radical López Anaut cavalierly replies, "He must have thought that it was unnecessary."

Finally, Radical Deputy Albarracín—a former military officer—criticizes de Tomaso for doubting the army:

I can firmly state that the army, by virtue of its traditions and its training, is an academy of civic virtues and culture that will never be properly appreciated. I am also within my rights to think it impossible that Colonel Varela, an honorable man and an official whose outstanding qualities and brilliant service record bring honor to the army, could have committed these reprehensible acts.

And now it's time for the vote. The Radicals reject the investigation. And they are in the majority.

The matter is referred to committee. In plain language, this means that it has been put to sleep. Those that are dead remain dead. No one will bring them back to life.

The one person left for whom the matter was not resolved was Commander Varela...

He neither receives a promotion nor was a statement issued in his favor. But while Hipólito Yrigoyen may squeeze his allies, he doesn't strangle them. His complicated tactics, his interminable and mysterious intrigues, have found a solution. In March, Varela is named director of the Campo de Mayo's Cavalry School. It's not much comfort, but at least he wasn't forced to retire.

And Yrigoyen would deal with the labor problems caused by the repression in Patagonia the same way he dealt with the military: Compromise, Yrigoyen's famous solution to all problems. I give in a little here, you give in a little there and then we'll meet in the middle.

It doesn't start out easy. With the FORA V, the anarchists, there's nothing to be said. They were filling the country with flyers on Santa Cruz, meetings, "lightning" protests, threats. With the executions in Patagonia poisoning everything, the social atmosphere resembled the days leading up to the Tragic Week. The syndicalist FORA couldn't let themselves be outdone in the eyes of the workers and so they also beat their drum—not as enthusiastically as the friends of Bakunin, but enough to save them from being criticized for passivity in the face of such a serious matter. But the massacre had also come home in a way, as it affected the Maritime Workers' Federation—the heart and soul of the syndicalist FORA—which had a paternal relationship with Patagonia's unions. The Maritime Workers' Federation itself, despite the friendship of its secretary-general with Hipólito Yrigoyen, fiercely criticized Commander Varela's actions in its official newspaper *La Voz del Marino*. Nobody wanted to take responsibility, but nevertheless somebody would have to pay the bill. They didn't want to have to confront Yrigoyen. So who could they blame, then? Varela, naturally. All the mud would be slung in his direction. This was the difference: while the anarchists aimed higher and directed their broadsides at the president, the pure syndicalists were content with the executioner, the man who commanded the firing squad, and ignored the intellectual author of the repression.

Besides, the men of the syndicalist FORA had to cover up their own complicity in the massacre, which made them a target for attacks from the anarchist FORA. If the strike ended the way it did, it was because the country's largest labor federation was looking the other way. They had left Antonio Soto alone, completely alone.

As much needed to be salvaged from this disaster as was possible. And it needed to be done as quickly and silently as possible. This was in the interests of the government, the syndicalist FORA, the army and the Rural Society. And Varela would receive each blow, like a circus clown.

One unresolved problem that kept the Patagonian repression a current issue was the fate of the prisoners. They had all been sent to Río Gallegos and were packed so tightly in the town's overcrowded jail that there wasn't even room for a pin to fit between them. And there wasn't enough food for all the peons who had been hunted down by Varela, Viñas Ibarra, Anaya, and Campos throughout the length and breadth of the territory. One hundred and eighty men were taken from the countryside and forced into a reeking, swarming mass. Despite their meekness, they were not spared punishment. Though some locals took pity on them and gave them a bowl of soup or a piece of bread when they were taken out to work in the streets, this situation couldn't last long. Besides, the union leaders who were deported to Buenos Aires before the conflict broke out had formed a committee to free the prisoners and lobbied the syndicalist FORA to intercede with Yrigoyen and ask for their release. The next congress of the syndicalist FORA was coming up and its leaders didn't want any problems.

The government understood that it has to do something to end the protests. The issue of Patagonia was a real son of a bitch and something had to be done to soften the fallout. Yrigoyen will arrange everything with consummate skill. Everyone agrees with his proposed solution: the syndicalist FORA, the Rural Society, the courts, the local government. There were only two obstacles left in his path, and they were to be left to the mercy of God: the dead—there was nothing more to be done for them—and Lieutenant Colonel Varela.

As always, the only dissidents would be the anarchists and the FORA V, along with all their flyers, newspapers, pamphlets, conferences, and plans to take justice into their own hands through direct action.

The proposed solution would rely on the territory's judge, Dr. Ismael P. Viñas. He will be assisted by his friend, Dr. José María Borrero, and by the silence of the Rural Society and all other interested parties. The only possible opposition in Patagonia would have come from labor organizations, which by now are nothing more than a memory.

When the repression began, there were three categories of strikers: the bad workers, who "died in combat"; the suspicious workers, who were imprisoned in Río Gallegos after being punished and humiliated; and the good workers, who were rescued by their employers.

The plan consisted of burying the past as quickly as possible, so the festering issue of the imprisoned peons needed to be addressed.

The prisoners had been handed over to the Río Gallegos police by the army—only rarely by the navy—along with a list of charges against them. The police then interrogated the prisoners. The interrogations were handled by Commissioner Fernando Wells, who was acting on the direct orders of Commander Varela or whichever officer was acting in his stead at a particular time. Reading these thick volumes of charges for sedition are not only proof that these poor prisoners lacked any legal protections, but to read them is to bear witness to a gory mockery of human dignity. All the confessions are the same. For example, those arrested in Punta Arenas repeat the official story established by Captain

Viñas Ibarra: the workers launched a surprise attack on the soldiers, whom they greatly outnumbered. The confessions of the workers arrested at La Anita are even worse: they state that they were "liberated by the army."

Commissioner Guadarrama, who was present during the interrogations, has told us that those peons who refused to cooperate were taken aside and had their memory "refreshed" with blows to the ribs. So true is this that in the file on the peon Pantaleón Sandoval González, it states that he "asked for permission to refresh his memory and confess." Permission was given, confessions were taken from the other prisoners in the meantime, and then Pantaleón returned and confessed perfectly, as required.

He who informed on his comrades was granted immediate freedom. Such was the case of Emilio Calisto, an eighteen-year-old peon who accused Zacarías González and Jacinto Murquin of being strike leaders and Zoilo Guerrero and Fortunado Pena of being key organizers. After signing accusations against these men, the boy was immediately released by Commissioner Fernando Wells.

But they weren't all that easy. Commissioner Guadarrama remembers the case of one Spaniard who was as hard as a rock. Though he was given more than his share of punishment, he refused to see the value of compliance. But then he was clearly one of those eternal contrarians. There was nothing to be done and they had to take down a statement—and while it is likely less complete than the prisoner may have wished, there's still enough for it to stand out from the rest. And so in the Sedition II file, a thirty-five-year-old Spaniard named Jesús Casas, who had been living in Argentina for the previous eleven years, declared that:

>...he came down from Buenos Aires in October and went around looking for work on a ranch but ended up joining a group of eighty striking workers. That this group was attacked by the army, who fired on them for a full fifteen minutes. That none of the strikers fired on the troops, and they hadn't attacked ranchers or taken hostages. That none of the group's

members were forced to join against their will and that they were all equals.

This statement completely contradicts the rest. But the police did well to include the words of this fanatical Spaniard—just as the exception proves the rule, so would the confessions of the other peons seem that much more truthful.

One detail here or there didn't matter—Judge Viñas wasn't going to analyze this mountain of paperwork anyway. Having just arrived from Buenos Aires, he would adopt a very expeditious method: release everyone! Even though ninety-nine percent of the strikers confessed to being bandits. There has never been a more inconsistent judicial process. The problem was political and it demanded a political solution.

On April 8th, 1922, Judge Viñas begins to act. Everything has already been arranged. Borrero will be the public defender. His defense strategy will be quite thin. While he does make a few mentions of injustice, at no point does he touch the issue of the mass executions. Instead, he makes a plea for clemency:

It would be a long and sorry task to describe the recent events that led to the imprisonment of my defendants, and even more so if we analyzed the outbreak of concentrated hatreds, the satisfaction of base passions, and the use of improper means that led these hundred-some honest and hardworking men to be deprived of their freedom for all these long, cruel months. They have repeatedly been subjected to all sorts of humiliation and mistreatment. I therefore feel that they ought to be considered as scapegoats and victims of the most small-minded vengeance, which is contrary to the most elementary rules of morality.

After outlining the events of the first strike, Borrero states:

The territory's acting governor, Captain Yza, ended the strike through an arbitrated settlement that both the bosses and the workers had agreed in advance to accept.

He says that the strikers only organized in response to the attitude of the ranchers, who had expelled them from their ranches. Faced with what he called "the material impossibility of coming to town," he argues that they were forced to band together due to their lack of resources.

His plea for the release of the prisoners is based on the idea that no crime had been committed—the prisoners were accused of having organized an armed uprising, yet "it's extremely strange that, though this is the main charge, these arms have not appeared anywhere, nor have they been placed at the disposal of the court."

On April 14th, Judge Viñas begins taking statements. He generally doesn't encounter any problems. The prisoners are exhausted and don't want any more trouble. But some of them are obstinate and retract their confessions or simply lift up their heads, demanding justice. The Spaniard Jesús Casas, for example, insists on reporting a theft. And he dares to accuse the Argentine Army. He reports that a guanaco-skin cape, a new poncho, a pocket watch, and a full set of horse tack were stolen from him by the soldiers while he was a prisoner at Punta Alta.

The gaucho Pantaleón Sandoval—the same one who asked for the chance to "refresh his memory" in the police report—rectifies his earlier confession, saying that it's not true that the workers fired on the troops at Corrales Viejos, "as it was the troops who attacked the workers, opening fire on anyone they encountered."

Juan Álvarez Delgado—a twenty-year-old Chilean—also wants to say something to the judge. He describes the murder of his friend Manuel Mansilla during the Corrales Viejos incident in Punta Alta. He says that Mansilla was "interrogated by Subcommissioner Douglas Price, who wanted to know the name of the group's ringleader." Mansilla answered that he didn't know, and so Commissioner Douglas Price "took out a revolver and shot him dead, for no other reason."Álvarez adds that "Pantaleón Sandoval and Jesús Casas can confirm this, as they were both there." His declaration goes on to say:

> …that he also wants to state that, upon being arrested by the soldiers, they were ordered to empty their pockets. He states that he was carrying 265 pesos, horse ownership certificates, and various other documents, none of which were returned to him.

As we can see, these are direct, concrete accusations signed by the victims. Not only is there the murder of Mansilla, where the murderer is mentioned by both his first and last name, but there's also the thefts committed by the 10th Cavalry. It would not have been difficult to investigate the alleged horse theft, as the thieves could have sold the animals if they possessed the ownership certificates. But Judge Viñas doesn't follow up on these allegations.

As the strikers are called before the judge, they increasingly find the courage to assert their rights:

Eustaquio Gómez, Argentine, forty-two years old, single, peon: "Upon being turned over to the authorities, the police stole his set of horse tack and a check for 13 pesos that was signed by Juan Bustamente, the administrator of the Stipicich ranch."

Santiago Gallardo, Chilean, twenty-four years old, single, peon: "At La Anita, the army stole four horse ownership certificates and a guanaco-skin cape."

Manuel Balderas, Chilean, eighteen years old, single, peon: "Upon being arrested at La Anita, they stole his horse tack and his pajamas."

Serafín González, Spaniard, thirty years old: "Officer Carrillo forced him to sign a confession under threat of violence."

Ramón Luna: "The army stole three horse ownership certificates and one saddle from him."

Taking into account the arguments of the defense attorney and the prosecutor's statement that there's no longer a reason to hold the prisoners, Judge Viñas frees all those he has seen up to this point, along with a few others—a total of twenty-one strikers. The prison is informed of his decision and the gauchos find themselves back on the street. Borrero advises them not to press their claims but instead to take advantage of the opportunity to leave the city as soon as possible, as "now is not the time to rock the boat."[9]

Poor devils! They were finally free but had no horses, no papers, not so much as a single peso in their pockets and nobody to turn to. Not even the Workers' Society was left to give them a hand. Governor Yza sees that this could soon create a problem and asks the federal government to cover their travel expenses so the peons can immediately return home.

After releasing the first prisoners, Viñas continues taking statements day and night. The questions he asks are routine and he never brings up the executions, even though it's the issue that has most stirred up the left-wing press in Buenos Aires. And it will be difficult for him. Although there's nothing that the prisoners want more than to be released, there are still a few malcontents who insist on denouncing the crimes that were committed against them. Let's look at a few more:

José Torres, a twenty-two-year-old Chilean horse-tamer: "The police stole twelve of his horses upon his arrest."

Florencio Avejer: "The soldiers of the 2nd Cavalry robbed him of a cape, a tarpaulin, two blankets, and a set of horse tack, which were taken to the police station."

Eduardo Avendaño: "The troops stole his saddle."

José Loza: "A soldier from the 10th Cavalry robbed him of 375 pesos, a cape, and a horse ownership certificate."

Basilio Listare: "The troops robbed him of a set of horse tack and a suitcase full of clothes."

José Ojeda Aquintín: "Officer Carreño stole all of his documents, including seven horse ownership certificates. When he asked them to be returned, the officer beat him."

Clodomiro Barrientos: "Upon being arrested by the 10th Cavalry, he was relieved of a guanaco-hide quillango, two horse ownership certificates, the clothes he was wearing, and some 100 pesos in cash."

José Miguel Aguilar: "The soldiers robbed him of a leather belt, five horse ownership certificates for individual horses, another for five horses, other personal documents, and 20 pesos."

Herminio Prieto: "The naval troops stole a set of horse tack and a quillango."

Ramón Rodríguez Vila: "The soldiers robbed him of his clothes and a set of horse tack."

Olegario Vázquez, Chilean: "Officer Carrillo asked him for his last name and ID number and he answered 'none.' The officer then beat him and the soldiers destroyed his personal documents."

Francisco Saldivia: "The soldiers destroyed his ownership certificates and stole three of his horses and his watch."

José Iglesias: "Captain Anaya's troops stole his quillango and a set of horse tack."

But one very serious accusation is made against Sub-lieutenant Frugoni Miranda—the man who allegedly distinguished himself by his flair for killing chilotes with a single bullet to the head. When the shepherd Juan Castrejas is called to make a statement, he insists that the army let him leave La Anita and that he went to work at Laguna Benito, where a group of soldiers from the 10th Cavalry Regiment arrived several days later. On the orders of a sub-lieutenant, they arrested him and took him to Laguna de Oro, where they tried to shake him down for 500 pesos. He told them that he had the money but would have to go to Río Gallegos to get it and the sub-lieutenant agreed to take him to town. He was finally given his liberty in exchange for 350 pesos in cash, which he handed over to the sub-lieutenant at the regiment's makeshift barracks. He says that there are no witnesses who can back up his story but shows the judge his safe conduct pass, adding that it wasn't enough to save him from arrest by the local police.

A safe conduct pass signed by Sub-lieutenant Juan C. Frugoni Miranda in Laguna del Oro on January 5th, 1922 can be found in Section VII, Page 2,032 of File 257/1922, the police file on sedition. The pass states that the bearer has permission to cross the border.

But Castrejas finds no outlet for his rage and impotence, as Viñas does little more than take note of what he says and file it away in the archives, even though there's enough evidence to begin criminal proceedings against the sub-lieutenant.

But at least now the judge will set them free and this includes—what a surprise!—four leading organizers for the Workers' Society: Pedro Mongilnitzky, Luis Sambucetti, Domingo Oyola, and Severino Fernández. How could this be, with all the charges against them? And what about Varela's argument that these people were bandits, arsonists, thieves? Now, with one stroke of a pen, the judge admits that they shouldn't have been arrested. What one hand writes is erased by the other.

The prisoners are ordered to be released on April 19th. Viñas continues working into the next day, suffering through another round of complaints:

Zoilo Guerrero, Chilean: "The soldiers of the 10th Cavalry stole his silver Longines watch and five horse-ownership certificates."

Eloy Fernández: "At La Anita, they stole six horse owner-ship certificates and a check made out to the bearer for 137 pesos, issued by the Las Vegas company."

Victorio Eugenin: "The 10th Cavalry robbed him of a check for 60 pesos from the Camusu Aike ranch, along with his identity papers and some blankets."

Federico Heerssen: "They stole three horses from him, along with their ownership certificates."

Juan Aguilar, Chilean: "They forced him to sign a declaration without reading it to him. At La Anita, the soldiers of the 10th Cavalry robbed him of a silver pocket watch, a check for 145 pesos from Rodolfo Suárez's Las Horquetas ranch, two horse ownership certificates, and his identity papers."

Elías López, Argentine: "At the Río Gallegos police station, they robbed him of his utility belt, a wallet with 20 pesos in it, and all his papers."

All of these men and a few more besides, twenty-two in all, are released on April 20th. Among this group are three members of El Toscano's Red Council: the Germans Raith and Heerssen and the Chilean Díaz.

The judge then turns to the prisoners arrested in northern Santa Cruz. Some of them will also report thefts and abuses by the soldiers.

Oscar Pereyra, Uruguayan, forty-four years old: Upon being arrested by Sergeant Dapazo, he was relieved of 400 pesos and his identity papers. He was to be shot but was saved by the women of the Hotel Cañadón León. He witnessed all manner of abuses, which "we will relate in another file that will be opened shortly."

Pedro Gutiérrez, Spaniard: "The naval troops robbed him of two horse ownership certificates, along with all his other papers."

Francisco Ragún, Argentine, twenty-five years old: "Sergeant Espídola of the 2nd Cavalry robbed him of a utility belt containing 823 pesos, two horse ownership certificates, his identity papers, and a set of horse tack."

Agustín Pizzo, Italian: "The 2nd Cavalry stole a set of horse tack and his quillango."

Benigno Prieto, Spaniard: "The troops stole his quillango."

Alberto Collier, Argentine, twenty-four years old: "The troops robbed him of twelve horse ownership certificates, along with all his other papers, and his personal revolver."

Enrique García, Spaniard, twenty-six years old: "He says that he signed a confession because they would punish him if he didn't. In San Julián, the troops robbed him of his blanket and his quillango."

Adolfo Boloqui: "He signed a confession out of fear of being beaten. He says that the strikers at Tres Cerros surrendered without firing a shot and that some of them were taken to San Julián, but no one knows what happened to the rest."

José Ornia, Spaniard, twenty-three years old: He says that his confession was false and was only made after Captain Anaya had him beaten with the rim of an automobile. The soldiers of the 2nd

Cavalry "stole a quillango, a saddlebag, a horse blanket, and all of the good reins and harnesses from his horse tack."

Zacarías González: "They stole the tack off his horse, along with a waterproof poncho, a penknife, and a knife with a silver handle and sheath."

Luciano Herrera, Uruguayan: "Upon being taken prisoner, they stole his belt, all of his papers, a complete set of horse tack and a penknife."

Venancio Montiel, Chilean: "Officer Carrillo stole a check from the Anglo Bank that was made out for 160 pesos and signed by the administrator of the Rincón de los Morros ranch. Carrillo then began to beat him for no reason. He later asked Carrillo to give him the check back but the policeman told him that he had lost it."

Santiago Oyarzún, Chilean: "They forced him to sign a statement drafted by the police. He says that it's not true that the workers fired on the army at San José. A corporal from the 2nd Cavalry also robbed him of a utility belt containing 100 pesos."

José Tellería, Argentine, twenty-four years old, peon: "Upon being arrested, a corporal from the 2nd Cavalry robbed him of his utility belt, which contained 100 pesos and had a silver belt buckle."

Francisco Rosa Silva, Portuguese, thirty-three years old: "They stole his quillango, horse tack, and clothes."

Aniceto Naves, Spaniard, thirty years old, farmer: "The troops robbed him of a silver pocket watch, a guanaco-hide cape, a complete set of horse tack, and his fourteen horses."

José Mancini, Italian, forty-five year old, peon: "A police officer robbed him of 100 pesos in cash."

Alfonso Vargas, tavern keeper, Chilean, thirty-one years old: "The troops robbed him of a complete set of horse tack, a utility belt containing 411 pesos, six horse ownership certificates, a gold wristwatch, a platinum tie clip, an 18-karat gold ring, a quillango, a suitcase filled with clothes, and a telescope."

Another fifteen prisoners are released on April 21st. They will continue trickling out until they're all free.

We've left the case of the shepherd José Liano for the end. He is one of the last to be summoned. It's clear that it's hard on him, but he finally gets the nerve to come forward as a victim. He asks for the return of his six sheepdogs, which the military stole from him at Fuentes de Coyle.

Anyone familiar with Patagonia and its rhythms of life knows that a shepherd is nothing without his sheepdogs—those shaggy, emaciated, restless mongrels that are quicker and more intelligent than their masters. All of a shepherd's capital, his sole tools, are his dogs. It would be impossible to herd sheep without them.

Poor Liano! They took everything from him (three horses and their ownership certificates, a quillango, a suitcase filled with 400 pesos worth of clothing, 233 pesos in cash, a pocket watch, all of the papers he was carrying with him, and a complete set of horse tack). But all that could be replaced. It represented his savings, his capital, everything he had accumulated after so many years— but he was used to these contingencies. Not even a beating was enough to scare him. But the dogs were something else. It was enough to make him want to slit his wrists.[10]

To whom could he protest? Who would ensure that justice was done? Only another José Hernández could do justice to these Patagonian Martín Fierros, who had been defeated, beaten, degraded, robbed and cast aside without a coin in their pockets or a shirt on their backs—even their dogs had been taken away from them. They had been humiliated and insulted. And by uniformed men from Buenos Aires who didn't know the first thing about Patagonia. By uniformed men whose only logic was that of the Mauser, the whip, the barked order. By those whose mouths were filled with the blue and white of the Argentine flag but who attended banquets organized by ranchers who sang foreign songs in their honor.

Judge Viñas orders all of these tremendous accusations against the soldiers, NCOs, and officers of the 10th Cavalry to be filed away. Accusations that, fifty years later, will be covered up by articles honoring the army's heroism and other such predictable nonsense. The truth will be covered up. This is the truth: theft, cruelty, and the murder of farmworkers.

Varela's patience is running out. His nerves are at the breaking point. The government refuses to come out in support of the Patagonia campaign. And the attacks are getting worse. Every day, without fail, the name of Lieutenant Colonel Varela appears in print next to the word "murderer." And not just in the anarchist press, which he can safely ignore, but in newspapers directed at the general public as well.

And Yrigoyen does nothing, as if it were but the sound of rain.

Varela has to react; he can't let the entire world insult him, vilify him, throw mud on his good name. They're cornering him like a bloodthirsty beast. And so he drafts a letter that ends up shedding a great deal of light on the events in which he took part:

Campo de Mayo
March 20, 1922
To the commander of the 2nd Army Division,
The events that occurred in Santa Cruz, in which the regiment under my command was called to intervene, are being exploited for propagandistic purposes by the party of disorder, which is thoroughly anti-militaristic. This propaganda consists of inexplicable and degrading attacks on the military, sometimes personally directed against me and sometimes directed against our military institutions as a whole. The newspapers *La Vanguardia*, *La Montaña*, and *La Crítica* have carried out a premeditated campaign to blacken the names of Argentina's military officers and their goal is to make the public believe that this public institution is a servile instrument used by third parties to destroy their enemies. In light of these facts, I would like to explain the following:
That the president has stated his approval of the actions taken by the troops under my command during the seditious movement in Patagonia. He has blocked any and all investigations into the actions of the troops and, in my presence, promised that

the war minister would study my reports and issue a decree praising the army's actions. The war minister, moreover, is in general agreement with my general course of action and the General Staff has published an elegy to a soldier who fell in the line of duty in *El Soldado Argentino*, along with praise for all the troops who served in the south.

While the aforementioned newspapers have undertaken a perfidious campaign to blacken the army's name in the foulest possible manner, which they have threatened to continue, the authorities have chosen not to intervene and the armed forces, the true strength of our nation, have remained silent and have instead only passively contemplated these insults directed at the army, our institution, and at the Argentine soldier who asks for nothing and gives his all to the fatherland. And while it's true that our sense of discipline demands steadfastness to weather the storms with which military life is filled, and that patriotic abnegation is a virtue that demands sacrifices that we must silently suffer, then let me state, as the commander of the division to which I belong, that I have the unshakable conviction that these newspapers are serving interests that are harmful to the fatherland, threatening both our national sovereignty and the discipline of the army. If the army does not definitively break its silence, then I am prepared to make whatever sacrifice is needed to save the honor and dignity of the officers who served under me, as well as that of the military institution itself, in the same manner in which I saved the nation's honor in Patagonia.

May God keep you.
Héctor B. Varela.
Lieutenant Colonel.

This letter, which can be found in the army's archives (S.C.1, RESTRICTED, Army, 2nd Division, 10th Cavalry), brings up a number of truths that are useful in investigating these events. In the first place, it states that President Yrigoyen approved of Varela's actions during the second strike. This is not something Varela can invent—he can't say things like this in a letter to a superior officer unless he is very sure of what he's saying. He knows that the letter will be forwarded to the war minister at the very least, and perhaps even to the president himself. And so he couldn't lie.

But there's something even more interesting. Commander Varela states that Yrigoyen "*has blocked any and all investigations into the actions of the troops.*" Here things get a little more suspect, because when charges of such seriousness are made, the proper course of action isn't exactly to block an investigation. When one has nothing to hide, the proper course of action is to order an investigation, or at the very least to publicly and categorically state that the army carried out no executions or that they had the full support of the government.

As can be seen, Varela's letter is that of a desperate man. He makes direct accusations against the government (or, as he calls them, "the authorities") by saying that "the authorities have chosen not to intervene" and against the army itself when he says that "the armed forces, the true strength of our nation, have remained silent and have instead only passively contemplated these insults…!"

What is the sacrifice that Varela offers to make? He does not say. It is a throwaway remark. But note that he never provides a rebuttal to the arguments of the journalists, he merely complains of their attacks. He does not say that he is willing to be investigated, that he is not afraid of the truth of his actions in Patagonia.

Lieutenant Colonel Varela's letter is received by General Dellepiane, the "hero" of the Tragic Week. But he simply forwards it to the General Staff without comment:

To the war minister. As requested by the commander of the 10th Cavalry Regiment, I have forwarded this letter to the officials in question. I am of the opinion that the ministry should take a position.

Campo de Mayo
March 21, 1922
General L. Dellepiane. Commander, 2nd Army Division.

The General Staff will take a position—though only on the anti-military campaign, not on Varela's mission in Patagonia. The army staff addresses the war minister in the following terms:

Restricted R-357
To the war minister:

The General Staff has closely monitored the active and continued propaganda carried out by the newspapers mentioned in the previous letter. Their attacks have been directed against military institutions in general and in particular against those regiments that intervened in Patagonia. Understanding the deep malaise that these newspapers are producing among a large section of the population, I hereby request that measures be taken against the aforementioned newspapers this January.

Being unaware of the decisions taken in response to the previous letter, it is my duty to inform you that it is the position of the General Staff to support the request made by the commanding officer of the 10th Cavalry Regiment and the arguments made by the 2nd Army Division, who feels that, while the Constitution may grant the freedom of the press, this freedom has not been granted to allow the press to denigrate the institutions created by the people to protect their own interests nor to slander the men who guide them.

The tenacious and socially destructive campaign that is being carried out by the extremist press has created a true danger to our country, as the General Staff has brought to your attention on several occasions. Though this danger was slow to take root, it has turned large sections of the population into sectarian rebels, even undermining a section of the teaching profession, whose task is to shape the hearts and minds of our young people into those of the nation's future citizens and soldiers. It cannot escape your attention that the army's mission of preparing the nation for war would be neglected if it did not pay heed to the aforementioned situations, as all will be lost if the people do not respond to the call to make sacrifices to defend the nation when the time comes.

Without seeking to be alarmist but convinced that this is a real and growing problem, the General Staff believes that it is its duty to warn you of the very serious threat represented by this antisocial campaign, which could reach crisis proportions in the event of war. We therefore strongly urge you to request that the proper government agencies take the repressive measures needed to guarantee internal order and the unity and development of the republic. Lastly, as it is the duty of our military institutions to safeguard the honor and reputation of its officers and soldiers when they have followed the orders of their superiors, as has occurred in this case, the Army Staff supports the request of the commanding officer of the 10th Cavalry Regiment on the understanding that any actions taken by the ministry will be beneficial to the morale of the officer corps and encourage them to do their duty and make sacrifices for the good of the nation. Issues 13, 14, and 15 of the magazine *El Soldado Argentino*, as referred to in the previous letter, are enclosed.

Buenos Aires
March 30, 1922
Pascual Quirós, Acting Commander of the Army Staff.

This letter draws back the curtain on one of the biggest mysteries in this entire affair: whether or not Yrigoyen gave orders to Varela. The General Staff directly told the war minister: "it is the duty of our military institutions to safeguard the honor and reputation of its officers and soldiers when they have followed the orders of their superiors." A warning to the politicians to not let their memory play tricks on them.

The army went on the offensive against the politicians, who wished to wash their hands of the matter. Here we can confirm two allegations: that orders were given and that, at least in private, Yrigoyen had stated his approval of Varela's actions.

But Yrigoyen was invincible in bureaucratic matters, as we have already seen. He would emerge unscathed here as well.

Before continuing with this exchange, let's examine an article from the General Staff's magazine, *El Soldado Argentino*. Its ultraconservative position and exaggerated language are startling, but this shows the political forces that were at work within the armed forces, evidently with the support of Yrigoyen. It should be kept in mind that *El Soldado Argentino* was a general magazine for conscripts and military academies. But its language was that of the Argentine Patriotic League. We have reproduced below one of the articles forwarded to the War Ministry to explain the position of the General Staff to the Radical minister. (Also observe that strikers are compared with Indians and bandits—a comparison also made by the anarchists for different reasons, comparing the strikers with the indigenous peoples exterminated by the white man and the gaucho rebels who fought against capitalist civilization.) The article first appeared in *El Soldado Argentino*, Vol. 2, No. 13, which was published on January 15th, 1922:

> The bandit of the valleys, canyons, and forests; the fugitive from justice, fleeing from his thefts and murders; the bloodthirsty outcast; the pariah without kin, home, religion, or fatherland; the assassin and the despoiler have risen up, like the Indian before them, to set fire to crops, attack ranches, and destroy what has been painstakingly built through forty years of continued daily labor. Who incited these bandits into taking such devastating actions? Who turned them away from the small thefts that were their daily bread and directed them towards terror on such a large scale? Who brought them together, armed them, and disciplined them when they couldn't even understand each other? We do not have to look far, they are the same enemy as always. Those who want to destroy the liberty that was secured by our forefathers, those who unfurl the banner of arson and destruction before the honest men who inhabit our rich land, those who speak of freedom while they light fires, murder and take prisoners. The usual enemies, to whom we owe the tragic events

of recent times, organizing unjustified strikes and leaving thousands of households without bread, have now incited the savage bandits of the canyons and forests by promising them a false and impossible paradise and then launching them on this bloody crusade. They are none other than the anarchists and communists that have been imported into our land.

But let's continue with the exchange. Here the military gets it wrong, right from the start. They play into Yrigoyen's hands. By appealing to the federal government, they have incited him to make another of his trademark moves.

Upon being received by the War Ministry, the letter is immediately forwarded to the Interior Ministry. It's all quite sober: "494 RESTRICTED. Forward to the Interior Ministry for their consideration. Guillermo Valotta. Secretary, War Ministry. April 4, 1922."

Time is not of the essence here. April goes by, then May and all of June. On July 5th—three months later!—there's finally a bureaucratic answer from the Interior Ministry. Dr. Isidro Ruiz Moreno of the National Territories Department has found a solution:

Dear Sir,

Regarding the information marked restricted that was gathered by the War Ministry following the receipt of a letter addressed to the commander of the 2nd Army Division by the commander of the 10th Cavalry Regiment regarding the articles published by several Buenos Aires newspapers, which constituted attacks on our military institutions and their representatives, the department I represent feels that the matter should be returned to the ministry that raised it in the first place. If examples can be provided from the newspapers *La Vanguardia*, *La Montaña*, and *La Crítica*, which were mentioned in the previous letter, it will be easier to determine it a crime has really been committed. If it has, then the matter should be referred to the Justice Ministry so that the prosecutor can draw up charges.

And so the problem is reduced to forwarding a few newspaper clippings. But the question went much deeper; Varela's request was made out of desperation. How can they ask for the newspaper clippings now, when the entire country is talking about it, when it's not a matter of figuring out who was right by reading different newspapers but of stating—without leaving room for doubt—if Varela had done his duty or not, if Varela deserved the thanks of his fellow citizens or not!

The paperwork then begins its return trip. The Interior Ministry sends a note to the War Ministry to forward some newspaper clippings, the War Ministry tells the General Staff to gather the clippings, the General Staff passes the order on to Varela and the Cavalry School. Varela, of course, doesn't respond. We can only imagine his rage.

But this exchange will prove to be less important than the one involving Captains Pedro Viñas Ibarra and Elbio Carlos Anaya. Because while Varela may have resigned himself to his fate, the captains have not. The insults directed at them in the anarchist press were not any kinder than those directed at their commanding officer. As young officers, they also want to meet with Yrigoyen and force him to take a stand. They first ask for the blessing of their commanding officer, Lieutenant Colonel Varela, who immediately grants it.

The two officers guardedly ask for an audience. They don their dress uniforms, with stiff collars and bow ties that make them feel even stiffer. And there they have the opportunity to get to know Yrigoyen's celebrated gift for making people wait. Not just a custom of his abortive second term from 1928 to 1930, the waiting room was already an institution in his presidency.

The two officers stand there, waiting. People wearing sandals, overweight NCOs, and women whose faces are painted in tropical colors come and go. The captains wait patiently, but it's clear that they feel out of place at the Casa Rosada. They remain silent as they eavesdrop on two government employees, who gossip as they drink coffee from cracked mugs. They gesture towards the officers and ask each other, "And those things, what are they waiting for?" The officers wait for three hours until one of the many bureaucrats and secretaries finally tells them, "No, look, the president won't be able to see you today."[11]

The same story repeats itself for a fortnight. The officers in dress uniform, waiting for Yrigoyen to receive them in his den. But Yrigoyen never appears. Sometimes they think they can glimpse the mysterious and much-admired man in a doorway and that he will come tell them, "I have been waiting for you." But it never happens. Every day it's the same: "No, look, the president won't be able to see you today."

They're not a pair of white collar beggars looking for government jobs, they're two army officers who want to be told if they acted correctly or not.

Days pass. The Santa Cruz affair slips off the front page. The only ones who keep hammering on about it are in the anarchist press.

It's now October 10th, 1922. Alvear will become president in two days and Yrigoyen will return to his house on Calle Brasil. They can't keep waiting any longer. Anaya and Viñas Ibarra write to Varela. Their letter exudes a barely concealed rage towards the president:

El Palomar.
October 10, 1922.
To the director of the Cavalry School, Lieutenant Colonel Héctor Varela.

Convinced of the material impossibility of decorously overcoming the obstacles that have presented themselves as an insurmountable barrier during our fifteen-day pilgrimage to the Casa Rosada, where we followed all the proper procedures to be granted an audience with the president (Article 308, Section D, Subsection V, Chapter IX, R.S.I.C.), we hereby write to you to inform you that we have done our duty, despite having been unable to meet with the president, which constitutes a breach of regulations (Article 320 R.S.I.C.) and an affront to our professional prerogatives. As the commanders of detachments under your orders, we had the honor to be deployed to Santa Cruz by the president in November 1921 to restore order and reestablish the rule of law, which had been utterly discarded in the desolate wastes of Patagonia. Our actions have become the subject of great controversy and special mention should be made of the insolence that has gone unanswered in parliament and unpunished in the anarchist press. Our sacrifice instead deserves the consideration and respect of civilized people, as the campaign in Santa Cruz exorcised a threat to the nation's social peace.

But it wasn't our intention to meet with the president so that he could praise us for doing our duty, especially when he tacitly recognized us by promising to issue a decree. Our intention was not to defend our personal interests so much as it was to defend the prestige of an institution that has been so unjustly attacked over the methods used by the troops under our orders. We were to petition the president for an immediate investigation that would categorically explain the actions and performance of the troops in accordance with the delicate and difficult mission that had been given to them by their superiors.

And, in conjunction with this request, which was inspired by our deepest convictions, we wished to convey to the president our own personal impressions as to the meaning and true causes of the subversive movement, from its origins to the question of responsibility.

May God keep you.

Elbio Carlos Anaya, Captain; Pedro Viñas Ibarra, Captain.

The tone of the letter, as we can see, is harsh. This is also the first time that one of the accused demands an investigation. Naturally, they could have been playing to the audience—mentioning it as a possibility that they would have requested an investigation if the president had received them, but never making a formal request to that effect. It may also have been a way of putting the government on the defensive, if it could be conclusively shown that Varela had been strictly following the orders given to him by the president. Lieutenant Colonel Varela will forward the letter from the two officers to the war minister one day later, on October 11th, 1922:

> To the war minister:
>
> I offer for your consideration this account by Captains Pedro Viñas Ibarra and E. Carlos Anaya so that you can judge the reasons behind their request to meet with the president and their failure to do so through proper legal channels, as established by current military regulations.
>
> As stated by these captains, the president ordered the war minister, in my presence, to draft a decree based on the dispatches sent to the ministry that would raise the prestige of the army and thank the officers, NCOs, and soldiers for their sacrifice and patriotism, which they demonstrated while fighting in the south to restore order and the rule of law.

These two documents are in themselves proof of two things:

1) That something abnormal and quite dark had occurred during the Santa Cruz campaign.

2) That Yrigoyen had initially promised Varela a decree but then decided to distance himself from the officer. If he hadn't, then why wouldn't he have seen the two officers, as he was legally required to do by military regulations? And he didn't just refuse to see them, but he made them do a fortnight of penance. Yrigoyen was not the sort of man to do such things gratuitously. It's clear that he was taking a position and that he wanted to make one thing clear: the president had not met with the officers responsible for repressing the workers of Patagonia.

One more thing: Varela does not say he endorses the request of his subordinates for an investigation, but only mentions the promised decree. The reason for this is probably that the captains were sure that they had faithfully followed the orders given to them by Varela, but had the latter followed the instructions that had been given—or insinuated—to him? Or had he overstepped his bounds?

This exchange is crucial. Because now we will see how General Agustín P. Justo, the war minister in the Alvear administration, will put an end to it all with one stroke of his pen. And here there's no delay.

First of all, General Aranzardi, the army's director of personnel, takes the letter to the war minister.

Then Minister Justo—after meeting with military auditor Risso Domínguez—promptly returns the letter with a note explaining that collective audiences are not permitted and adding, as if to definitively end the matter, "THIS LETTER SHOULD HAVE NEVER REACHED MY DESK." And then he signs it: Agustín P. Justo.

Maybe now they'll finally stop fucking around with the damned question of Santa Cruz. Neither Alvear nor Justo wanted to inherit such a disagreeable matter.

This was a harsh blow for Varela and his two officers. The authorities had come up with a pedantic pretext—audiences with the president must be individual and not collective—to tell them to shut their mouths once and for all. And they understood. Nothing more would be said of the matter until January 25th, 1923—just three months later—when Wilckens's bomb puts the massacre in Patagonia back on the front page.

CHAPTER SEVEN

THE AVENGERS

"The British residents of Santa Cruz honor the
memory of Lieutenant Colonel Varela, a paragon of
honor and discipline in the performance of one's duty."
Plaque placed on Commander Varela's tomb,
September 22, 1923

"Foreign gaucho! Brother Wilckens, receive the
embrace of your comrades from La Pampa, who
consider you to be a paragon of the people's justice."
La Pampa Libre, newspaper printed in General Pico,
La Pampa,
February 15, 1923

Commander Varela is dead. His body bears seventeen wounds:
twelve from shrapnel and another five from bullets (two of them
pierced his aorta). Wilckens didn't tremble as he pulled the trigger. He has delivered what the anarchists call proletarian justice.
With this assassination, he has avenged the hundreds killed in
Patagonia. Now death has leveled them. Like his victims, Commander Varela has been left dying on the ground, gasping for
breath.

The news spreads from mouth to mouth: Commander Varela
has been killed. The site of the attack turns into a gathering place
for the curious, numbering in the hundreds.

He's taken to the barracks of the 2nd Infantry Regiment on a stretcher. They place his body on a table in the officer's lounge and cover it with a sheet.

The cavalry officers feel a profound bitterness as they watch their commander's body being brought in. Captain Anaya and the other officers of the 10th Cavalry soon arrive from Campo de Mayo.

The atmosphere is tense. Nobody is thinking about the anarchist. While they don't justify his action, they recognize that he followed his own laws, those of the underdogs. For these young officers, those responsible are located much higher up. And they generalize: the politicians. Incidents like this will prepare them for a confrontation that will repeat itself over the coming decades, with an ever-increasing level of violence each time. The military will speak of "the politicians" with contempt, as if defining a type, one of Argentina's endemic diseases. And the politicians will speak of "the military" between winks and flattering smiles.

With their commanding officer dead, these cavalry officers need an explanation. They already know some of the details and suspect many more. Lieutenant Colonel Varela was used by the politicians. He risked his life for them. Whether his actions were right or wrong, he was following orders. He was no statesman, and he wasn't intelligent enough to issue himself with orders and act on his own. It's possible that he misinterpreted his orders. But those who gave the orders made no effort to correct Varela's "exaggeration." The interior minister, El Tuerto Gómez, did not speak up. Neither did War Minister Julio Moreno. Nor did the former president, Hipólito Yrigoyen.

They gave Varela a free hand. And they abandoned him as soon as he put things back in order. They left him on his own. "He went too far," said the ministers. "He went too far," said the committee leaders. "He went too far," said the ward bosses.

Yrigoyen remained silent for the rest of his term in office. Alvear continued this silence. And when it came time to make a decision and promote Varela to the rank of colonel—as was merited by his seniority and service record—the paperwork stalled in the Senate. "It's in committee," the politicians pompously explained. And Commander Varela, with his fierce gaze and his angular jaw, had to suffer in silence after risking his life and reputation for the politicians and for those who controlled Patagonia's wealth.

But now he has been assassinated. Now he is no longer inconvenient. Now it's time to take a stand. Let's see what Yrigoyen and Alvear do now!

Things have changed: Yrigoyen leads the opposition to Alvear. He feels betrayed by his former ambassador to France, now anointed president. The time of factional struggles within the Radical Civic Union has begun.

Marco T. de Alvear appears unexpectedly at the barracks of the 2nd Infantry Regiment at 11 that morning. His demeanor is serious, his face like marble. He silently salutes the officers surrounding the body. It's a difficult moment. But the officers are satisfied and have more than a little hope. Will justice be done? Will he be promoted *post mortem*? Will the president sing the commander's praises?

No…they were mistaken. No statements will be made. The Patagonia tragedy will be resolved by other means. By gunfire. Justice will be done without turning to the authorities, who will remain silent. They will refuse to come down in favor of either side.

At the same place and time in which Marcelo T. de Alvear pays his respects to Varela, there is an incident involving the journalists and a strange, vehement young man with curly hair and piercing eyes. No one knows how he entered the barracks. He wants to prevent the journalists from entering the room where the corpse lies. He shouts at them, threatening to shoot the journalists if they continue. He's a member of the Argentine Patriotic League. His name is Jorge Ernesto Pérez Millán Temperley and he will be the protagonist of another chapter in this bloody sequence.

The Alvear administration's decree according full military honors to Varela couldn't be more insipid. There is neither a posthumous promotion nor even praise for his service to the country. But there is the strange and imposing presence of former president Hipólito Yrigoyen at the wake. In absolute silence and acting properly austere, Yrigoyen and those who served under him are there to mourn their former colleague. When Alvear makes his appearance, Yrigoyen lingers for a few minutes longer and then he departs, his entourage following.

Those in the know interpret this incident as clear proof of the division between the two Radical leaders. Some Yrigoyenist officers, however, take it as a sign of Yrigoyen's disapproval of Alvear's decision to not posthumously promote Varela.

Out in the street, Yrigoyen is greeted by party members who reach out their hands to touch him. He gets into a car with Elpidio González and loudly tells the driver to take them to La Chacarita, where the National Cemetery is located. But despite showing up to the wake, Hipólito notes a coldness among the officers crowded around the coffin. It's as if they felt betrayed.

They have not left the coffin for two days, following Varela's body from the barracks to his family home on Calle Fitz Roy. They leave at eight in the morning on Friday the 26th—in the midst of an atmosphere of indescribable exasperation—and take him to the morgue for an autopsy. From the morgue, the body is taken to the Military Circle, where it's watched over by a special delegation of soldiers and sailors. The Jockey Club is present, represented by Dr. Joaquín de Anchorena. And so is the Argentine Patriotic League, whose delegation is led by the inevitable Manuel Carlés—dressed in a black jacket with a white shirt, a bow tie, and a top hat—followed by Lieutenant General Pablo Ricchieri and representatives of the Ladies' Fatherland Defense Association, the Chilean Patriotic League and the Argentine Equestrian Club.

At 4:30 p.m., in the stifling January heat of almost 40°C, the coffin leaves the Military Circle. Everyone is sweating, both the officers in their heavy uniforms and the politicians in their stuffed collars and uneasy consciences. The funeral procession heads down

Calle Florida through a multitude of onlookers. What are the good people of Buenos Aires thinking as they crowd together on the sidewalk, wearing the straw hats then obligatory during the summer? What is it that provoked this motley crowd to brave the sun's destructive rays in order to see them bury Commander Varela? What is it? Curiosity? Indignation? What irony did they see in the sight of so many officers passing by with downcast expressions, so many politicians pretending to be hurt? There goes Varela, shot five times and his body full of shrapnel, they're taking him away. The poor man was nothing more than the meat sandwiched between so many political and economic interests. At least he'll have a state funeral with full honors.

At La Chacarita, it's none other than War Minister Agustín P. Justo who presides over the burial, the same man who so harshly rejected the requests of his subordinates. His words are well chosen and full of praise for the deceased, but in the end they're nothing more than words. Of the expected posthumous promotion, nothing.

Lieutenant Colonel Julio Costa also speaks on behalf of the army, as does Frigate Captain Eleazar Videla for the navy, General Ezequiel Pereyra for the Military Circle, Manuel Guisbed Blanck for the Radical Civic Union, Atilio Larco for the Center for Revolutionary Veterans (who says unbelievable things like, "The deeds of tradition and patriotism become visible in the romance of justice—these present times, which tremble with cowardice, must be vindicated with a new epic"), and Manuel Carlés for the Argentine Patriotic League. The concluding remarks are given by the one who will tell the truth: Captain Elbio Carlos Anaya, Varela's second-in-command in Patagonia, one of those men who risked their lives. Anaya's speech goes off script. Without naming names, he attacks Alvear, Justo, and Yrigoyen. And, with the hoarse voice of a veteran, he concludes his speech by clearing up all doubts regarding the responsibility for the massacre in Patagonia: "Lieutenant Colonel Varela always acted within the strict confines of the orders he was given."

There is an uncomfortable silence during Anaya's speech. The crowd disperses once the coffin is in the ground, feeling somewhat relieved.

History continues with its forward march. Life continues with its forward march. Varela is just another casualty. And he has been laid to rest.

In the meantime, Wilckens has to endure the inevitable consequences of his action. They begin to soften him up from the moment he arrives at the station. He responds courteously to all their questions. He identifies himself as Kurt Gustav Wilckens, thirty-six years old, the son of August Wilckens and Johanna Harms. His mother has passed away but his father is still alive in Germany, where he lives with his brothers Otto, Max, Paul, and Franz. He was born on November 3rd, 1886 in Bad Bramstedt, in the Segeberg district of Schleswig-Holstein (in northern Germany, near the border with Denmark). He is 1.76 meters tall, of average build and has blond hair, blue eyes, and a high forehead. And, most importantly for the police, he has a criminal record: he is listed as Political Offender No. 44,797 and his file describes him as an anarchist. He has also used the names Christensen and Larson in anarchist circles. Why did he use these names? Because even though Wilckens has only been living in Argentina for a few short years, he has already been threatened with deportation as a foreign agitator.

Thanks to his criminal record, the police investigating the attack on Lieutenant Colonel Varela are able to reconstruct the German anarchist's life story. He emigrated from Germany to the United States at the age of twenty-four. Back home, he had lived the tough life of a Silesian miner. In the United States, he adopted the lifestyle of so many Scandinavian and German immigrants (described so well in Knut Hamsun's book *Landstrykere*): that of roaming around the country with a bundle over one's shoulder and harvesting crops or working any other odd job that requires the use of one's hands. Wilckens arrived in the United States with a grounding in Marxism and the class struggle. But there his traveling partners found their sustenance in anarchism, and so he began to read and developed an interest in libertarian ideas, particularly those of Tolstoy. With the passing of time, he became a pacifist.

His first conflict with the repressive arm of the United States government came after he led a curious protest in a fish cannery. There were two lines of products: the best quality fish was put in luxury packaging and sold in bourgeois stores, while the leftovers were sold in working-class neighborhoods. Wilckens spoke with his coworkers and they decided to reverse the procedure: the best fish went into the cheapest packaging and the leftovers were treated as a luxury product.

Afterwards, Wilckens returned to his old trade as a miner. In 1917, he participated in a miner's strike in Bisbee, Arizona. He spoke at all the assemblies because he could speak and write well in English. But as the United States was at war, it could not permit strikes, and 1,168 miners were deported from Arizona to a concentration camp in Columbus, New Mexico. He tried to escape but was captured. As a German citizen, he was convicted of high treason and taken to the prisoner of war camp at Fort Douglas. He managed to escape on December 4th, 1917 and headed to Washington State, where a group of German and Swedish farmers took him in and gave him work. He set out for Colorado in 1919 to find work as a miner but was captured by the police and deported to Germany on March 27th, 1920. He arrived in Hamburg on April 8th and went to his hometown of Bad Bramstedt. His mother died days after his arrival and he returned to Hamburg to get in contact with the city's anarchist groups.

But Wilckens was not cut out for urban life. He loved nature and hated cities. Tolstoy had made a deep impression on his thinking: he was a pacifist and an anti-militarist. The anarchists in Hamburg told him that there was a large libertarian movement in Argentina and so he decided to travel to that unknown country. He left from Amsterdam on the steamship *Brabantia* with all his documents in order, including a German passport issued in Segeberg and a certificate of good conduct issued in Bad Bramstedt. He arrived in Buenos Aires on September 29th, 1920. He traveled to Río Negro in search of new pastures and found work picking fruit in Cipoletti. Once the harvest was over, he headed to Ingeniero White, where he worked as a stevedore and made contact with rural workers and their labor organizations. After the harvest, he worked as a gardener in Bahía Blanca. But he was nostalgic for his North American comrades in the Industrial Workers of the World, in which he had done so much organizing that left an indelible mark on his memory. He returned to Buenos Aires in May 1921 to sail back to the United States. He was well aware of the difficulties he would face in trying to reenter a country from which he had been deported. As he was preparing for his journey, he stayed at a small hotel on Avenida Leandro N. Alem, which was run by a fellow German named Hoff, and spent his time at the anarchist social center on Calle Estados Unidos 1056. And then another event occurred that would change the course of his life.

On May 12th, 1921, Kurt Gustav Wilckens went to wait for some friends at the La Brasileña café on the corner of Estados Unidos and Bernardo de Yrigoyen. While he read, someone sat down at his table and told him that they were a fellow anarchist. With his characteristic candor and naivety, Wilckens greeted him warmly. They talked. The stranger wanted to hear his life story, the state of the anarchist movement in Germany, etc.

Wilckens, who spoke Spanish poorly, answered his new comrade's questions as best he could. He told him of his adventures in the United States and even showed him a newspaper clipping that included his photograph and called him "the most dangerous Red in the West." After a lengthy conversation, the stranger invited him to come over to his house and look at some books. Wilckens accepted. But the "house" turned out to be the 16th Precinct. And his "comrade" was none other than Mauricio Gutman, Agent No. 838. The clever policeman had been following the lonely foreigner around after seeing him enter the anarchist social center several days beforehand. He suspected that the foreigner would be a big catch right from the start. He wasn't just anybody, he had an intelligent gaze and a gentle face.

The police immediately stripped him of his belt and shoelaces and locked him in a cell. As he had not committed any crimes, they charged him with carrying a weapon: "The suspect was found with a knife in his belt."

And so Wilckens, the pacifist, was accused of being unlawfully armed. The matter was passed on to the National Immigration Board, along with Mauricio Gutman's statement and the newspaper clipping. While deportation proceedings for violation of immigration law got underway, Kurt Wilckens was taken in handcuffs to the Central Police Department and then to see the warden. When asked what he was doing at the anarchist social center, the German answered that he had gone looking for a friend who had promised him a free place to store his luggage. But the newspaper clipping was proof of his ideology and political activities. The deportation process, however, took a long time.

Wilckens filed an appeal of *habeus corpus*, which was rejected by Judge Jantus. But in a very controversial move, a federal court overturned the judge's decision, ordered Wilckens to be immediately released and slapped National Immigration Board Director Remigio Lupo with a 1,000-peso fine for having exceeded his jurisdiction.

Wilckens had proven to be a working man and not a paid agitator, as he belonged to the Bahía Blanca Port Workers' Society. This was confirmed by the leader of the port workers in Buenos Aires, who affirmed that Wilckens was a stevedore and a card-carrying union member.

He was released on December 6th, 1921 after four months in prison. The anarchist newspaper *La Protesta* saluted their German comrade with a December 9th article entitled "A Dangerous Suspect":

This German comrade, who speaks several languages, was imprisoned for carrying a clipping from a U.S. newspaper in his pocket. That was his crime. The police, whose ignorance is chronic, neither knew the language the newspaper was written in nor the sort of revolutionary Wilckens is. And to investigate the matter, they shuttled him from the precinct to the prison and then back again until our comrade finally escaped their clutches. We won't fall into the trap of getting indignant and protesting this incident, because we're no longer frightened by anything and we know—we are convinced—that the police cannot help but act arbitrarily, and that actions that are not arbitrary cannot have been committed by the police.

To your health, Comrade Wilckens! You now have something to remember Argentina by!

This adventure changed his plans. In prison, Wilckens had met a group of anarchists who were being held on a variety of charges. The historian Diego Abad de Santillán, who was living with Wilckens at the time in a humble apartment on Calle Sarandí 1461, has shared his reminiscences:

Wilckens met several comrades in prison, in particular those who had been implicated in the Calle Estados Unidos bomb case, and he also always talked enthusiastically of Silveyra.[1] Upon his release, one comrade found him a job washing cars and he spent almost all of his wages helping his former fellow inmates. He often went hungry so he could keep sending money to his comrades locked away in the National Prison. Silveyra and the others never suspected the sacrifice that was involved because he never said a word to anyone. When we realized the reason why he sometimes disappeared from the room we lived in on Calle Sarandí, we encouraged him to think about himself a little more, telling him that the Prisoner Solidarity Committee was there to take care of our political prisoners. But it seems that there was one visiting day when the comrades from the committee hadn't shown up, which led him to believe that the prisoners had been forgotten about. He said that our prisoners should be the priority of those of us who were free and he led by example.

Then came a period of unemployment. He went months and months without being able to find work. He managed to keep going with what he earned from the occasional odd job. He lived in misery but never asked anyone for help as it was hard for him to accept anything. He never seemed worried about his own fate.

After this period, Wilckens—who remained unable to find a steady job—went back to Ingeniero White to work as a stevedore. But he soon suffered a fairly serious accident: he was hit by a dock shunter, badly wounding one of his arms, and he had to be hospitalized. An anarchist named Siberiano Domínguez brought the news to Buenos Aires.[2] Abad de Santillán had this to say:

> We knew that Wilckens wouldn't say a word himself about his situation, nor would he ask anybody for help, even though he really needed it. We couldn't sleep until he was back in Buenos Aires again, so we turned to the Prisoner and Deportee Solidarity Committee for help.

In the first months of 1922, news of the massacre in Patagonia was beginning to reach Buenos Aires:

> Wilckens closely followed the movement in Patagonia with intense hopes. He barely knew Spanish but he always made an effort to read news of the Varela expedition.

Wilckens was actually a correspondent for two German newspapers: Hamburg's *Alarm* and Berlin's *Der Syndikalist*. His dispatches can be found in the archives of both papers. The first was the official publication of the Federation of Libertarian Anarchists and Libertarian Communities of German Workers, and the second was the publication of the Free Workers' Union of Germany, Anarcho-Syndicalist.

News of the executions in Patagonia shook Wilckens, who had no tolerance for injustice. He had met Patagonian workers and the men of the Argentine countryside when he was working in Río Negro and Villa Iris in southern Buenos Aires province. He dearly loved them for their sense of friendship and hospitality, their humility and their unassuming ways. Santillán again:

> We suspect that he was thinking about killing Varela from the moment he heard about the events in Patagonia. I hadn't seen him since March 1922 and I still remember the last day I saw him. Wilckens had gone down to the port, his arm still in bandages, to bid me farewell.[3] Perhaps he had foreseen that we would never see each other again. But even if we had kept sharing that tiny room on Calle Sarantí, he never would have told me his thoughts on Varela. He would have done whatever he could to keep from turning me into an accomplice.

Wilckens stopped frequenting libertarian circles at this time. He continued living in the same room on Calle Sarandí but managed to throw the police off his tracks. None of his neighbors knew his real name. He had to be careful because there was someone who still had their eye on him: Officer Mauricio Gutman, who almost managed to get him deported. Gutman was able to place him at the offices of the Association of Car Washers and Bronze Polishers on Tacuarí 653. In his police report, Agent No. 838 mentions that "at the hiring hall, Wilckens went by the name of Larson." And so Wilckens stopped working as well. Santillán writes:

> About eight weeks before January 25th, 1923, a comrade from Buenos Aires asked us about his whereabouts. No one had seen him for several months and there were rumors that he had left for the United States or Mexico. What had actually happened was that he was preparing to avenge the dead in Santa Cruz and had therefore isolated him himself from everybody, making

himself invisible so as not to compromise his comrades when Lieutenant Colonel Varela's final hour arrived.

It's clear that Wilckens made contact with some of the groups of expropriators that operated within the anarchist movement. He didn't know how to build a bomb and had never even picked up a gun, much less learned to shoot. But the idea that guided him, above all his other libertarian principles, was that of anti-militarism. He believed that all military men—without exception—were conscious of the uselessness of their profession, but had only realized this when it was already too late. This is why they felt such hatred towards the common man: they developed a complex, having felt betrayed by the parents or teachers who had encouraged them to sign up. Those who knew Wilckens say that whenever he saw men in uniform, he stopped to stare at them with a look of pity and sorrow in his face. Deep down, he considered them to be humanity's most unfortunate victims—but victims who had become the executioners of humanity, of their own brothers.[4]

Wilckens always had respect for the two wings of anarchism: the pacifists and the expropriators. He never scorned the expropriators, nor did their actions scandalize him. Though he was a pacifist, he understood that men could be driven to violence by the violence of society. Reliable witnesses have told us that Wilckens was friends with Miguel Arcángel Roscigna and it was surely either him or a member of his group who built the bomb and gave Wilckens the gun. Roscigna was a quiet man who carried out "direct actions." Emilio Uriondo, one of the few survivors of Roscigna's group, has told us that it was Andrés Vázquez Paredes—who was Roscigna's inseparable companion—who provided the materials for the bomb that killed Varela. Emilio Uriondo accompanied Wilckens and Vázquez Paredes to a place near Puente Barracas where they held bomb practice. The German anarchist took the opportunity to explain his theory that actions targeting an individual should only involve one man, as it would be more effective and wouldn't compromise others. But he didn't tell them anything about his plans.

Wilckens's attitude towards the expropriators was similar to that of Bartolomeo Vanzetti: he treated them as equals, considered them his comrades and, if need be, helped them as best he could.[5]

But now he's been taken prisoner and things couldn't be worse. Defenseless, he's confronted by men who want to know everything, who demand to know everything. His captors mistreat him. Their imperative and over-familiar questions herald the slaps, punches, backhands, and kicks to come, always skillfully and joyfully delivered.

After meticulous searching his person, all the police are able to find is an ordinary-looking wallet containing 1 peso and 50 centavos, a prescription issued by the German hospital, two needles and some black thread, a black handkerchief, a trolley ticket, a nickel-plated watch, one large key and one small one, a penknife, a German-Spanish dictionary, the day's issue of the *Deutsche La Plata Zeitung*, a box of matches, some string, a cravat, and a book entitled *Das Anarchistische Manifest*.

They force him to stand for three hours straight. Even though his broken bones dig into his muscles and tissues and threaten to break through his skin, and even though his left foot is nothing more than a bloody mess, they don't give him a chair or even let him lean against the wall. But the German is tough. His bad Spanish is good enough to allow him to answer all their questions about his identity. But when they begin to interrogate him about the assassination, he seems to suddenly forget the language, unable to say more than, "I was alone. Intellectual author. I made the bomb without help. Individual act."

And that's all. He doesn't understand any of the other questions. They can't get anything else out of him. Besides, he's lost a lot of blood. He's about to pass out and can't think straight.

The press, in general, severely condemns the anarchist's attack. Surprisingly, the Yrigoyenist newspaper *La Época* mounts a defense of the deceased officer. But then, as if responding to Captain Elbio Carlos Anaya, who loudly and emphatically stated before all those gathered to mourn his deceased commander that

Varela had been following the orders of the president, they clarify their position the following day, trying their best to dot their i's and cross their t's:

> We regret that we must condemn another treachery, and of the worst sort, by reporting that it has been said that Lieutenant Colonel Varela had been given decisive orders from the president in his second expedition to the south, which is a malicious way of saying that his orders corresponded to the incidents that certain sectors of the press have dishonorably attributed to him. This is false, absolutely false. Lieutenant Colonel Varela received the same orders from the war minister as he did during the first expedition, which were in accordance with the administration's policy of peacefully resolving all of the country's social and political problems. And so if it can be proven that Lieutenant Colonel Varela committed any or all of the incidents that have been malevolently attributed to him in the press, then he would have recklessly disobeyed the orders he was given by the federal government.

Let's make things clear, then: if there were executions, then it's the responsibility of Varela and not the Yrigoyen administration.

It seems as if the responsibility of all those who owed something to Varela, of those who benefited from his actions, ended with his death and with the words spoken and the ink spilled in condemning his assassination. Nobody so much as lifts a finger. Not the Río Gallegos Rural Society, nor the Association of Southern Ranchers nor any of the other forces at play in Patagonia. Even the homage to the fallen officer in the Chamber of Deputies in the first legislative session following his death is remarkably cold. A sole deputy, the Yrigoyenist Felipe Alfonso from Buenos Aires, says barely four words, all of them clichés like the well-worn descriptor "honorable serviceman." And nothing else. No other deputy participates in the homage, neither the majority leader nor a single committee leader, no one.

There's an awkward silence and then the chamber moves on to other items on the agenda. And in the Senate, not a single word is spoken in tribute.

The ones who don't forget about Varela are the British. They express their gratitude for everything the Argentine officer did for them. On Saturday, September 22nd, 1923, a bronze plaque is affixed to his headstone. It reads, "The British residents of Santa Cruz honor the memory of Lieutenant Colonel Varela, a paragon of honor and discipline in the performance of one's duty." British diplomat Allan M. McDonald, speaking on behalf of Argentina's British residents, says a few words during the ceremony:

> It's a great honor to represent the British ambassador at this homage. Heo requested that I speak on behalf of my fellow countrymen before the tomb of this honorable serviceman. (…) Our homage to Varela goes beyond the parameters of this intimate ceremony. We speak for the very souls of each and every Briton who has worked to build a future for themselves on the immense pampas of Patagonia. I say with pride that, as your brothers, we have known to respect and admire the example of Lieutenant Colonel Varela's performance of his duty.

It was another chorus of "For He's a Jolly Good Fellow," this time as a eulogy.

Six days after the assassination, Judge Malbrán orders that Wilckens be denied bail and that his assets be seized. In the judge's view, there is a "criminal association of anarchists" behind the assassination.

In mid-April—three months after the assassination—Wilckens is finally able to stand with the help of crutches. Either his wounds were very serious or no one concerned themselves with his recovery. According to the last doctor to see him before his transfer to the prison on Calle Caseros, he will have to use crutches for the rest of his life. And he's right. But then, he doesn't have much longer to live.

No longer under medical supervision, Wilckens is placed in jail and assigned to Cell Block Two, which consists of twenty-four cells on the ground floor and three on the second. This is generally where prisoners with proven good conduct are held, not violent offenders. It's impossible for Wilckens to escape; a convict has never been seen to escape on crutches. He's held in the first cell on the ground floor.

Diego Abad de Santillán has written about his imprisonment:

Once Wilckens had somewhat recovered from his injuries, his greatest torment was the lack of good reading: for many revolutionaries, prison is a university. There they study, meditate and find new sources of strength for the difficult struggle for freedom. Wilckens worried little about his fate or the outcome of his trial, he only suffered from an absence of books. When they transferred him to the Federal Prison and he was given permission to read, he drew up a long list of books he wanted to be ordered from Germany. He was constantly sending me lists of books and was forever updating them: he asked for books by Bakunin, Kropotkin, Stirner, Dostoevsky, Zola, Ferrer... but, above all (as he was constantly reminding us), by Tolstoy and about Tolstoy. He was a fervent admirer of his thinking, which he could reflect on in the relative peace of his cell. Poor Wilckens! He received some books, but the ones he wanted most—the works of Tolstoy—arrived too late...the reactionaries had already committed their crime.

Wilckens was a deeply committed anti-militarist and he followed the radical anti-militarist campaign of Pierre Ramus with great interest. He was also overjoyed by Rocker's speech against war production at the conference of arms industry workers (1919).

If Wilckens had Radowitzky's luck, then after adding a page to the history of anarchism with his execution of Lieutenant Colonel Varela, he would have shared his magnificent thoughts with us, and the readers of tomorrow would have basked in the afterglow of his extraordinary heart and his limitless love for oppressed humanity.

Some of the letters he wrote in prison have survived. Wilckens sent two letters to Abad de Santillán, then in Berlin, which were published in German by the newspaper *Alarm*. The first of the letters sent from the Federal Prison is dated May 2nd, 1923:

Comrade Santillán:

I arrived here last Thursday. It's better than the prison hospital, where I could neither read nor rest. Things are going well, all in all. Physically I'm regaining my strength, as my comrades are caring for me like a child, but I've nevertheless lost a lot of blood. The operation—the removal of a ten-centimeter-long bone fragment and the stitching of my muscles and skin—was very painful and performed without chloroform or injections, but in my opinion it went well. I was treated humanely by the doctors and nurses. I use crutches to walk now, which is difficult but painless. My case is advancing slowly. I have little interest in it, as I don't concede the court the right to judge me. If I had a thousand lives, I would gladly give them all to the cause.

Now to the books, as I'm allowed to read in here. Above all, I should like old Tolstoy, as Ramus recommends: *The Four Gospels Unified and Translated*, *What Is Art?*, *Anti-War Speeches*, *A Confession*, *Resurrection*, *Anna Karenina*, *What I Believe*, Schmitt's *Leo Tolstoy and His Works*, *The Intimate Diary of 1898*, and others. *The Modern School* by F. Ferrer, *Force and Matter* by Buchner, *Errico Malatesta: The Biography of an Anarchist* by Max Nettlau, something good by Leonhard Ragaz (advertised in *Erkenntnis und Befreiung* No. 23), something beautiful like Helene Stöcker's *Love*, anything by Kropotkin except for *The Conquest of Bread* or *Anarchist Morality*, *The Ego and Its Own* by Stirner, anything by Mackay, the works of Bakunin. Barrera will send money for the books. Also, *Christ, the Priest and the Peasant* by Ramus and *Germinal* by Zola.

Libertarian greetings, Kurt G. Wilckens.

The other letter was written just days before his death. It was mailed from the Federal Prison on May 21st, 1923:

Comrade Santillán:

Yesterday I received your letter dated April 23rd. Writing in my cell is not very pleasant.

I do not feel as if I have been accused of a crime and I will not present myself to the authorities as the accused but as the accuser. The courts, like all government institutions, do not represent the people. No, they are their executioners and they always have been. Only an imbecile could hope for justice from the representatives of Roman law. Was there ever a time when they were anything but the assassins of justice? It would be laughable if it weren't so sad. Justice is blind for they have blindfolded her. I am firm in my struggle and I have never attempted to defend myself. I only marvel at the cowardice of the representatives of justice and the court's doctors. Typical representatives of a cowardly and deceitful system. How sure of themselves they seem with their hidden foot soldiers in the Patriotic League! But the courage of the cowardly Carlés is based on the criminal ignorance of his fanatical followers. Physical and spiritual prostitution hold their orgies. To know them is to despise them.

But let's not speak of revenge. It wasn't revenge; I didn't see Varela as an insignificant officer. No, he was everything in Patagonia: judge, jury, and executioner. I aimed to strike at the naked idol of a criminal system. But vengeance is unbecoming of an anarchist. Tomorrow, our tomorrow, does not promise quarrels and crime and lies, it promises life, love, and science and we must work to hasten the coming of that day.

Can we not see that the organizations for the struggle of the oppressed are in a sad state of affairs? Are mutual aid and solidarity anything more than words and cowardly lies for many unions? All those who aspire to dominate must resort to calumny, deceit, and other such vile means. Education, patience, and respect for the truth are what is needed. We must not act like the enemies of *La Protesta* and pick apart everything that seems wrong about an action or phrase that seems unclear to us. He who goes looking for evil is generally incapable of a generous thought. Perhaps unconsciously, hate turns supposed revolutionaries into enemies of revolution. Only those who fight lies can love truth.

Ramus's interpretation of Tolstoy's anti-militarism is our only hope. *Erkenntis und Befreiung* points true north.

Greeting to all enemies of slavery.

Kurt G. Wilckens.

I anxiously await the books.

On his life beyond bars, we have the testimony of some of his fellow anarchists. This article, entitled "Kurt G. Wilckens in Prison" and signed by M. González, provides several interesting details:

Wilckens was seriously wounded by the shrapnel from his bomb. This injury ruled out any attempt to escape. He had to empty his revolver to finish off the beast of Santa Cruz, so he was arrested on the spot without putting up resistance. Handcuffed, he was taken to the precinct, where they kept him standing on his broken leg. He lost so much blood that it brought him to the point of collapse, but even when his body wavered, his spirit remained strong. He unhesitatingly answered all of their questions while maintaining his personal integrity and he responded to the insults of the "high" representatives of the army and the war minister with his trademark smile. The torture was prolonged, but his stoicism overcame the pain.

The judges ordered that Wilckens be taken to the hospital of Argentina's most dangerous prison as a precautionary measure. He was separated from his fellow inmates and held in a large room for ten days under heavy guard. His lawyer, Juan A. Prieto, met with him on behalf of the Prisoner Solidarity Committee. Although he was still very weak from his wounds, Wilckens gave the same answer to everyone who questioned him: he was an anarchist and therefore an enemy of violence. He spoke with many journalists who questioned him about his ideas and his action and he disarmed all his enemies with his good-natured serenity, winning the sympathy of all who approached him.

As a "security measure," the court ordered that he be imprisoned and held in isolation throughout his convalescence on the pretext that he had to be kept apart from the other inmates. His guards were told not to exchange even so much as a single word with him. But Wilckens didn't see the evil in anyone, he thought they were all good men. Despite the harsh orders of the warden, he was admired by everyone around him for the greatness of his soul.

When the Prisoner Solidarity Committee was able to establish direct contact with Brother Kurt, they noticed the hero's simplicity. His food was simple and healthy: Graham bread and fruit. He never ate meat or drank alcohol. This undoubtedly helped accelerate his recovery, which was quite rapid.

After two months of imprisonment, he had overcome his isolation to earn the love of all his fellow inmates. They idolized him, and the general sympathy with which they saw him spurred the warden to ask for him to be transferred to the Caseros prison on the argument that he had not yet been convicted of a crime.

Late one night, Wilckens was silently taken to the jail and placed in one of the cells reserved for "distinguished" inmates.

Another article, published in the Montevideo newspaper *El Hombre* (No. 252, June 1923) and entitled "Kurt Wilckens, Impressions from Prison," recounts the following:

We have received a letter from a dear friend of ours who, like Wilckens, is an inmate of the Federal Prison in Buenos Aires.

It shows the impression that the arrival of Wilckens made on our friend: "Life in prison has its surprises. Kurt has been the prison's guest for two or three days now. He's being held in isolation, but I don't know if it's out of their interest in him or as a simple security measure. You can guess how I felt. My days were spent in the midst of a profound worry, far from the somewhat brutal distractions of the other inmates. Kurt stirred up warm feelings in me, as his heart is loyal, his expression is honest and his nature is calm and generous. I would have liked to once more hold his hands in mine and open our hearts to each other. But the prison wardens, taking up their usual business of being inappropriately severe, have not allowed so natural and simple a thing. He doesn't display the conceited attitude of the hero. He is an anarchist. Moving slowly on his crutches, he even seems indifferent to the prison itself. His eyes always glow with kindness and his face likewise shows his serenity and decisiveness. When the guards lead him past my cell, he always greets me by my first name. There is a depth of feeling in his soft voice. He can only stand upright with the aid of his crutches as his wounds are quite serious. But even as a cripple, Kurt radiates heroism. He has a place deep in our hearts. This is how the youth, the young anarchists, must see him. He has captured the attention of an entire generation of proletarians, not just out of sympathy but out of admiration for his heroism in the midst of the deep tragedy of the past two decades, which have been marked by the convulsions of a younger generation that has not been able to properly express its desires and its idealism.

It's now June. The prosecutor has asked for a seventeen-year prison sentence. The verdict is to be announced sometime in the next couple days. On Thursday the 14th—visiting day—Wilckens is seen by his lawyer, Dr. Prieto, and two friends from the Prisoner Solidarity Committee. They bring him some fruit. They're worried because Wilckens has been receiving death threats. Some of the prison guards have said that someone might try to poison his food and that the Argentine Patriotic League is planning to murder him. Even though Wilckens tries to play down these rumors, Dr. Prieto reports the matter to the prison warden and demands tighter security measures.

But the plot to kill the German worker has already been set in motion and his lawyer's demands have the opposite effect: instead of canceling their plans, the conspirators act with greater urgency.

The evening of Friday the 15th is just another night for Wilckens. In accordance with prison regulations, he is in bed by 9 p.m. He gazes one last time at the walls that enclose him, a nomad, a libertarian. He has all of his possessions with him: the two sawhorses that hold up the pallet upon which his straw mattress rests; the shelf containing Goethe's *The Sorrows of Young Werther* and *Hermann and Dorothea* and Knut Hamsun's *Hunger*, which are his favorite non-political books, plus a Spanish textbook; the bags of fruit brought by his faithful Spanish comrades in the Prisoner Solidarity Committee.

Wilckens sleeps with the infinite exhaustion that overcomes prisoners and caged birds at this hour. He will wake up only to die.

The plot has been painstakingly prepared. It will be executed by Jorge Ernesto Pérez Millán Temperley, a veteran of the first strike's Battle of El Cerrito. The scion of an aristocratic family, he is a member of the Argentine Patriotic League and has a loose family connection to Lieutenant Colonel Varela (his sister married Captain Alberto Giovaneli, the brother of Varela's widow). He is ready to act.

The cells and hallways of the prison are very cold. The cells of the inmates who have earned the guards' trust have been left open so they can use the communal toilets. A nervous man walks down the hallway in the uniform of a prison guard, but he has nothing in common with the institution's other employees. He's a tall, thin young man with a pale complexion, almost girlish in appearance with his refined face and large, restless eyes. It's his first round in that cell block. Through the half-open door, he carefully observes the inmate asleep in the first cell: Kurt Wilckens.

It's twenty minutes before his shift ends. Now is the time. He stealthily enters the illuminated cell—in accordance with prison regulations, all of the inmates have to sleep with the lights on; they can never enjoy complete darkness.

There lies the foreign anarchist. One of his crutches leans against the wall and the other lies by the side of the bed, within his reach. Pérez Millán Temperley grips his Mauser with both hands and shoves its barrel into the back of the sleeping man, who sits up with a start, as if he had received an electrical shock, and stares at the guard.

"Are you Wilckens?"

"*Jawohl*," the startled prisoner responds in German.

And then Pérez Millán's finger squeezes the trigger. The bullet strikes Wilckens in the chest, point blank, entering his body slightly above the heart, tearing apart his left lung and going out the other side.

Such was the death of Wilckens, the avenger of the Patagonian strikers of Patagonia. His chest was completely torn apart. The crime was committed with total impunity. The barrel of the gun was pressed hard against his body to ensure the success of the plot. The gunshot echoed through the hallways of the cell block like a dull drumbeat. The inmates began to stir and the guards have been alerted.

Pérez Millán is very nervous. He makes for the cell door, as if to close himself inside and thus conceal his crime. Inspector Luis Conti will later say that, when asked what happened, Pérez Millán's first words will be, "I served under Commander Varela, who is my kin. I have avenged his death."

He sounds like he's about to burst into tears and adds that he woke the prisoner and asked for his name before firing.

The prison doctor, Dr. Maza, arrives minutes later. The victim is still alive, he says, but won't last more than a couple hours. They take him to the infirmary and leave him there, taking his pulse every once in a while to see if he's still alive. But the anarchist refuses to give up. His lawyer arrives at seven in the morning.[6] His eyes light up. Wilckens will hold on for the rest of the day, breathing his last breath on Sunday at 3:10 a.m.

The news spreads through Buenos Aires from mouth to mouth: Wilckens was shot in his cell while he slept. Though the newspapers don't have time to run a story, there isn't a single anarchist social center or union hall that the news hasn't reached by midday.

"The workers will cause trouble," President Alvear is told. When he hears the news, the president is disgusted and takes it out on his assistants.

A fine development! Now everyone will think that the government ordered the assassination of Wilckens. How could Pérez Millán get a job as a prison guard? And how did he get himself assigned to Wilckens's cell block? Clearly this cannot be explained by chance, nobody would believe it. But something has to be done to save the prestige of the government, placate public opinion and explain things to the workers. Alvear issues a decree launching an immediate investigation into the incident.

That the president has to intervene in this affair speaks to Wilckens's importance and the impact his assassination had on the public, as we shall soon see. But the decree doesn't seem to placate the workers, much less the anarchists among them.

To the contrary. As the hours pass, the anger grows on that cold June morning. By ten o'clock, *La Protesta* and *La Antorcha* have already printed declarations of war.

For the anarchists, Kurt Wilckens is a hero and a martyr, loyally rising to meet the usual fate of those who stake their lives on the vindication of man, the guardians of the living flame of liberty. The majority of the anarchists are in such an agitated emotional state that they can only talk of declaring an indefinite general strike.

The police are unable to prevent *La Protesta*'s broadside from flooding the Avellaneda, Nuevo Pompeya, and Mataderos neighborhoods. The broadsides even reach the cafés on Avenida de Mayo and Calle Florida.

And then a spontaneous movement breaks out across the country. Without waiting for orders, the workers begin to put down their tools, *motu proprio*. The first to stop work are the bakers. The union leadership immediately endorses their action. Their decision is so spontaneous that *La Protesta*'s broadside hadn't even been printed yet: it includes an announcement at the bottom of the page stating, "While we went to press, we were informed that the bakers had just voted to go on strike."

La Protesta's broadside reads: "Wilckens was Murdered in the Federal Prison. A cowardly and despicable act of vengeance. We must declare a general strike, starting immediately, to protest this treacherous crime. ANARCHISTS! WORKERS! Dignified men, show your repudiation of this infamous act of cowardice! We must vindicate the sacred name of the avenger!" The language is that of war:

> We must initiate a general strike, starting immediately. The proletariat must not remain indifferent to this nameless infamy. Kurt Wilckens was treacherously murdered in the Federal Prison. His death cannot go unpunished.

As the broadsides circulate, workers continue to empty out on to the streets. After the bakers, it's the turn of the chauffeurs, painters, sawyers, brickmakers, fuel deliverymen, construction workers, and metalworkers.

At noon, the FORA V officially declares a general strike and invites the entire population to take to the streets:

> Workers! Let nobody remain silent. To not protest in the midst of this emergency would mean solidarity with the barbarous events in Patagonia and the repulsive murder committed in the Federal Prison.
>
> Comrades, proletarians, men of conscience, to the streets!

And then the major newspapers invade the streets with their evening editions, providing two completely contradictory versions of the incident. As *Crítica* senses that its readers are sympathetic to Wilckens, their headline reads, "Wilckens Was Cravenly Attacked Today in the Federal Prison" with "The Incident Has Deeply Moved the Workers" printed below it. Meanwhile, the conservative newspaper *La Razón* prints, "Pérez Millán Has Avenged the Death of Commander Varela."

One after another, the unions unanimously declare their support for an indefinite general strike. The largest union federation, the Argentine Syndical Union (USA), formerly the FORA IX, cannot appear weak and also declares its support for the strike. The death of Wilckens has achieved the impossible: it has united the divided Argentine working class.

The post office refuses to deliver the FORA's telegrams informing its affiliates elsewhere in Argentina of the indefinite general strike. The pot is about to boil over. The police begin to worry about the atmosphere at the offices of the bakers' union on Plaza Once.

The federal government strives to appear as if it's not taking sides. Justice Minister Marcó personally inspects the cell where Wilckens was shot, as if to reassure the public that justice will be done and that a thorough investigation will be carried out.

That night is one of tense expectations. Wilckens is still alive, although nobody has any hope that he'll pull through. Only his physical strength prolongs the inevitable end.

At Bartolomé Mitre 3270, where the FORA has its headquarters, union delegates gather, representing the bakers, chauffeurs, metalworkers, construction workers, brickmakers, tillers, painters, coffinmakers, and stonecutters. There has been a great deal of activity throughout the night and into the early hours of the morning. By contrast, the headquarters of the USA at Rioja 800 are quiet: the union has also gone on strike but has instructed its members to remain at home and refrain from participating in the demonstrations.

When the news that Wilckens has died reaches the FORA, they begin preparations for a mass demonstration to accompany the remains of their martyred comrade. They also receive some good news: the proletariat in Rosario has unanimously supported the call for a general strike, there isn't a single vehicle on the streets of Avellaneda, and the grocery stores have closed their doors. But the police haven't been caught sleeping; dozens of workers have been arrested and their homes have been searched for weapons and explosives.

But the most meaningful and human gesture is the unprecedented hunger strike declared by all of the inmates of the Federal Prison, who ceased their usual activities and refused to eat after hearing of the death of Wilckens.

The FORA issues another statement upon hearing of his passing:

> Wilckens went to his death with the same pride and magnanimity with which he lived. The FORA hopes that the blood of our beloved martyr will inspire us to unwaveringly continue our crusade.

The police, meanwhile, waste no time. Dr. Prieto files the paperwork to claim the body. But though Judge Carlos Martínez tells him that he can come back to pick up the body in the afternoon, Commissioner Duffey—on the orders of Justice Minister Marcó—makes the body disappear.

At 11:00 a.m., a Black Maria leaves the police garage on Paseo Colón and Belgrano. It heads towards the morgue on Viamonte and Junin, where two officers have already arrived with a pinewood coffin. Subcommissioner Dante Buzzo—who remains extremely nervous throughout the operation, afraid that the workers could show up at any moment—orders the body to be placed in the coffin, which is then driven to Chacarita. By noon, Wilckens has been buried in an unmarked grave. Several days later, a shrewd journalist will discover where his body is buried: Path 3, Row 4, Grave 57, in a section set aside for paupers.

That afternoon, the anarchist delegates wait for the judge to release the body of their comrade. Judge Martínez continues to make promises, dragging things out and confusing the nervous union leaders. He will later apologize and say that the police hadn't asked him for permission to inter the body, which had instead been granted by Judge Luna Olmos, who was in charge of the Pérez Millán case. But the truth is that the orders came from much higher up, from the federal government itself.

That Sunday, while a group of determined men take shelter in the union hall on Plaza Once as they await the body of their comrade to arrive, there are others who have their attention elsewhere: Argentina is playing against Scotland. There's faith that the Argentine team will be able to defeat the masters of soccer. But the Scots win.

While cheers for the Argentine players can be heard in the stadium, there are other, hoarser cheers in the union hall. They have just received a message from the Uruguayan Regional Workers' Federation (FORU) that states, in the characteristic language of the times:

> Wilckens' heart has stopped beating, but an ideal of love continues to beat in the breasts of his brothers, who will ensure that justice is done. They have killed our comrade and the crime demands that we immediately strike against the cowering beast.

Minute by minute, new unions announce that they will join the strike: the carters and taxi drivers have stopped work and the newspaper vendors have announced that they won't sell any papers that side with Pérez Millán, which essentially means that they will only be distributing *Crítica*. The stagehands have also stopped work, leaving Buenos Aires without entertainment, and they draft the following manifesto:

> KURT WILCKENS! With your virile, heroic action, with your sacrifice, you have avenged the deaths of over 1,500 of our brothers who were murdered, like you, at the hands of a mercenary hired by those who freely buy and sell our fatherland. A

grotesque caricature embodying the prototype of the cowardly and ignorant assassin, he leaped on to the national stage by treacherously murdering you as you slept—dreaming, perhaps, of the sweet and sacred dream of our future society.

When they hear that the body has been stolen, a group of hotheaded Spaniards and Italians head out to stop the city's trolleys. They break their windows, beat their guards and drivers, and are about to set them on fire when the police show up. The police lay siege to the union hall, blocking the exits and cordoning off the block. Nobody can leave. They take a couple bloodied Spaniards to the police station and a couple strikebreaking trolley operators to the hospital.

In the meantime, news of the strike continues to arrive. There's a general strike in every port in the country: stevedores have stopped work in Tandil, Mar del Plata, Bahía Blanca, Ingeniero White, San Juan, Mendoza, Tucumán, and Necochea. The Balcarce Farmworkers' Association declares their solidarity, as do the stonecutters of Cerrito and Afirmado, the Amalgamated Trade Union of Arteaga (Buenos Aires province), the Regional Workers Federation of Tres Arroyos (seconded by the workers of Copetonas, Orense, Coronel Dorrego, and Oriente), the workers of Córdoba, the bakers and construction workers of Pergamino, the bakers and deliverymen of Chacabuco, the bakers of Bragado, the Local Federation of San Fernando and Tigre, the Workers' Center of Quemú-Quemú (La Pampa), the construction workers of Darragueira (Buenos Aires province), the Amalgamated Trade Union of Santa Rosa (La Pampa), the Regional Workers' Federation of Villa María (Córdoba), the Local Workers' Federation of Lomas de Zamora (seconded by the workers of Adrogué and Temperley), the maritime workers of Paraná, the Local Workers' Federation of Río Cuarto, the workers of Alejandro (Córdoba), etc.

On Monday, the city is paralyzed. Not a soul can be seen in downtown Buenos Aires. Things are not looking up for Alvear. The president of the Labor Association, Dr. Joaquín de Anchorena, visits the Casa Rosada to lobby for the energetic intervention of the government. Finance Minister Rafael Herrera Vegas states that the biggest impact of the strike can be seen in the shipping industry and the ports. In the city of Santa Fe, there's a shootout in front of the Emile Zola Workers' Library, a common gathering place for anarchists. Five workers have been wounded and a police horse is killed. The police report also mentions total work stoppages in Rosario and Mar del Plata.

The president of the Argentine Patriotic League, Manuel Carlés, offers Police Chief Fernández the use of forty-three civilian brigades to help restore order.

At the beginning of the day, the trolleys run normally, albeit under heavy guard. But the drivers and guards walk off the job after being attacked by groups of workers.

The "pure" syndicalists, socialists and communists also join the struggle. The USA issues a statement asserting that:

[Wilckens] belongs to all proletarians. Our brave comrade Wilckens, who has the ineffable gratitude of all the republic's workers and with whom we have taken on a debt of solidarity, has been treacherously shot by a man who added to his repulsive occupation as a prison guard by becoming a hired killer for the bourgeoisie. To remain silent now would imply solidarity with his killer and would undermine the sympathy of the working class with the heroic attitude of the avenger of the massacres in Santa Cruz. This cowardly aggression is an attack on all workers.

The FORA accepts this unexpected show of solidarity from the syndicalist union, but remains suspicious. So much so that they issue a warning to the workers that Monday, in the midst of the general strike:

Workers! Abide by the resolutions of the strike committee. No worker should resume their labors until the strike has been officially called off by the joint resolution of all participating unions.

The order to return to work cannot be issued by those sectors who were dragged into the struggle by the course of events, but only by those who knew what attitude to take from the moment they heard of the barbaric martyrdom of the avenger, Kurt Wilckens.

This is a shot across the bows of the Argentine Syndical Union. The FORA plans a major demonstration for Tuesday the 19th at 2 p.m. in Plaza Once, just a few meters away from where the police have the bakers under siege. There's no question that there will be a battle.

The USA foresees this and orders its members to return to work that same day, June 18th. Their leaders imagine that if things continue as they have, the events of 1919 will repeat themselves and there will be another Tragic Week. By calling off the strike, they divide the movement and dampen the spirit of the workers. The FORA knows that it's a minority within the labor movement and that the desertion of the USA will leave the anarchist workers without support. But after a tumultuous assembly, the FORA's union delegates resolve to keep the strike going until the bitter end.

The USA posts a broadside all over the city that admittedly does sound very combative, but which announces the definitive end of the strike. Words like these are wasted:

The murderers of our heroic comrade Kurt Wilckens have received a warning in the attitude of the proletariat, a warning that the organized proletariat will always be ready to fight off the criminal cowardice of the liberticides. Workers, unite and fight!

And then they call for a return to work.

On Monday night, the police make a smart move. They lift their siege of the bakers' union, whose hall had become the FORA's base of operations. The idea is to eliminate a potential flashpoint during the demonstration that the anarchists will hold the following day.

But they're mistaken. Thousands of workers gather in Plaza Once that afternoon, concentrating near the union hall. The police control practically all the rest of the plaza, as well as the surrounding streets. They arrest the troublemakers and confiscate their flags.

And then the trouble begins. Nobody knows who started it. The police will say that it was the anarchists.

The shooting starts as the police move on the union hall. Enrique Gombas, a Spanish baker, leads the defense of the building. The workers return the direct fire of the police with a variety of short-range weapons. The anarchists are disorganized and use up all their bullets in just five minutes. The police wait for reinforcements and then storm the building on horseback. They clear the premises of the fanatics, who defend themselves with clubs and iron bars. The police continue firing and chase the workers down Calle Anchorena towards the Once de Septiembre station.

And when it's all over, the ground is stained red. Enrique Gombas lies dead, with two bullets in his head and another in his right eye. Further away, the body of another proletarian—a street food vendor named Francisco Facio—has been trampled by horses (the police will later say that he was trampled to death by runaway horses that simply happened to be in the area).

The earliest reports mention many dead and wounded. A genuine battle has taken place and it's a miracle that the denouement wasn't more tragic than it was. In any case, the workers have been taught a harsh lesson. Besides the two casualties, there are seventeen people with serious injuries and another 163 have been arrested, all of them badly bruised or beaten.

The wounded are a sight to behold. The baker Emilio Tiraboschi, for example, is admitted to the Ramos Mejía Hospital with his nose split in two by an ax; the baker Ricardo Cabo has been shot in the face; the Russian Nikifor Cholowsky is unrecognizable from all the contusions and open wounds on his face.

But the police didn't emerge unscathed. Four policemen have been shot. One of them, Security Officer José Arias, received three bullets in the abdomen and will later die in the Ramos Mejía Hospital.

The FORA valiantly marched out to fight without thinking of the consequences. The USA, however, was untouched. They paid their tribute to public opinion and supported the strike, but also knew when to call for calm. And so they won't have to deal with the problems of prisoners, hospitals, or police raids.

A few desperate souls continue attacking the police and laying siege to trolley lines throughout the night. Down at the port, a trolley is burned and the driver killed for resisting.

The rest return to work, as ordered by the USA. The FORA makes an anguished call to continue the strike:

> Comrades! Proletarians! The barbarians have not sated their bloodlust. Despotism and the most barbarous reaction have been unleashed upon the workers. Today, at 2:30 p.m., there was a massacre near Plaza Once. Will the proletariat let this new massacre go unpunished? The FORA Strike Commit-tee appeals to the dignity of labor and to the conscience of the unions to continue this strike against the unprecedented outrages of police despotism. Brothers, returning to work and allowing this new massacre to go unpunished is tantamount to complicity in police vandalism.

The USA obviously could not ignore the Plaza Once incident nor the deaths of the two workers. They could not risk a confrontation with the bakers, who saw one of their leaders shot to death. And so they adopt a Solomonic approach. Though they went back to work the day of the Plaza Once shootout, they commit to stop work for the funeral of those who were killed.

While the FORA continues with the strike, they make preparations for a mass demonstration to accompany Gombas's funeral. But one smart move by the police undoes all their plans. The body disappears and Gombas is buried in an unknown location because "he has no close relatives."

And then something truly outrageous occurs. The USA, after making their usual protests, lifts the strike. They had committed to stop work the day of the funeral. And as there will be no funeral, there will be no strike.

On June 20th, the FORA publicly attacks the rival labor federation:

> And now that the USA has committed yet another act of treason, abandoning the proletariat at its moment of greatest crisis. We must directly address the workers affiliated with the association and ask them to defy the will of their leaders, the Judases that exploit them and trick them, and fraternally struggle for justice alongside us, dying for freedom if they must.

The strike continues: the cordwainers, chauffeurs, painters, stevedores, brickmakers, winch operators, coach drivers, tobacconists, fuel deliverymen, electricians, oil merchants, etc. all remain impassive.

But despite all their efforts and sacrifices, weariness sets in. For every worker who wants to continue the strike, there are ten unemployed workers who will apply to cover the vacancy. The FORA can't fight alone against both the government and the USA. And there's also concern about unions disaffiliating themselves. The strike is finally lifted at 6 a.m. on Thursday the 21st.

There are two unions, more Catholic than the Pope, that continue the strike on their own. The "only ones to remain faithful to the memory of Wilckens" are the upholsterers and the tilers. But after seventy-two hours they too come to recognize that they can't change the world, and return to work.

On the 21st, the Socialists drop Wilckens from the front page of their newspaper, *La Vanguardia*. For them, the issue of the budget is much more important. Their headline that day reads, "The Chamber of Deputies Held a Spectacular Session Yesterday."

The memory of Wilckens is already beginning to fall under the shadow of forgetfulness. And just as the politicians have to face more pressing issues than the rehabilitation of Varela, so the workers will have to deal with the disagreements and mutual recriminations that take up so much of their time. There won't be any energy to spare for a blond foreigner who thought he could redeem his class by throwing a bomb.

But it's worth spending a few paragraphs on describing the impact his death had on the public. Perhaps the image of a prisoner dying in his cell and the underlying sympathy for all those who rebel in isolation, attacking a powerful figure without harming bystanders, earned him the sentimentality and admiration of the mass of people who never openly complain but nevertheless critically observe the men in charge.

Kurt Wilckens was a source of inspiration for *payadores* for many years.[7] He captured the attention of Luis Acosta García, one of the authentic *payadores* of Buenos Aires province and the most celebrated individual from his hometown of Coronel Dorrego.[8] Acosta García had won the payador competition in Parque Gaol on Plaza Lorea and was that emblematic Buenos Aires venue's most lauded payador during the 1920s. On the night of Saturday, June 16th, 1923—Wilckens had been attacked early that morning—Acosta García stepped on stage and, in the midst of the auditorium's religious silence, launched into this song:

The enormous building, all draped in darkness
The prison slept in the greatest of silence
But from time to time a sound could be heard,
Repeated and repeated by a alert guard,
A voice from far off that would turn your heart cold,
All of a sudden, a jailer moves stealthily
Approaching a cell where an invalid sleeps.
Who are you? He asks him mysteriously
Kurt Wilckens, the prisoner answers meekly
And with one gunshot, the entire city awakes.
After the stampede, they discover the deed
Fearful and confused, the guards have come running

And find Kurt Wilckens, shot through the chest.
A wounded lion, he roars, clutching his breast
While in the doorway stands Pérez Millán, smiling.
What have you done? They ask the unrivaled cretin
What have you done? They repeat indignantly
I did my duty, says the criminal, patriotically
I am a loyal soldier and I killed the assassin
Who murdered Varela, my colonel, the lion.
Swine, low-born bastard, destiny's abortion,
You have profaned the flag of our nation,
By invoking the land Ameghino
The birthplace of Moreno, where Bernadino
Gave the criollos culture and education
And the men of distant lands, what will they see
As they dream of America, of humanity
But learn that we mistreat our prisoners
As we are known to have jailers
From well-placed families in high society.
Assassin! Your victim was convalescing
But you repugnantly turned criminal
By killing a man, defenseless and sleeping
Only a beast with no soul, his heart rotting
Could commit such an act *plus ultra natural.*
Not even Enrique, who mutilated Conrado,
Nor that fearsome beast, the criminal Mateo,
Nor Lauro nor Salvado have ever committed
A crime so iniquitous as that perpetrated
By the cruel jailer of nineteen twenty three.[9]
You killed Kurt Wilckens, that living flame
The martyred apostle of high ideality
Without seeing that far away, in another century
Another man, blond like him, had the same idea
And honored with his death all of humanity.
And to bring more shame to your cruelty
You have proclaimed the name of Argentina

And as an Argentine, this I must deny
For Juan Bautista Alberdi, in the name of Sarmiento
I name you a fool, without nationality!

The value of these verses is their spontaneity, their contemporary references and metaphors, their generous naivety. But they're little more than a blind romance lacking literary value, albeit meaningful for the masses. It was sung around campfires and in tenement patios throughout the 1920s and even into the 1930s, becoming a favorite of servants and working class girls. It was no longer strictly anarchist, in other words, but had entered the popular songbook.

That night, the police entered Parque Gaol. Luis Acosta García was used to being forced off the stage because of his lyrics, however, and carried on singing until the two officers took him away.

The assassination of Varela also inspired Martín Castro, a famous payador of the 1920s.

Fernando Gualtieri's poem "The Hero," written in October 1924, was obligatory reading at literary gatherings for over a decade. It's a curious poem, perhaps without literary value, but it nevertheless powerfully expresses the sentiments of the era. Huri Sosa de Portela, the principal of the elementary school in Los Antiguos, Santa Cruz, transcribed the poem in 1972, verse by verse, as he heard it recited by an elderly man named Gabino Pérez in 1972. The old criollo sang the verses while accompanying himself on the guitar. Fifty years had left no mark on his memory.

The Hero

I

When the people have been crushed
By repression, brutal and unjust,
The bard, fiery and strong,
Must sing and shout a new song

Come and hear the song of those
Who have been scorned and hated.
His is a powerful and savage cry
That proudly condemns the mighty!

II

In a far-off region of Argentina,
A vast territory to the south,
In the year nineteen twenty one,
A strike broke out in Santa Cruz.
From there it quickly spread to elsewhere
Like a burning dust storm, without compare,
And our great continent took up the standard
of the revolution, of the Social Vanguard.
A shadow of fear, of doubt,
Was seen in the camp of the bourgeoisie,
And panicked, they raised the alarm:
"They have insulted the flag of our country!"
And that was when, with irate gestures
The eternal architects of evil
Gathered their damned followers
And told them of their tragic plan

III

Under the command of Héctor Varela,
From this hospitable city, this grand capital,
A thousand vain soldiers departed
With an air both solemn and martial.
And they arrived to where there gathered
The proletarians, united peacefully,
Who with the strike defended
Their daily bread, which was a misery.
Ambushes, treason, and violence,
The tools of every good soldier,
Were the arms that were utilized

By those sent to put out the fire.
Unable to appreciate the beautiful
Or to understand greatness or the joy of life,
The soldier, instead, follows his evil tastes
and chooses to imitate the example of Cain.
And then they warmed up their Mausers
Spitting out lead, murderous and infernal,
Thinning the ranks of the workers
With a rage so beastly and cynical.
Many a hairy chest, filled with bravery,
Dreaming of a world filled with love,
Was targeted by the soldier's weaponry
Infamously given to them by the State.
And there fell hundreds upon hundreds,
Two hundred, five hundred, a thousand,
These sons of their elderly mothers,
These fathers of their precious cherubim.

IV
What infamy the state has committed!
How much blood it has spilled without end,
Since remote times, long since passed,
When the globe first began to spin!
The soldier is the most ignoble being,
The cruelest, the foulest, and most vile,
His school is the school of crime
And the barracks his only teacher.
He doesn't work, doesn't laugh, doesn't love,
He has no time for sweet pleasures,
He only ever submits (obedient slave)
To the discipline imposed by his officer.
And this is why each and every soldier
Will eventually turn tyrant and hangman,
Becoming the scourge of the people,
Snuffing out the flames of rebellion!

And so, with a hand made of iron,
Like a blacksmith forging a cross,
They thought to try, without pity, the idea
Of binding the hands of the men of the south.
In vain, I repeat were the efforts of the mercenaries
Who would see force triumph over reason!
In vain, I repeat, were all their efforts,
For ideas cannot be silenced by cannon.
A man, if shot, may be killed,
Such as was the fate of Ferrer,
But an idea, like God, is immaterial,
It does not die with him, nor can it be destroyed!

V

Here, skulls crushed and discarded,
There, dreadful torsos, disembodied,
Blood and tears, cries and moans,
All around the rule was pain!
Who was responsible for this crime,
So horrible, sinister and brutal?
That there, far away—so very far!
Created a scene so infernal?
The answer is concrete, it's quite simple:
All those in power, who command others,
Bear the direct responsibility
For this barbarous crime of yesterday.
More than a year of bloody struggle,
More than a year of dogged pursuit,
And we have learned that the Argentine saber
Has severed one thousand five hundred heads.

VI

What a paradox! Look, what a paradox!
When an army is on the battlefield,
Is it possible to defeat the enemy

Without losing a single soldier?
Is it possible for a thousand men to fall,
A thousand workers, in an uneven struggle,
Without wounding so much as a single soldier
Who fought on behalf of the state?
It's quite clear that there were no battles…
Nothing more than an abundance of crime,
Soldiers massacring our defenseless brothers
On the orders of a colonel so vile.
And then the heroes come sailing back home,
Triumphantly returning to the capital
With laurel branches upon their temples,
Drunk on their barbarous instincts.
And the valiant lieutenant, Varela,
Who fought under the flag of Argentina,
Receives the salutes and cordial applause
Of Yrigoyen, Elpidio, and Carlés.

VII

But there was one, a man of courage, a brother,
A faithful son of the faith of anarchism,
Who was outraged by this unspeakable crime
That was the end of so many workers like him.
And so he said to himself: he who kills
Without reason or justification
Cannot be allowed to go on living!
Cannot be allowed to live among us!
And so once, twice, three times and four,
Patiently, calmly and well-positioned,
He lay in wait for the brutal colonel.

VIII

The twenty-fifth of January. Morning.
A quiet street comes to life.
The majestic sun shows its face.

Varela awakes, vaguely afraid.
His conscience is screaming at him:
Tyrant! Murderer! Thief! Criminal!
And he shakes and shakes from fear.
He no longer walks as before, martially.
And then suddenly, strikingly, elegantly,
A round object flies through the air...
...and justice, long awaited, has been done!
Kurt Wilckens has avenged the affront!
The people of Argentina can feel free
Their noble spirit has at last been cleansed
Of the tenacious stain that man represented
And they can show their faces with dignity.
But our hero, the redeemer of that morning,
Who took up his cross quietly, with calm,
Was also wounded by his own bomb
Whose light reached off to the horizon.
He endured, Christlike, the mockery,
the insults, and the official ridicule
And serenely, calmly and happily
Withstood the hatred of the state.
And the law, that one-sided law
That is never used on the lord and master,
Punished he who killed but one man
While respecting he who ordered
The deaths of one thousand.
And so the hero was incarcerated
His body suffering, wracked with pain,
And he waited, patiently waited,
For his punishment, atrocious and inhumane.

IX
The sixteenth of June. Night.
Dense shadows. There's no light in the prison.
A poisonous reptile glides

Across the stones of that mansion.
He approaches the cell of a weary man,
His tranquility written on his face,
His mind lost in a peaceful dream.
Crossing the threshold of the cell,
The man steps forward, his voice ringing:
"Are you Kurt Wilckens, the prisoner,
Who sullied the honor of our nation?"
The wounded man replied, "I have avenged
A vile, despicable act of repression..."
But his sentence was left unfinished,
He was cut off by the sound of a gun.
And this Christ, this hero, this brave man
Lowered his head one last time
As a cowardly and murderous bullet
Tore apart his generous heart.
A terrible clamor arises among the people
As they awake to hear the ghastly news,
They desire to have at their mercy
Pérez Millán, that infamous villain.

X

Who put the gun in the hand of the criminal?
Who followed his orders so very well?
Was it his patriotism that drove him to murder?
Or was he but the tool of another?
No, there's no room for doubt—in life, Kurt Wilckens
Was a shining star, an emblem, an icon of justice.
Out of love, he bore his cross for us!
And so the state and the clergy,
The armed forces and even the bourgeoisie
Had to join forces and arm the hand
Of an idiot, an imbecile, a patsy!
And now that it's all over, two faces remain:
Kurt G. Wilckens and Pérez Millán!

Who is with the noble altruist?
And who is with Pérez, the dog?

XI

Noble people of Argentina!
Your brow has been cleansed of all shame:
But never forget the hero of January
Whose altruism in blood was paid!
Never forget him! Ponder the deed
Of this martyr, whose equals number just one:
Noble Simón Radowitzky
Who still rots in his infernal prison.
Two heroes, two great men of nobility,
Two stars shining brightly above,
Who have pointed the way, happily,
With their bombs, thrown with love.

If we hadn't personally collected the testimonies, flyers, communiques, etc., we wouldn't have believed that, even in the most remote corners of the country, there were people who felt the need to express their support for the anarchist avenger and their anger at his murder. The railway workers of Añatuya, Santiago del Estero, for example, distributed a flyer retelling his life story that referred to him as "a symbol of Freedom and Justice." Or there's the Anarchist Thought group in Comodoro Rivadavia, which called him "the bravest man to have ever emerged from the ranks of the people." Or the Amalgamated Trade Union of Tamangueyú, which promised Wilckens that they would avenge his death. Or the anarchist group in General O'Brien (Buenos Aires province) that organized a protest, or the union that made a proclamation in distant Oran, or in La Rioja, where there wasn't even a union, but a group of workers nevertheless got together and publicly stated, "May the blood of this stoic martyr increase the dynamism and moral force of the libertarian red flag." Or in General Pico (La Pampa), where a young Jacobo Prince—who would later become one of the leading thinkers of the libertarian movement—was imprisoned for organizing a public event in homage to Wilckens.

The same thing occurred abroad, where none of the anarchist publications of Europe, Asia, and the Americas failed to provide in-depth coverage. But the country where the news caused the greatest impact, of course, was Germany. In Berlin, the Koensigsstadt beerhall hosted an event protesting "the murder of the revolutionary Kurt Wilckens in a Buenos Aires prison." The event was organized by the Berlin Anarcho-Syndicalist Federation's hiring hall and featured speeches by Rudolf Rocker and Augustin Souchy. The posters advertising the event read:

> Wilckens was murdered in prison before he could face trial. Argentina's reactionaries were afraid that the trial would expose the bestial methods they had employed to repress the proletariat. Workers, protest against international fascism with your presence!

There was also a public meeting held in Hamburg. More than eight hundred people showed up at the Vaterland assembly hall. The *Alarm* devoted five whole pages to the life of Wilckens and the speeches made at the popular assembly, which was presided over by C. Langer, the newspaper's editor and a close friend of the assassinated worker. Langer's speech was a beautiful farewell to a comrade who had perished in a distant land. He described the massacre of the workers in Patagonia, the general strike that was spontaneously declared after Wilckens was killed, and the shootout in front of the union hall, while criticizing the Argentine authorities for refusing to turn over the body of the murdered anarchist. He finished the speech by quoting the last words of one of the Chicago martyrs, the German August Spies: "The day will come when our silence will be more powerful than the voices you strangle today."

The German libertarians printed eight thousand handbills explaining the attitude of Wilckens and the massacre in Patagonia.

Another two thousand, bearing his portrait, were sent to anarchist groups across Europe.

Remember that, in those years, Germany was suffering from hunger and continuous political strife. They were years of misery and bloodshed. This makes it all the more remarkable that Germany's anarchists still had time and energy to spare on an event that had occurred thousands of miles away. And there was an incident that speaks of their German precision: upon learning that the Argentine Navy training frigate *Presidente Sarmiento* would be visiting Hamburg, anarchist workers boarded the ship and distributed the following flyer (written in Spanish, of course) among the crestfallen cadets:

> Argentines! Your capitalist government has treacherously murdered our comrade Kurt Wilckens, the assassin of the bloodthirsty Colonel Varela. Varela ordered the execution of 1,500 striking workers in Patagonia. Kurt Wilckens freed your land and your people of this beast. We sympathize with the revolutionaries of Argentina and we send fraternal greetings to her oppressed people. In turn, we have nothing but contempt and abhorrence for her government and dominant class.
>
> THE REVOLUTIONARY WORKERS OF HAMBURG
> (Free Anarchist Federation)

Later on, the federation will print postcards with his portrait and distribute them around Europe and the Americas so that his action will not be forgotten. The *Alarm* will also run a drawing of Wilckens on its front page.

German workers will organize a third meeting commemorating Wilckens's death, in the city of Elberfeld, where the union hiring hall drafts a resolution protesting the assassination and forwards it to the Argentine ambassador.

The secretariat of the International Workers Association (IWPA), based in Berlin, will draft a manifesto entitled "Kurt Wilckens, Murdered in the Dungeons of Argentina." Translated into several languages, it will be reprinted in labor newspapers around the world.

But the protests were not limited to Germany. In Austria, during a general assembly of the Federation of Libertarian Socialists, the anti-militarist thinker Pierre Ramus gave a talk entitled "Kurt Wilckens and the Reaction in Argentina":

> The name of Kurt Wilckens, like that of August Reinsdorf, another noble avenger, deserves to live on in the memory of the German proletariat, spurring it on to liberate itself from the idiocy of German nationalism. In Wilckens, we venerate a treasure of our international movement. His self-sacrifice on behalf of his Argentine brothers has made him into one of the leading lights of the German proletariat.

In Norway, the union hiring hall in Christiana, as Oslo was then called, held a protest on July 4th denouncing the death of Wilckens and the execution of workers in Patagonia, forwarding a written protest to the Argentine ambassador in Norway.

In Chile, Wilckens's death will have a special impact. After all, the German had avenged the deaths of countless chilotes in the south. A public meeting is held on Sunday, June 24th at 4 p.m. in Santiago—in the Alameda, at the foot of the statue of O'Higgins—as part of the preparations for a four-hour work stoppage that Tuesday. At the meeting, a variety of speakers attest to "the horrific crimes committed by the sinister Colonel Varela in the Magellanic region, crimes that were avenged by the hand of Wilckens, who banished this repugnant uniformed assassin from the face of the earth."

The anarchist even receives his tributes in Iquique, in the pages of the weekly newspaper *El Sembrador*.

Before we finish our commemoration of Wilckens, we would like to reprint four short texts that were written about him, forming a sort of small anthology.

The first offers a somewhat religious image, with his image and the following epigraph printed on the obverse side:

KURT WILCKENS—Hero and Martyr
(Treacherously murdered by the patriotic hordes in the hours
before dawn on June 16th, 1923, while he slept in the Federal
Prison).

And on the reverse, there is a pagan prayer:

THE PEOPLE SING!
Wilckens! The first image that flowers in the mind is the
heart of Jesus, open to the world.
Wilckens! And we see the open hearts of the people, freeing
our brother Simón.[10]
Wilckens! And amidst the mists of the past, there appear,
radiant and vigorous, the heroes who have been ignored and
forgotten: Lingg,[11] surrounded by bombs in his solitary cave;
Bresci,[12] facing Umberto with his smoking revolver; Caserio,[13] smiling, looking for the heart of Sadi Carnot, his dagger
hidden in a bouquet of freshly cut flowers; Angiolillo;[14] Orsini;[15]
Ravachol…![16]
The people sing their song of death after valiantly struggling
in the fight for progress. Sing! And when it's not Jesus who
comes to us down the years, with the bloody heart of a pariah, it's
Wilckens, supremely tragic, destroying himself in one fatal push
designed to ensure the freedom of lives that are just now beginning, their dreams in the making, their hopes radiating from the
beautiful lips, the beautiful eyes of a young girl.
The people sing their song of death. And amidst the tears of
mothers, the illusions of brides, and the portentous yearnings of
the young, the world embraces the heart of Jesus and the bomb
of Wilckens.

Hail Anarchy!
GRUPO CLARIDAD

The next reading comes from the pen of the playwright
González Pacheco:

THE DEATH OF KURT WILCKENS

And so Wilckens, in turn, has also been killed. It seems that this could have been foreseen and that perhaps he himself even expected it: a life for a life, a death for a death. Only those murderers who are lost in the shadow of their crime try to avoid the consequences, lying in wait and striking out at their pursuers. They must be killed like vipers, hiding in the crevices of their instincts, or like wild beasts, in the wilderness of their conscience...

Wilckens was not one of those. His comrades know that he was a noble man: his blue eyes kissed the mountaintops, his spirit soared like gossamer in the wind. That he was a good man, sensitive and responsible. And that once he entered into the terrible trance of the avenger of the people, he surely foresaw that it would be his downfall.

Yes. Wilckens knew all this. Every great man can feel his destiny as if it were a bird of prey tearing out his entrails. He knew that, sooner or later, he would be captured, that he would destroy himself, falling at the feet of a tyrant or dying on the barricades. And so he took no stock in his own death.

Wilckens knew. He who doesn't know, who is but a poor fool, is his murderer. Small-minded and vicious, observe him trying to feign madness, clumsily alleging hallucinations. Now a hero to the military, they will soon see him as a vulgar, irresponsible exhibitionist. He scorns the gravity of his action, even his motive, to play the fool before the judges. Take him away, gentlemen!

Our history has no need to remember this treacherous scoundrel. It needs neither another martyr nor another prisoner. The images of Kurt Wilckens and Simón Radowitzky are engraved on our hearts!

If the people can be said have a face, a soul, and a will, then these men are the people of Argentina. We recognize ourselves in them and we progress through them. Youth and maturity, fervor and reflection, tenderness and strength: they find their unity at two different ages, like the march of the ideal down the years...

Wilckens, like Radowitzky, foresaw prison and death. They were great men. And all greatness is fatal. Onward!

R. GONZÁLEZ PACHECO

This next text appeared on the second anniversary of the death of Wilckens, in June 1925. By Severino Di Giovanni, it was originally written in Italian and published in his magazine *Culmine*. It is the first piece that the violent Italian anarchist wrote on Wilckens. We have decided to reproduce it for the sole reason that it was written by the anarchist expropriator, a man who has gone down in history as a gunman, a common criminal. *Culmine* printed an engraving of Wilckens by Lluch, accompanied by the inscription "GIVE FLOWERS TO THE FALLEN REBEL" and followed by Di Giovanni's article:

WILCKENS

Let us remember each stage of his industrious, heroic life: let us remember him as a simple soldier in far-off Germany, let us remember him in the heart of the mines of the Ruhr, let us remember him as a rebellious agitator in the state of Virginia. Obscure and anonymous in his demolition work, visionary in the colossal work he accomplished. A conscious and humane vigilante, he jeopardized his own life to save a little girl who had innocently put herself in danger. And, though wounded, in his constant obsession with punishing the butcher, he fired several shots from his revolver after throwing his bomb.

Beautiful and terrible, kindly and vengeful, this is how we remember him on the second anniversary of his death.

Glory, oh Kurt Wilckens, valiant hero!

We too, a rebel phalanx of miners in the dark belly of humanity, beat our destructive pickaxes against the iron walls of prejudice by the weak light of a lamp. In this dark and dreadful cavern, we cannot help but raise our metallic voices so we can at least hear their echo, which brings with it a virile awakening.

And if the surviving butchers of the 1,500 proletarians dismembered in the distand land of Santa Cruz haven't been defeaned by this year's protests, this doesn't mean that the immense, nameless masses—who have lived through frightening times and who have been rescued from the immense blood sacrifice ordered by Colonel Varela and his men, all of them drunk on hate, wine, and blood—have forgotten their avenger, the selfless Wilckens.

They tremble with fear, the intellectual authors of that bloody orgy that brought such shame on our...democratic land, which owes its very existence to Bernadino Rivadavia. Those who managed to save themselves, living ghosts who have been reduced by your terror to the most pitiable misery, pay homage in these days to the executioner of Varela and unfurl the black flag of human revolt.

The last piece on Wilckens that we wish to cite was published by the newspaper *La Antorcha* on Friday, September 14th, 1923:

THE GRAVE OF KURT WILCKENS
Path 3, Row 4, Grave 57

A young comrade and I spent many hours trying to find the poorest, least hospitable and most isolated grave in the cemetery, certain it would be that of Kurt Wilckens. Our thoughts turned to the words written by Eugenio Noel after visiting the grave of Francisco Ferrer. Accompanied by a group of young republicans, he too searched in the most miserable and desolate part of the civil cemetery. We cannot help but be humbled, which is deeply human and even necessary. Men of action would rather forget the hard ground that will one day cover them. The urgency of their lives demands it. You can therefore be sure to find the resting place of a man who sowed many seeds, who gave his all for the young, for freedom, and for life in a cold grave unadorned by flowers and memorials. We had no way of being sure of the exact location of his grave. We unfolded an old, deteriorating page from a newspaper offering the workers a guide to his tomb as a memorial to a bygone struggle. Path 3...Path 3 is the section for the poor, the terminally ill, the ground meat produced by the jails and hospitals. Of course it had to be here: there was nowhere sadder or more desolate. After crossing and recrossing the endless rows and stopping before innumerable graves, always the most sordid, we finally found a clue. At the back of the cemetery, near the perimeter wall and just one hundred meters away from the railway tracks whose strident whistles constantly interrupt the peace of the dead, Path 3 can be found. Here you will not find the cheerful, infantile assortment of white tombstones scattered at the foot of the low, rolling hill. This is a wasteland, a desert. Old dirt, barren and yellow, covers everything. On the hill, among the graves of the rich, trees are cared for almost religiously. Here there are no trees. There are only small, rustic crosses battered by the wind and a few scrawny plants piously placed on the graves. This is the free section, the one filled with nameless suicides, the one giving the vagabond a resting place, the merciful common grave, the dirt that will cover up those exiled from the hospitals and jails. Path 3, Row 4...we're now at the very back. It won't take long to find his grave. It must be in this unforgiving soil. Row 4 is some twenty steps from a path that goes off to the old cemetery wall. Here is where we will look for the grave of our comrade. Row 4 is a small, rectangular elevation of land some thirty meters long. On each side, in two parallel lines, are the graves. Overturned crosses, withered flowers, brass plaques painted black with names and dates scrawled in white. In Row 4, there are three or four bodies per grave. One grave is dug each day and it will be filled by nightfall. Path 3, Row 4, Grave 58...at the far end of the row, next to a small garden, there's one pile of earth that stands out. It's marked with a brass plaque. We advance slowly along the narrowed path, which has been turned to mud by the recent rains. There are no flowers in this garden, nothing more than a few lifeless shrubs and a crude brick border separating them from the barren earth. Here is Grave 58, and here the flesh of Kurt

Wilckens decomposes. The ephemeral rejoins the eternal energy of life. When the rage of the workers overflowed into the streets, the police quietly buried his body. Then, as the days went by, when peace and calm reigned once again, anonymous hands provided a few flowers for the rough garden that covers his grave. We read upon the plaque that "KURT WILCKENS DIED ON JULY 18, 1923 AS A CONSEQUENCE OF HIS BELIEFS. HIS ACTIONS LIVE ON IN THE MINDS OF HIS COMRADES." We remain there for a while, one or two hours, silently standing before Grave 58. An infinity of ideas and memories arise in our minds. Those anonymous hands, the hands of the workers, the hands that procured flowers for his grave and wrote the memorial, are symbolic of an ideal that will never die, that will always be ready to spring to life.

How beautiful and simple it all is!

It's like the story of that Russian peasant who, when Kropotkin died, crossed the steppe on foot to help dig his grave in the hardened, icy ground. He knew that a saint had died and that the grave of a saint should be dug by the rough arms of a peasant. Our presence, that of two young men standing before such a pitiful grave, awakens the curiosity of two or three other mourners. One of them approaches and reads the name of Kurt Wilckens on the plaque. Silently, he takes a violet from the bouquet he carries and places it on the grave.

The morning is a cold one and the sky is filled with black clouds. A persistent gale continuously lashes out at us. Trains speed by on the nearby tracks. Mud sticks to our boots and climbs its way up our pant legs. We head back to town. The words we exchange on our return journey, spoken slowly and sadly, capture the desolate vision of the third path, whose barren, yellow soil is nourished by the remains of a comrade whose life can be summed up in the greatness of two dates: January 25th, 1923 and June 16th, 1923. We return to town somewhat troubled but also filled with hope, reminiscent of that sunny morning in which Kurt, face to face with the beast, made the air ring out with the thundering, avenging voice of dynamite.

—H. An. Jover

But anarchists have never placed much importance in graves. They have always preferred cremation and scattered ashes. For them, cemeteries and their upkeep are irrational and senseless. A dead body has absolutely nothing to do with the memory or emulation of heroes. This is why the above article is so surprising, as is the one commemorating the assassination published five years later in *La Protesta*, although the author of the latter will apologize for his sentiments even as he expresses them:

We would like to say one more thing. And this is of a more intimate nature: without being idolatrous, as we are the only family of the avenger of those massacred in Patagonia, we would have liked to preserve the grave of our unforgettable comrade in the same way that Chicago's Waldheim Cemetery has preserved the memory of its five martyrs with a small monument. Nobody has thought of this detail, and perhaps the hour is now too late to do the same with the grave of our poor friend. We aren't idolaters, but perhaps it would have been preferable for the anarchists of Argentina to have conserved for posterity the location where Wilckens's remains were buried in the dark of the night. Future generations would not have been able to pass in front of that modest tomb without thinking of social justice, just as no one can walk through Waldheim Cemetery without clenching their fists at the memory of that infamous judicial crime in Chicago.

La Protesta will print the following, one year later:

We are iconoclasts in our house, we do not recognize any idols. But when our comrades arrive, the first thing they notice is the portrait of Kurt Wilckens that we have prominently displayed where all visitors can see it. We are right to take pride in our hero, in his private life, and in his long history of revolutionary activity, which culminated in a deed that was both vengeful and deeply human. Although it has not been long since Wilckens left our side, he appears as a symbol, a legendary figure.

We loved him as a brother before January 25th, 1923. We learned to admire him after that memorable date and we have venerated him, almost as if he were a saint, since June 16th of that same year.

We have never met another man of such moral purity. His life was a continual torment because few men are as good as him, and because life is full of such pain that a man with his temperament must have felt the victim of endless lacerations. He was a man who treated others as if we were already living in the society of tomorrow. His kindness, his honesty, and his nobility almost bordered on mysticism, but behind his evangelical softness, he had an energy and a firmness of steel. Those who didn't know him well never suspected it.

That same issue of *La Protesta* also carries the following report:

We have been told that the pariahs of the great estates in the far south idolize Wilckens and that there is a mountain, whose name we cannot recall, where an anonymous hand has carved the name of our friend into stone: it will be many years before that inscription is erased. But it will be even more years until the proletariat forgets the righteous vengeance of Kurt Wilckens.

In the panorama of Argentina in the 1920s, so worthy of Edgar Allan Poe, we have somehow managed to overlook the figure of Jorge Ernesto Pérez Millán Temperley.

What was this that aristocratic youth doing in the uniform of a prison guard, assigned to watch over Wilckens? Is this all a coincidence, or is there something stranger at work here? But if we go back further, what was Jorge Ernesto Pérez Millán Temperley doing in Santa Cruz in 1920, disguised as a gendarme? And what was Jorge Ernesto Pérez Millán Temperley doing at Commander Varela's wake, shooing away reporters?

Jorge Ernesto Pérez Millán Temperley deserves close study because he is a prototypical figure of the far right. Here we are referring to the members of those right-wing "self-defense" forces that almost always serve as the civilian wing of military dictatorships and the secret police.

Pérez Millán's crime is only comparable to those committed by torturers or those hunters who enjoy watching their game suffer, helpless, before they die. He resembles those fox hunters in the south who skin their prey alive, making the animals suffer because—according to them—they are "vermin," when in reality it's only because of their sadistic temperament.

Pérez Millán acted sadistically and derived pleasure from the kill. Omnipotent, he knew that he would be well protected, that his victim didn't even have so much as a penknife to defend himself. And that he would not only be cornered, he would be asleep.

Pérez Millán must have enjoyed preparing for the kill. Knowing that Wilckens would be left to his mercy and his alone must have given him a special pleasure.

Pérez Millán, the son of Ernesto Pérez Millán and Florencia Temperley, was twenty-four years old when he killed Wilckens. In his adolescence, his parents worried about his wild character. He dropped out of school and ran away from home. The police brought him back, but it was no use. He was determined to make a name for himself, one way or another. He was obsessed with guns. He collected firearms catalogs from all over the world. He was something of a specialist. A devout Catholic—he was fond of waking early to attend mass at 6:30 a.m., going to confession, and then taking communion—a nationalist and an "anti-liberal," at the age of twenty-one he joined an organizing committee of the Radical Civic Union. There he often handled security. He stood out because of his family background. When the organizing committee began recruiting gendarmes for the south, Pérez Millán was one of the first to sign up—not out of need, but out of a thirst for adventure.

He fought at El Cerrito, but his performance was rather lackluster. He was wounded and immediately surrendered, joining El Toscano's hostages.

Liberated by Lieutenant Colonel Varela when the strikers agreed to the settlement, Pérez Millán returned to Buenos Aires. At the beginning of 1922, while Varela was liquidating the last rebel workers, Pérez Millán used his Radical friends to get a job as a coast guard cadet. He was assigned to the customs authority. He liked wearing a uniform and belonging to a militarized service corps. But he was fired after eleven months for misconduct—he had many conflicts with his colleagues and superiors—although he will insist that he resigned.

Again he turned to his Radical friends, who offered him a job selling advertisements in the party newspaper, *La Época*. He worked at the newspaper for quite a while but never felt comfortable there. Besides, he had found a new group of friends in the Argentine Patriotic League. He had become a fanatical follower of Dr. Manuel Carlés.

And then Commander Varela died on January 25th, 1923. Pérez Millán felt deeply indebted to the officer for having rescued him from the strikers in Santa Cruz. He also felt like they were much more closely related than they actually were—as we have said, their only kinship ties were through marriage. At the wake, he refused to leave the coffin and, with his hands shaking but his voice roaring, he told everyone who approached that he would avenge the officer's death.

And here begins a very shameful tale. Prison guards must be approved not only by the warden, but by Justice Minister Marcó himself. And what's more, Pérez Millán's application was accepted on January 27th, the day after Varela's funeral and two days after the assassination. It's clear that the plot was first prepared while the body was still warm, but that someone then decided to postpone it. Pérez Millán begins working at the jail where Wilckens is being held on February 9th. But then something must have happened or somebody must have opposed the plan, because then Wilckens is transferred to the prison on Calle Caseros, where Pérez Millán "coincidentally" follows him two weeks later. It's clear that there is more than one person involved, and that someone very powerful is pulling the strings. Pérez Millán works there until June 2nd, when he is given ten days off. He reappears on the 16th and is assigned to the cell block where Wilckens is imprisoned. And then he shoots his victim in cold blood.

Pérez Millán Temperley will be rescued. To start with, he isn't treated like a dangerous criminal. They don't even handcuff him. On the morning of the crime, he has his picture taken, striking arrogant poses and wearing a bandolier filled with cartridges, which makes him look more dignified. Then, accompanied by another prison guard, he marches off in military step. He's handsome and keeps his back straight, but his pallor and refined manners remain inescapable. *Crítica* alleges that Pérez Millán is homosexual. If true, it wouldn't make his crime any better or any worse.

The first articles that appear in conservative newspapers try to understand him and look for extenuating circumstances. *La Razón* states that, while he was guarding Wilckens, Pérez Millán was yearning for his girlfriend and had a hallucination: he thought he saw one of the inmate's crutches pointing at him and heard the sound of a rooster crowing. This more or less resembles Pérez Millán's initial statement to the police, which is nevertheless somewhat less fantastic:

(The undersigned) was on duty when he heard a noise that seemed to come from one of the first cells, which added to the memories of his past suffering and the stress he had been under since he began working as a prison guard. Upon investigating the first cell, which was occupied by Kurt Wilckens, he saw the inmate sitting up in his bunk and, staring directly at the undersigned, pointing or directing something at him that cast a horizontal shadow. Not knowing if he was in grave danger or was merely the victim of a powerful hallucination, the undersigned instinctively fired his Mauser with the speed and dexterity of a veteran soldier. The sound of the gunshot startled him. When he realized that he had wounded Kurt Wilckens, he uttered phrases that surprised even him.

Pérez Millán begins to feign madness. He has been counseled well. His friends know that he could be imprisoned for life for such a cold-blooded crime. For the moment, the forensic specialist Dr. Vailatti notes that:

> Pérez Millán, who has been subjected to a psychiatric examination, shows symptoms of having experienced a light nervous breakdown. At certain points of the examination, he showed signs of memory loss and had difficulty remembering certain periods of his life, which is uncharacteristic of the subject and his level of education.

Pérez Millán is taken to Precinct 28 and then to the National Prison instead of the city jail, which is where he should have been held while awaiting trial. He is not held with the other inmates and his cell is under constant guard. There are fears of a revenge killing.

Judge García Ramos then sentences him to eight years in prison, basing his decision on:

> Pérez Millán's statements concerning his past activities, his adventures, his idealism, his artistic inclinations, his neurasthenia, his participation in the struggle against the revolutionary strikers in the south and the vandalism he witnessed there, his passionate love affair with his first girlfriend, his attraction to the nomadic life, and the lack of a harmonious relationship with his family.

As we can see, these are very idyllic motives for murdering a defenseless prisoner. According to the judge, "his preexisting psychological anomalies, his unimpeachable prior conduct and his youth move us to impose the minimum sentence: eight years."

The verdict is announced fourteen months after the crime. Such a simple matter, with a clearly identified killer, is dragged out until the public forgets about it. The Court of Appeals will later confirm the sentence.

In April 1925, Pérez Millán is transferred to the mental hospital on Calle Vieytes. His friends and family believe that he will be safer there. To facilitate the transfer, a medical report is prepared stating that, "Pérez Millán suffers from a delirium of systematic persecution, characteristic of degenerates." With this diagnosis, he can be transferred to the mental hospital and is placed in the wing for well-behaved patients, the ones from good families. He shares a cell with José Eugenio Zuloaga, another scion of high society. On November 8th, Pérez Millán and Zuloaga get into a fistfight and have to be separated. The former is taken to the cell across the hall. All of these cells can be accessed from a wing housing eleven patients of limited means. Among them is a twenty-six-year-old Yugoslav from Dubrovnik named Esteban Lucich. He is short and is slightly hunched over. Everyone treats him like he's harmless, even though he's there for having shot Dr. Francisco de la Vega to death six years beforehand. Lucich had been the doctor's servant, but was fired when his master began to notice signs of madness. The Yugoslav's reaction was to kill him and he was sentenced to seventeen and a half years in prison. After a few months' imprisonment, however, he was transferred to the mental hospital on Calle Vieytes because of his evident madness.

Despite his appearance, Lucich is one of the mental hospital's most beloved patients. He earns a little money by working as a servant for the more well-off nurses. He shines their shoes, he makes beds for them, he sweeps the floor. He never gets upset and no one sees him as anything but "the good lunatic." This lasts until the morning of November 9th, 1925.

That spring day, Pérez Millán seems edgy and ill at ease. He has been writing at his desk since very early that morning, not even bothering to eat breakfast. He carries on until lunchtime, when he puts down his pen and eats silently before continuing with his letter.

At 12:30, Lucich, "the good lunatic," asks with his characteristic humility to enter the wing housing the well-to-do patients. He normally doesn't even bother to ask and simply goes in. No one has any objections, so he heads towards Cell 3, which had been occupied by Pérez Millán until the day before. He asks for him. Zuloaga tells him that they moved his former cellmate to Cell 4, across the hall. Lucich crosses the hall and looks through the doorway to see Pérez Millán writing at his desk. Lucich steps forward, draws a pistol from his pocket, aims at Pérez Millán and tells him, "This is from Wilckens!"

Startled, Pérez Millán turns around and takes a bullet in the chest. He throws himself to the floor like a cat, saving himself from the second gunshot. The bullet lodges itself in the wall. He grabs the hunchback by the arm and pulls him to the ground. Lucich fires again, the bullet grazing Pérez Millán's pelvis and lodging itself in his left thigh. But the victim has managed to take control of the situation. He disarms the Yugoslav and starts beating him. A nurse arrives, alerted by the hysterical cries of the patients, and saves Lucich from Pérez Millán.

Lucich is put in a straitjacket while Pérez Millán is taken to the emergency room. The wound in his chest is quite serious, but the doctors are confident they can save him. After the operation, Pérez Millán is given thirty days of bed rest.

The gunshots in the Las Mercedes Mental Hospital reawaken a story that had been buried by the government and the army. It's a taboo subject because no investigation has occurred and no explanation has been given; everyone skirts the issue whenever some naïve soul dares to ask what really happened in Patagonia.

It all comes flooding back: the images of the executions in the far south, the controversial figure of Lieutenant

Colonel Varela and the strange Nordic worker who avenged his copper-skinned brothers.

But how wasa new episode in this never-ending story possible? How could Pérez Millán have been attacked when such pains had been taken to place him beyond the reach of the long arm of vengeance? Was he not being held in the safest of places?

But had Lucich decided on his own to kill Pérez Millán? No. This was a plot that could only have been hatched by those incredible anarchists who never give up, no matter how many times they've had a lesson beaten into them. Is Lucich an anarchist? No. He was a member of the FORA when he was working as a servant, but that's not enough to define him ideologically. It's clear that Lucich was armed by someone else, that he was used as a tool. Straitjacketed, Lucich is interrogated. But no matter how many times he's beaten, he continues to parrot the line it seems he had been told to memorize: "I found the revolver on Pérez Millán's desk. When he started hitting me, I shot him in self-defense."

The interrogation has to be brought to a halt because the lunatic is in such a state of excitement that it's impossible for him to have an orderly conversation. But the investigation is in the hands of none other than Inspector Santiago, the chief investigator for the Buenos Aires police. He is lucid, quick on his feet, and has the nose of a bloodhound. Possessing the mentality of the capital city, he knows when it's time to shoot and when it's time to go soft. A Radical with his own brand of politics, he's not above playing the numbers games organized by the local party boss. He has a deep understanding of human nature and won't let those responsible for the events at the mental hospital get away so easily. He realizes, after interrogating him for only two minutes, that Lucich did not act alone. Behind him there's someone bold and intelligent who managed to overcome every barrier to the vengeance promised by the anarchists. Santiago asks for a complete list of the mental hospital's patients and employees. He scans the list and suddenly jumps up from his seat, as if everything had been cleared up, shouting, "Boris Wladimirovich!"

Exactly: Boris Wladimirovich. It couldn't have happened any other way. As if we were living through a tale of the Russian Revolution, full of Bulgarian conspirators or Serbia's Black Hand. The Las Mercedes Mental Hospital has been treating none other than Boris Wladimirovich, who was transferred from Ushuaia just two months earlier. But how did Boris Wladimirovich end up at the asylum on Calle Vieytes?

Boris is brought in on a stretcher because he's all but paralyzed. The police officer and the enigmatic anarchist are face to face. The shrewd officer looks ready to eat him alive. Boris Wladimirovich smiles back at him, as if to say that he's already won this round.

And who is Boris Wladimirovich? He's a true anarchist, an import, a White Russian with decades of agitation and conspiracy under his belt. He resembles a character from Hemingway, Melville, Jack London, Joseph Conrad with his large black mustache, wavy hair, and penetrating eyes. This is how the newspaper *La Prensa* describes him:

> The agitator Germán Boris Wladimirovich, imprisoned for having robbed the Perazzo currency exchange, is not a common criminal. Highly educated, he has written several books, taught university-level classes, and participated in the most important anarchist congresses organized by Russian exiles in Europe before the revolution, but the abuse of alcohol and tobacco had turned him into a shell of who he once was by the time he arrived in our country. The attempted robbery of the Perazzo currency exchange, carried out with the goal of acquiring funds to start a subversive newspaper, shows his instability. When he's at his best, however, he reveals himself to be an educated man capable of persuasively expressing his ideas and winning people over. He has recently been transferred away from Ushuaia as his mental state remains unstable and he has lost the use of his lower extremities. Currently in treatment, he spends most of the day in bed as it is difficult for him to walk for any length of time.

The assessment of *La Prensa* is accurate for the most part, although the article does contain a few errors that will later be rectified. It seems that Wladimirovich isn't crazy but only wants to appear that way. And he robbed the Perazzo currency exchange not because he was unstable but because he wanted to put his ideals into action. He's an intellectual, it's true, but he also has one quality rarely seen among intellectuals: a love for action. Wladimirovich is one of Europe's most experienced terrorists, responsible for a string of bombings in Moscow, Leningrad, Paris, and Barcelona.

But let's go back a bit. We can learn more about this outlandish character by examining the events of May 1919. He tries to rob the Perazzo currency exchange in Chacarita. He fails. The three robbers must flee. One of them kills a police officer and wounds another but is captured when he runs out of bullets. He turns out to be Andrés Babby, a thirty-year-old anarchist from Bukovina with a long record as an agitator. Babby says that he doesn't know the identities of his two companions and refuses to say another word. An anonymous informant tells the police that he lives at Corrientes 1970. The building manager is forthcoming: a person with the last name Babby does live there, sharing a room with a professor, Germán Boris Wladimirovich. The police ask to speak with the professor. No. Impossible, the professor hasn't been seen since May 19th—the day of the attempted robbery—and he left carrying suitcases.

When shown a photo of Boris Wladimirovich, the employees of the currency exchange identify him as one of the robbers. He's also a known anarchist. It's also known that he's a cosmography enthusiast and that he makes periodic visits to the observatory in La Plata, where he has several friends. At the observatory, they find Boris Wladimirovich's suitcases, which are full of anarchist publications and books, his letters and his own writings. An employee of the observatory and a friend of Boris, who never suspected the Russian heretic's other activities, says that he doesn't know where to find him but that Juan Matrichenko, a Ukrainian who lives in Berisso, might know. The investigators seek out Matrichenko and tell him that they wish to discover the whereabouts of the fugitive, claiming that they fear he has been kidnapped. The naïve, concerned Matrichenko rapidly consoles them: he referred the professor, who had told him that he needed to rest, to a friend in San Ignacio, Misiones. He adds that the chauffeur Luis Cheli might know which day he left, as Wladimirovich always uses his services.

Two birds with one stone. While they search the home of the chauffeur, they telegraph the police in Posadas.

They find anarchist literature in Cheli's room and the employees of the currency exchange recognize him as the man who drove the getaway car. Everything has been cleared up. But the main protagonist of the early years of the anarchist expropriators is still at large.

Wladimirovich is finally arrested in San Ignacio, Misiones. The police don't understand how this man could be a criminal. He looks like a professor, an intellectual. He's good-natured and has intelligent eyes, though his face shows what seems to be a great deal of personal suffering. His arrest causes such a stir in Posadas that the governor of Misiones himself, Dr. Barreiro, comes to the police station and converses with the anarchist for several hours. And when a group of police officers under the command of Commissioner Foppiano arrive from Buenos Aires to retrieve the prisoner, the governor decides to accompany them back to the capital by train.

Before departing, the police and the provincial authorities take a picture for posterity. All of them are seated, acrimonious and haughty, while Boris Wladimirovich stands behind them. The prisoner, who has a Nietzschean look, appears to be meditating, unconcerned with what's going on around him, while the important government functionaries stare tensely at the camera.

In the meantime, the police have successfully confirmed his identity. He is Russian, forty-three years old, a widower and a writer by trade. *La Prensa* informs its readers in more detail:

Boris Wladimirovich has many interesting characteristics. He is a doctor, a biologist, and a painter; he has made a name for himself in Russia's avant-garde circles. Though the police have him listed as a draftsman from Montenegro, he is in fact Russian, from a noble family. In his twenties, Boris got engaged to a young revolutionary and soon after renounced his title. It is known that he was a man of good fortune but that he renounced it all for the sake of his ideals. He is a doctor and a biologist but, aside from a temporary teaching position in Zürich, he has never exercised his profession. On the train back to Buenos Aires, Dr. Barreiro listened to him discuss several scientific theses that had captured his attention. In Russia, Boris was a social democrat and served as his country's delegate to the 1904 socialist congress in Geneva.

The police continue to investigate: Boris is the author of many publications, including three books on sociology. He has mastered German, French, and Russian and is familiar with most of his mother country's dialects. He expresses himself relatively well in Spanish. He is a Sunday painter and has left behind twenty-four canvases in Buenos Aires, among them a self-portrait. He has also given talks on anarchism in Berisso, Zarate, and the capital.

But how did this man, an active participant in the European revolutionary movement, end up in Argentina?

Little by little, more details come to light. The death of his wife and the tremendous failure of the Russian Revolution in 1905 take their toll on his spirits. Melancholy to begin with, he finds solace in vodka after suffering a cardiac collapse. He donates his house in Geneva to his comrades—he has already been converted to libertarian ideas—and heads to Paris, where he decides to undertake a long journey to lift his spirits. One of his friends has a brother with a ranch in Santa Fe, Argentina and recommends that he visit him. Boris Wladimirovich arrives in the country in 1909 and makes contact with immigrant labor activists soon afterwards. After resting awhile on his friend's brother's ranch, he heads to

Chaco, where he will spend the next four and a half years. He lives off his meager savings and devotes his time to studying the region, traveling from Paraná to Santiago de Estero, focusing on the Patiño estuary. He lives frugally, but his vodka consumption continues to increase. When World War I breaks out, he finds himself in Tucumán. From there he returns to Buenos Aires. *La Razón* recounts his activities in the capital:

> In Buenos Aires, he was welcomed with open arms by those activists who, despite his long absence from organizing, could not forget his role in the libertarian movement in his home country, which gave him the halo of a prophet, made brighter by his exile. And so he returned to his propagandistic activities, giving talks and recruiting people for the movement, without regard to the size of the venue. When the Vasena strike broke out in January 1919, Boris went to Chacarita to organize a revolutionary committee with a solid base, but the people he found there were completely incompetent, unable to stick to a plan and doing little more than recklessly shooting their guns in all directions at once. His disappointment was immense.

After the Tragic Week, Boris becomes obsessed with Carlés and his followers' threat to "kill all the Russians." "Going Russian hunting" was a popular expression among the young men of the upper and middle bourgeoisie of Buenos Aires who enlisted in the Civil Guard and the Argentine Patriotic League that bloody week in January, committing iniquities in Jewish neighborhoods—for many Argentines, there was no difference between the two.

Boris meditates on this threat and feels it is his duty to warn his countrymen living in Argentina. He must also explain to them the meaning of the October Revolution, which he believes will set men free. And so he becomes obsessed with having his own publication. As he explains in the weeks following his arrest, when he is finally allowed to speak, a newspaper is key because "those who come to Argentina from Russia are the dregs of the people, many of them Jews, and they form an incoherent mass incapable of committing to a serious revolutionary plan, much less implementing a grand theory."

But to publish a newspaper, you need money. He has two options: he can rely on the spare change of the Russian workers and the odd intellectual who is willing to fast for two or three days to help pay for the printing costs of the first issue, or he can set his sights higher. And his family background has left him unaccustomed to making do with little. Though he lives off of what paintings he can sell and the occasional language class, whenever he has money he dines at Marina-Keller, a German restaurant on Calle 25 de Mayo that has an authentic European ambiance and serves genuine Russian vodka. So when he plans to start a newspaper, he feels it necessary to have real money at his disposal. And he begins to hatch a plan. He speaks with Negro Cheli, the anarchist chauffeur who always takes him home when the vodka leaves him unable to find his way on his own. Cheli is a man of action who fought alongside him during the Tragic Week. The chauffeur knows where they can steal the money.

Wladimirovich can also rely on his roommate, Babby, an anarchist who admires him and sees him as his mentor. He's capable of giving his life for the professor.

But it's all in vain. Now all three have been imprisoned. When the police bring Wladimirovich back from Posadas, he confesses to the attempted robbery and claims to bear full responsibility for the crime. He does it to save Babby, who could face the death penalty for having killed a police officer.

Involuntarily, Boris has created a legal controversy. He has turned out to be such an interesting person that, though he's been prevented from speaking to the press, he's nevertheless visited by the interior minister and several Radical legislators who wish to get to know him for themselves. They spend hours conversing with the anarchist intellectual. The interior minister tells the press that the prisoner calmly answered all the questions he asked. This angers the judge overseeing the case, who reminds the government that the prisoner is being held incommunicado and is therefore not allowed to have visitors.

The future does not look bright for these frustrated criminals. Especially for Babby, who has killed a police officer. The Jockey Club has begun collecting money for the family of the officer, whom they describe as having been killed by "an anti-Argentine gang." They gather 2,010 pesos on the first day alone.

La Razón questions Wladimirovich's story that he wanted money for written propaganda. They allege that his goal was to acquire the raw materials needed to manufacture bombs. *Crítica*, on the other hand, describes the three men as resembling the Bonnot Gang, the group of French anarchists who robbed banks across France and Belgium at the turn of the century.

During the opening statements of the trial, the prosecutor, Dr. Costa, asks for the death penalty for Babby, fifteen years for Germán Boris Wladimirovich, and two years for Cheli.

After several long months of imprisonment, Judge Martínez sentences Babby to twenty-five years, Boris Wladimirovich to ten years, and Cheli to one year. On appeal, the prosecution simply asks that Judge Martínez's sentence be upheld. But then something unexpected happens: The judges of the Court of Appeals prove to be more Catholic than the Pope and give the death penalty not only to Babby, but also to Wladimirovich.[17]

(Here we can see the blindness of justice: Wladimirovich, who had committed a robbery but had killed no one, as the shootout between Babby and the police occurred elsewhere, is condemned to death—but Pérez Millán Temperley, who murdered a sleeping man in cold blood, abusing his privileges as a prison guard, only received eight years.)

The death sentence imposed on Wladimirovich proves to be very controversial. The anarchist newspapers describe it as the "class vengeance" of the judges. Court insiders appear surprised by the decision. They feel that it's fair in Babby's case, but Wladimirovich hadn't even fired a weapon. The trial judge feels the same way:

Each man must answer for the consequences of the actions they committed individually. Boris can therefore not be held responsible for the later actions of Babby—which led to the death of Officer Santillán and the wounding of Officer Varela—as there was neither prior conspiracy nor the direct participation of Boris Wladimirovich.

The Court of Appeals instead makes use of the following argument:

The court has shown that the accused formed a conspiracy and a criminal association, as established by Article 25 of the Penal Code. Although Boris Wladimirovich did not participate in the murder of Officer Santillán, he nevertheless bears responsibility for this murder, as the law understands that there is absolute solidarity among the crimes of the conspirators, drawing no distinction between perpetrators and accomplices. (…) Regarding the fact that the prosecutor himself requested a lesser punishment, it is the prerogative of the court to enforce the law, a power that cannot be limited by the requests of the prosecutor.

The decision is signed by Ricardo Seeber, Daniel J. Frías, Sotero F. Vázquez, Octavio González Roura, and Francisco Ramos Mejía.

In a joint statement signed by Manuel Carlés, Admiral Domecq García, and Drs. Mariano Gabastou and Alfredo Grondona, the Argentine Patriotic League expresses its satisfaction with the decision and praises the judges as good Argentines who know that weeds should be pulled out by the root.

But their celebrations are cut short, as two members of the Court of Appeals—Drs. Eduardo Newton and Jorge H. Frías—prove to either be more just or less Argentine, as they refuse to sign off on the sentence. This saves Babby and Wladimirovich from being executed, as the court finds itself forced to issue the following statement:

In light of the inability to impose the death penalty under Article 11 of the Penal Code, which demands the unanimity of the court, Babby and Boris Wladimirovich are hereby sentenced to life in prison.

In Ushuaia. Worse, much worse, than death. Too harsh a punishment for what the Russian émigré had done. That same year, there are common criminals with prior convictions who are condemned to only two or three years in prison. Wladimirovich had no prior convictions, unless you count his participation in social struggles.

When informed of his sentence, the professor Boris Wladimirovich blithely states, "The life of a propagandist such as myself is prone to such contingencies. It's as true today as it will be tomorrow. I know that I will not live to see the triumph of my ideas, but sooner or later others will come along to take my place."

And he leaves behind a statement for the press, written in rather good Spanish. The police seize it and only release the final paragraph, written in a clear, firm hand:

(This incident) will be more easy to understand after the events to come than it was during the trial... I urgently needed money to defend the life of the Russians in Argentina from the crimes committed by the Patriotic League... Here, any and all means are acceptable! I did not hesitate to personally participate in the robbery, as someone else would perhaps not be able to explain their actions to humanity... And my conscience is clean.

—Germán B.

Tomorrow will never come for Zürich's former biology professor. Months later, he will be taken to Ushuaia in shackles, mixed in with a group of common criminals. Although he once ran the risk of being sent to Siberia, it's possible that he never dreamed of being imprisoned in an equally desolate region of such a far-off country.

His health, already broken, went into a rapid decline. Those who knew him in prison have stated that he continued to propagate his ideas among the inmates. His end was approaching, hastened by the poor food, the cold, and the beatings that were the prison's daily bread in those dark years. But, before dying, he will embody the long arm of vengeance against the hero of the Patriotic League, Kurt Wilckens's executioner.

This won't be the last time that the strange figure of the professor Wladimirovich will appear on the front page of Argentina's newspapers (*La Razón* calls him a "curious, sinister, fantastic character").

And now, six years later, Germán Boris Wladimirovich smiles at the threats of the chief investigator. For a police officer as shrewd as Inspector Santiago, the presence of the Russian anarchist in the Las Mercedes Mental Hospital cannot be a coincidence. How did he end up here? He begins to review the institution's files. When Wladimirovich began to "lose his mind" in Ushuaia, Pérez Millán had already been in the asylum on Calle Vieytes for a month and a half. It's clear that Boris had heard the news. According to the doctor in Ushuaia, he showed clear signs of derangement: he didn't eat, he sang old Russian songs, he gesticulated wildly, he couldn't walk, and he spent the day praying on his knees, which could only be a sign of incurable madness for an anarchist...

As Ushuaia was also home to "Saint" Simón Radowitzky—who was explosive enough on his own—the warden didn't have any problems with requesting that Wladimirovich be transferred to Buenos Aires so he could be treated in an asylum. And the only institution that accepted the criminally insane was the one on Calle Vieytes, as Wladimirovich knew quite well.

And so after all the paperwork was filed, the anarchist was transferred to Las Mercedes Mental Hospital. There he was held in a wing housing sixteen criminals until he was brought out on a stretcher to see Inspector Santiago. He's placed face-to-face with the police officer. He looks like a ghost. He's barely forty-nine years old but he looks like he is in his seventies. The only thing he has left is his penetrating gaze. Years of imprisonment have broken him physically, but his eyes still have their old fire.

Although the police officer is convinced that Wladimirovich is the intellectual author of the attack on Pérez Millán, it will be very difficult to prove it. Especially if the attacker—Lucich—only ever repeats that he found the gun on the victim's desk. And so Wladimirovich continues to smile. They can't prove anything. And so his revenge for Wilckens's death is complete.

And it really is all over. The bullet that pierced Pérez Millán's chest was deflected into his abdominal cavity, injuring his stomach and intestines. Though the operation was declared successful, the patient slowly begins to lose strength. His father and Dr. Manuel Carlés remain by his bedside. His heart begins to fail at midnight. At 5:35 the next morning, Pérez Millán dies. Vengeance has taken another life. And the curtain falls on the fourth act of the drama that began in distant Santa Cruz.

Pérez Millán Temperley is buried in La Recoleta Cemetery. His coffin is covered in white flowers tied together with blue and white ribbon, the colors of the Argentine flag. His body is taken from the funeral home at Calle Calao 418 amid hoarse cries of "Long live the army and the fatherland" and "Death to anarchism, maximalism, and agitators." All throughout the night, his coffin had been watched over by a group of young men belonging to the Friends of Order, an affiliate of the Patriotic League.

At the cemetery, these young men are joined by a group of army officers, policemen, prison guards, priests, and Pérez Millán's family. Dr Manuel Carlés is the first to speak, hailing Jorge Ernesto Pérez Millán Temperley as a martyr to patriotism, tradition, family, and God. He's followed by Colonel Oliveros Escola, who repeats several times that the murder will not go unpunished. The final speech is given by Sergeant Eduardo Romero.

When the ceremony is over, the young men leave the cemetery with their teeth clenched and with more hate in their hearts than ever for those workers who dared to rise up against the established order.

The police—as always—are under pressure to clear things up as quickly as possible. Santiago has but one meager trump card, but Wladimirovich proves to be a tough nut to crack. They work him over at the station, trying to soften him up. But the anarchist is accustomed to the cold, hunger, and lead-tipped clubs of Ushuaia and finds it easy to hold up to the lack of sleep, sudden change of cells, starvation, wet floors, and kicks he receives in Buenos Aires.

Inspector Santiago is beginning to sweat ink, but then he receives some unexpected help. A young man who was known as El Tanito in the mental hospital shows up, smiling and acting deferentially. His name is Alejandro Orselli. A twenty-year-old Italian, he has been diagnosed as feeble-minded, although he doesn't look it with his sharp eyes. He saw it all and repeats everything to the eager police officer: "On Sunday, a group of three men came to visit Boris Wladimirovich during visiting hours. One of them gave him a pistol. Taking advantage of the confusion in the hospital that day, Boris went up to Lucich and gave him the gun, putting it in his trouser pocket."

Santiago quickly gets to work. He doesn't need any more details. Who were the three men who visited Boris Wladimirovich? The register is right there. Their names are Timofey Derevianka (Russian), Simón Bolkosky (Russian), and Eduardo Vázquez (Spaniard). Two truly suspicious nationalities.

A dragnet is organized. Their prior records are enough to establish them as co-conspirators. See what angels they are:

Simón Bolkosky, single, Russian, born in 1894. A known anarchist agitator and a member of the South American Russian Federation, he was part of the group that burned down the Church of the Sacred Heart during the Tragic Week. In 1919, the police tried to deport him under the Residence Law, but Yrigoyen let the process get tied up in paperwork.

Timofey Derevianka, Russian, born in Kiev in 1892. During the Tragic Week, he spoke at an anarchist assembly (at which—naturally—the police had a spy), saying that his friend Wladimirovich had recommended that they immediately turn to violence. He added that Wladimirovich knew how to make bombs and that such expertise needed to be spread at larger assemblies. Derevianka was arrested in 1921 for his role in a strike. When Wladimirovich was sent to Ushuaia, Derevianka collected funds for his imprisoned comrade.

Eduardo Vázquez Aguirre, another known anarchist agitator, came to the country in 1906. He led the Trolley Workers' Union's resistance society and was at the offices of the Chauffeurs' Union on May 21st, 1921, when it was attacked by a group of young men from the Patriotic League. Vázquez wounded one of the attackers in the arm. He has been imprisoned more than once. On May 9th, 1923, he shot the stationmaster of the Caballito Station over work-related issues and was sentenced to a year and two months in prison. He had been a security guard for the Anglo-Argentine Tramway Company but was fired for his role in the Tragic Week. He also supplied the strikers with explosives and was caught scattering tacks in a rental car lot when the chauffeurs went on strike.[18]

All three are arrested and interrogated for days on end. But Santiago knows that none of them will talk. They all insist that they brought Wladimirovich fruit and not a revolver. But the one who begins to talk now is Lucich, the man who killed Wilckens's murderer:

> When I killed the doctor, they held me in Cell Block 15 of the jail, along with Boris Wladimirovich. That's where I met him. I was happy to see him on September 12th, when he showed up at the mental hospital. We saw each other every morning after that. After all, he's a learned friend who can speak many languages.

Wladimirovich was unable to enter the wing where Pérez Millán was being held. Lucich was the only one with access, thanks to his job working as the servant of the nurses. The only way that the long arm of vengeance could reach Pérez Millán was through Lucich. For the anarchist, avenging Kurt Wilckens's death was a matter of prestige. The first step was to smuggle in the weapon. One of the three visitors took care of this. Then Wladimirovich spoke with the unstable Lucich—over whom he had a great deal of influence—and gave him instructions on how he was to kill Pérez Millán. He even told him which words to say to make it clear that it was a revenge killing: "This is from Wilckens!" And that once it was all over, he was to say that Pérez Millán had attacked him and that he had defended himself with a revolver he found on his victim's desk.

It couldn't have happened otherwise. According to the doctors, Lucich had too childish a mentality to have planned it all himself. But despite all the evidence, Wladimirovich will not be convicted. The only two witnesses are mental patients: Orselli, the Italian, and Lucich himself. Their statements would not hold up in a court of law. And there was no way to break the spirits of the three anarchists who had smuggled in the weapon.

Days pass. There are no further developments. Besides, nobody wants to make too much of the matter, not even Carlés. The Pérez Millán affair had always been rather thorny, indefensible, unpleasant, irritating.

Boris Wladimirovich will never leave prison. His mistreatment by the guards, which only increased after the Pérez Millán affair, hastened his death. In the last months of his life, he was paralytic from the waist down and had to drag himself around on the floor of his cell, soiled with his own excrement. A Dostoevskian end, copied straight from *The House of the Dead*. Pious women would say that God had taken care of his punishment.

UNMARKED GRAVES

"I have seen the small cemetery of the executed
strikers in Santa Cruz, between the mountains and the
sea. Badly buried in the graves they themselves dug,
the tips of their shoes emerge from among the dirt and
the lizards."
Raúl González Tuñón,
El Cemeterio Patagónico

We have reached the end of our study, the product of seven years
of research. I hope it serves a purpose. I believe it will. At the very
least, I believe it will shed some light on the most cryptic event in
the history of the Argentine proletariat in the twentieth century.
The 1921 massacre of the rural workers of Patagonia is no longer
a taboo subject, mentioned as if it were but a legend. Now we
know what happened, who was responsible, why it occurred and
the reasons behind its cruelty and terror. By drawing back the curtain on this tragedy, we can expose its methods, subterfuges, lies,
and crimes.

It was an overwhelming task. The difficulties were numerous. But even more numerous were those men of good will who
came forward to help. They have my thanks. As for the rest—
particularly those who did everything in their power to send me
to prison—I reserve my tolerance and forgetfulness.

We insist that two crimes were committed in Patagonia: the execution of prisoners and the use of force—giving orders is the use of force—to require young men who were barely twenty years old—the soldiers—to take human lives, making them bear that stain on their conscience until the day they died. This may have been the greatest crime committed in those years by the government and the military commanders who carried out their will.

The responsibility for the massacre lies with the government, but this does not relieve Varela of his share of the guilt. If we start by making excuses for him, then we will have started down the road that ends with accepting the arguments of the Auschwitz Guard Battalion.

Conclusions? There can be no conclusions, save our ever-increasing amazement at God's equanimity, that equanimity that rewards the powerful and abandons the weak. And if there is still any doubt, let's go back to the very first pages of this book, in which we examined the life of a powerful man, taken at random: Mauricio Braun, the son of a Russian immigrant named Elías Braun, whose hard work and drive amassed one of Patagonia's greatest fortunes.

When the strike had been completely forgotten, when there was no longer anybody left who knew the names of Wilckens or Facón Grande, Outerelo, or Wladimirovich, when the Patagonian wind had blown away every last trace of the graves of the executed men, there was one man who was honored across southern Argentina and Chile. It was 1967. Ceremonies were held in his honor, attended by governors, ministers, chiefs of police, military officers, subprefects, bishops, priests, office workers, and families in their Sunday best: in every branch office of La Anónima, the centenary of the birth of Mauricio Braun was observed. Hundreds of newspaper articles were written in his memory and, throughout Patagonia, dozens of masses were said for his soul.

Read these lines, written by none other than the Salesian priest Raúl Entraigas, one of Patagonia's most renowned historians. Here is what he wrote on the Braun-Menéndez marriage, which united the two greatest fortunes in Patagonia:

The couple radiated goodness throughout the long road that they traveled together. After fifty happy years of marriage, they invited me to say the mass for their golden anniversary. And their prayers that day were full of emotion and affection. The Basilica of San Carlos overflowed with the faithful. Those days were also graced by an exquisite gift of providence: the birth of their fiftieth grandchild. Fifty years of marriage and fifty grandchildren to kiss their gray brows... When the mass was over, a bishop who was a friend of the family administered the sacrament of confirmation to those of their grandchildren who had not yet received it. That afternoon, in the family's ancestral home on Calle Ayacucho in the heart of Buenos Aires's Barrio Norte, a French play was performed in Mauricio Braun's honor. The cast was made up of every one of his grandchildren who were capable of performing on a stage. It was at this party where Josefina Menéndez Behety, the wife of Mauricio Braun, confided a secret in me: once their golden anniversary celebrations were over, their home would be demolished and a temple raised in its place, embodying the gratitude felt by two equally pious souls for the blessings they have received over half a century of fruitful living. This is the story behind the beautiful St. Joseph's Parish Church. Josefina Menéndez Behety de Braun wanted it to be dedicated to her patron saint.[1] I have seen Mauricio Braun several times since then, always with that trademark smile on his lips that so perfectly expresses his personality, as if his eyes were radiating the kindness of his soul. With all justice, we could call him MAURICIO THE GOOD.

This is reality. Kurt Wilckens has a piece of metal marking his grave and a name that is no longer remembered, he is absolutely unknown to the younger generations of workers and students. There's not a single line about Antonio Soto in all the histories of Argentina's labor movement. The Spaniard Outerelo, the gaucho Facón Grande, the German Schulz, the Chilean Farina, Albino Argüelles...names that resounded without an echo in the loneliness of Patagonia. Germán Boris Wladimirovich died a cripple, like a stray dog cast on a garbage heap with maggots in its snout. No barefoot friar erected so much as a wooden cross in their memory. No "Our Father" was rapidly muttered so that God would forgive them for being so weak as to champion the poor, the wretched, the unwashed.

But José Menéndez will forever be remembered by the St. Joseph's Parish Church at the site of his ancestral home at Ayacucho 1064, in the heart of Buenos Aires's Barrio Norte.

EIGHTY YEARS LATER:
PERFIDY AND POETRY

It was an incredible coincidence. I was approached by the daughter of a war criminal and then, three days later, by the daughter of one of that very same war criminal's victims, executed during the strike in Patagonia eighty years earlier. Eighty years that have not managed to erase the pain, which has instead remained constant, present, and unforgettable, bearing the face of the victims.

One Saturday morning in December 2001, I went to a bookstore in San Isidro to participate in a meeting between various writers and the public. As always, I was the first one there. And while I was waiting for my colleagues to arrive, I ordered a coffee in the bookstore's leafy, illuminated patio. I was lost in thought, reflecting on recent political events, the premonitions of the street protests to come. And then I was approached by a woman of a certain age, who addressed me in a grandiloquent voice: "I am the youngest daughter of the late General Anaya, whom you called a murderer and accused of executing workers in Patagonia. I have come to demand the documents that you stole from him. I live across the street from this bookstore and when I saw your name in the store window, I resolved to come and fulfill the dying wishes of my father, the general."

The woman, though elegant and well-dressed, was noticeably nervous. I asked her to have a seat and tried to calm her down.

I realized that this seventy-four-year-old woman hoped to win the argument with her theatricality and embarrass me in public—the outcome of this unusual encounter was being furtively awaited by the bookstore's customers. And so I responded firmly but respectfully: "To begin with, madam, you are slandering me. I haven't stolen any of your father's documents. I don't need his personal documents to prove that, back in 1921, your father murdered agricultural workers in the most cowardly and despicable manner imaginable. But before I say any more, I would like to ask you what General Anaya said to you on his deathbed."

"Before dying, he gathered all of his children together and told us that we have to struggle against you, recover the documents that you had stolen from him, and prove that he was no murderer."

"It's very interesting," I responded, "that General Anaya waited until he was at death's door to accuse me of stealing his personal documents, and even more that he asked his children to prove that he wasn't a despicable murderer. It's even comical—he had many years to file charges against me for theft or sue me for slander. Look, your father and I already had a public debate back in 1974, in the newspaper *La Opinión*. I proved that he ordered striking workers to be executed in the Patagonian countryside, with no legal justification. And I refuted his clumsy accusation that I had stolen his personal documents, which was nothing more than an attempt to distract the attention of the gullible. Your father died in 1986. He had twelve years to defend himself, in other words. And you yourself have said that he waited until he was on his deathbed to tell his children to take care of this for him. So for twelve years, he kept his mouth shut. And what's more, it has now been fifteen years since his death—fifteen years in which his children have ignored their father's last wishes. You only came here to confront me because you saw my name in the window of the bookstore across the street from your house. Quite convenient. A strange way to carry out the wishes of a dying man. Your father was the only officer from the Patagonia expedition to make the rank of general. He participated in the 1943 coup d'etat and—through corruption and a cruel magical realism—he was named justice and education minister. The murderer of 1921, justice minister. Argentine reality. Then he participated in Aramburu's coup d'etat in 1955. *La Nación* wrote, "General Anaya didn't hesitate to give his approval to the 1956 extrajudicial executions that claimed the lives of dozens of soldiers and civilians, including General Valle."[1] When Anaya died, General Juan Carlos Onganía, the former dictator, spoke at his funeral. And there you have his life. And now it's 2001, and you've come to accuse me of stealing his personal documents. But a researcher would never steal documents because that would take away their value—they could no longer be cited as a source. Photocopies of all the military documents I cited were provided by General Juan Enrique Gugalialmelli, the director of the School of Advanced Military Studies. There you can find your father's documents.

The general's daughter went away enraged. I thought of how dramatic it must be to be the child of torturers, kidnappers, genocidaires. Their actions curse their families for generations.

But three days after this Argentine magical realism, I was offered compensation. A journalist from *Página/12* told me that there was someone who wanted to see me. It turned out to be the daughter of Albino Argüelles, the leader of the peons in San Julián who had been executed by Elbio Carlos Anaya. It was eighty years after the massacre and I spoke with the daughters of the murderer and the victim within a few short days of each other.

In Palermo, I was welcomed by Irma Dora Labat. She told me that she was the natural daughter—the love child—of Albino Argüelles and Carla Irene Labat, her mother.

"My father never knew me," she said. "They fell in love and I was conceived before my father left for Patagonia. I was born one month before he was killed by General Anaya, which occurred on December 18th, 1921. Today is December 17th, 2001—it's been exactly eighty years. My father learned of my birth just weeks before his death. My mother received a letter from San Julián that contained a poem he wrote about me. I memorized it when I was a little girl and I have never forgotten it."

She looks at me excitedly. This is the best possible homage to her father, who was killed for defending the rights of those who work the land:

You are left with the solace
Of our fruit, our beloved
And you will find in her bright face
The payment for your sleeplessness
Always maintaining present
Our young daughter's memory
And may you glorify her brow
Your kisses covering her constantly

After she finished, there was silence. The elderly Irma Labat was in tears. Looking at her face, I was filled with a profound sense of affection for her, perhaps in silent protest.

She told me that her mother went down to the port with the other women every time a ship arrived from Patagonia because rumors would circulate that there were prisoners aboard. But the ships came in and the hopeful women waited until the docks were empty. No, he never arrived. They had shot him. They had shot him alongside so many of his comrades.

Later, they learned the details. That Albino Argüelles didn't want to fight the army, but to discuss the implementation of the previous year's labor settlement—which was the law of the land— with the officers. And that Captain Anaya had them imprisoned in a corral and ordered them to be ferociously beaten with saber blows before they were shot. A cowardly, despicable act.

"My mother never married," Irma Label told me. "She lived off the memory of my father. He was very young (only twenty-seven when they killed him) and was full of good humor. Socialists and anarchists don't marry, love is enough to keep them together. My father was a socialist and *La Vanguardia* published a very sad account of his death. The International Socialist Party also kept his memory alive."

His killer became a general, and even justice and education minister. The students, teachers, and democratic citizens of San Julián must reclaim the figure of this labor leader who fought to implement the first labor settlement reached with the peons. He led by example, using the power of his words. He killed nobody and never fired on the army. He was killed because he was intelligent, because he understood, body and soul, the value of justice and solidarity with the underdog. There should be a street named after him, a monument marking the place where his body lies next to those of his comrades.

Time always tears down the curtain that tries to hide the truth. A crime can never be covered up forever.

Osvaldo Bayer
December 27, 2001

Endnotes

Introduction

1 R. Munck, with R. Falcon. & B. Galitelli, *Argentina from Anarchism to Peronism* (Atlantic Highlands, NJ: Zed Books, 1987).

2 A. Gomez Mueller, *Anarquismo y anarcosindicalismo en America Latina: Colombia, Brasil, Argentina, Mexico* (Medellin: La Carreta Editors, 2009).

3 A. Marti, *La biografía del anarquista Simón Radowitzky: del atentado a Falcón a la Guerra Civil Española* (La Plata: De la Campana, 2010).

4 E. Gilimón, *Hechos y comentarios y otros escritos: El Anarquismo en Buenos Aires (1890–1915)* (Buenos Aires, Distrito Federal: Libros de Anarres, 2011), 99. (Original work published 1911.)

5 D. Abad de Santillán, *La FORA: Ideología y trayectoria del movimiento obrero en la Argentina* (Buenos Aires, Distrito Federal, Argentina: Libros de Anarres, 2005), 207. (Original work published 1933.)

6 D. Rock, *Politics in Argentina 1890-1930: The Rise and Fall of Radicalism* (Cambridge: Cambridge University Press, [digital ed.] 2009), 27. (Original work published 1975.)

7 Abad de Santillán, *La FORA*, 235.

8 Rock, *Politics in Argentina 1890-1930*, 89–90.

9 Ibid, 129-131.

10 H. Ricardo Silva, *Días Rojos, Verano Negro: Enero de 1919, la semana trágica de Buenos Aires* (Buenos Aires, Distrito Federal: Libros de Anarres, 2011), 244.

11 Ibid, 235–236.

12 J. Carulla, *Al filo del medio siglo*, (Buenos Aires, Distrito Federal: Editorial Huema, [2nd ed.], 1964), 309. (Original work published 1951.)

13 L. Lugones, "The Ayacucho Address," in G. Kirkpatrick (ed.) & S. Waisman (trans.), *Leopoldo Lugones: Selected Writings* (New York: Oxford

University Press, 2008), 82.

14　Carulla, *Al filo del medio siglo*, 273–274.

15　Angel Cappellett & Carlos Rama, *El anarquismo en América Latina* (Caracas: Biblioteca Ayacucho, 1990), 78.

16　Abad de Santillán, *La FORA*, 235.

17　M. Caminos & G. Leza, "Osvaldo Bayer, a 40 años de 'La Patagonia Rebelde': Censura, exilio y anécdotas inolvidables," *La Nación*, November 7, 2014. Retrieved February 15, 2016, from http://www.lanacion. com.ar/1741493-ob-el-radicalismo-deberia-hacer-una-autocritica- por-la-patagonia-y-el-peronismo-por-lopez-rega-ob-a-40-anos-de-la -patagonia-rebelde-censura-exilio-y-anecdotas-inolvidables.

18　G. Flores, "Entrevista a Osvaldo Bayer historiador, escritor y periodista," *Río Negro*, June 21, 2012. Retrieved February 15, 2016, from http://www.rionegro.com.ar/diario/entrevista-a-osvaldo-bayer-histori- ador-escritor-y-periodista-902477-9574-nota.aspx.

19　J. D'Andrea Mohr, *Memoria Debida*, 1999. Retrieved February 15, 2016, from http://www.desaparecidos.org/nuncamas/web/investig/dan- drea/memoria/memori11.htm.

20　O. Bayer, "A treinta años de aquellas humillaciones," *Página/12*, March 13, 2004. Retrieved February 15, 2016, from http://www.pagina12.com. ar/diario/contratapa/13-32583-2004-03-13.html.

Prologue

1　This little girl was named María Antonia Palazzo. Ten years old at the time, she was the daughter of Roque Palazzo. Her family lived at Calle Santa Fe 4858, Buenos Aires.

2　This incident has been reconstructed from the witness statements featured in Case File No. 3776 (Trial Court No. 9, which was then located at Albarracín 64, but has since moved to Albarracín 126). The examining judge was Manuel P. Malbrán and the sentencing judge was Carlos M. Martínez. Complementary details were taken from the reports published in the newspapers *La Nación*, *La Prensa*, and *Crítica*.

Chapter One: Argentina's Far South

1　The data taken from the 1920 census (Vol. II, Page 227) can lead us to the wrong conclusions if we take it at face value. According to these figures, 47 percent of the population of Santa Cruz is Argentine, 20 percent Spanish, and 10.7 percent Chilean. But we should pay attention to what Horacio Lafuente says in his essay *Santa Cruz 1920/21*: "If we analyze the economically active population, we will see that the Argentine population drops to 30 percent. To the extent that the number of Argentines decreases as the population ages, the number of foreigners increases. The size of the immigrant population between twenty and forty years of age approaches that of the group of citizens of the same age, only to later decline." Furthermore, to analyze who really does the work in Patagonia, we have to take into account the nationality of the region's seasonal laborers, not just the nationality of those with an address in Patagonian territory. Here the best statistics can be gathered from police and military reports on the strikes that occured from 1915 onwards, when information on the nationality of workers began to be included (see, for example, *Los Bandoleros*, Vol. 1, Chapter 2: "Pequeñas Historias de Locos e Ilusos," published by Editorial Planeta). Let us cite another paragraph from Lafuente's excellent report: "The active population of Santa Cruz is divided by trade into 3,297 day laborers, 1,178 skilled laborers, 1,055 office workers, 706 merchants, and 671 ranchers. Oddly, we find 4,432 workers with an unspecified trade; presumably this is where the rural peons are categorized." The same thing happens with the landowners. Lafuente again: "In 1920, over 20 million hectares were divided into 619 ranches, of which only 189 were owned by Argentines, while 110 were owned by Spaniards, eighty-one by Englishmen, fifty-three by Chileans, forty-two by Frenchmen, and thirty-seven by Germans." We feel that this breakdown is not entirely accurate due to the existence of the so-called *palos blancos*—individuals who were officially listed as the owner of a ranch, but who were in fact representatives of corporations or large landowners. The *palos blancos* were a major institution throughout Patagonia and research on the true landowners in southern Argentina has yet to be undertaken.

2   *Chilote*: Literally the indigenous people of Chile's Chiloé Archipelago, but the term is used as an insult in Argentina [—Translator].

3   In honor of Elías Braun, his father.

4   The company's full name in Spanish is Sociedad Anónima Importadora y Exportadora de la Patagonia [—Translator].

5   Borrero mentions massacres of Indians and other methods; longtime residents attribute it to their factories and brothels, as well as to smuggling, land seizures, and the exorbitant rescue fees they charged for those shipwrecked on Isla de los Estados and all throughout the dangerous maritime route from the Atlantic to the Pacific.

Chapter Two: The Whites and the Reds

1   Universal *male* suffrage, that is.

2   The Interior Ministry directly administered Argentina's territories. Residents of Santa Cruz could not elect their governor or representatives, who were instead appointed by the federal government in Buenos Aires. Santa Cruz did not achieve provincial status until 1957 [—Translator].

3   The white beret is the symbol of the Radical Civic Union.

4   It was this military dictatorship that made torture official policy and institutionalized the use of the *picana*, that notorious Argentine invention developed by Polo Lugones, son of the famed author Leopoldo Lugones.

5   The Patriotic League played a key role in the repression of the labor movement in the 1920s, years in which—as a consequence of Russia's October Revolution—there was a tremendous wave of revolutionary movements around the world. What's most important here is the Patriotic League's presence in the country's most isolated towns, its role in giving bosses and property owners a sense of unity, and its influence on the authorities, the armed forces, and the police.

6   The FORA V championed anarcho-communism.

7   Although there were socialists and communists (International Socialist Party) among the organization's members, their mouthpieces (*La Vanguardia* and *La Internacional*) were critical of many of the measures taken by the union, which was largely dominated by "pure syndicalists"— apolitical reformists, in other words.

Chapter Three: Dawn for the Wretched

1   This is typically anarchist. Just think about the riskiness of a strike in a place where jobs are extremely scarce, where all the bosses know each

other, and where nobody will hire a disobedient worker. And that these somber men—peons, bellboys, and stevedores—would take such a risk on behalf of someone who had died eleven years before in a far-off land. That these proletarians—most of them illiterate—took such a risk to commemorate the founder of the Modern School!

2 From his monograph entitled *El espíritu obrero en la Patagonia*. Río Gallegos, 1921.

3 A "hotel for Chileans." These establishments, then plentiful throughout Argentine Patagonia, offered both food and lodging.

4 Wooden bed frames, stacked one on top of the other, with sheepskins for mattresses and blankets. These bunks were crammed into narrow rooms with very little space between them. Borrero offers a detailed description of the bunk system in chapter 9 of his book *La Patagonia Trágica*.

Chapter Four: Happy Ending: A Good Prelude to Death

1 All of the details of Micheri's mission are taken from the inquiry into the events at El Cerrito and the statements made by Officer Garay and Sergeant Cancino (Archives of the Supreme Court of Santa Cruz).

2 *Ibid* for all of these details, as well as the story that follows.

3 From the file on the El Cerrito incident: statements made by Sergeants Peralta and Montaña.

4 Camporro received no reward for his mercy. He was executed by the military during the second strike.

5 Evidently, Senecovich did indeed work for the police. His name is included on the list of officers fallen in the line of duty at the Río Gallegos Police Headquarters.

6 Blankets consisting of a patchwork of animal hides, traditionally made by the indigenous people of Patagonia.

7 Even Judge Viñas, who had so openly supported the workers, felt that things were slipping out of control. He sent a telegram calling for military intervention to Justice Minister José Salinas.

8 Soto had taken shelter in a small house on the outskirts of Río Gallegos, owned by a commanding Galician woman. She was known as Doña Máxima Lista—a nickname she earned as a maximalist, a synonym for

"Bolshevik," because, despite being an anarchist, she supported Lenin and the Russian Revolution. But these ideological differences did not prevent her from helping fugitives. The Patagonian writer Alfredo Fiori thus describes her: "Spanish by nationality and a native of the Galician province A Coruña, this tiny woman, nearly eighty years old by 1920, was so sprightly and restless that she could be seen going all over town in a single day. She could be found wherever someone was sick, wounded, or imprisoned, bringing them a gift of mate, cheese, or sausage. Where did Doña Carmen get the money to pay for all these gifts? From her job, which could not be more respectable. She ran a guesthouse for workers, where she did the work of ten ordinary women.

"And where did she get so much energy and such an innate sense of justice, far beyond that of most mortals? I discovered that Doña Carmen had two adult sons and that one of them, the eldest, had lost his mind. As the mental health facilities in Río Gallegos in those days were rather primitive and left much to be desired, mental patients were held at the jail. And the police, clearly, had neither the resources nor the space to treat them humanely. Doña Carmen constantly visited her son at the jail, sometimes twice a day, which is how she developed her own personal, balanced, and humane conception of justice. After Doña Carmen lost her eldest son to drink, she began to feel that she was the mother of all those unfortunates who had become prisoners for one reason or another, feeling that they were as innocent as her lost son. And though she was illiterate, she felt a special predilection for political prisoners.

"Police officers and prisoner guards had a fearsome adversary in Doña Carmen. The slightest abuse of a prisoner was enough to get her to launch into a tirade, telling the wardens that their mothers had surely repented of having given birth to such unjust sons. Doña Carmen was unable to overlook the slightest injustice and was constantly entering the prison without asking permission of the guards, who often preferred the corporal punishment of their superiors to the verbal punishment they would have received from the elderly woman. I should add that I'm not familiar with a single case where a prison guard was punished for letting her pass, as even judges were afraid that she would force them to face their consciences. Doña Carmen, if you are in heaven and you can read my thoughts, you will know that I am grateful for your heroism and your divine pacifism. All the more so because it provided an example to follow on how not to be unjust with one's fellow man, which has helped heal my own wounds."

9 Report by Officer Martín de Beguiristán to the Santa Cruz police chief, March 23rd, 1921.

10 This episode has been reconstructed from the file on Commissioner Nicolía Jameson's dismissal (Archives of the Supreme Court of Santa Cruz).

11 General Anaya in an interview with the author.

Chapter Five: The Long March Towards Death

1 Magazine published by the Army General Staff [—Translator].

2 From a speech given by General Elbio C. Anaya at a conference held at the Center for Military Studies from October 29th to November 2nd, 1965.

3 The list of conditions included in the Yza Settlement, which was later ratified by the National Labor Department in Buenos Aires, tacitly accepted all of the workers' economic demands. It only came into conflict with the Workers' Society on two points: back pay for days lost to the strike (workers would only be given half a day's pay for each day of the strike) and the problem of ranch delegates, in which Yza decided not to get involved and instead gave both sides a free hand.

4 The original copy of this contract can be found in the archives of the Supreme Court of Santa Cruz and its text was previously reproduced by José María Borrero in his book *La Patagonia Trágica*.

5 Statement made by Antonio Fernández of Río Gallegos, who was present.

6 The second car carried Pedro Mongilnitzky Kresanoscki (a single, twenty-nine-year-old Polish mechanic and spokesman for the Workers' Federation), Luis Sambuceti Vernengo (a single, twenty-three-year-old Argentine electrician and note-taker for the Federation), Zacarías González (a rural delegate), and Severino Fernández (a thirty-four-year-old Spaniard and spokesman for the Federation).

7 Without providing any testimony or documentary proof, of course.

8 We have copied out Varela's itinerary because these paragraphs are essential in proving that the Chilean government collaborated in the persecution of the strikers and did not, as some claim, foment chaos.

9 In official documents, he's listed as "Simón Mesor, Russian, forty-eight

years old, married, peon on the Esperanza Douglas ranch."

10 Eight days after the "Battle" of Punta Alta, the Syrian merchant Fortunato Nasif appeared before the Río Gallegos police. He said that Commissioner Douglas told him that his brother, Juan Nasif, had died at Corrales Viejos. Commissioner Samuel Douglas Price's report literally states that "the subject Juan Nasif" died during "a treacherous attack on the federal forces" and that "his body had been left at the scene." A later police report states that, on November 24th, "five bodies, all males, were found fifty meters from the peons' quarters, buried in a shallow grave. The merchant Nasif recognized one of the bodies as that of his brother Juan (Syrian, twenty-three years old, a resident of Argentina for the past eight years, single). No documents or objects were found on his person. He had three wounds, located in the carotid region, the precordial region, and the right intercostal space. No objects or documents were found on any of the other four men, who had wounds on various parts of their bodies. They were immediately reburied and the police retreated out of fear of being captured." Observe one detail: the police themselves certify that the deceased had nothing on their persons. Which means that the victims had been stripped of all their documents—so they could not be identified—as well as all their valuables. As we will see, the army and the police will be accused of looting.

11 The official list of the soldiers in the 10th Cavalry Regiment includes Octavio Vallejos.

12 Sergeant Francisco Esperguín and Corporal First Class Eulalio Sosa.

13 Juan Nasif.

14 Previously, there had only been a Fatherland Defense Association in town.

15 This figure has been corrected in ink from the original typewritten number, which seems to be eight.

16 This system was adopted to make any escape attempt more difficult.

17 Armando Camporro, who had participated in the El Cerrito incident.

18 The rancher Hospitaleche, whose account of the incident we will examine later, argues that this report was made hastily and that the rape never occurred.

19 This was a nickname; their real names were José and Pendino Fernández García.

20   In Patagonia, the adjective "green"—aside from meaning "inexperienced"—also means "timid," "inhibited," and "awkward."

21   Interviewed in December 1972 on his farm on the outskirts of Gobernador Gregores.

22   Read *Los degolladores* by Juan M. Vigo: "Slitting the throats of human
beings was an authentic Argentine passion." *Todo es Historia* No. 3, July
1967, edited by Félix Luna.

23   But the telegram reproduced by *La Nación* states: "Argüelles, Jara, and
eighteen others"—twenty casualties, in other words.

24   This sense of justice probably helped Captain Anaya's career. As a general, he held the position of justice and education minister in the regime
that came to power in the 1943 military coup.

25   This mass grave was useful in covering up other murders of peons that
occurred later. One of these cases is known as "the crimes of Valenciano." This police officer found an easy way to make money. Valenciano
acquired a black notebook and spread a rumor among the peons that
it had been left behind by Lieutenant Colonel Varela and contained a
list of strikers who had been condemned to death. He was assisted by
Sergeant Ludovico Tjetjan. Tjetjan went looking for "the condemned,"
whom he then brought to the station. There, Valenciano showed his victim the black notebook and told him to prepare to die. When the victim
had said his last prayer and was taken out to be shot, he was offered "one
last chance"—the chance to give Valenciano half of what he had earned
during the shearing, in other words, or a reasonable percentage of his
wages if he was paid monthly. The condemned not only paid up, but
even thanked Officer Valenciano and Sergeant Tjetjen for their mag-
nanimity. Of course, more than a few of their victims were stubborn
and refused to hand over a single centavo, and so the two police officers
strictly complied with the orders left behind in "Commander Varela's
black notebook." They executed the shepherds León Dehesa and Mateo
Albarracín and the shearer Antonio Crocha. Their bodies were taken to
the mass grave at El Perro to make it seem as if they had "fallen in combat." These two murderers were never punished. To the contrary—many
years later, Félix Valenciano was named justice of the peace for the Lago
Buenos Aires region by Governor Gregores. And a logical question aris-

es: if Captain Anaya could become justice and education minister for the entire country, then why can't Officer Valenciano become a justice of the peace? This is the logic of this entire tragic, dirty episode.

26   Alberto Francisco Lada, sixty-four years old in 1972, was then twelve. His mother, a widow, was the owner of a fleet of carts in San Julián that were used for transporting wool. Alberto Lada, still a child, always traveled with the carts. In December 1921, the strike takes them by surprise while they're at La Anita and they are forced to remain on the ranch. He had vivid memories of the strikers, their assemblies, and above all of Antonio Soto, whom he described as a fiery speaker whose words always commanded an attentive silence. He told us that the strikers were well supplied and were good cooks. During his entire time on the ranch, until the army's arrival, he witnessed no vandalism, looting, or brawls. He said that the hostages were kept apart but that they were in no way mistreated. One curious fact Lada mentioned is that Antonio Soto never slept with the strikers at La Anita—he always disappeared at nightfall, probably to visit the La Leona group. One morning, Soto was beaming as he returned to camp. He promptly called an assembly where he announced that victory was near. He had received news that Outerelo had just occupied Paso Ibáñez. There was a great deal of rejoicing in those days, but this hope would soon dissipate.

27   It's possible that his last name was Otto Kulinnen, the only peon registered with this first name.

28   Hobo.

29   Commissioner Guadarrama has explained that when Viñas Ibarra was faced with the two Chilean delegates, he was able to silently order their execution without even so much as moving his arm: he only indicated the number four with his right hand. The nearest NCO would understand that this meant four shots. Not a single bullet was wasted.

30   Other witnesses claim that there were forty-seven or even a hundred men who followed Soto. It's possible that there were other groups that fled before or after Soto's departure. But there were only twelve men in his group.

31   As reported by Walter Knoll.

32   Robert Ridell, who had replaced Angus Show.

33 He spoke of "hundreds of households" despite stating that he liberated exactly one hundred hostages (the exact number of hostages at La Anita was eighty).

34 Alberto Lada's testimony doesn't lose its relevance here: "I was a witness to the fact that they executed close to twenty-five strikers (some ten from the first group and some thirteen from the second). Then the ranchers selected all of the peons they considered to be 'good.' Isolated shots could be heard after that, especially after the 'good' peons had been taken away by the ranchers. There was a great deal of confusion. I think that not even Viñas Ibarra knows exactly how many men were executed."

35 No wounded prisoners ever reached Río Gallegos. Neither the jail nor the public assistance office ever reported their arrival. The lists of prisoners prepared by Viñas Ibarra for official use make no mention of wounded prisoners. So what happened to those wounded in battle? Was there ever a battle? No. There were executions.

36 The final bastion of the Río Gallegos Workers' Society had fallen on November 25th, long before Varela's arrival, with the eviction of a clandestine printing press on Calle Sarmiento, near the intersection with Mitre, that was set up by Luis Santamaría. The room was rented under the name of Isabel Purrúa, a widow. The eviction "decree"—as it was called by the police—stated that the room was "the nerve center or headquarters of a group of recalcitrant elements." Besides a small printing press and a few boxes of type, the police seized the following subversive publications: *Anarchist Morals, Men and Prisons, Humanity of the Future, The Eternal Intelligence, Society's Parasites, Towards a Moral Without Dogmas, The Universal: Origin and Doctrine, What Will The Future Be Like?, Marvels of Life*, and *The Physiology of Living Beings*, along with the newspapers *La Protesta, La Antorcha*, and Punta Arenas' *El Trabajo*, etc. They also found the draft of a flier that hadn't yet been printed, which read as follows: "Comrades, we must remain firm and continue the strike until we triumph. We shall once again prove that we are men and that we will never forget it, no matter the cost. The exploited should not be ashamed of their unions. And it will never be said that we fell silent when struck by the policeman's whip." They also found a copy of an article against

obligatory military service, originally written by Count Leo Tolstoy and copied out in what was determined to be Antonio Soto's handwriting. The final police report on the raid stated, "Among the documents seized, we can note an appreciation for the Russian Revolution and its benefits, both in general and especially in our own immediate environment, as well as veiled attacks on the federal government and insults directed at the army."

37   The rancher Jenkins told me in May 1971 that three strike leaders were executed around Christmastime in 1921 and buried at his father's ranch, located on the south side of the Río Deseado.

38   Whether or not Font was misguided, this phrase shows that he felt the struggle meant something and that it was about more than just "terrorizing" the population, as Varela stated in his dispatch. That he was thinking of the future of the children shows that he was conscious that things needed to change.

39   Ruso Manchado's name was Paulino Kapeluj and he was twenty-six years old. He had arrived in Patagonia only eleven months before. He was born near Moscow. He had been rounding up livestock when he joined the strike. In 1974, his nephew was working in the Puerto Deseado railway station. Stationmaster Carlos Gómez Wilson introduced us to him.

40   Without this woman, perhaps the shootout at Tehuelches never would have taken place, as Varela only dared to attack Facón Grande after receiving information about where his men had set up camp. If this woman had told Font that it was the army that was approaching, there would have been no misunderstandings. She knew that she was dealing with the army, as she had been informed of their arrival by the Fitz Roy stationmaster. Elsa Minucci de Gamarra now lives in Puerto Deseado. We asked to interview her. She flatly refused. She was the only witness we encountered during our research who refused to tell us her perspective on the events in which she played such a crucial role. We understand this silence. Who knows what feelings guided her spirit during this tragic episode? She also refused to speak with Rodríguez Moro, the director of the Puerto Deseado newspaper *El Orden*. The Patriotic League publicly recognized her role in eliminating Facón Grande and his men.

Josué Quesada—the secretary of Manuel Carlés—wrote about her in an article entitled "A Heroic Woman": "The bandits had cut off all lines of communication. This girl repaired them by climbing the telegraph poles herself and informing Varela that Facón Grande was nearby. Thanks to this information, Varela was able to make the proper preparations. She asked for a weapon to fight with. Officers and conscripts alike were visibly moved by this mother, worried for her children, who had done so much to assist them in their sacred duty of fighting for the fatherland" (*El Nacional*, Río Gallegos, April 21st, 1922).

41 Facón Grande's possessions were clearly seized by his enemies. As we have mentioned, the gaucho owned a fleet of carts. Commissioner Albornoz merely stated that "four carts and some eighty horses" had been found. By the time an investigation was opened (File No. 13/22, Santa Cruz), there were only two carts and twenty-five horses left. Captain Anaya was asked about the missing carts and replied that the NCO who was in charge of guarding them was "missing." Judge Viñas finally named Commissioner Albornoz, a member of the Patriotic Leauge, to administer the property of the deceased. Then, silence. The last page of the dossier states that Commissioner Albornoz took Facón Grande's carts and horses back to his own ranch.

42 The prisoners were forced to squat and their hands were placed behind their backs and tied to their feet in such a way that their bodies remained tense and they could only move by rolling around.

Chapter Six: The Victors (For He's A Jolly Good Fellow)

1 Another newspaper, Puerto Deseado's *El Orden*, adds another detail: "Mr. Herbert Elbourne told Varela of the gratitude of the British community and, as if to answer the commander's complaints about their lack of Argentine sensibilities, asked his countrymen to sing the children's song 'For He's a Jolly Good Fellow,' a request that was answered by the twenty-some Englishmen present, who sang at the top of their lungs."

2 Testimony of his sister, Delfina Varela Domínguez de Ghioldi, a celebrated educator. The other Varela was a Federalist guerrilla who led an armed rebellion against the Unitarian government in 1866.

3   See the newspapers *La Prensa* and *La Nación* on January 26th, 1922.

4   Here de Tomaso is referring to the list of demands drafted by Outerelo in Puerto Santa Cruz. The other columns of strikers merely demanded the release of the prisoners and the implementation of the Yza Settlement.

5   This was but one of the crimes committed by Commissioner Sotuyo of Puerto Santa Cruz. If it hadn't been witnessed by naval personnel, it would have been covered up like the rest. The full details can be read in the trial record (File 4826, Folio 478, Court of Santa Cruz, 1921) and in the report filed by Frigate Captain Dalmiro Sáenz (Interior Ministry No. 442, Classified, and Naval Ministry File 1 - B—24, 1922, Classified). Two members of the Workers' Society had remained in Puerto Santa Cruz: a Spaniard named Domingo Islas and a Russian named Miguel Gesenko, who was the construction workers' delegate. The latter had disarmed Dr. Sicardi, the local president of the Patriotic League, during the previous year's May Day celebration. When Sotuyo arrested these two workers, he invited Dr. Sicardi to the police station. Witnesses have stated that they heard Sicardi say, "The union members must be eliminated." Turning to the prisoners, he told Islas, "You will be shot like your compatriot Francisco Ferrer." Sotuyo told Gesenko, "Your life is over." Then he ordered Islas to be given fifty saber blows. Islas collapsed after thirty-five and he was given the rest while lying on the ground. Then Sergeant Sánchez kicked him to his feet and made him walk back to his cell, where he was put in shackles. The next morning, when they went to take him out to be shot, they realized that he had died during the night. They took his body to the beach, bringing Gesenko along with them. They drew their weapons and forced the Russian construction worker to drag his comrade's body into the sea. Once Gesenko was waist deep in the water and the body of Islas was beginning to float, the police—on Sotuyo's orders—began to shout, "He's escaping! He's escaping!" Between the shouts, they opened fire on Gesenko, who tried to dodge the bullets as he rose and fell with the waves. Eight rifle shots were enough to finish off the Russian anarchist. Once his still-warm body was brought back to the beach, Sergeant Sánchez finished him off with a bullet in the back of the head. Unfortunately for Sotuyo, the

entire scene was witnessed by the naval troops. But the court spared Dr. Sicardi, while Commissioner Sotuyo was sent to Chubut for trial. But sometimes there's no justice like the people's justice. While sailing to Chubut, Sotuyo—who had complete freedom of movement aboard the ship—drowned after being thrown overboard by a group of anarchist sailors (File 10.251, Court of Santa Cruz).

6 Inspector Marcelo Pierucetti's report on the repression in Puerto Santa Cruz states, "The prisoners chosen for extortion were forced to witness the punishments inflicted on the other prisoners, who after being beaten and exhausted from pain and hunger, were then forced to bring buckets of gravel from the beach to the police station. This sorrowful caravan resembled nothing so much as the tragic processions of Christians being whipped forward by the Armenians."

7 As told to the author by General Elbio Carlos Anaya.

8 This section has been reconstructed from the transcripts of the 1922 legislative sessions held in the Chamber of Deputies. The atmosphere in the room was described by former senator Bartolomé Pérez, who was then present as a spectator (in 1922, he was the Radical leader in Santa Cruz).

9 According to a statement made by the shearer Viriginio González of Puerto Natales.

10 Here we should add a few words on the fate of Antonio Soto, the man who refused to surrender at La Anita. We had last seen him fleeing into Chile over the Centinela pass. After being pursued for five days by the Argentine military and the Chilean carabinieri, Guatón Luna's group made it to Puerto Natales. There they were smuggled aboard a schooner and taken to Punta Arenas, where they were given refuge by the Magallanes Workers' Federation. The crew of the steamship *Argentino* tried to stow Soto aboard and take him to Buenos Aires, but the plan failed when someone tipped off the police. He finally made it from Punta Arenas to Valparaíso by hiding in a laundry basket. From there he headed farther north, to Iquique, where he worked in the nitrate mines, but he was badly burned in an accident and returned to Valparaíso after a long convalescence. But he constantly thought about returning to Río Gallegos to explain his actions during the 1921 strike. Twelve years later, he got his wish. He crossed the border and stayed at the Hotel Miramar

in the capital of Santa Cruz. After reestablishing contact with his old comrades, he organized a meeting that turned out to be a resounding failure. Times had changed. In Patagonia, ideas of unionism and social struggle had been drowned in blood and it would remain that way for over half a century. Even though Soto gave the best speech of his life, the only people who came to listen were a small group of Spaniards who had miraculously survived the massacre in 1921. Soto was immediately deported by Governor Gregores, who also gave the order to permanently ban him from ever setting foot on Argentine soil again. Soto remained faithful to his libertarian ideals until the day he died, although he no longer acted on them publicly. Towards the end of his life, he purchased a small hotel in Punta Arenas that became a gathering place for journalists, artists, freethinkers, and Spanish Republicans. His body was accompanied to the graveyard by a sizable entourage, led by the flagbearers of the Spanish Republican Center, the Red Cross—of which he was a member—and the Galician Center. They were followed by student groups, who honored Soto as the inspiration behind the first student strike in Punta Arenas, which secured an increase in the meager pay of the town's teachers.

11   As told to the author by General Elbio Carlos Anaya in May 1968.

Chapter Seven: The Avengers

1   Ramón Silveyra, an anarchist baker who became famous for his daring prison breaks.

2   His real name was Severiano, but he had changed it to Siberiano in tribute to the Russian anarchists imprisoned in Siberia.

3   Abad de Santillán traveled to Europe in 1922.

4   As told by Emilio Uriondo, La Plata.

5   Miguel Arcángel Roscigna, one of the most prominent anarchist expropriators in the River Plate region—whose story has been told by the author of this book in *The Anarchist Expropriators*—described the personality of Kurt Wilckens in an article entitled "Once Again, Regarding Expropriation," which was published by Severino Di Giovanni in *Anarchia*. A response to the Italian theorist Hugo Treni, the article mentions Wilckens in the following paragraph: "I'm not speaking to

you of a Wilckens, an expropriator and adjudicator, I'm not speaking to you of a Nicola Sacco, a fierce, proud expropriator who managed to terrify the proud, barbarous Yankee upon whom he declared war, nor of the unsurpassable Ravachol, I'm speaking of the thousands of Ravachols you don't know. Like the grand tramp Kurt Wilckens, they carry their possessions on their shoulders but remain unvanquished and unadapted to wage slavery, refusing to contribute a single cent towards what you call *benessere di tutti*, and so they wander around the world, using a thousand different means to attack that false principle that holds the people in subjection: authority." In turn, Severino Di Giovanni, the anarchist expropriator executed by General Uriburu in January 1931, took Kurt Wilckens as his model. He left behind an unfinished article entitled "The Heralds of the Storm: Kurt Wilckens in Thought and Action." In this article, Di Giovanni stated that Wilckens "was the prototype of the anarchist expropriator, the man of action who was always willing to take responsibility for what he had done. A man of few words, he had a serene and devastating spirit."

6   The Hamburg newspaper *Alarm* reported that the prison authorities initially tried to keep the assassination a secret until they could consult with their superiors and devise a more acceptable story of what had happened. But their cover-up was unsuccessful because of a fortuitous accident: a dentist showed up early that morning with written permission to see Wilckens, which had been obtained for him by *La Protesta*. When the authorities refused to let him pass, he vehemently insisted. The warden, not wishing to appear an accomplice of Pérez Millán, was forced to show his face and explain what had happened.

7   A type of gaucho troubador [—Translator].

8   Atahualpa Yupanqui composed a minor gem entitled *Cantor del Sur* memorializing Luis Acosta García, the *payador* of the humble folk of the countryside.

9   "Enrique, who mutilated Conrado" refers to the famous Palermo Lakes crime. The Mateo referred to here is Mateo Banks, who murdered his entire family, while Lauro and Salvato were the ones who killed Frank Livingston. All of them were common criminals, in other words.

10   Simón Radowitzky, the assassin of Colonel Falcón.

11 Louis Lingg, German, one of the Chicago martyrs. Before he was scheduled to be hanged, he committed suicide with explosives that had been smuggled into his cell.

12 The anarchist Gaetano Bresci killed King Umberto I of Italy. He died in the Santo Stefano prison under mysterious circumstances in 1901.

13 Sante Geronimo Caserio killed French President Sadi Carnot. He was guillotined in Lyon in 1894.

14 Michele Angiolillo killed Spanish Prime Minister Antonio Cánovas. He was garotted in 1897.

15 Felice Orsini tried to assassinate Napoleon III in 1858, armed with a bomb he made himself. Weeks later, he and his comrade Andrea Pieri were guillotined.

16 Ravachol was a French anarchist who carried out a series of bombings from 1891 to 1892. He was guillotined in Montbrisson on July 11th, 1892.

17 The death penalty had not yet been abolished in 1919.

18 Eduardo Vázquez's son has told us that, shortly before he died, his father confessed that if the plan they concocted with Wladimirovich failed, the anarchists were ready to attack the Las Mercedes Mental Hospital, kidnap Pérez Millán Temperley, and hang him in the Plaza de Mayo.

Epilogue: Unmarked Graves

1 St. Joseph—San José in Spanish—in honor of her father José Menéndez.

Eighty Years Later: Perfidy and Poetry

1 The story of some of these executions is told in Rodolfo Walsh's book *Operation Massacre* [—Translator].

Index